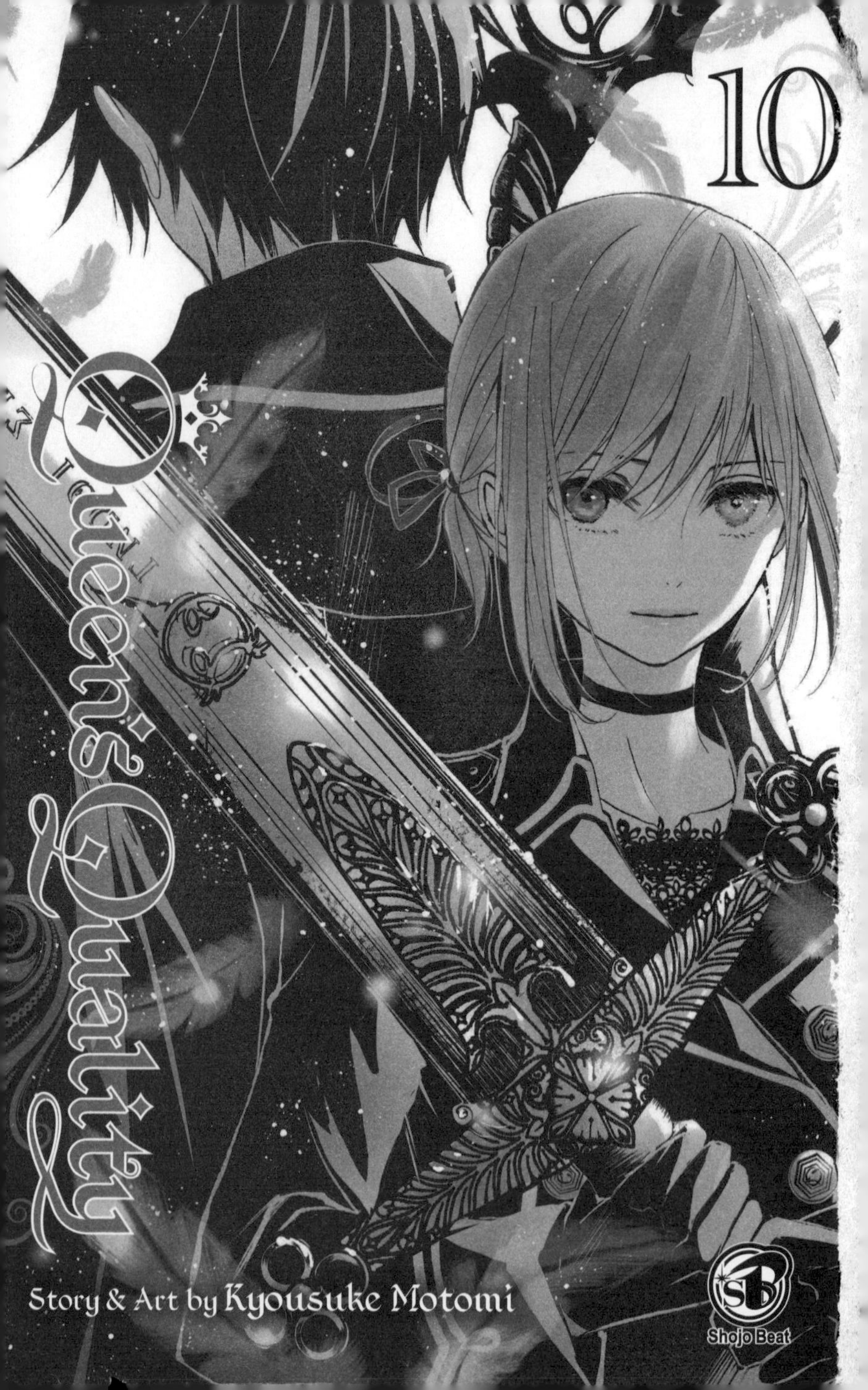
10
Queen's Quality
Story & Art by Kyousuke Motomi
Shojo Beat

Queen's Quality

CONTENTS

10

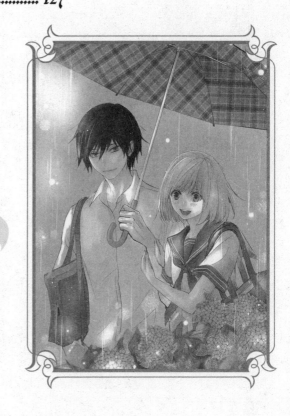

Cast of Characters

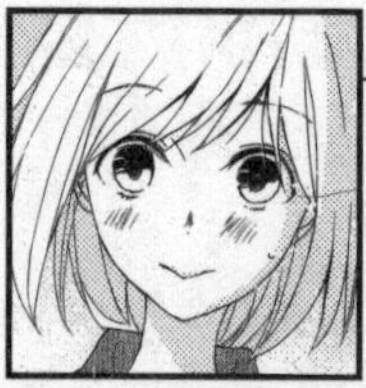

Fumi Nishioka

An apprentice Sweeper with the powers of a Queen, this second-year high school student dreams of finding her very own Prince Charming.

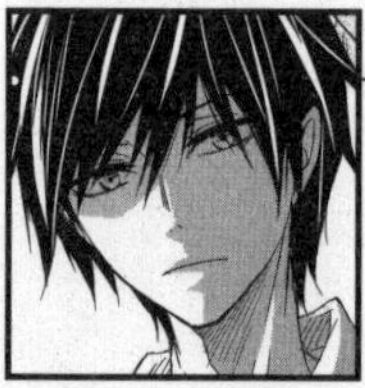

Kyutaro Horikita

A mind Sweeper who cleanses people's minds of dangerous impurities. Although incredibly awkward with people, he and Fumi are now dating.

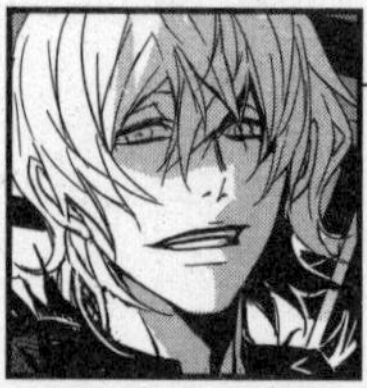

Ataru Shikata

A former bug handler who uses bugs to manipulate people. Saved by Fumi and Kyutaro, he has joined the Genbu Clan.

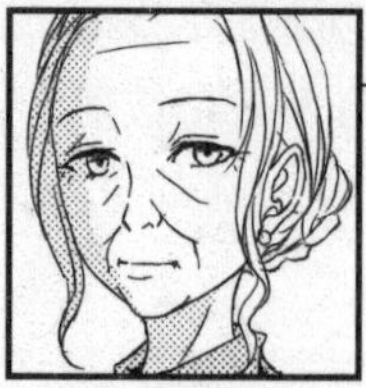

Miyako Horikita

The prior head of the Genbu Gate Sweepers. She can be both strict and kind, and she watches over and advises Fumi.

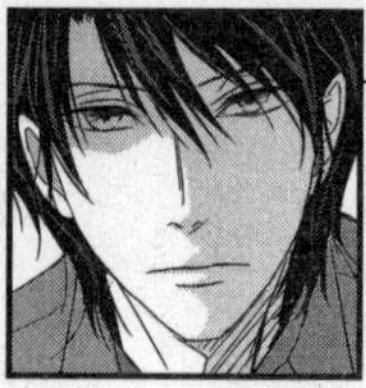

Koichi Kitagawa

The chairman of the school Fumi and Kyutaro attend. He's a Sweeper as well as being Kyutaro's brother-in-law.

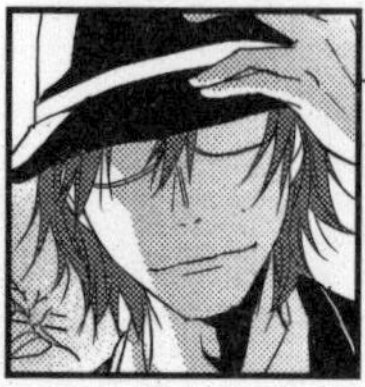

Takaya Kitahara

One of the Genbu Clan, he was originally a member of the main Byakko Clan. He's an expert with suggestive therapy and is actually Fumi's uncle.

Story Thus Far

The Horikitas are a family of Sweepers—people who cleanse impurities from human hearts. After seeing Fumi's potential, they take her on as an assistant and trainee. Within Fumi dwells the power of both the White and the Dark-Gray queens, both of whom have the ability to give people immense power.

Having paid the compensation demanded by the White Queen and completed the training in Seichi, Fumi and Kyutaro are finally on the same page emotionally and are now in a relationship! Fumi, giddy with happiness, is determined to channel her feelings into the strength she'll need for the challenges that still lie ahead...

MONTHLY BETSUCOMI SALE DATE NOTICE ON TWITTER

CHAPTER 45

THIN GYOZA WRAPPERS GET SO NICE AND CRISP WHEN YOU FRY THEM, BUT...
...THE LARGER, THICKER ONES ARE EASIER TO USE, AND ONLY GRANNY AND I ARE ANY GOOD AT MAKING GYOZA...
Fumi's probably as bad at it as Koichi is...
HE'S THINKING SO HARD AND LOOKS SO SERIOUS...!
He's almost as focused as when he cleans!

I'M PRETTY GOOD AT MAKING GYOZA! I LIKE TO ADD A LITTLE MISO PASTE TO THE FILLING.

LET'S SEE... WHAT'S UP IN *QUEEN'S QUALITY* THIS MONTH?
(1) AFTER ALL'S SAID AND DONE, I THINK THEY PROBABLY WILL SLIP HIM ONE. (HIS LIFE IS VERY HARD.)
(2) KYUTARO MANAGES GYOZA QUALITY CONTROL IN THE HORIKITA HOUSEHOLD.
(3) KOICHI, HOW MANY TIMES HAVE I TOLD YOU NOT TO WEAR THAT SHIRT WHEN YOU HAVE SOMETHING SERIOUS TO SAY?

THIS NEW VOLUME BEGINS ON A COZY DOMESTIC NOTE.

I SEND OUT TWITTER UPDATES LIKE THIS EVERY MONTH. YOU CAN READ SOME OF MY OTHER MUTTERINGS THERE TOO.

@motomikyosuke

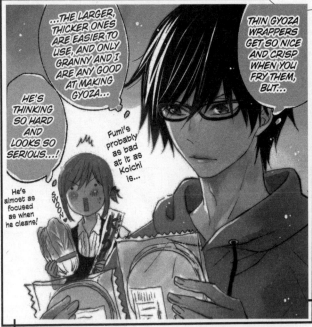

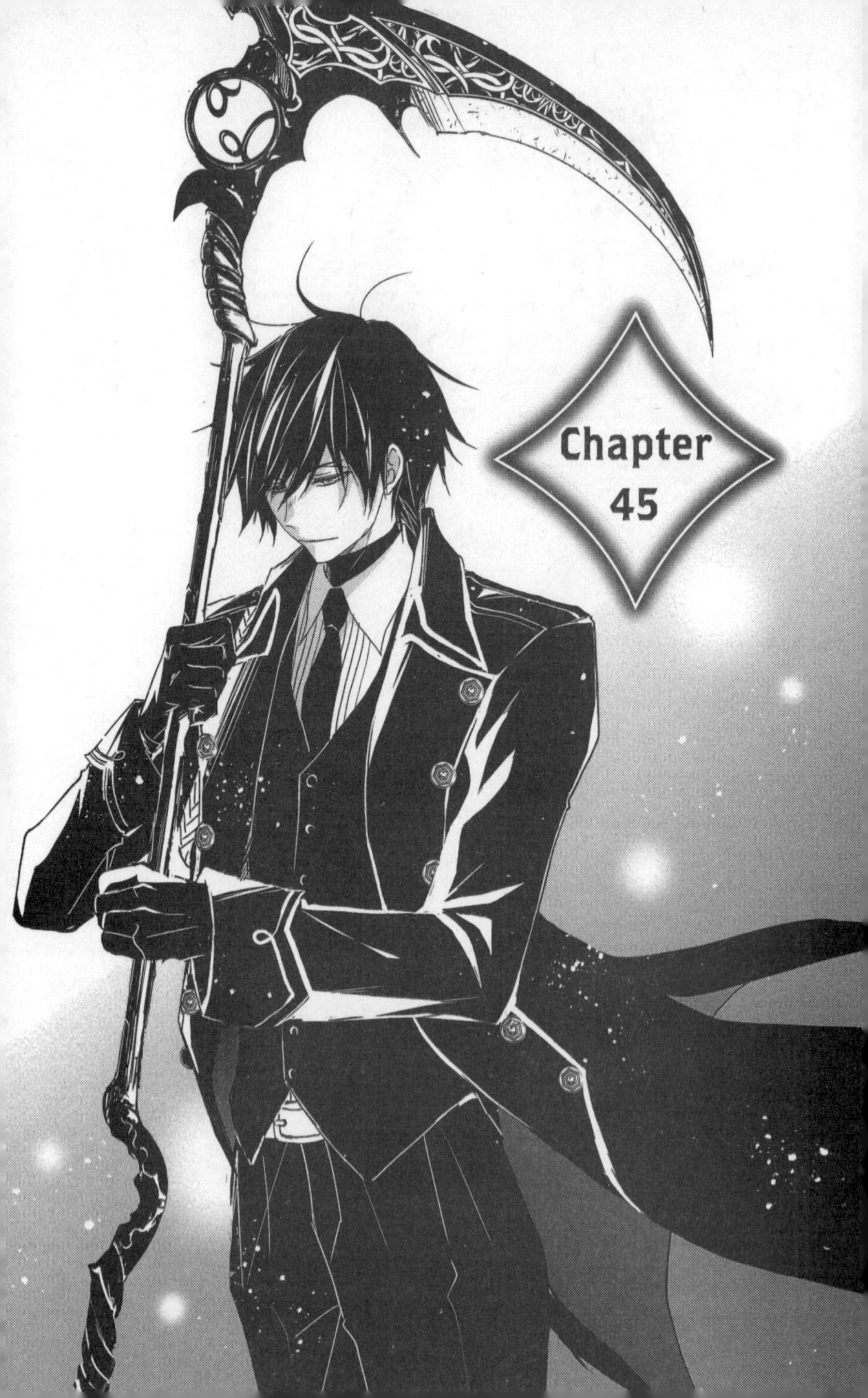
Chapter
45

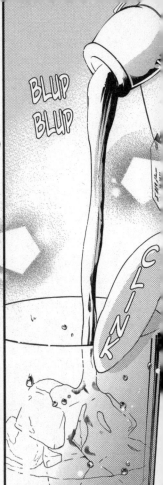

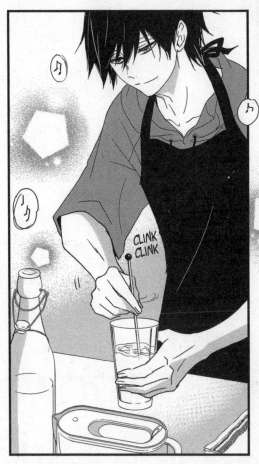

CLINK
CLINK

BLUP
BLUP

CLINK

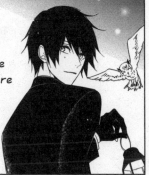

Hello, everyone! This is Kyousuke Motomi. This is the tenth volume of *Queen's Quality,* which has me all emotional. If you factor in *QQ Sweeper,* that puts us at 13 volumes. I've made it this far thanks to all of you out there reading along.

There's a whole new development starting in this volume, and I hope you'll look at it through that lens as you read!

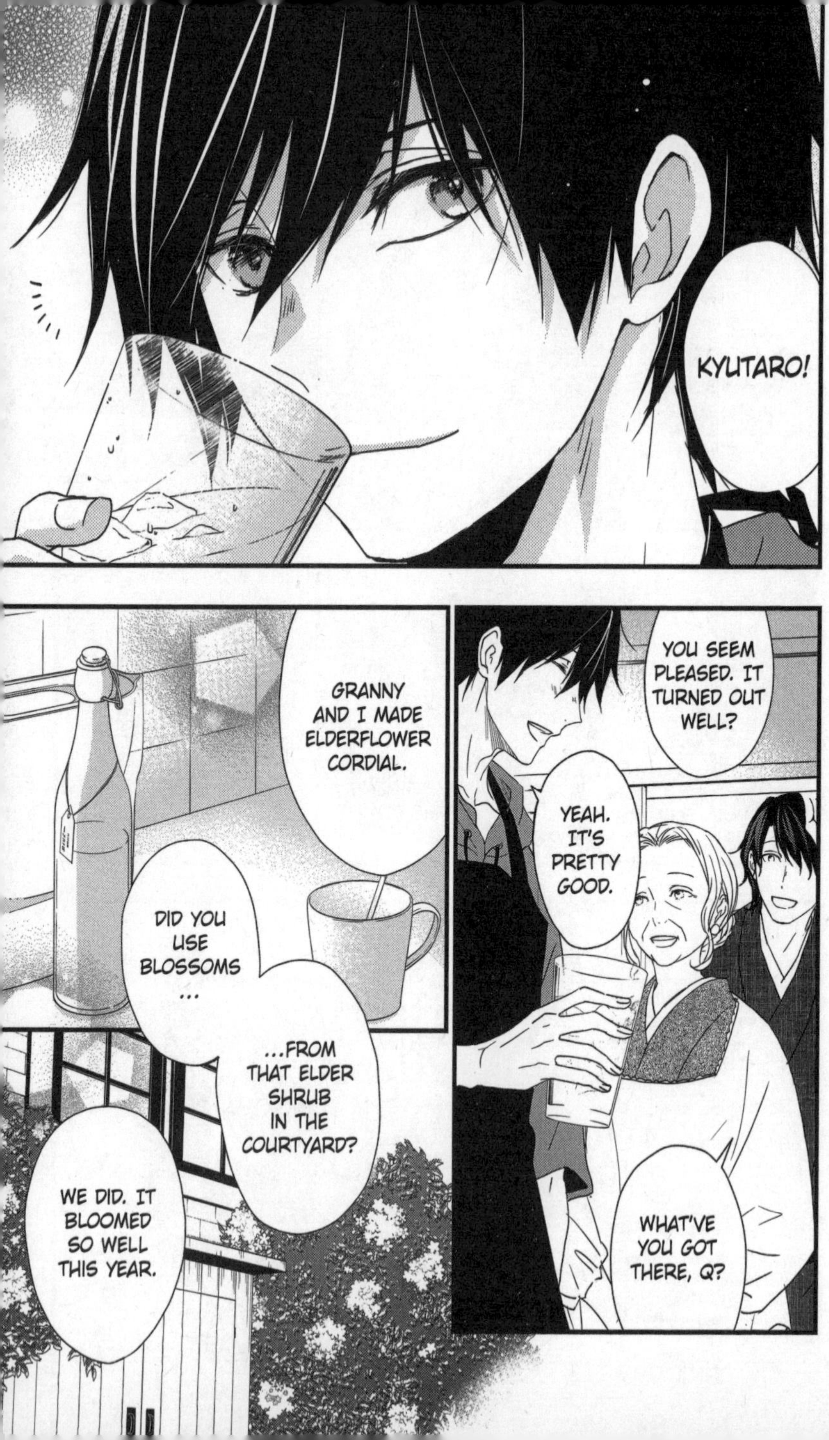
KYUTARO!
YOU SEEM PLEASED. IT TURNED OUT WELL?
YEAH. IT'S PRETTY GOOD.
WHAT'VE YOU GOT THERE, Q?
GRANNY AND I MADE ELDERFLOWER CORDIAL.
DID YOU USE BLOSSOMS ...
...FROM THAT ELDER SHRUB IN THE COURTYARD?
WE DID. IT BLOOMED SO WELL THIS YEAR.

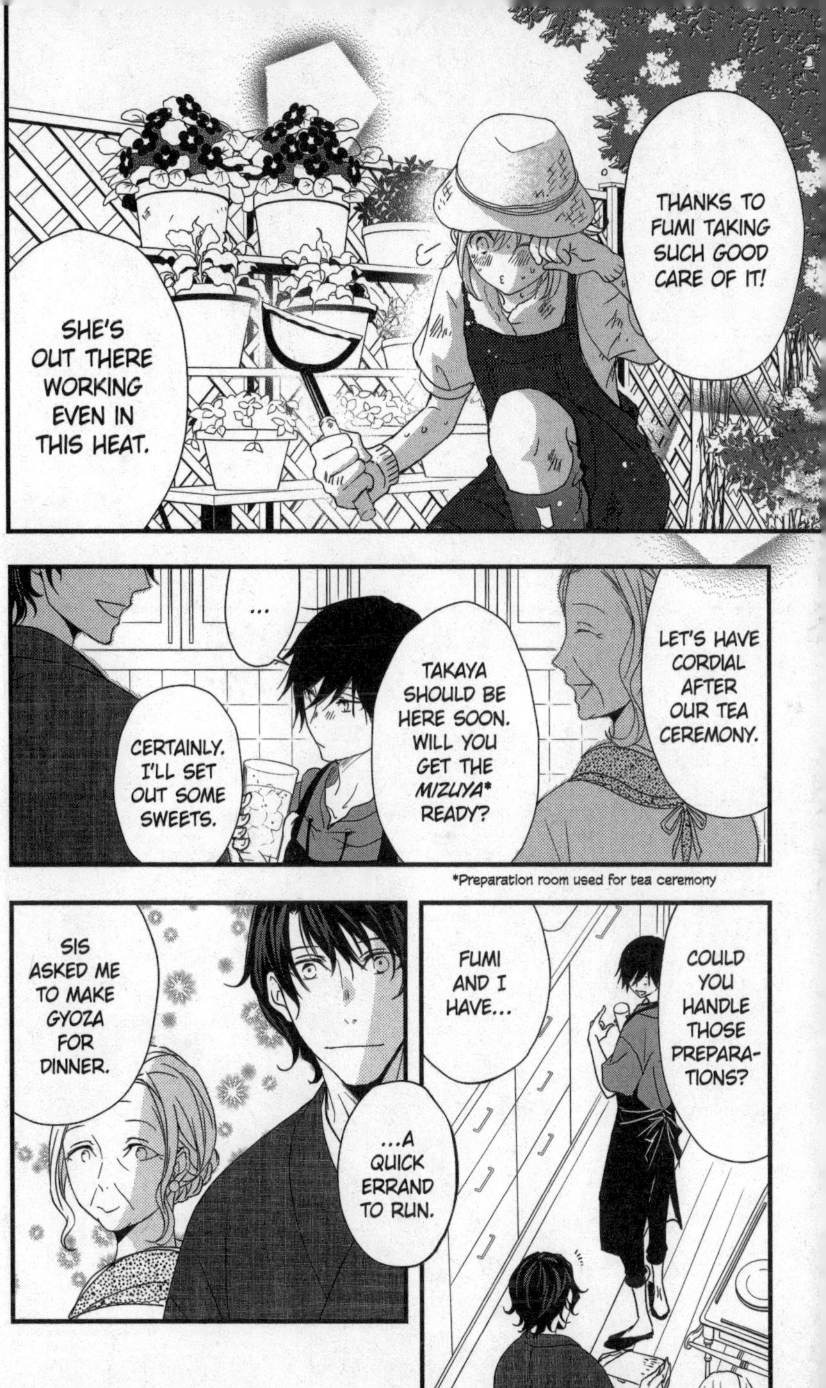
THANKS TO FUMI TAKING SUCH GOOD CARE OF IT!
SHE'S OUT THERE WORKING EVEN IN THIS HEAT.
LET'S HAVE CORDIAL AFTER OUR TEA CEREMONY.
TAKAYA SHOULD BE HERE SOON. WILL YOU GET THE *MIZUYA** READY?
...
CERTAINLY. I'LL SET OUT SOME SWEETS.
COULD YOU HANDLE THOSE PREPARATIONS?
FUMI AND I HAVE...
...A QUICK ERRAND TO RUN.
SIS ASKED ME TO MAKE GYOZA FOR DINNER.

*Preparation room used for tea ceremony

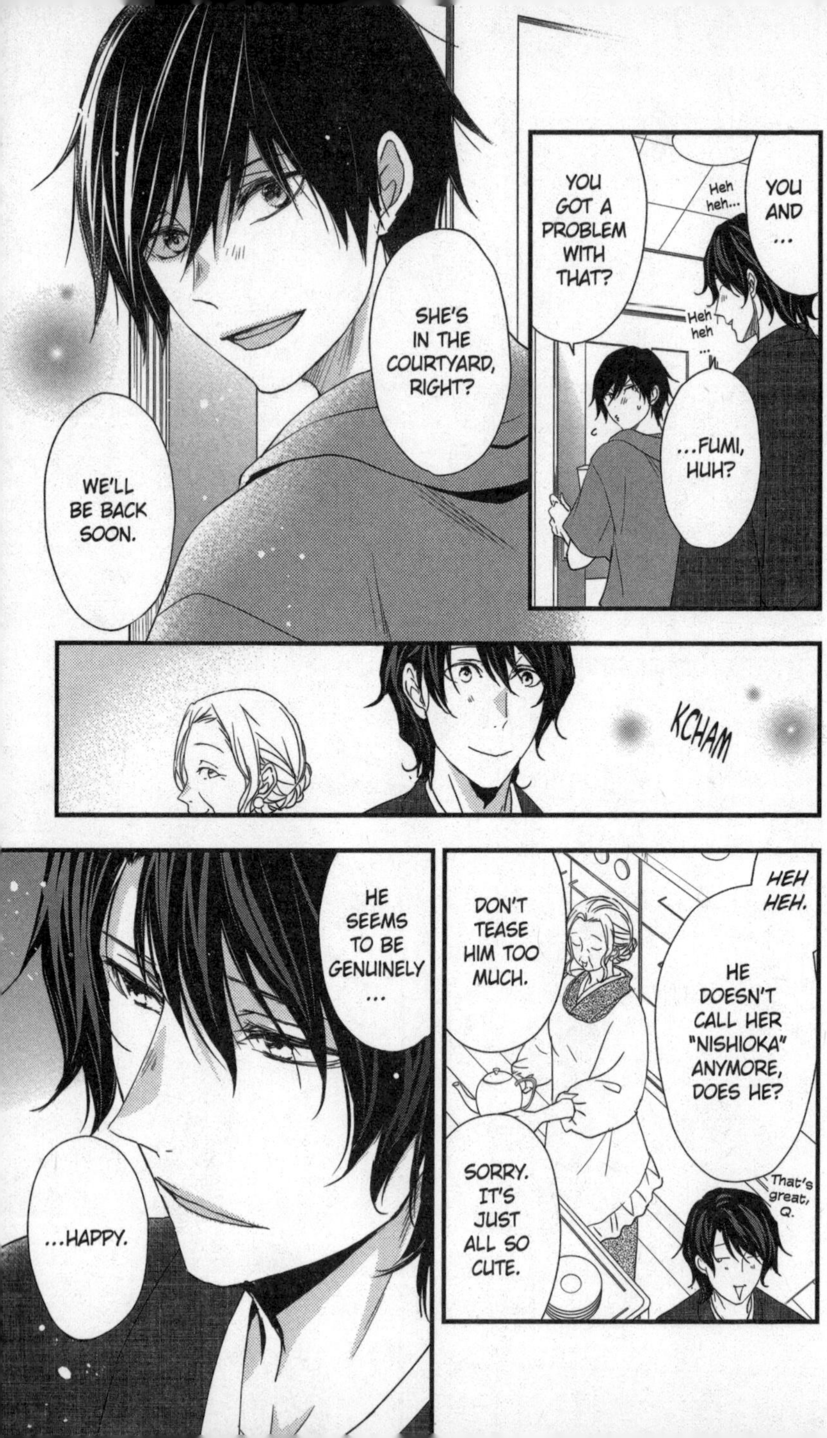
YOU AND ...
Heh heh...
Heh heh ...
...FUMI, HUH?
YOU GOT A PROBLEM WITH THAT?
SHE'S IN THE COURTYARD, RIGHT?
WE'LL BE BACK SOON.
KCHAM
HEH HEH.
HE DOESN'T CALL HER "NISHIOKA" ANYMORE, DOES HE?
DON'T TEASE HIM TOO MUCH.
That's great, Q.
SORRY. IT'S JUST ALL SO CUTE.
HE SEEMS TO BE GENUINELY ...
...HAPPY.

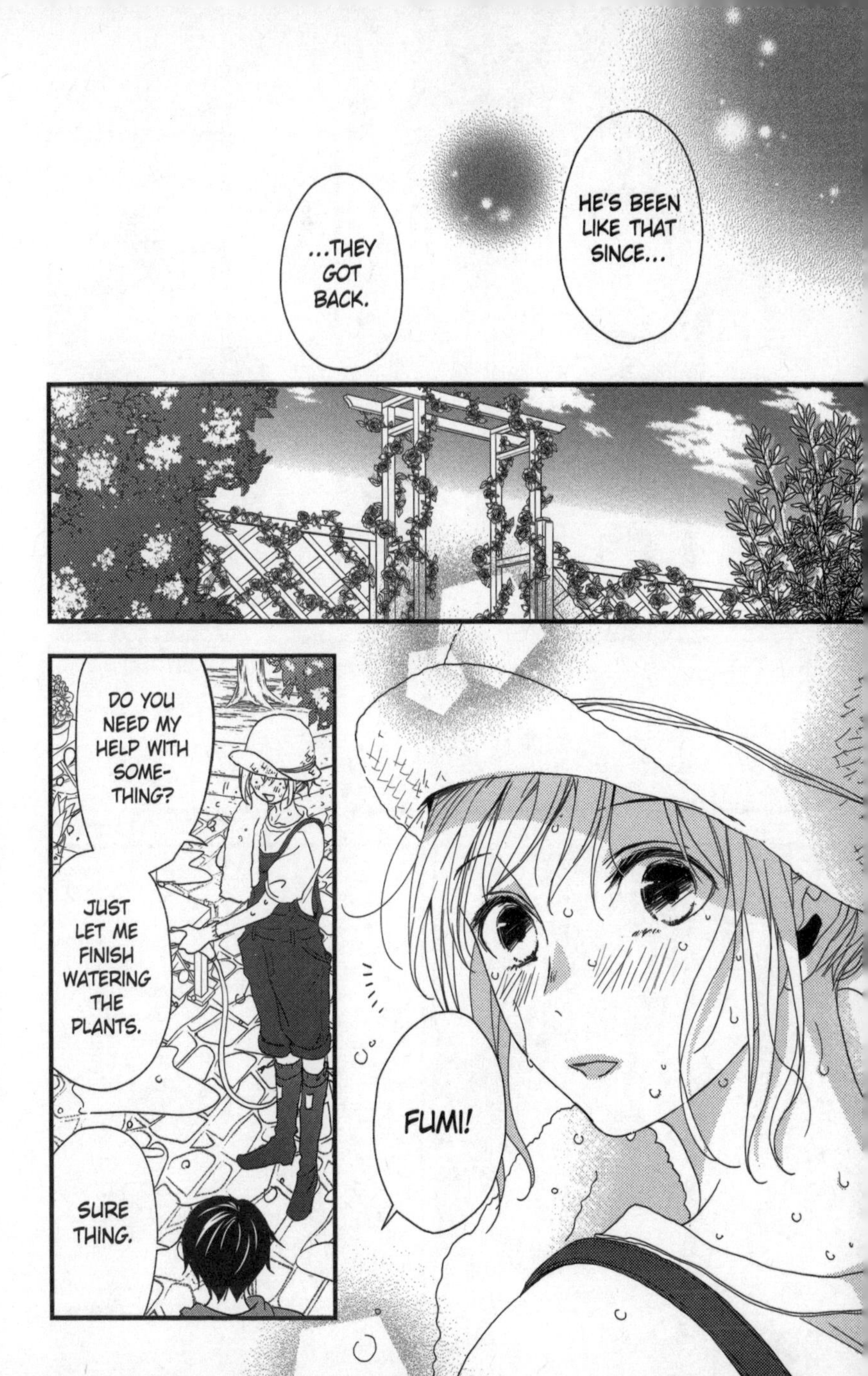
HE'S BEEN LIKE THAT SINCE...
...THEY GOT BACK.
FUMI!
DO YOU NEED MY HELP WITH SOME-THING?
JUST LET ME FINISH WATERING THE PLANTS.
SURE THING.

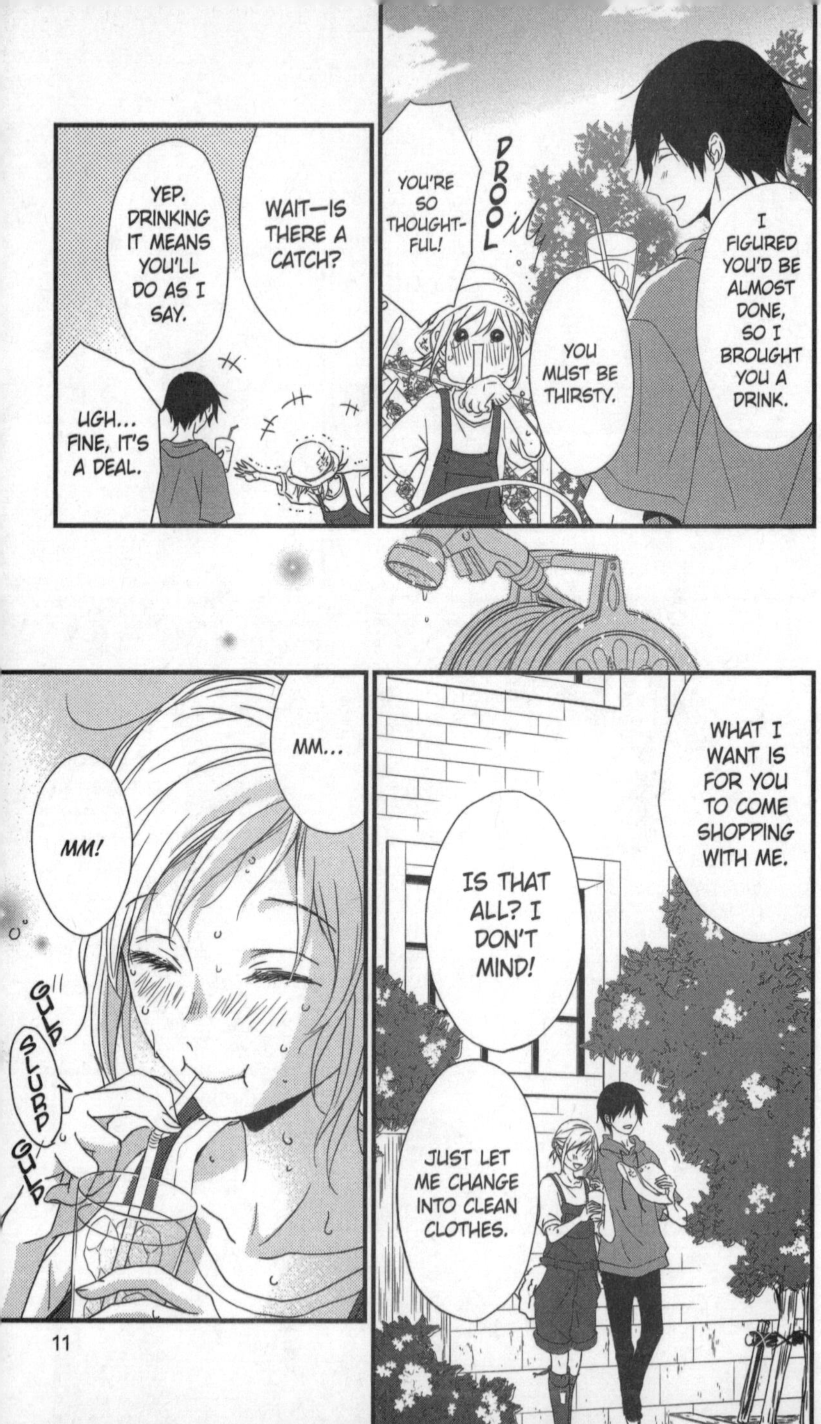
I FIGURED YOU'D BE ALMOST DONE, SO I BROUGHT YOU A DRINK.
YOU MUST BE THIRSTY.
DROOL
YOU'RE SO THOUGHTFUL!
WAIT—IS THERE A CATCH?
YEP. DRINKING IT MEANS YOU'LL DO AS I SAY.
UGH... FINE, IT'S A DEAL.
WHAT I WANT IS FOR YOU TO COME SHOPPING WITH ME.
IS THAT ALL? I DON'T MIND!
JUST LET ME CHANGE INTO CLEAN CLOTHES.
MM...
MM!
GULP
SLURP
GULP

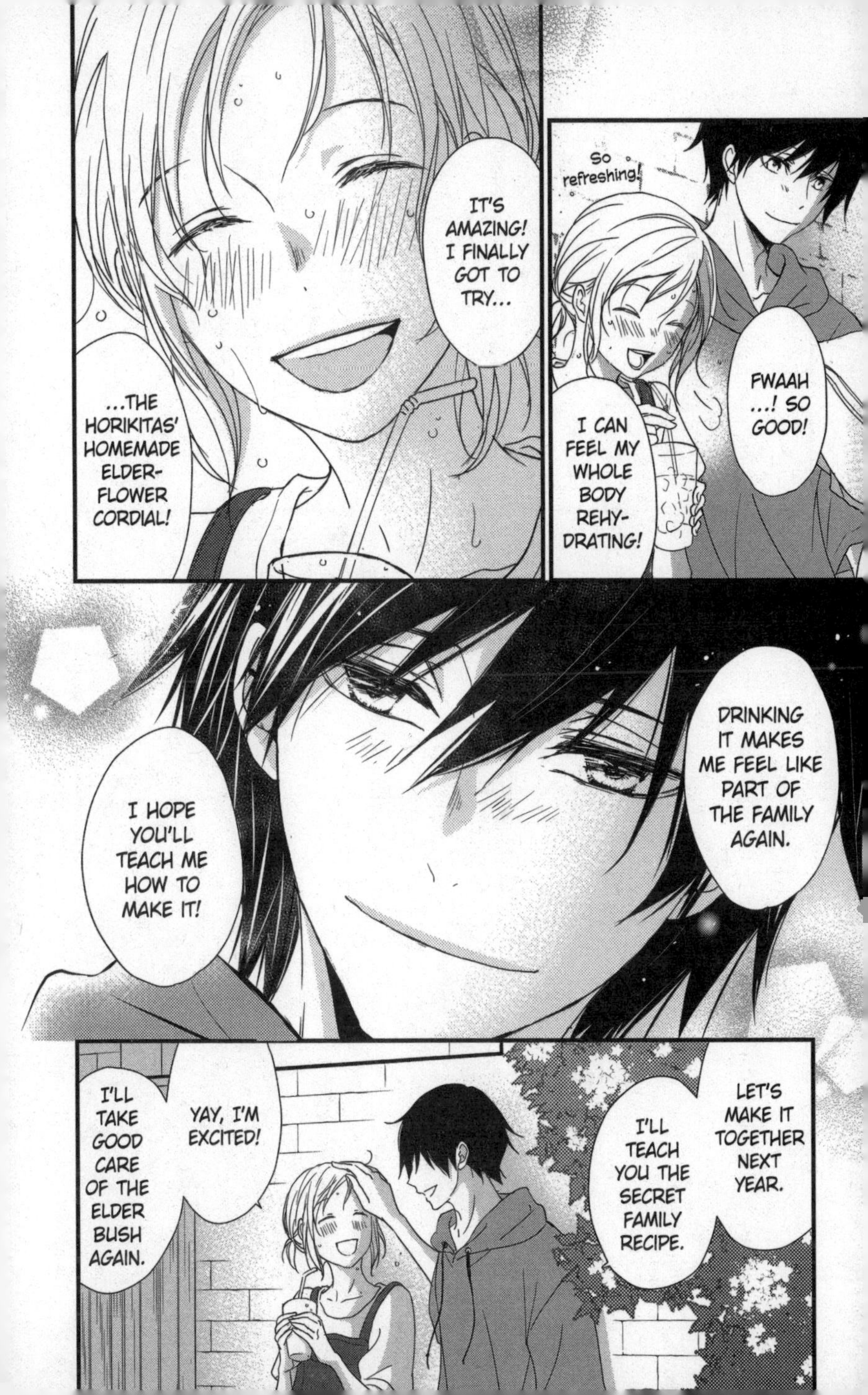
So refreshing!
FWAAH ...! SO GOOD!
I CAN FEEL MY WHOLE BODY REHYDRATING!
IT'S AMAZING! I FINALLY GOT TO TRY...
...THE HORIKITAS' HOMEMADE ELDERFLOWER CORDIAL!
DRINKING IT MAKES ME FEEL LIKE PART OF THE FAMILY AGAIN.
I HOPE YOU'LL TEACH ME HOW TO MAKE IT!
LET'S MAKE IT TOGETHER NEXT YEAR.
I'LL TEACH YOU THE SECRET FAMILY RECIPE.
YAY, I'M EXCITED!
I'LL TAKE GOOD CARE OF THE ELDER BUSH AGAIN.

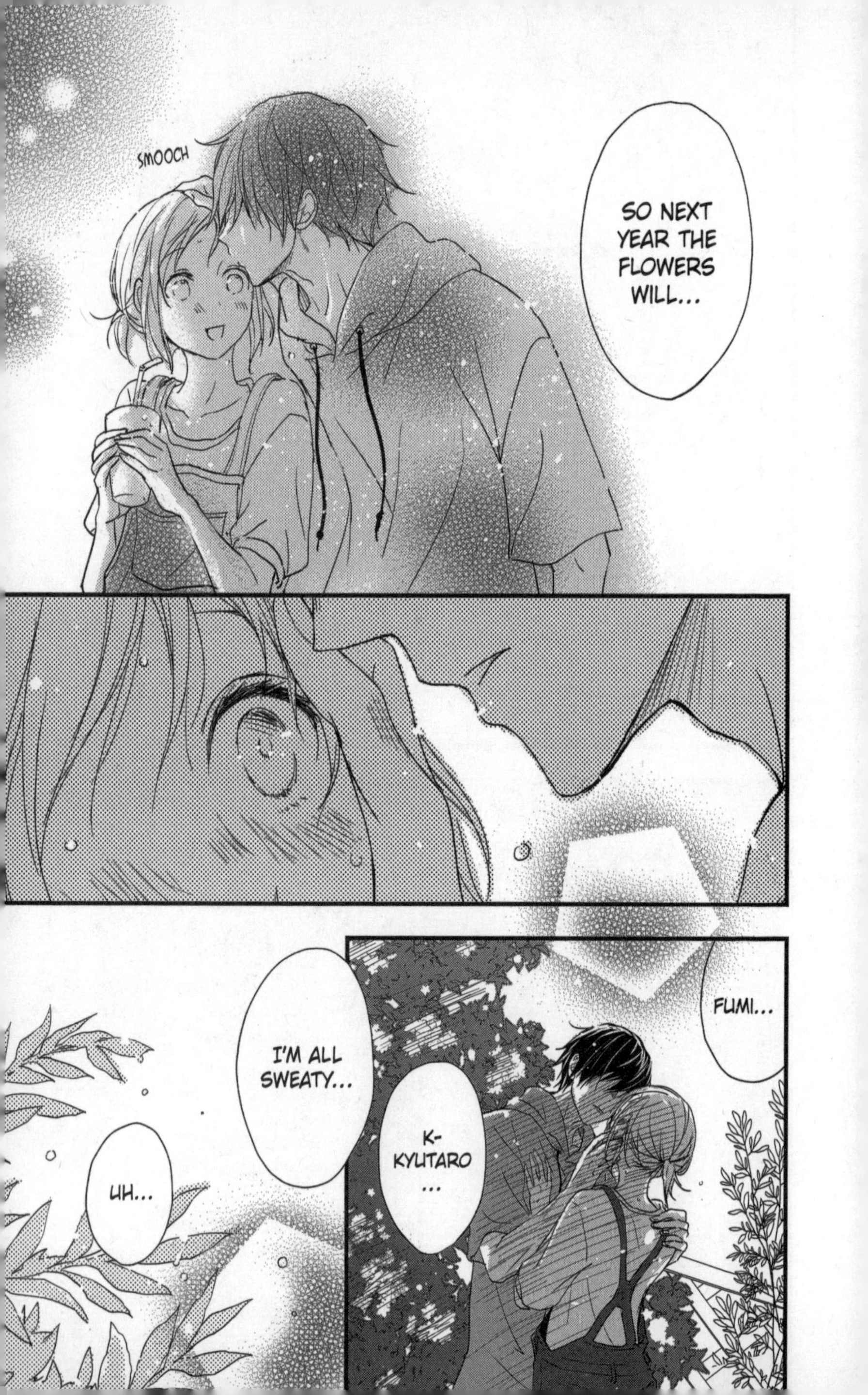
SO NEXT YEAR THE FLOWERS WILL...
SMOOCH
FUMI...
K-KYUTARO ...
I'M ALL SWEATY...
UH...

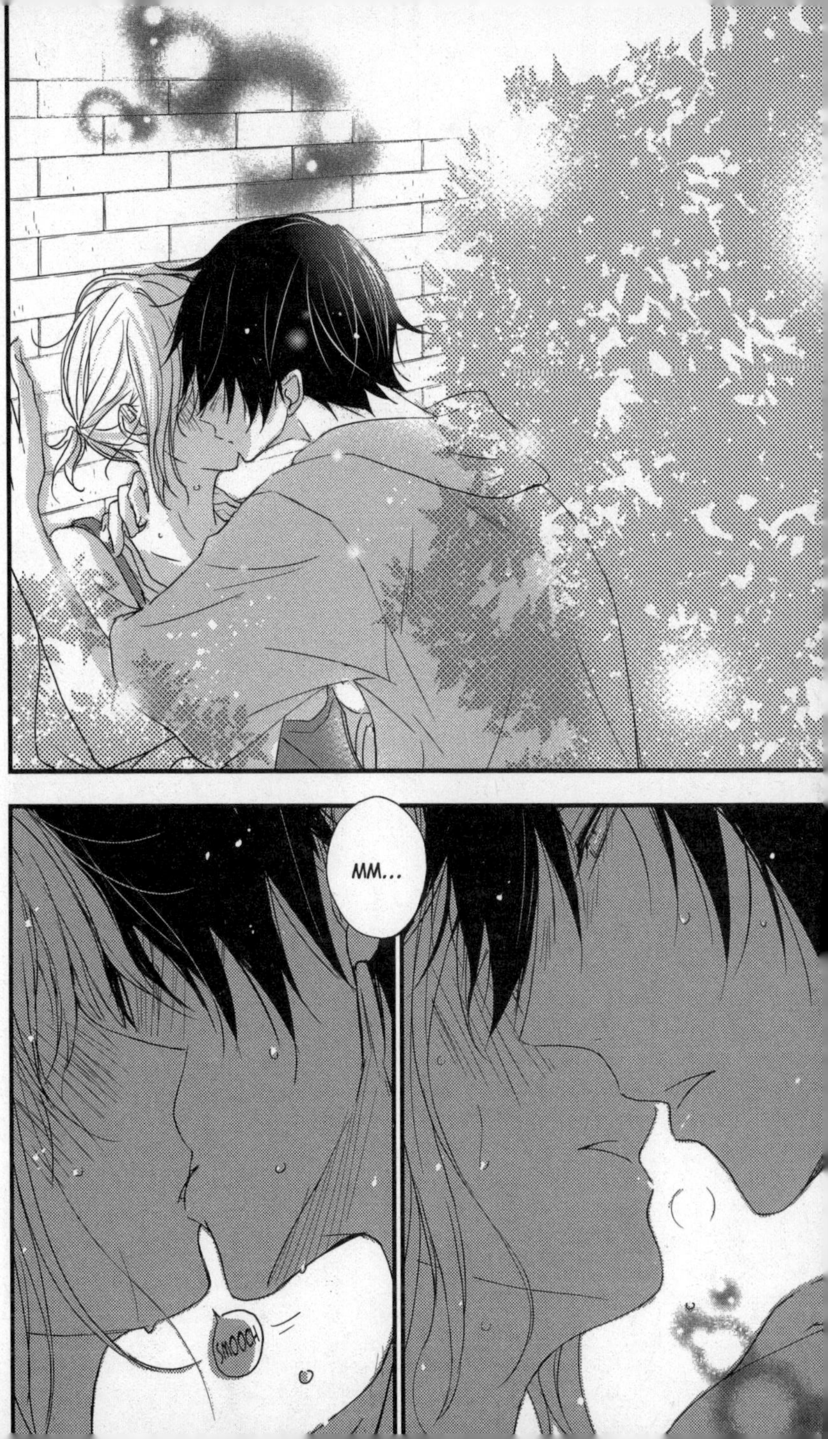
MM...
SMOOCH

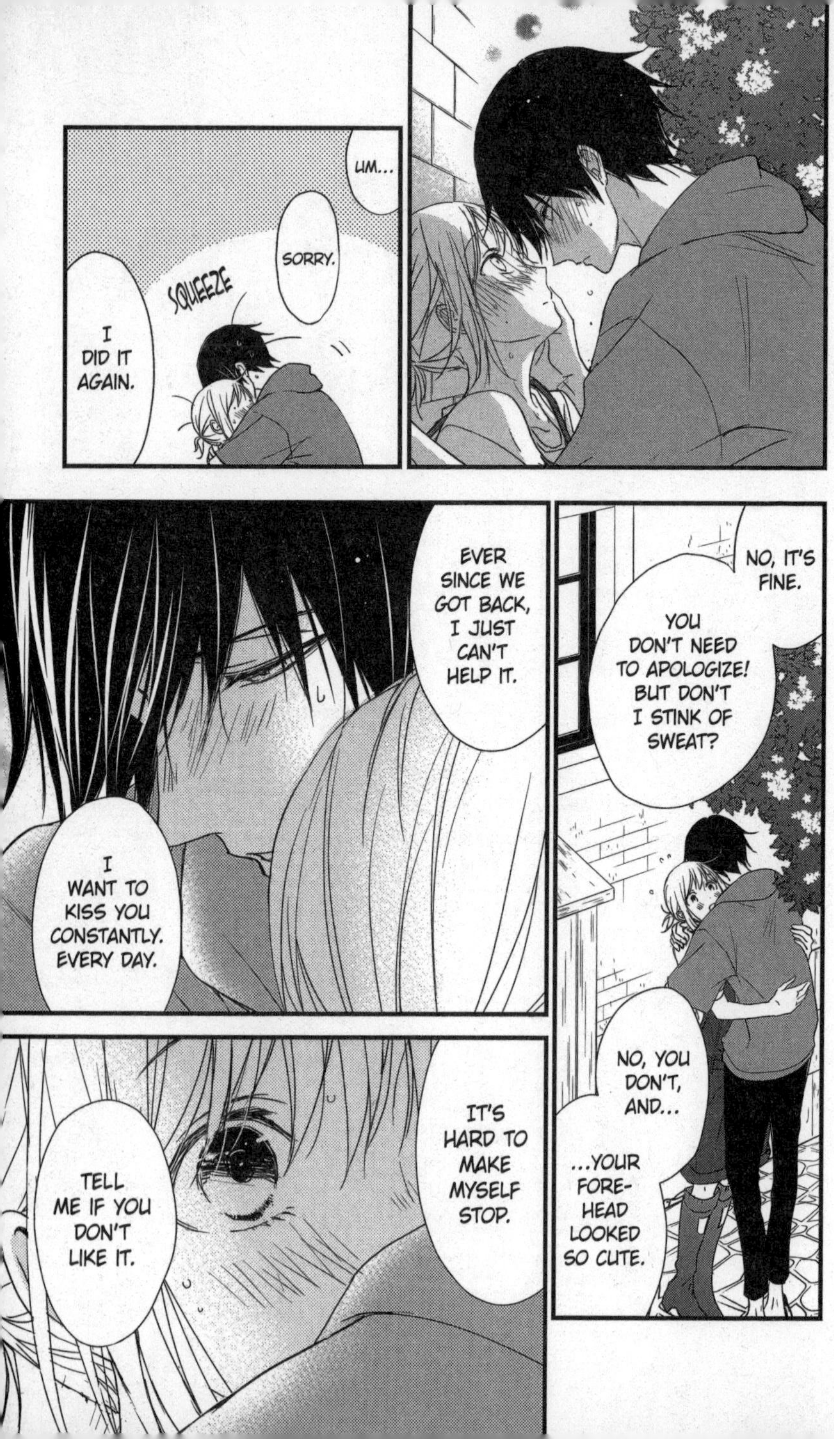
UM...
SORRY.
SQUEEZE
I DID IT AGAIN.
NO, IT'S FINE.
YOU DON'T NEED TO APOLOGIZE! BUT DON'T I STINK OF SWEAT?
NO, YOU DON'T, AND...
...YOUR FORE-HEAD LOOKED SO CUTE.
EVER SINCE WE GOT BACK, I JUST CAN'T HELP IT.
I WANT TO KISS YOU CONSTANTLY. EVERY DAY.
IT'S HARD TO MAKE MYSELF STOP.
TELL ME IF YOU DON'T LIKE IT.

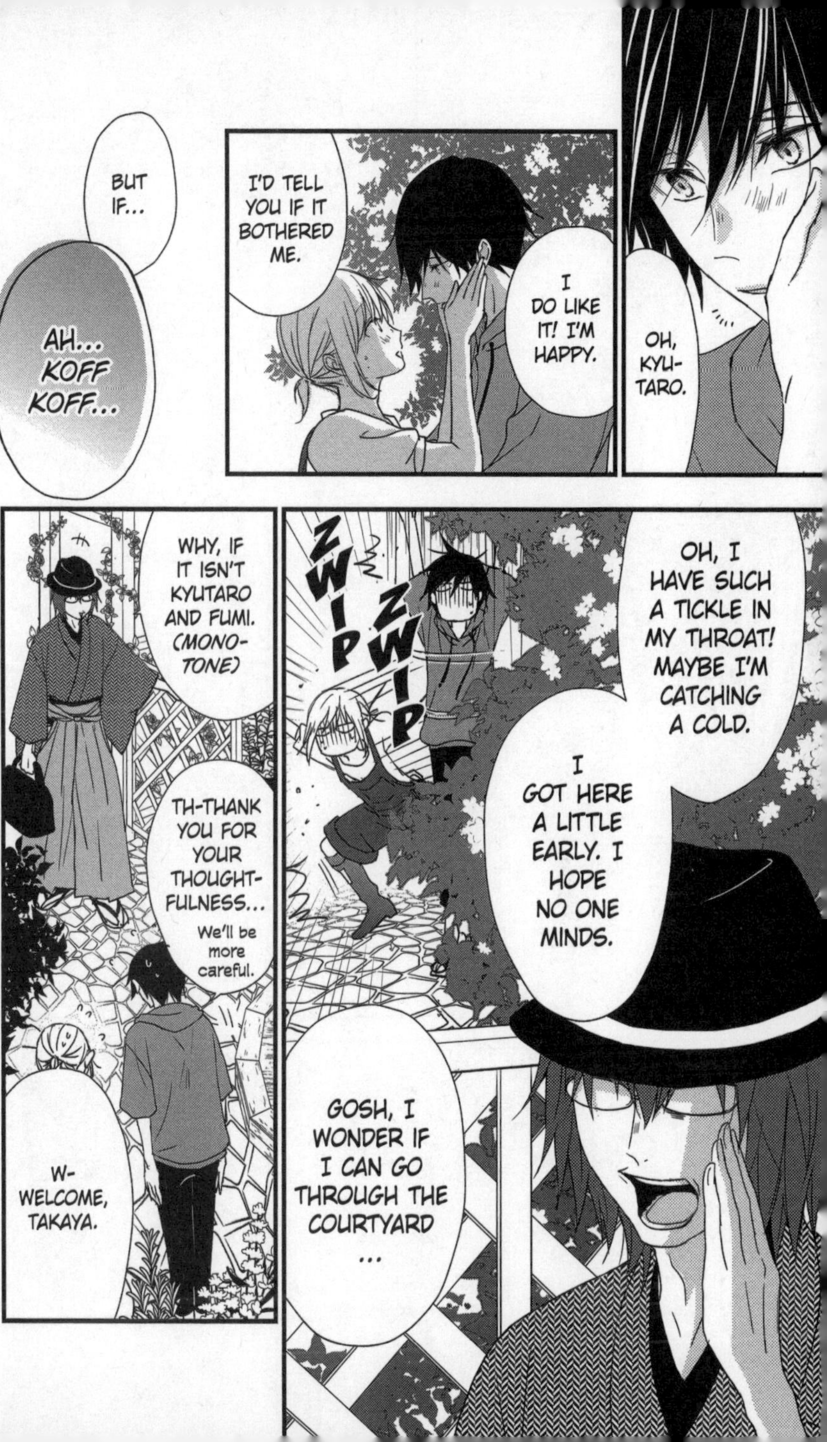
OH, KYUTARO.
I DO LIKE IT! I'M HAPPY.
I'D TELL YOU IF IT BOTHERED ME.
BUT IF...
AH... KOFF KOFF...
OH, I HAVE SUCH A TICKLE IN MY THROAT! MAYBE I'M CATCHING A COLD.
I GOT HERE A LITTLE EARLY. I HOPE NO ONE MINDS.
ZWIP
ZWIP
GOSH, I WONDER IF I CAN GO THROUGH THE COURTYARD...
WHY, IF IT ISN'T KYUTARO AND FUMI. (MONOTONE)
TH-THANK YOU FOR YOUR THOUGHTFULNESS...
We'll be more careful.
W-WELCOME, TAKAYA.

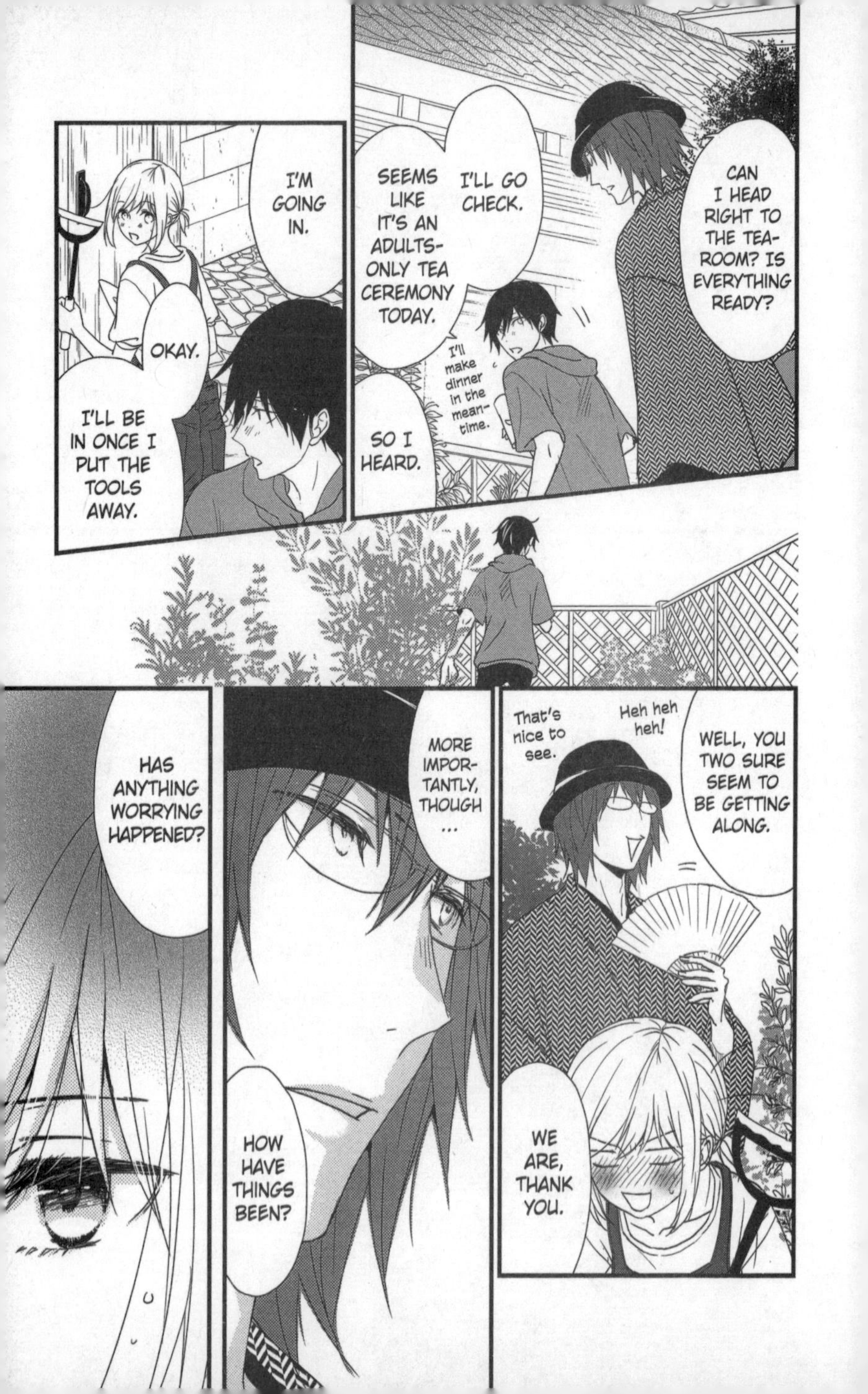
CAN I HEAD RIGHT TO THE TEA-ROOM? IS EVERYTHING READY?
I'LL GO CHECK.
SEEMS LIKE IT'S AN ADULTS-ONLY TEA CEREMONY TODAY.
I'll make dinner in the mean-time.
SO I HEARD.
I'M GOING IN.
OKAY.
I'LL BE IN ONCE I PUT THE TOOLS AWAY.
WELL, YOU TWO SURE SEEM TO BE GETTING ALONG.
Heh heh heh!
That's nice to see.
WE ARE, THANK YOU.
MORE IMPORTANTLY, THOUGH ...
HOW HAVE THINGS BEEN?
HAS ANYTHING WORRYING HAPPENED?

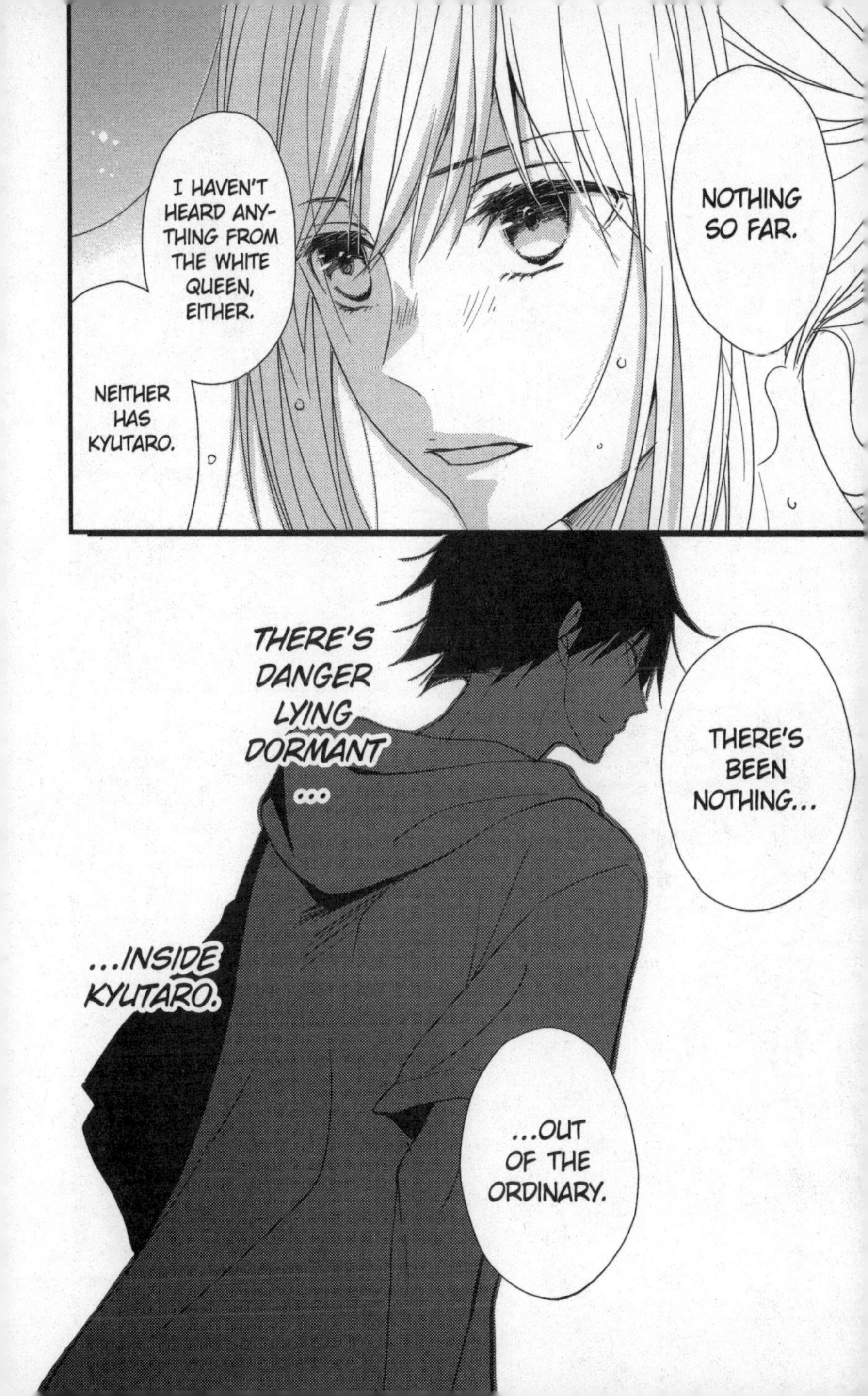
NOTHING SO FAR.
I HAVEN'T HEARD ANY-THING FROM THE WHITE QUEEN, EITHER.
NEITHER HAS KYUTARO.
THERE'S BEEN NOTHING...
...OUT OF THE ORDINARY.
THERE'S DANGER LYING DORMANT...
...INSIDE KYUTARO.

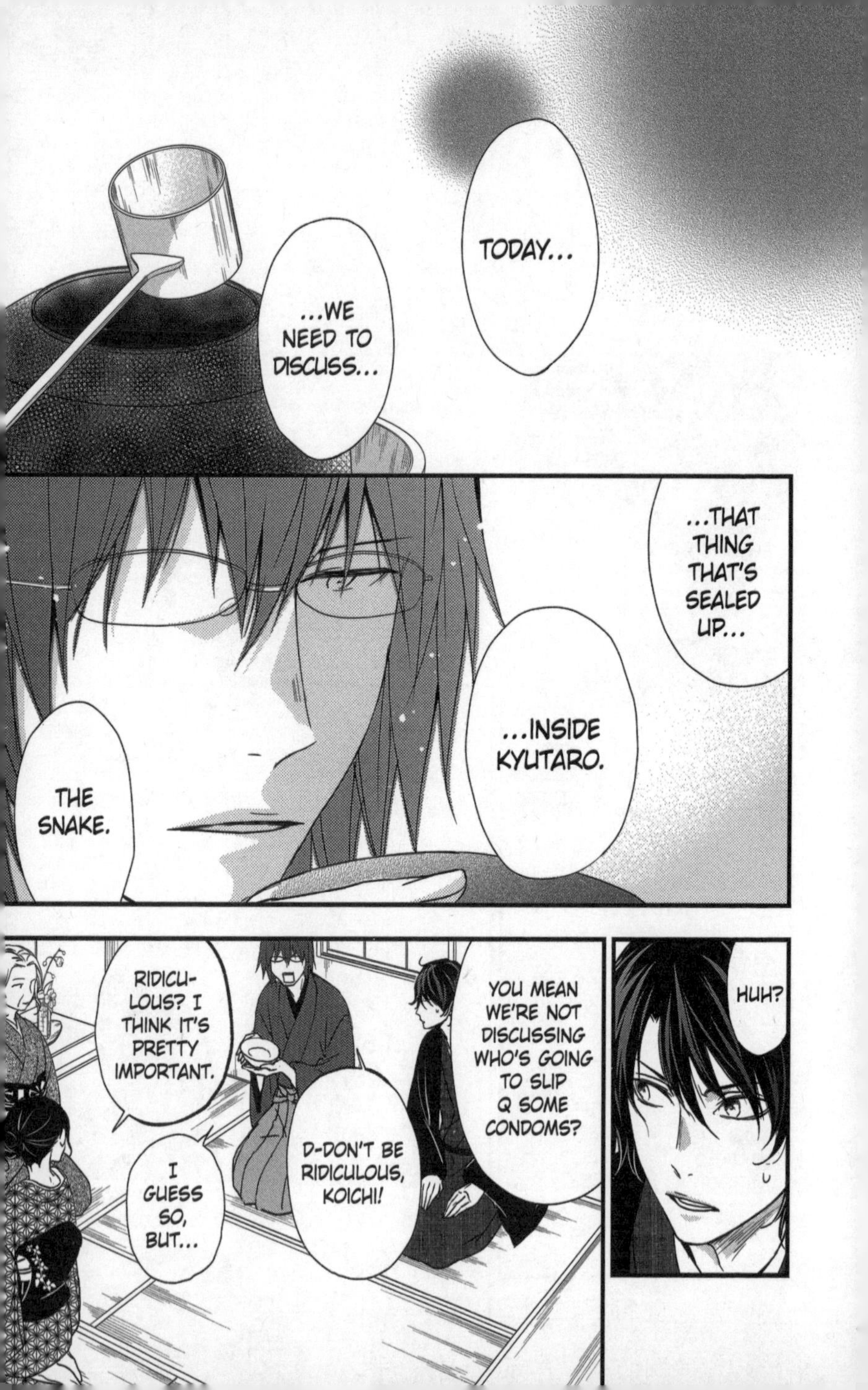
TODAY...
...WE NEED TO DISCUSS...
...THAT THING THAT'S SEALED UP...
...INSIDE KYUTARO.
THE SNAKE.
HUH?
YOU MEAN WE'RE NOT DISCUSSING WHO'S GOING TO SLIP Q SOME CONDOMS?
D-DON'T BE RIDICULOUS, KOICHI!
RIDICULOUS? I THINK IT'S PRETTY IMPORTANT.
I GUESS SO, BUT...

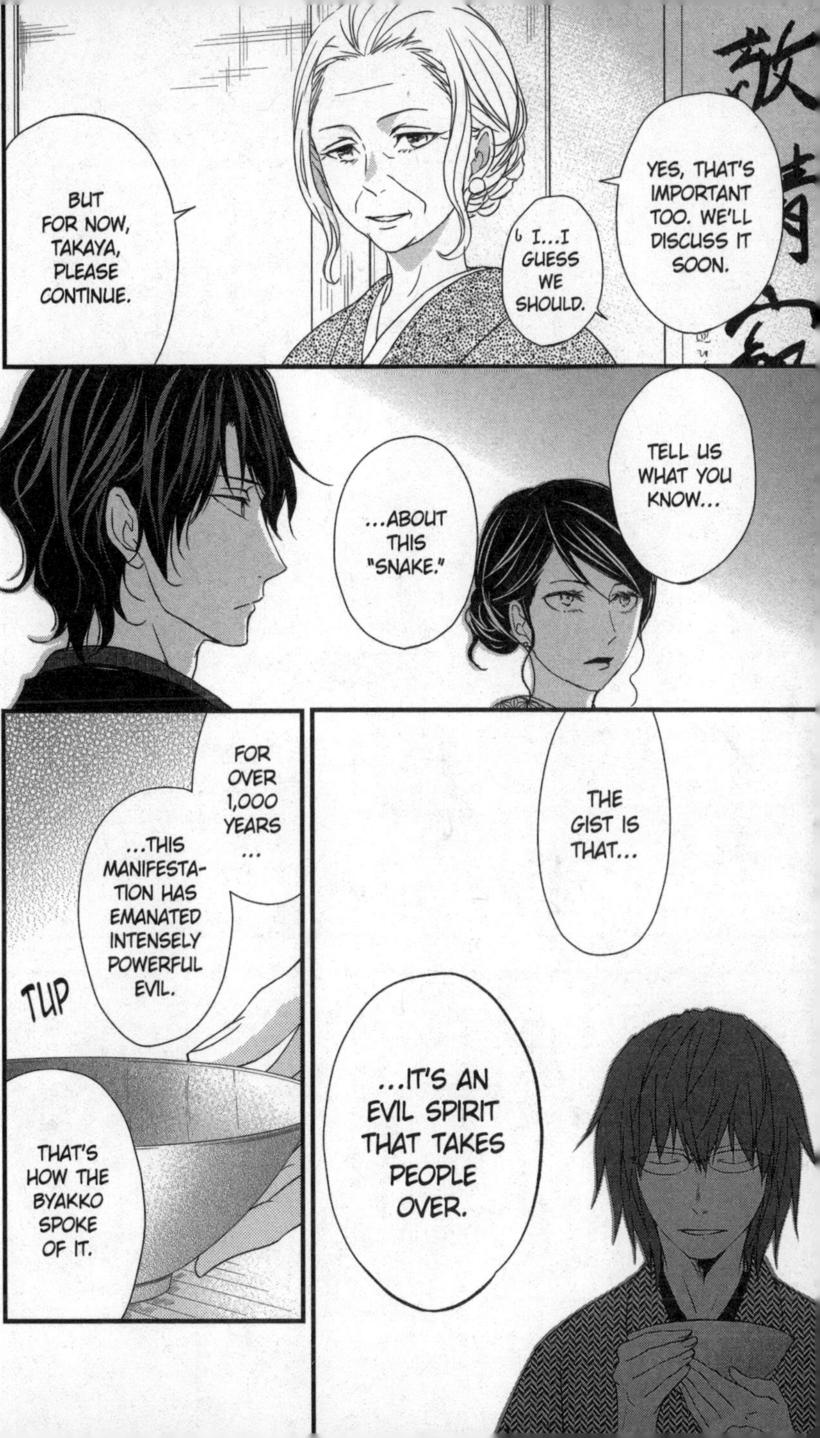
YES, THAT'S IMPORTANT TOO. WE'LL DISCUSS IT SOON.
I...I GUESS WE SHOULD.
BUT FOR NOW, TAKAYA, PLEASE CONTINUE.
TELL US WHAT YOU KNOW...
...ABOUT THIS "SNAKE."
THE GIST IS THAT...
...IT'S AN EVIL SPIRIT THAT TAKES PEOPLE OVER.
FOR OVER 1,000 YEARS...
...THIS MANIFESTATION HAS EMANATED INTENSELY POWERFUL EVIL.
TUP
THAT'S HOW THE BYAKKO SPOKE OF IT.

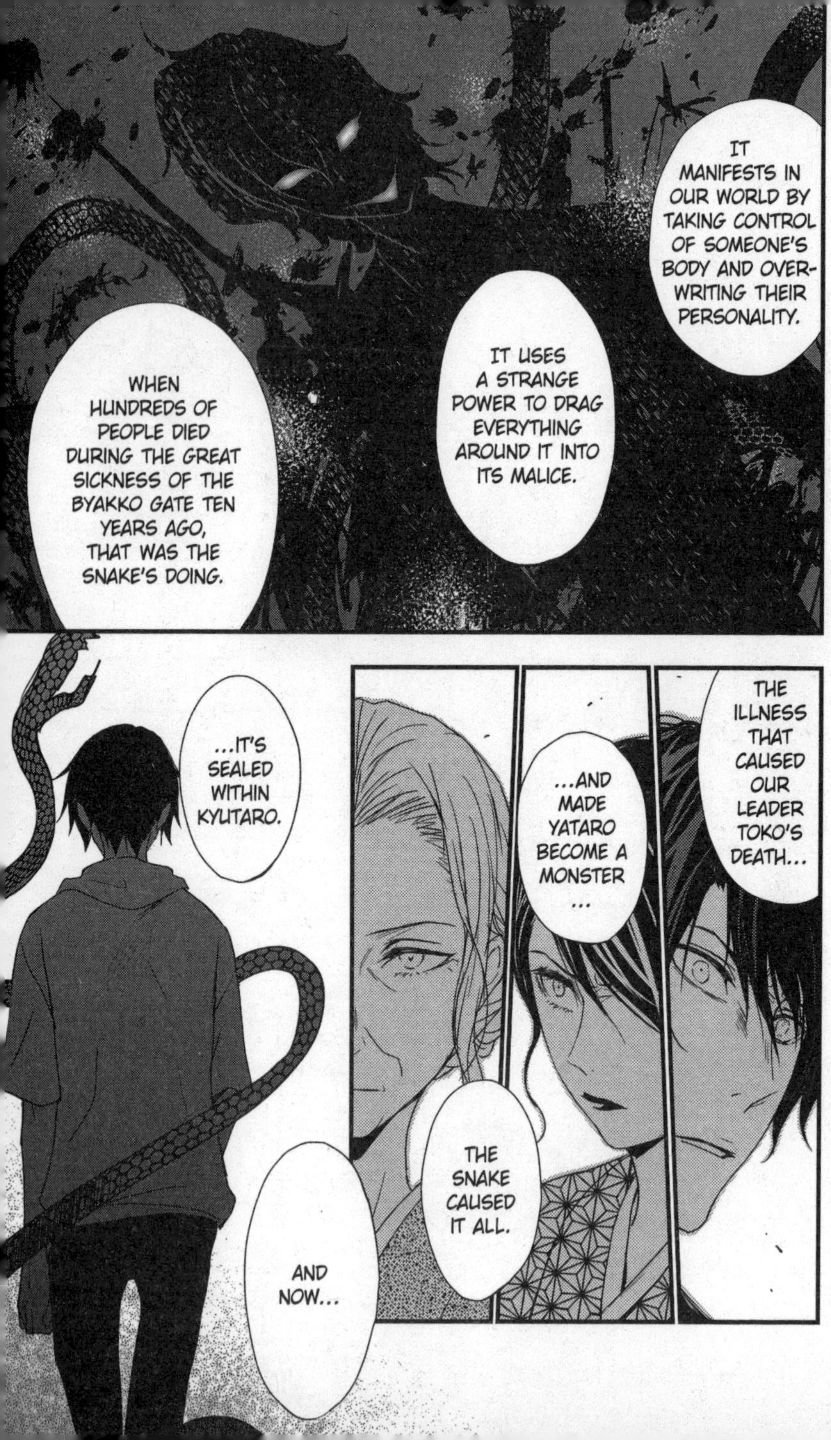
IT MANIFESTS IN OUR WORLD BY TAKING CONTROL OF SOMEONE'S BODY AND OVER-WRITING THEIR PERSONALITY.
IT USES A STRANGE POWER TO DRAG EVERYTHING AROUND IT INTO ITS MALICE.
WHEN HUNDREDS OF PEOPLE DIED DURING THE GREAT SICKNESS OF THE BYAKKO GATE TEN YEARS AGO, THAT WAS THE SNAKE'S DOING.
THE ILLNESS THAT CAUSED OUR LEADER TOKO'S DEATH...
...AND MADE YATARO BECOME A MONSTER...
THE SNAKE CAUSED IT ALL.
...IT'S SEALED WITHIN KYUTARO.
AND NOW...

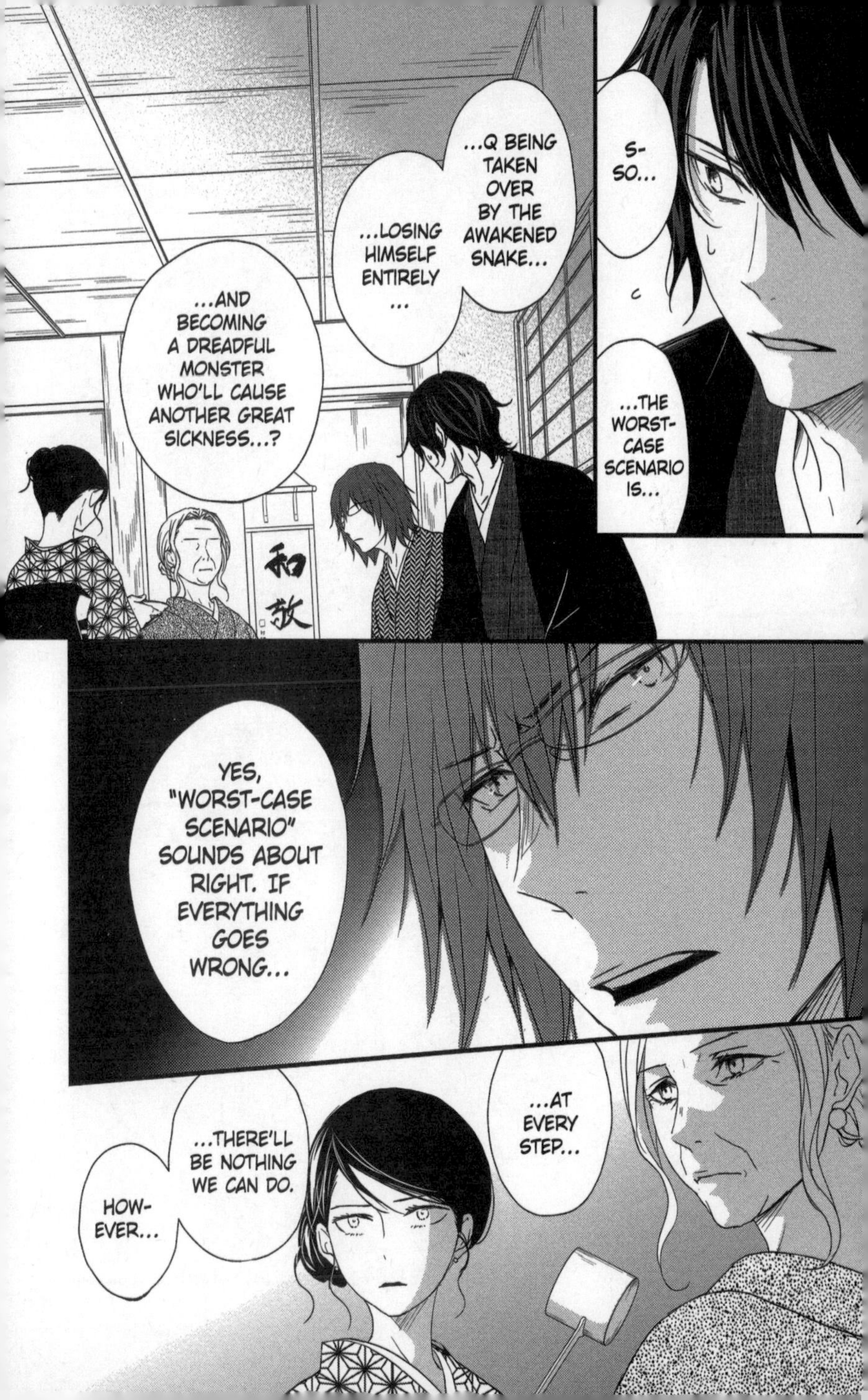
S-SO...
...THE WORST-CASE SCENARIO IS...
...Q BEING TAKEN OVER BY THE AWAKENED SNAKE...
...LOSING HIMSELF ENTIRELY...
...AND BECOMING A DREADFUL MONSTER WHO'LL CAUSE ANOTHER GREAT SICKNESS...?
YES, "WORST-CASE SCENARIO" SOUNDS ABOUT RIGHT. IF EVERYTHING GOES WRONG...
...AT EVERY STEP...
...THERE'LL BE NOTHING WE CAN DO.
HOW-EVER...

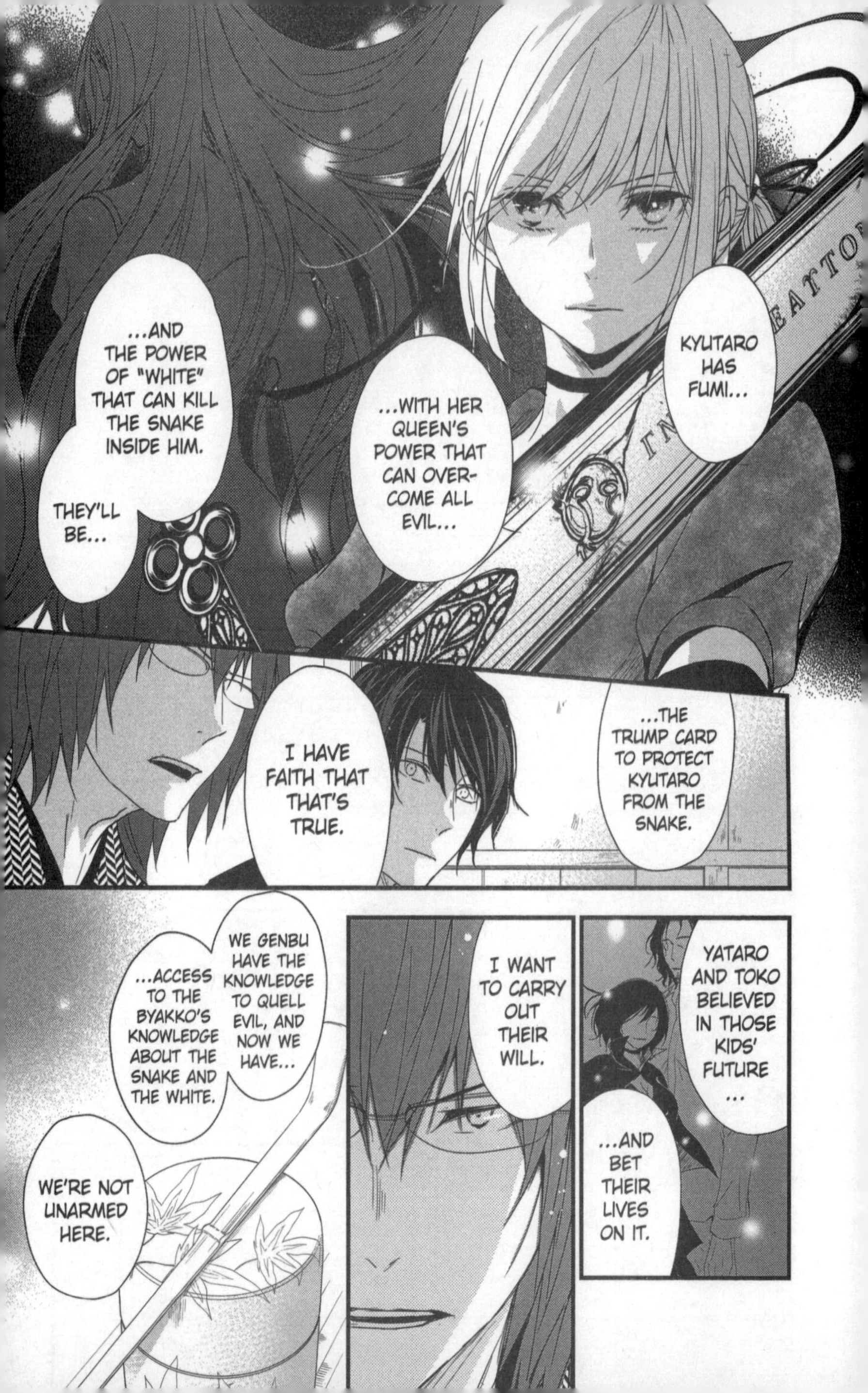
KYUTARO HAS FUMI...
...WITH HER QUEEN'S POWER THAT CAN OVER-COME ALL EVIL...
...AND THE POWER OF "WHITE" THAT CAN KILL THE SNAKE INSIDE HIM.
THEY'LL BE...
...THE TRUMP CARD TO PROTECT KYUTARO FROM THE SNAKE.
I HAVE FAITH THAT THAT'S TRUE.
YATARO AND TOKO BELIEVED IN THOSE KIDS' FUTURE...
...AND BET THEIR LIVES ON IT.
I WANT TO CARRY OUT THEIR WILL.
WE GENBU HAVE THE KNOWLEDGE TO QUELL EVIL, AND NOW WE HAVE...
...ACCESS TO THE BYAKKO'S KNOWLEDGE ABOUT THE SNAKE AND THE WHITE.
WE'RE NOT UNARMED HERE.

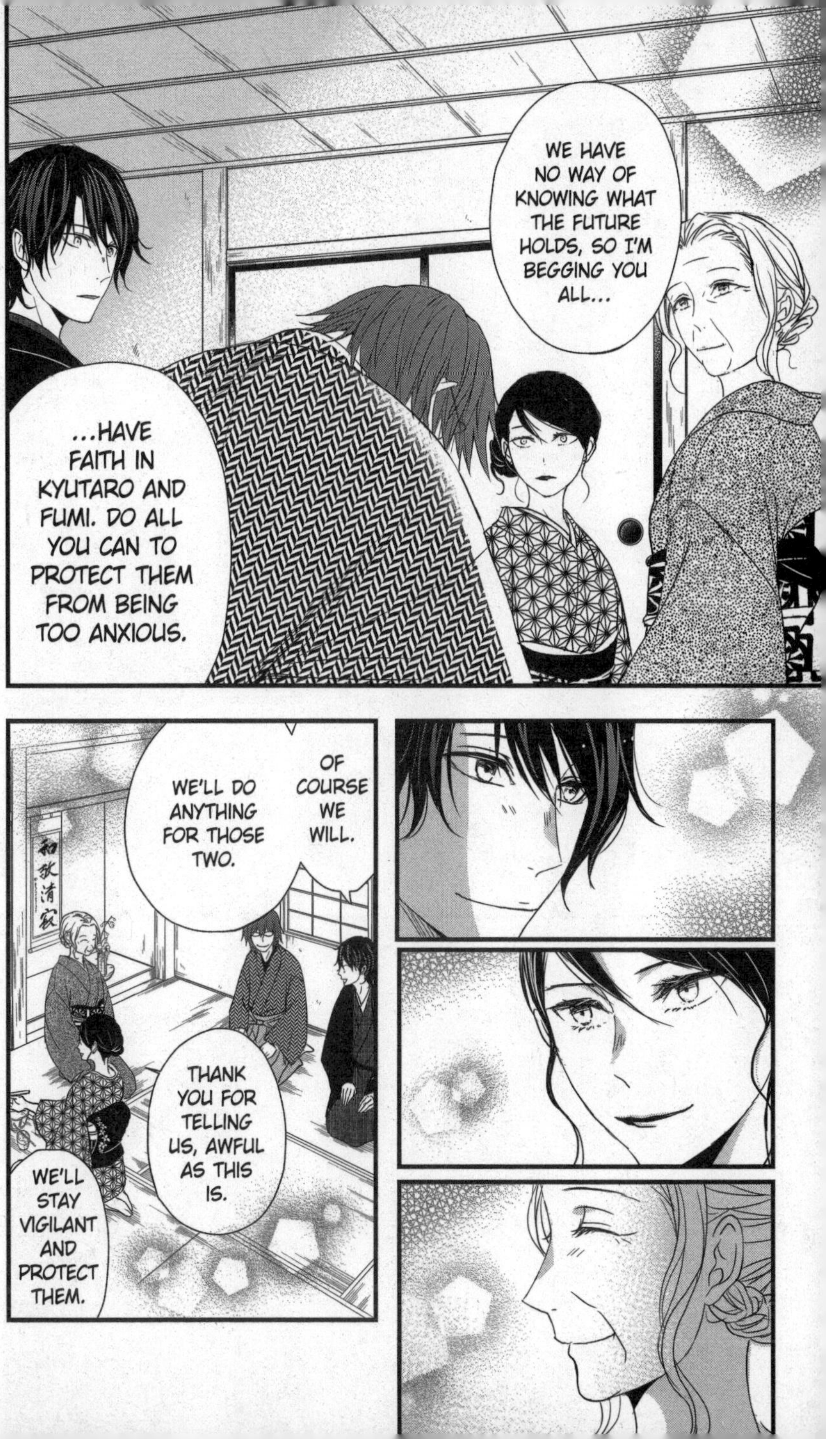
WE HAVE NO WAY OF KNOWING WHAT THE FUTURE HOLDS, SO I'M BEGGING YOU ALL...
...HAVE FAITH IN KYUTARO AND FUMI. DO ALL YOU CAN TO PROTECT THEM FROM BEING TOO ANXIOUS.
OF COURSE WE WILL.
WE'LL DO ANYTHING FOR THOSE TWO.
和敬清寂
THANK YOU FOR TELLING US, AWFUL AS THIS IS.
WE'LL STAY VIGILANT AND PROTECT THEM.

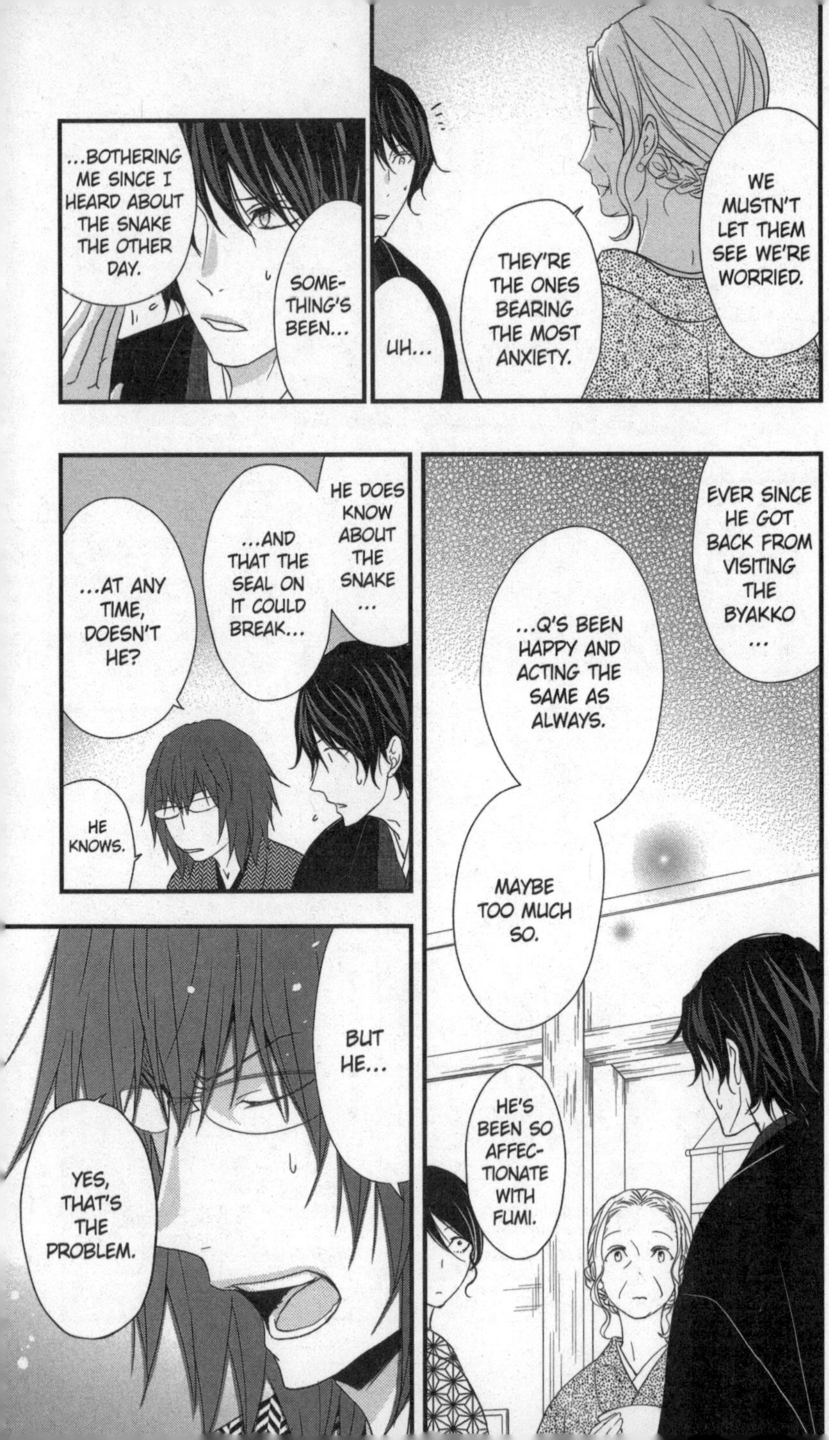
WE MUSTN'T LET THEM SEE WE'RE WORRIED.
THEY'RE THE ONES BEARING THE MOST ANXIETY.
UH...
SOMETHING'S BEEN...
...BOTHERING ME SINCE I HEARD ABOUT THE SNAKE THE OTHER DAY.
EVER SINCE HE GOT BACK FROM VISITING THE BYAKKO...
...Q'S BEEN HAPPY AND ACTING THE SAME AS ALWAYS.
MAYBE TOO MUCH SO.
HE'S BEEN SO AFFECTIONATE WITH FUMI.
HE DOES KNOW ABOUT THE SNAKE...
...AND THAT THE SEAL ON IT COULD BREAK...
...AT ANY TIME, DOESN'T HE?
HE KNOWS.
BUT HE...
YES, THAT'S THE PROBLEM.

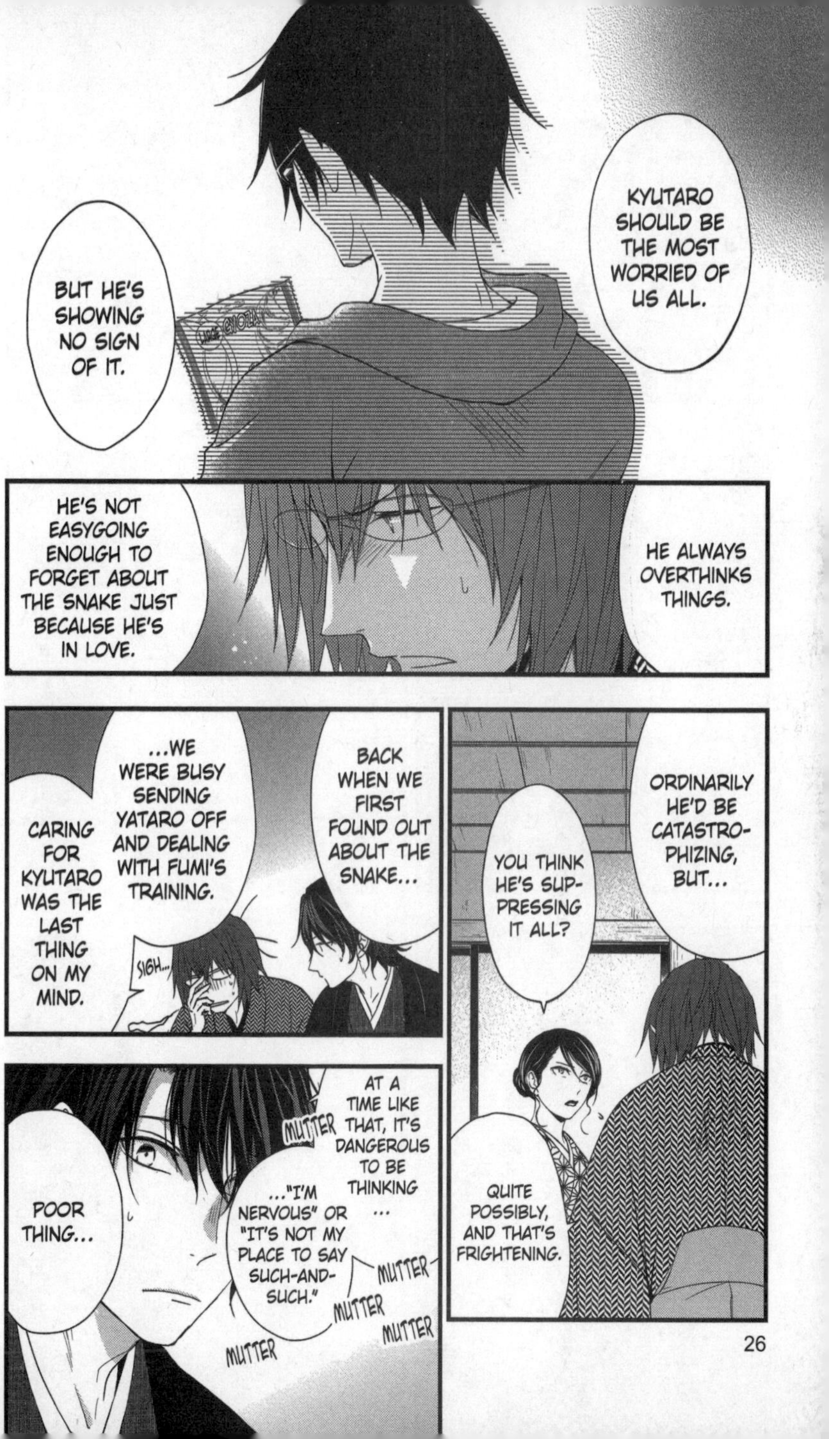
KYUTARO SHOULD BE THE MOST WORRIED OF US ALL.
BUT HE'S SHOWING NO SIGN OF IT.
HE ALWAYS OVERTHINKS THINGS.
HE'S NOT EASYGOING ENOUGH TO FORGET ABOUT THE SNAKE JUST BECAUSE HE'S IN LOVE.
ORDINARILY HE'D BE CATASTRO-PHIZING, BUT...
YOU THINK HE'S SUP-PRESSING IT ALL?
QUITE POSSIBLY, AND THAT'S FRIGHTENING.
BACK WHEN WE FIRST FOUND OUT ABOUT THE SNAKE...
...WE WERE BUSY SENDING YATARO OFF AND DEALING WITH FUMI'S TRAINING.
CARING FOR KYUTARO WAS THE LAST THING ON MY MIND.
SIGH...
AT A TIME LIKE THAT, IT'S DANGEROUS TO BE THINKING...
MUTTER
..."I'M NERVOUS" OR "IT'S NOT MY PLACE TO SAY SUCH-AND-SUCH."
MUTTER
MUTTER
MUTTER
MUTTER
POOR THING...

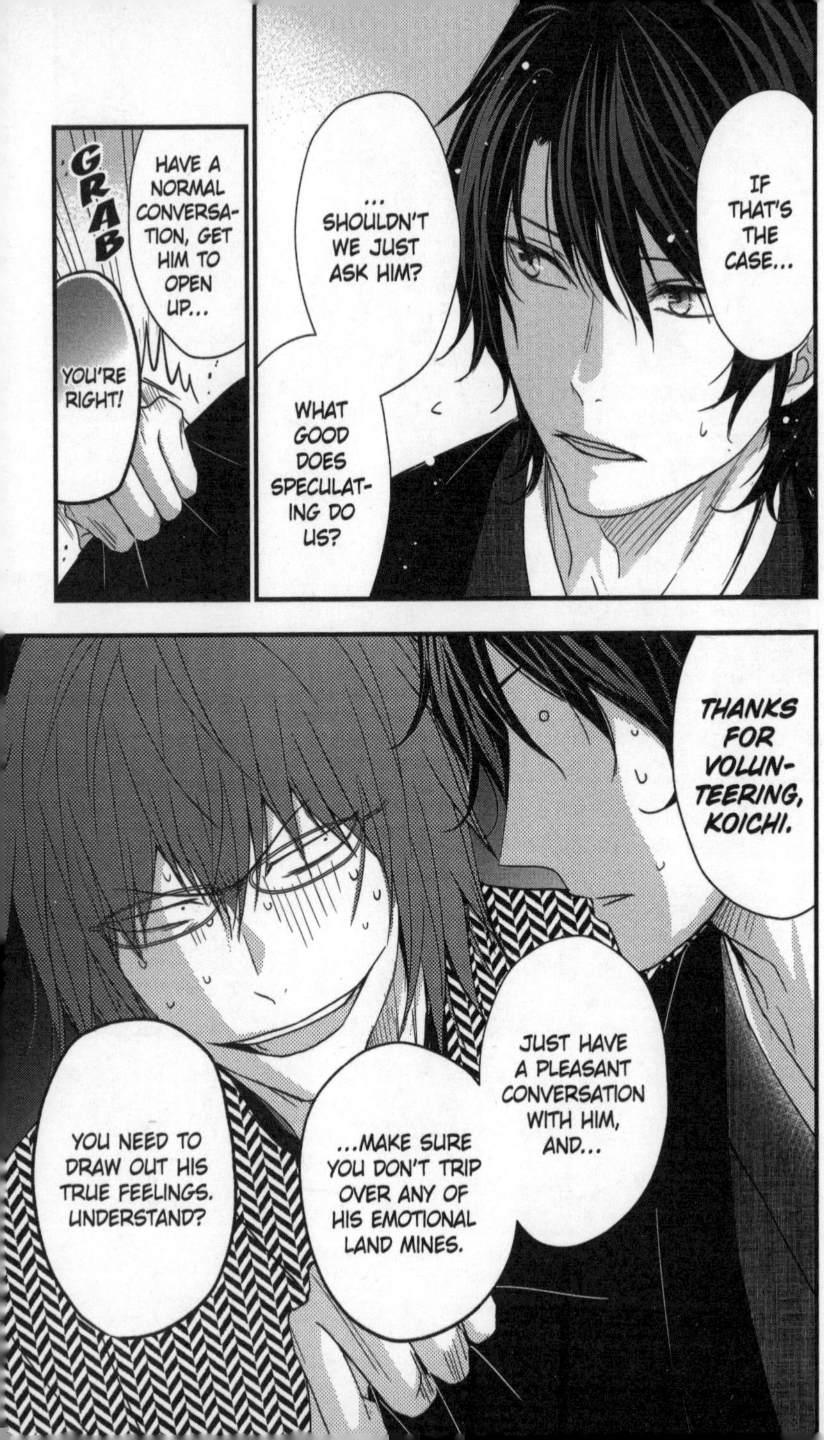
IF THAT'S THE CASE...
... SHOULDN'T WE JUST ASK HIM?
WHAT GOOD DOES SPECULATING DO US?
HAVE A NORMAL CONVERSATION, GET HIM TO OPEN UP...
GRAB
YOU'RE RIGHT!
THANKS FOR VOLUNTEERING, KOICHI.
JUST HAVE A PLEASANT CONVERSATION WITH HIM, AND...
...MAKE SURE YOU DON'T TRIP OVER ANY OF HIS EMOTIONAL LAND MINES.
YOU NEED TO DRAW OUT HIS TRUE FEELINGS. UNDERSTAND?

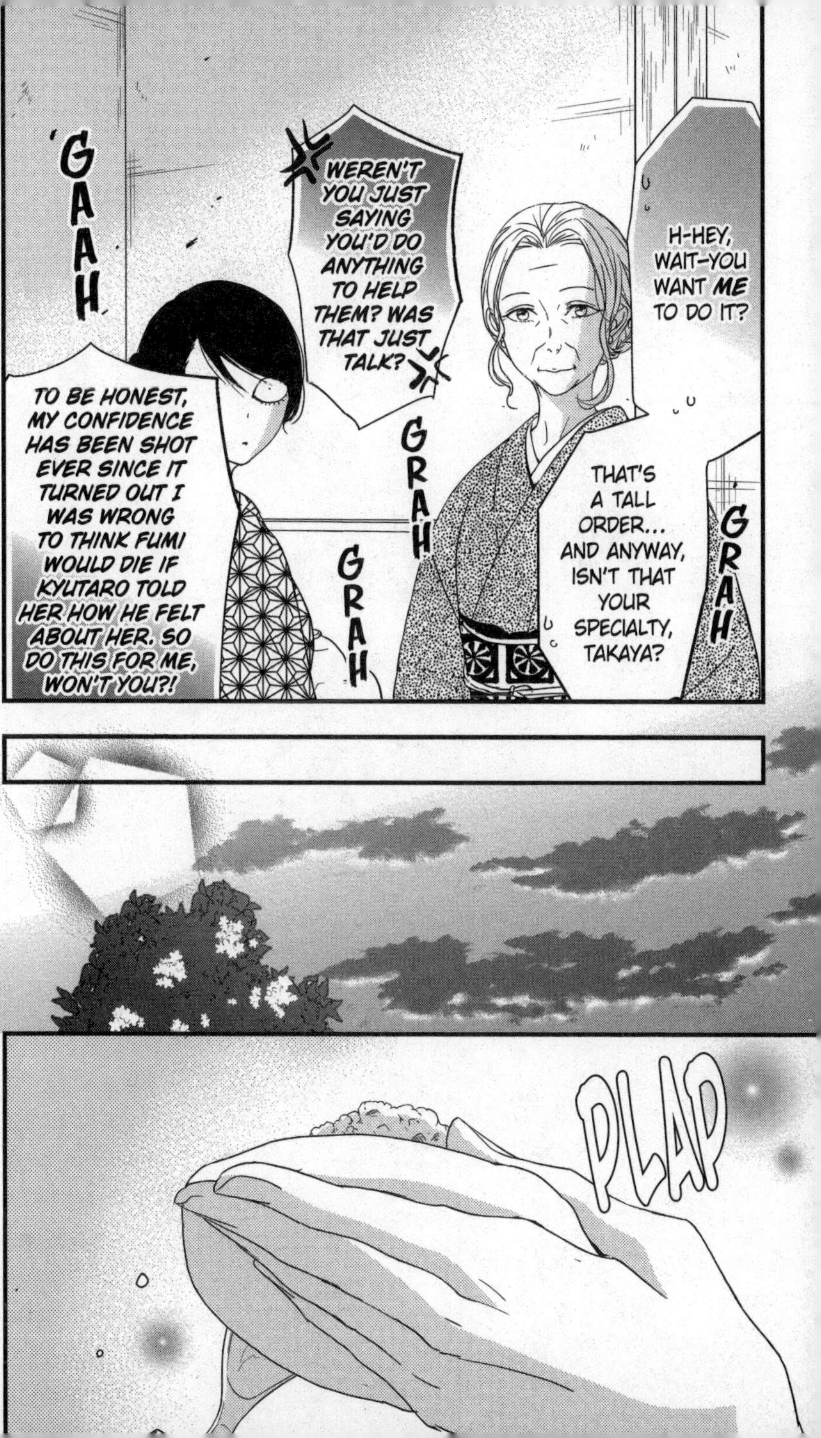
H-HEY, WAIT—YOU WANT ME TO DO IT?
THAT'S A TALL ORDER... AND ANYWAY, ISN'T THAT YOUR SPECIALTY, TAKAYA?
GRAH
WEREN'T YOU JUST SAYING YOU'D DO ANYTHING TO HELP THEM? WAS THAT JUST TALK?
GRAH
GRAH
TO BE HONEST, MY CONFIDENCE HAS BEEN SHOT EVER SINCE IT TURNED OUT I WAS WRONG TO THINK FUMI WOULD DIE IF KYUTARO TOLD HER HOW HE FELT ABOUT HER. SO DO THIS FOR ME, WON'T YOU?!
GAAH
PLAP

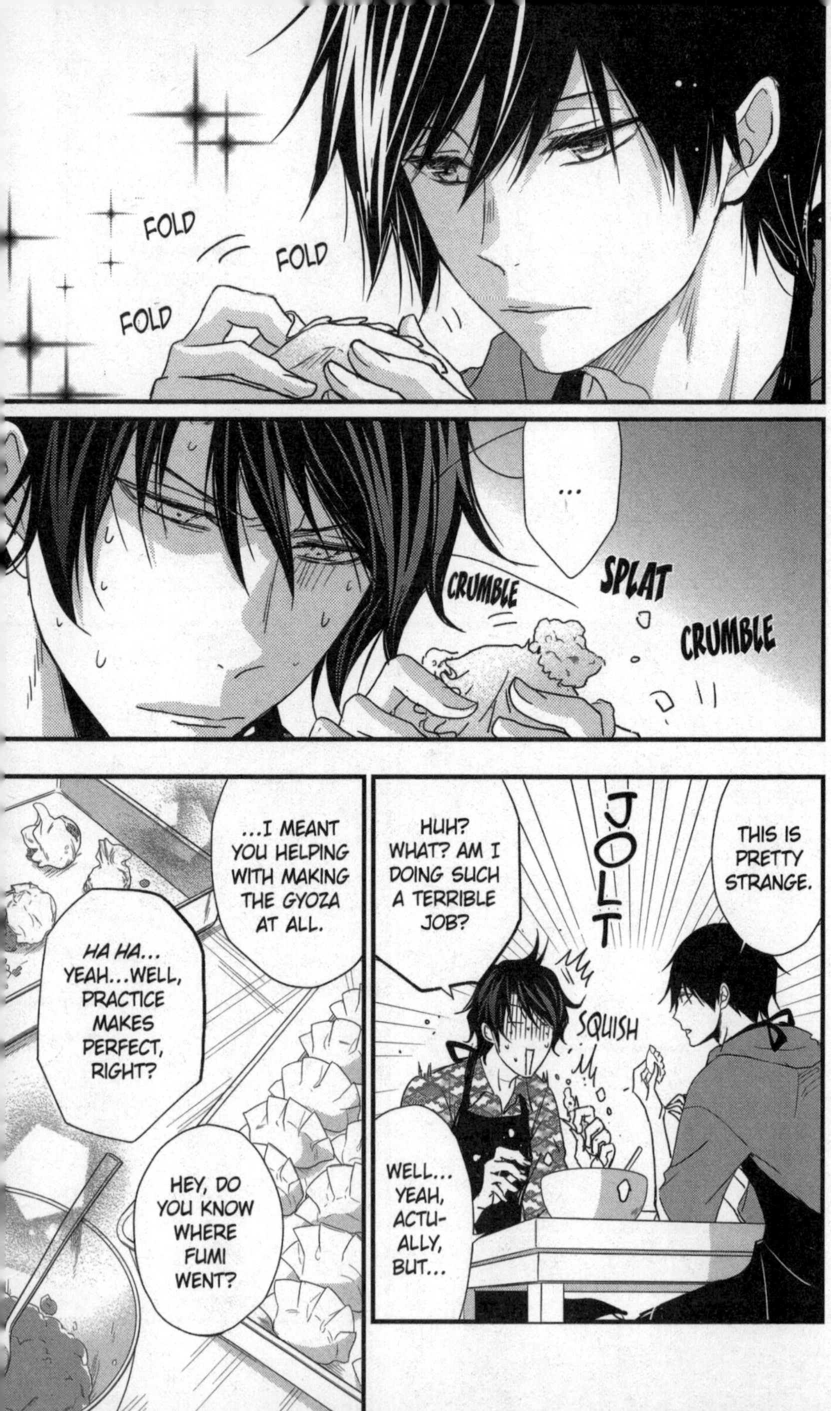
FOLD
FOLD
FOLD
...
SPLAT
CRUMBLE
CRUMBLE
THIS IS PRETTY STRANGE.
JOLT
HUH? WHAT? AM I DOING SUCH A TERRIBLE JOB?
SQUISH
WELL... YEAH, ACTU-ALLY, BUT...
...I MEANT YOU HELPING WITH MAKING THE GYOZA AT ALL.
HA HA... YEAH...WELL, PRACTICE MAKES PERFECT, RIGHT?
HEY, DO YOU KNOW WHERE FUMI WENT?

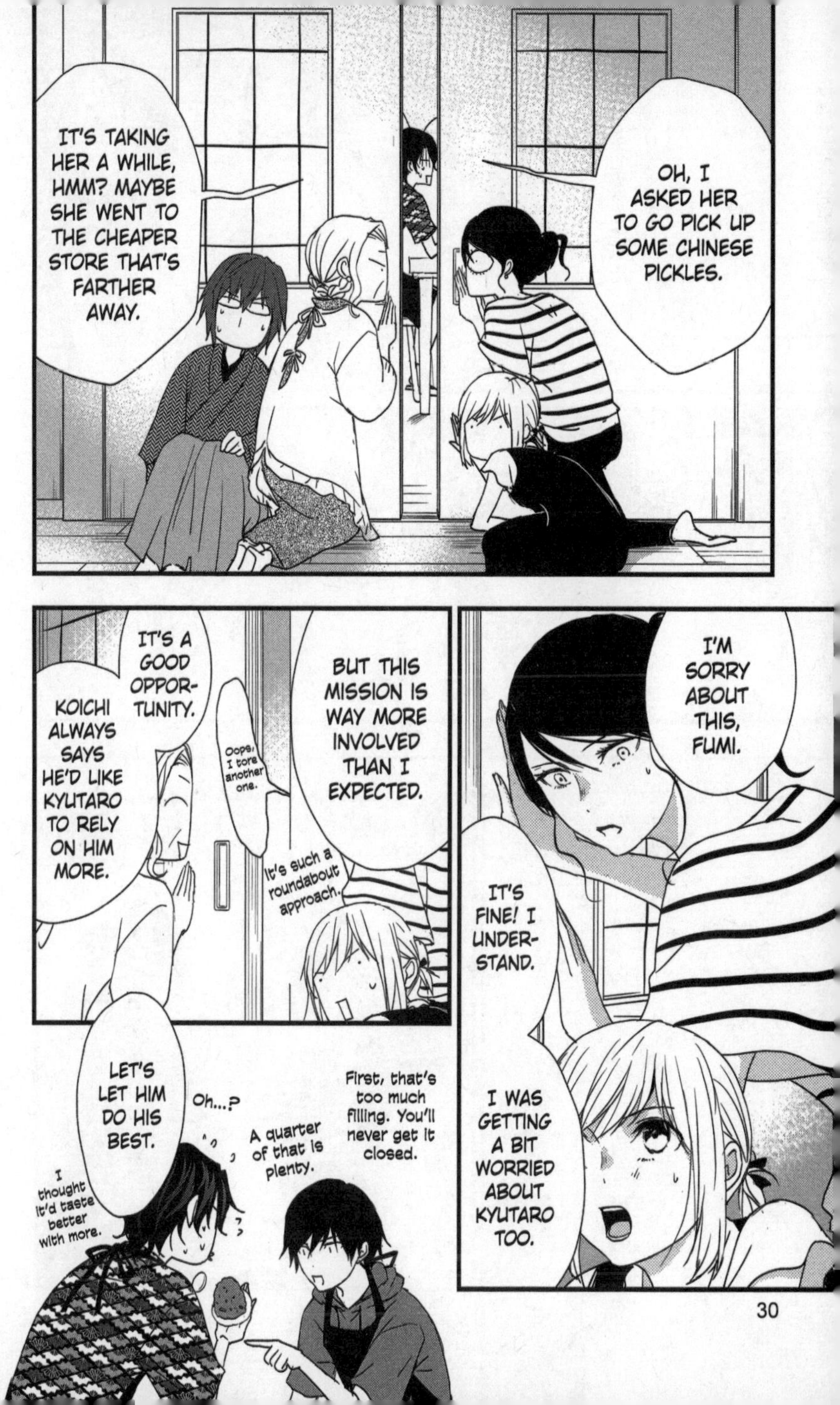
IT'S TAKING HER A WHILE, HMM? MAYBE SHE WENT TO THE CHEAPER STORE THAT'S FARTHER AWAY.
OH, I ASKED HER TO GO PICK UP SOME CHINESE PICKLES.
I'M SORRY ABOUT THIS, FUMI.
IT'S FINE! I UNDERSTAND.
I WAS GETTING A BIT WORRIED ABOUT KYUTARO TOO.
BUT THIS MISSION IS WAY MORE INVOLVED THAN I EXPECTED.
Oops, I tore another one.
It's such a roundabout approach.
IT'S A GOOD OPPORTUNITY.
KOICHI ALWAYS SAYS HE'D LIKE KYUTARO TO RELY ON HIM MORE.
LET'S LET HIM DO HIS BEST.
First, that's too much filling. You'll never get it closed.
A quarter of that is plenty.
Oh...?
I thought it'd taste better with more.

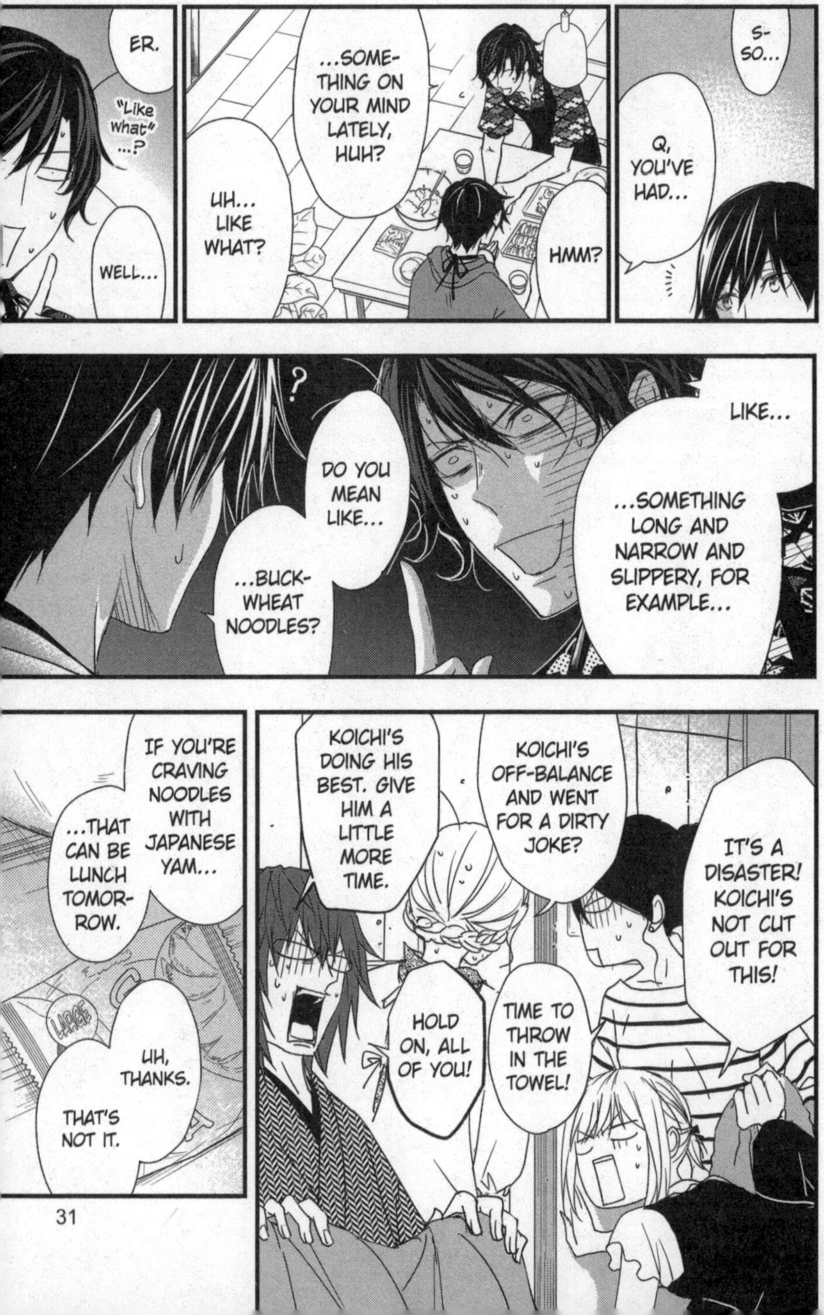
S-SO...
Q, YOU'VE HAD...
...SOMETHING ON YOUR MIND LATELY, HUH?
HMM?
UH... LIKE WHAT?
ER.
"Like what" ...?
WELL...
LIKE...
...SOMETHING LONG AND NARROW AND SLIPPERY, FOR EXAMPLE...
DO YOU MEAN LIKE...
...BUCKWHEAT NOODLES?
IT'S A DISASTER! KOICHI'S NOT CUT OUT FOR THIS!
KOICHI'S OFF-BALANCE AND WENT FOR A DIRTY JOKE?
KOICHI'S DOING HIS BEST. GIVE HIM A LITTLE MORE TIME.
TIME TO THROW IN THE TOWEL!
HOLD ON, ALL OF YOU!
IF YOU'RE CRAVING NOODLES WITH JAPANESE YAM...
...THAT CAN BE LUNCH TOMORROW.
UH, THANKS.
THAT'S NOT IT.

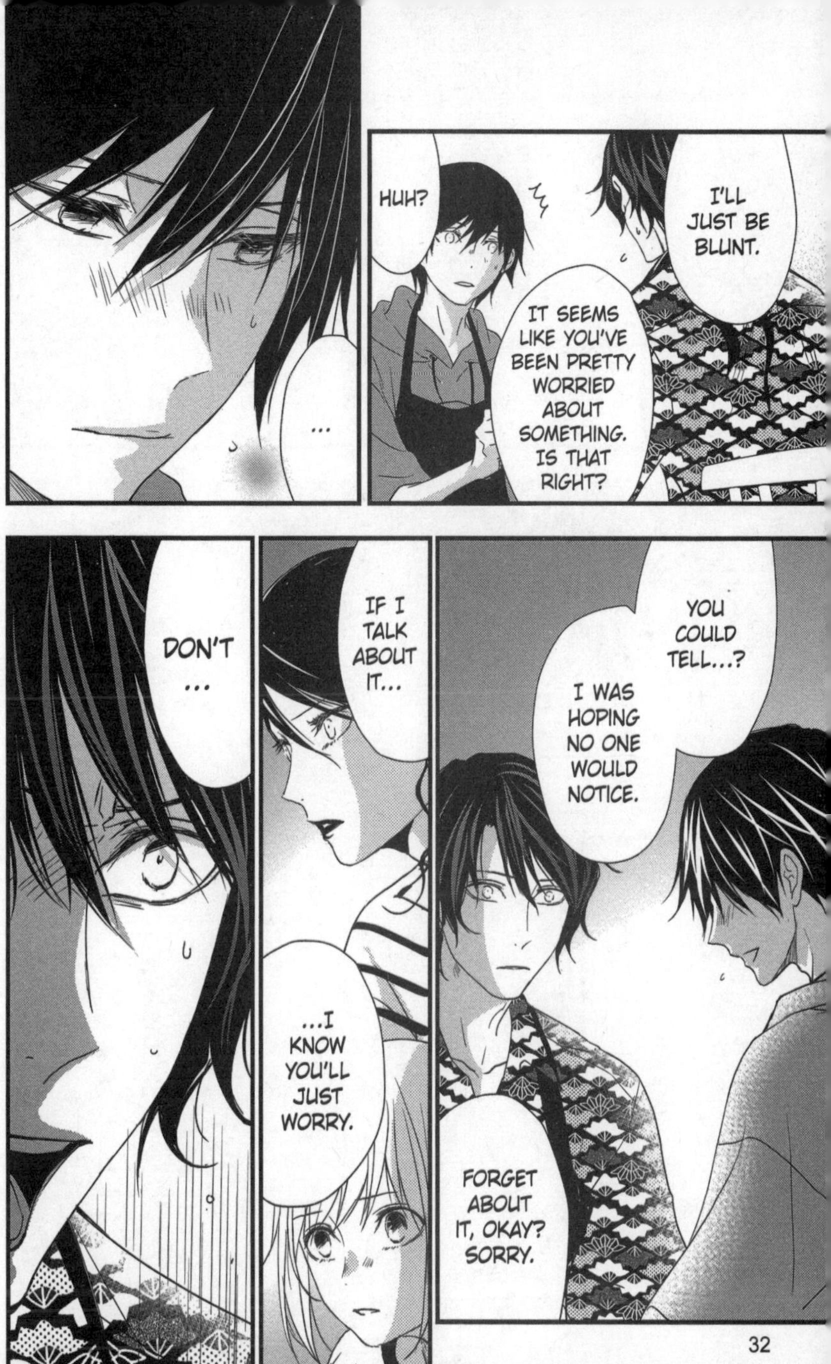
I'LL JUST BE BLUNT.
HUH?
IT SEEMS LIKE YOU'VE BEEN PRETTY WORRIED ABOUT SOMETHING. IS THAT RIGHT?
...
YOU COULD TELL...?
I WAS HOPING NO ONE WOULD NOTICE.
FORGET ABOUT IT, OKAY? SORRY.
IF I TALK ABOUT IT...
...I KNOW YOU'LL JUST WORRY.
DON'T ...

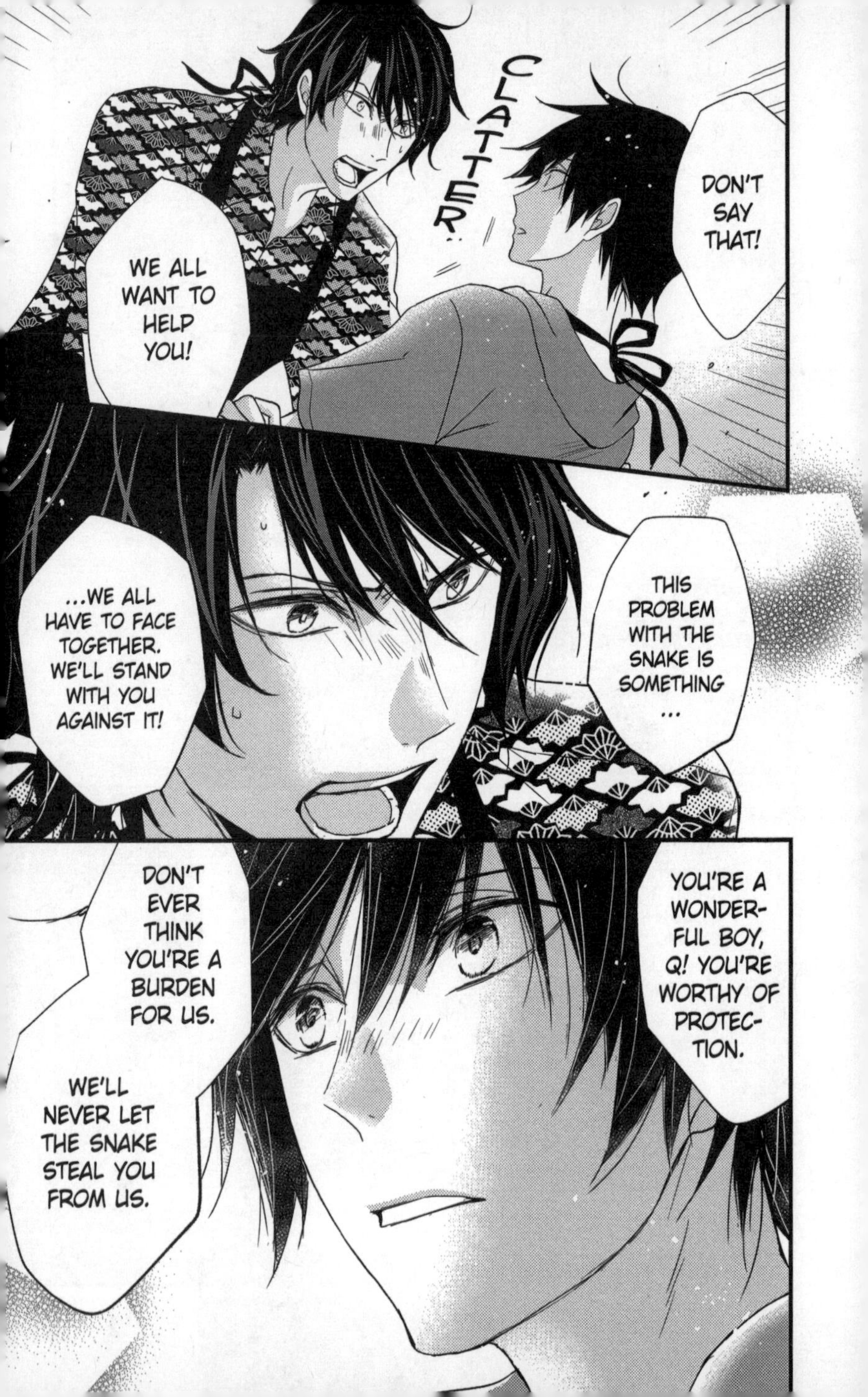
DON'T SAY THAT!
CLATTER!!
WE ALL WANT TO HELP YOU!
THIS PROBLEM WITH THE SNAKE IS SOMETHING...
...WE ALL HAVE TO FACE TOGETHER. WE'LL STAND WITH YOU AGAINST IT!
YOU'RE A WONDER-FUL BOY, Q! YOU'RE WORTHY OF PROTEC-TION.
DON'T EVER THINK YOU'RE A BURDEN FOR US.
WE'LL NEVER LET THE SNAKE STEAL YOU FROM US.

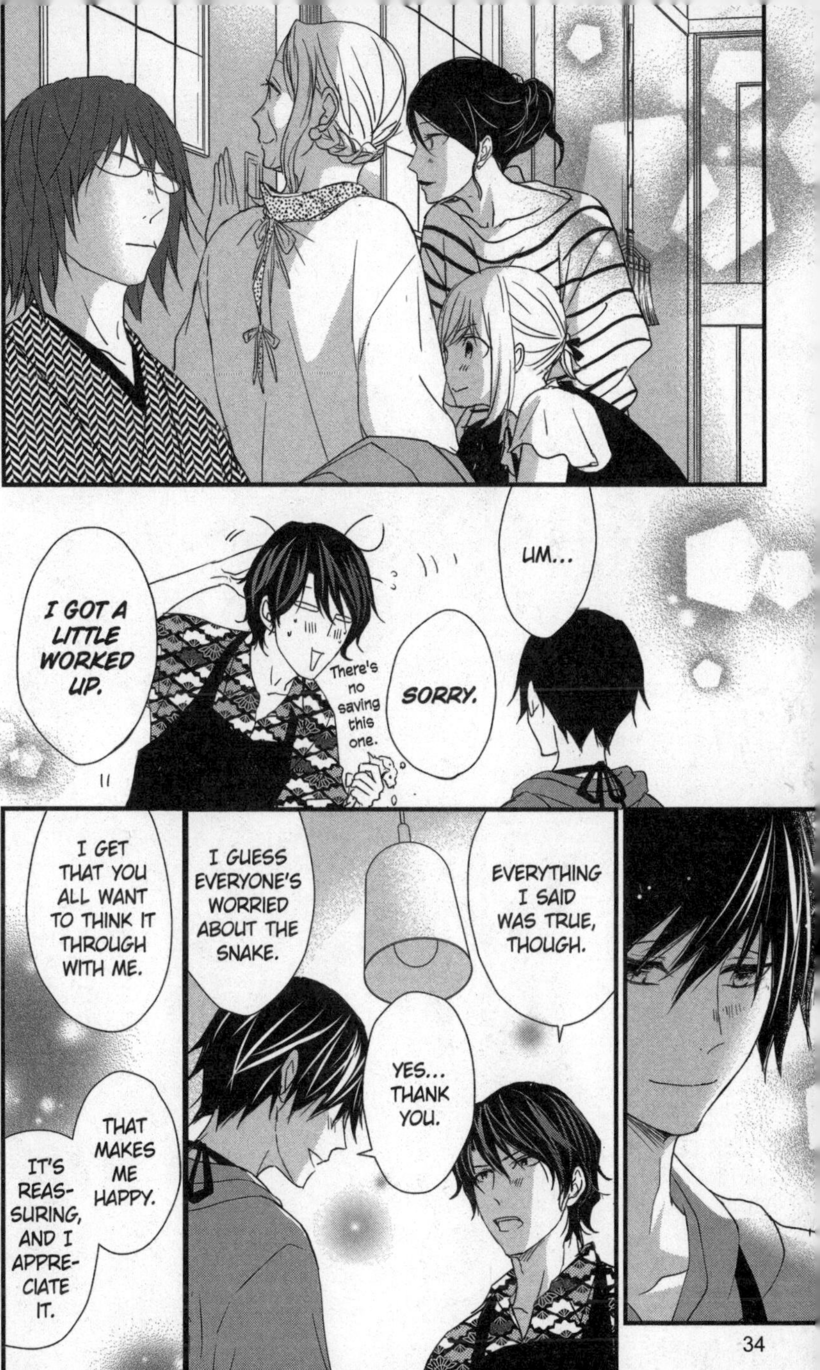
UM...
SORRY.
There's no saving this one.
I GOT A LITTLE WORKED UP.
EVERYTHING I SAID WAS TRUE, THOUGH.
I GUESS EVERYONE'S WORRIED ABOUT THE SNAKE.
YES... THANK YOU.
I GET THAT YOU ALL WANT TO THINK IT THROUGH WITH ME.
THAT MAKES ME HAPPY.
IT'S REAS-SURING, AND I APPRE-CIATE IT.

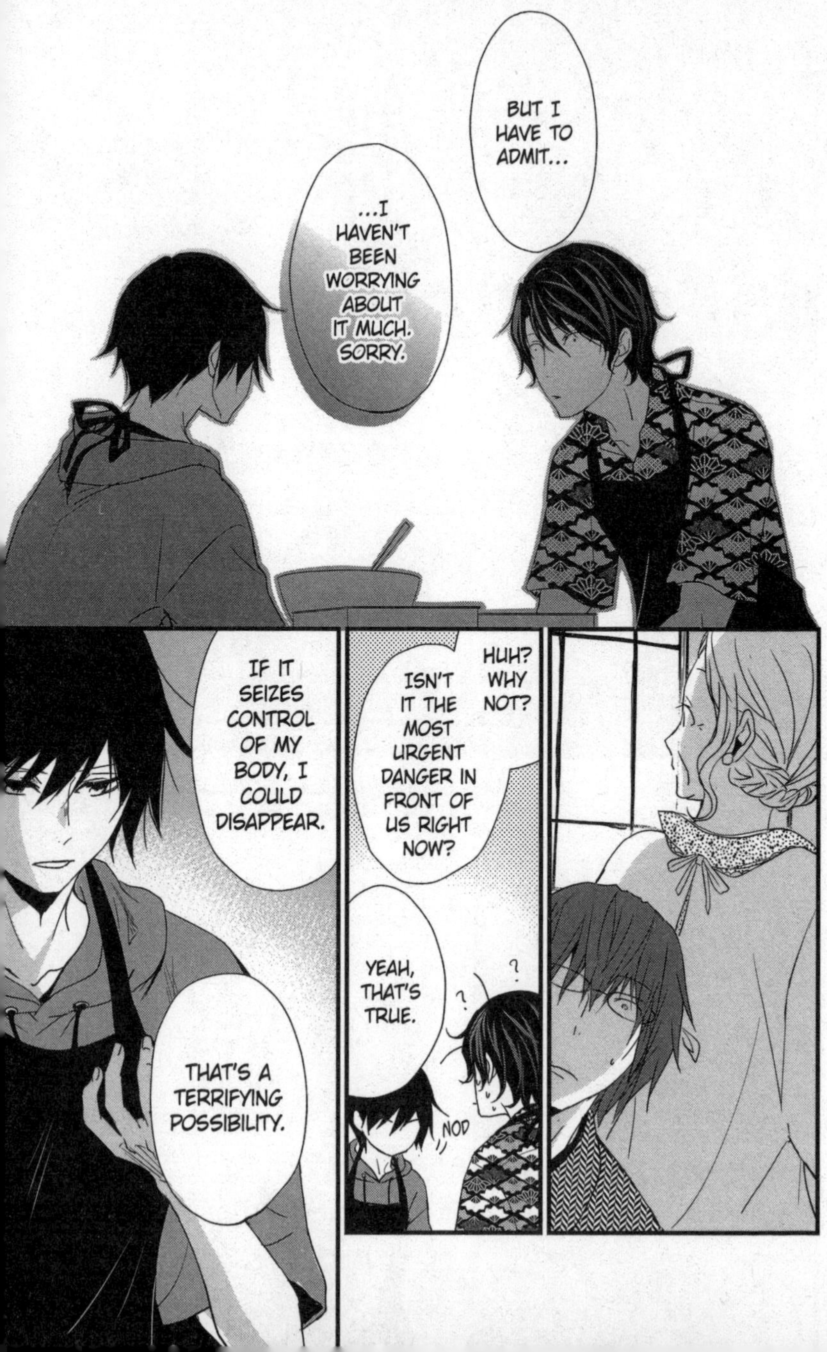
BUT I HAVE TO ADMIT...
...I HAVEN'T BEEN WORRYING ABOUT IT MUCH. SORRY.
HUH? WHY NOT?
ISN'T IT THE MOST URGENT DANGER IN FRONT OF US RIGHT NOW?
YEAH, THAT'S TRUE.
?
?
NOD
IF IT SEIZES CONTROL OF MY BODY, I COULD DISAPPEAR.
THAT'S A TERRIFYING POSSIBILITY.

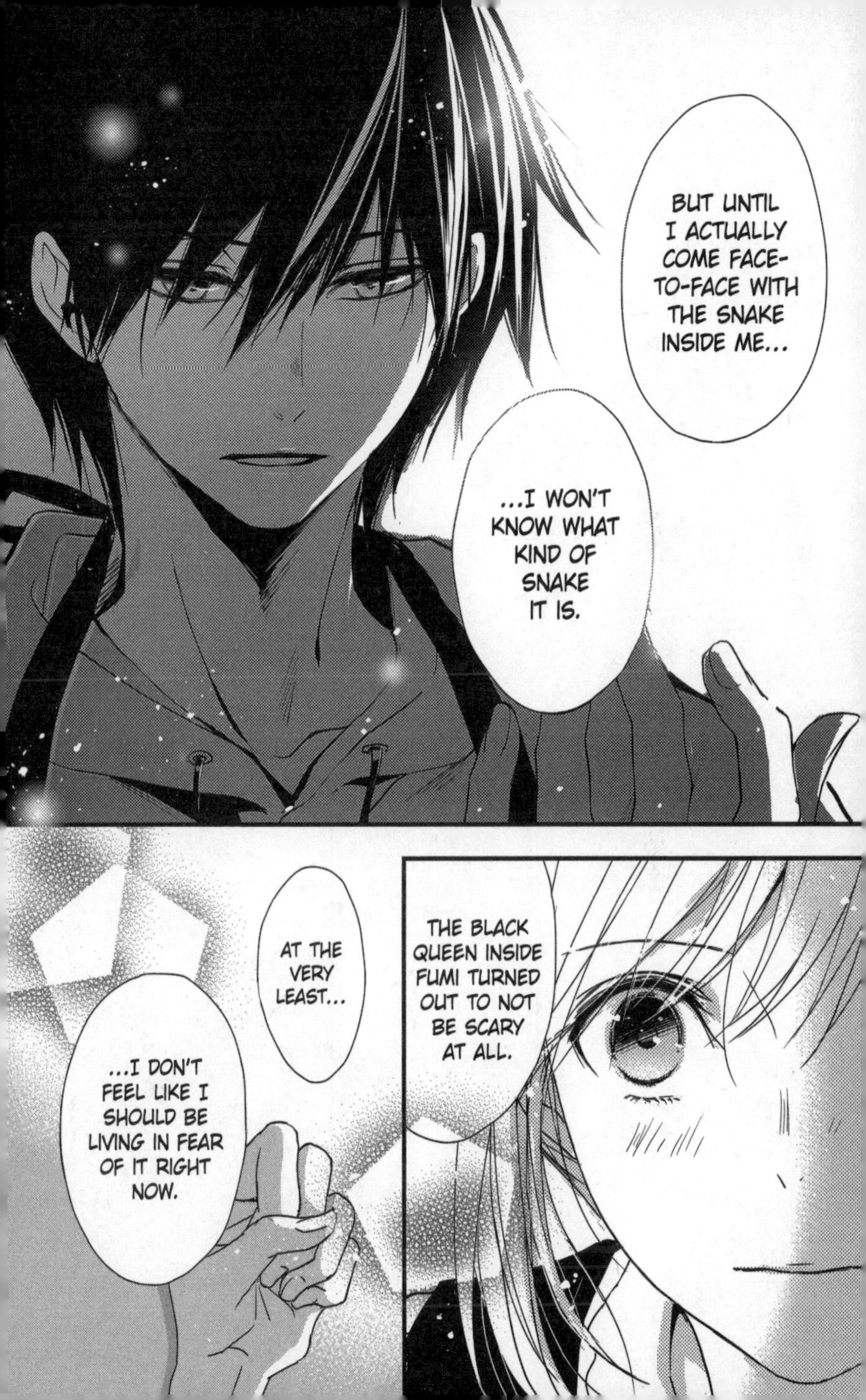
BUT UNTIL I ACTUALLY COME FACE-TO-FACE WITH THE SNAKE INSIDE ME...
...I WON'T KNOW WHAT KIND OF SNAKE IT IS.
THE BLACK QUEEN INSIDE FUMI TURNED OUT TO NOT BE SCARY AT ALL.
AT THE VERY LEAST...
...I DON'T FEEL LIKE I SHOULD BE LIVING IN FEAR OF IT RIGHT NOW.

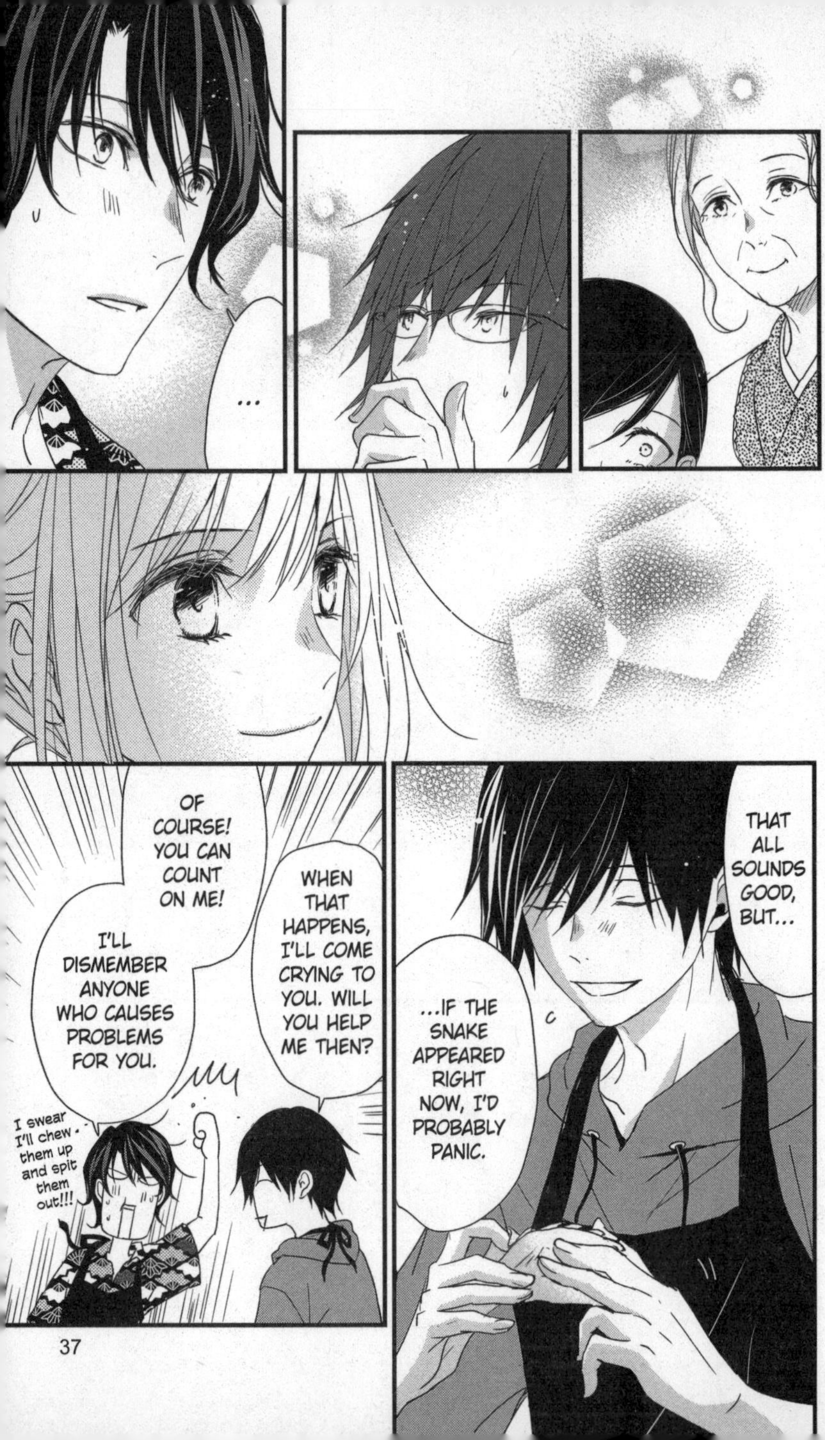
...
THAT ALL SOUNDS GOOD, BUT...
...IF THE SNAKE APPEARED RIGHT NOW, I'D PROBABLY PANIC.
WHEN THAT HAPPENS, I'LL COME CRYING TO YOU. WILL YOU HELP ME THEN?
OF COURSE! YOU CAN COUNT ON ME!
I'LL DISMEMBER ANYONE WHO CAUSES PROBLEMS FOR YOU.
I swear I'll chew them up and spit them out!!!

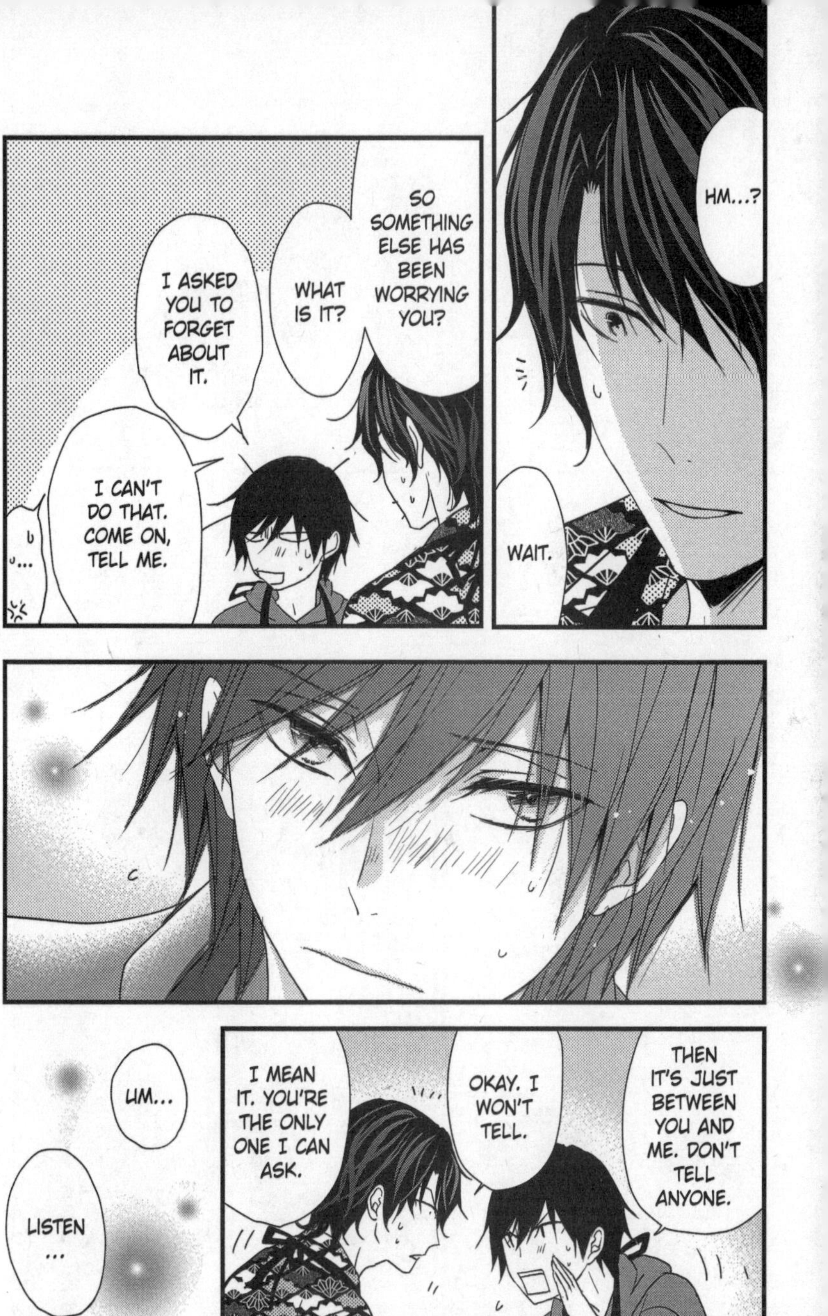
HM...?
WAIT.
SO SOMETHING ELSE HAS BEEN WORRYING YOU?
WHAT IS IT?
I ASKED YOU TO FORGET ABOUT IT.
I CAN'T DO THAT. COME ON, TELL ME.
U...
THEN IT'S JUST BETWEEN YOU AND ME. DON'T TELL ANYONE.
OKAY. I WON'T TELL.
I MEAN IT. YOU'RE THE ONLY ONE I CAN ASK.
UM...
LISTEN...

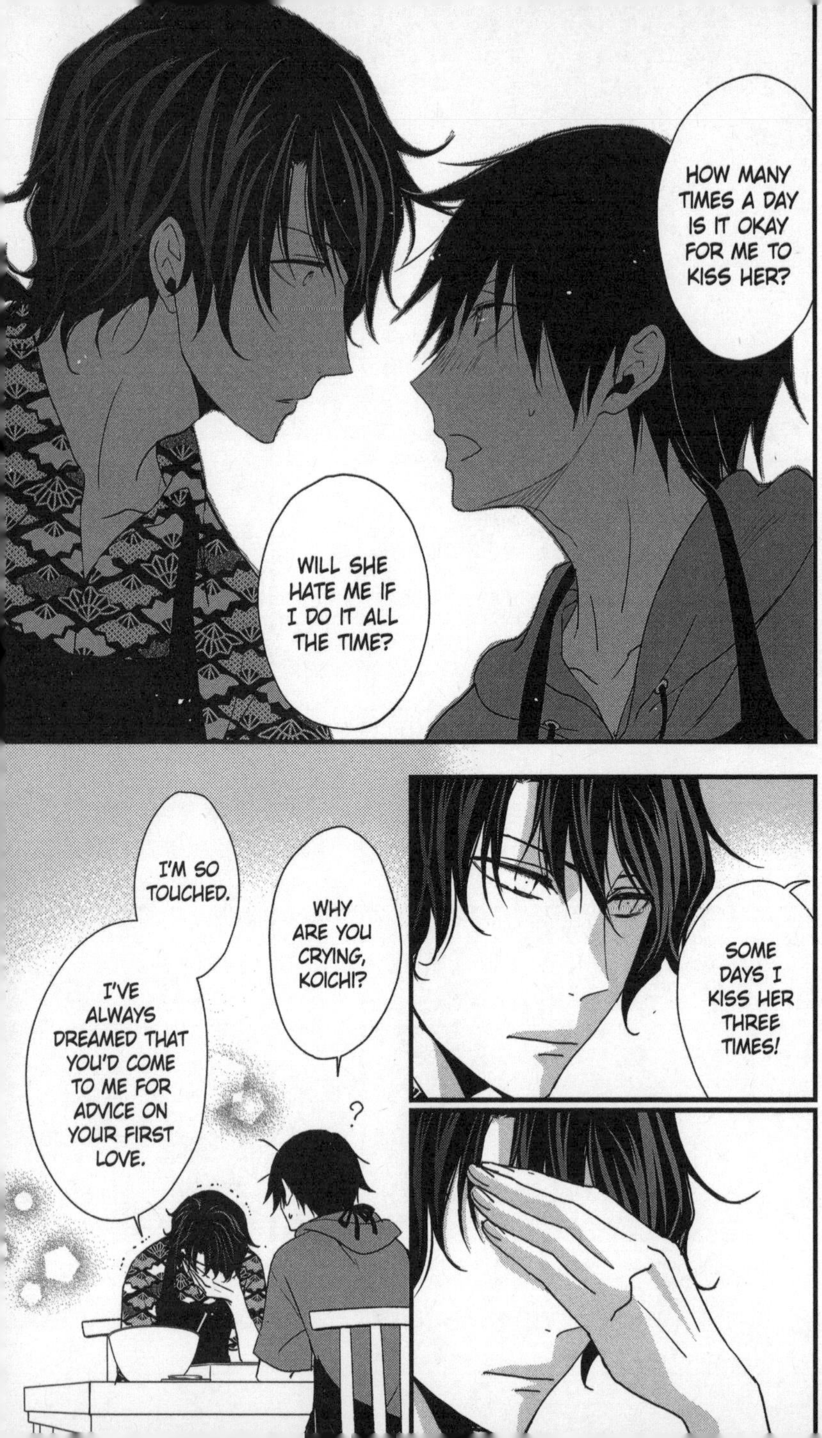
HOW MANY TIMES A DAY IS IT OKAY FOR ME TO KISS HER?
WILL SHE HATE ME IF I DO IT ALL THE TIME?
SOME DAYS I KISS HER THREE TIMES!
WHY ARE YOU CRYING, KOICHI?
?
I'M SO TOUCHED.
I'VE ALWAYS DREAMED THAT YOU'D COME TO ME FOR ADVICE ON YOUR FIRST LOVE.

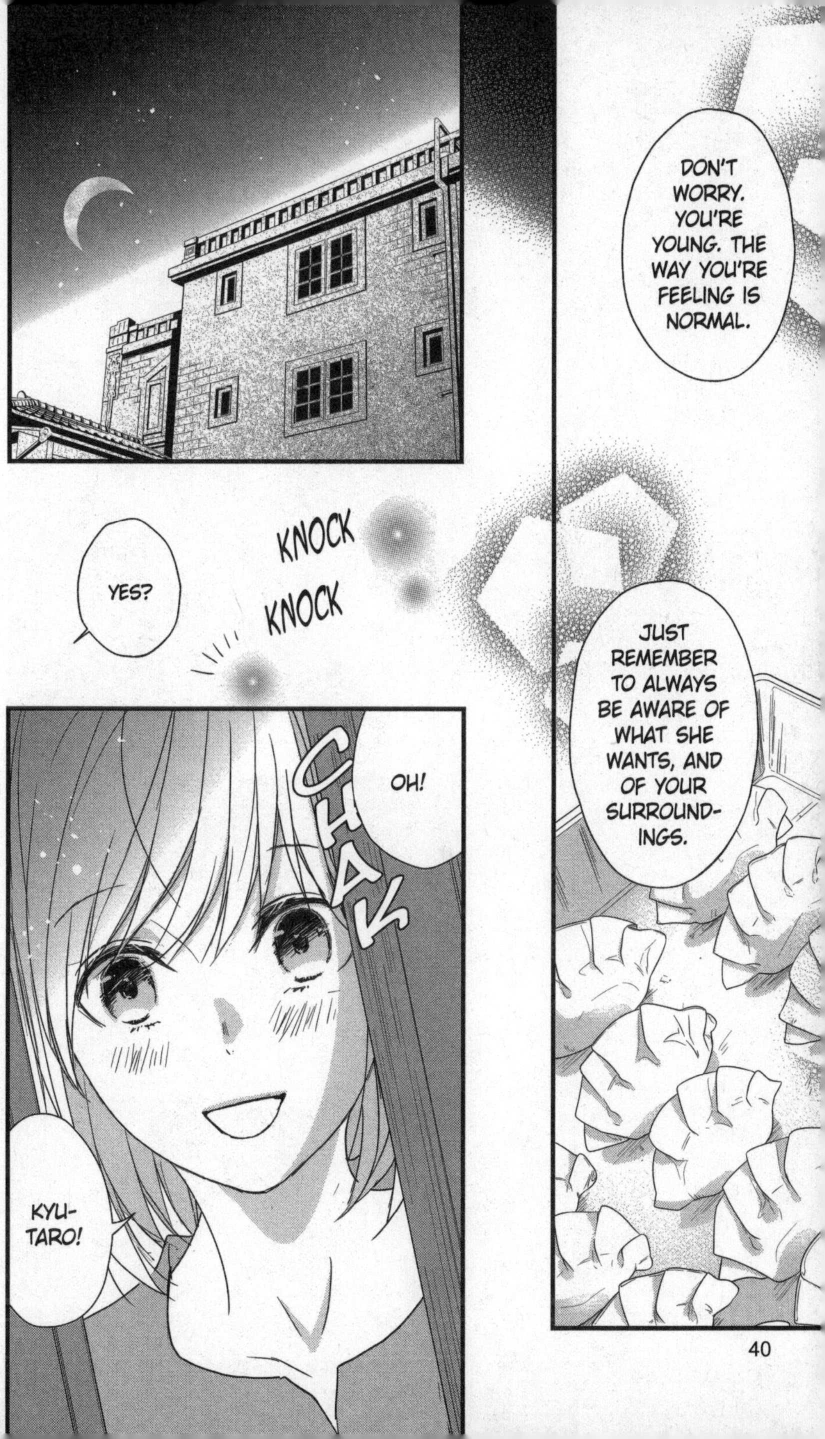
DON'T WORRY. YOU'RE YOUNG. THE WAY YOU'RE FEELING IS NORMAL.
JUST REMEMBER TO ALWAYS BE AWARE OF WHAT SHE WANTS, AND OF YOUR SURROUND-INGS.
KNOCK
KNOCK
YES?
CHAK
OH!
KYU-TARO!

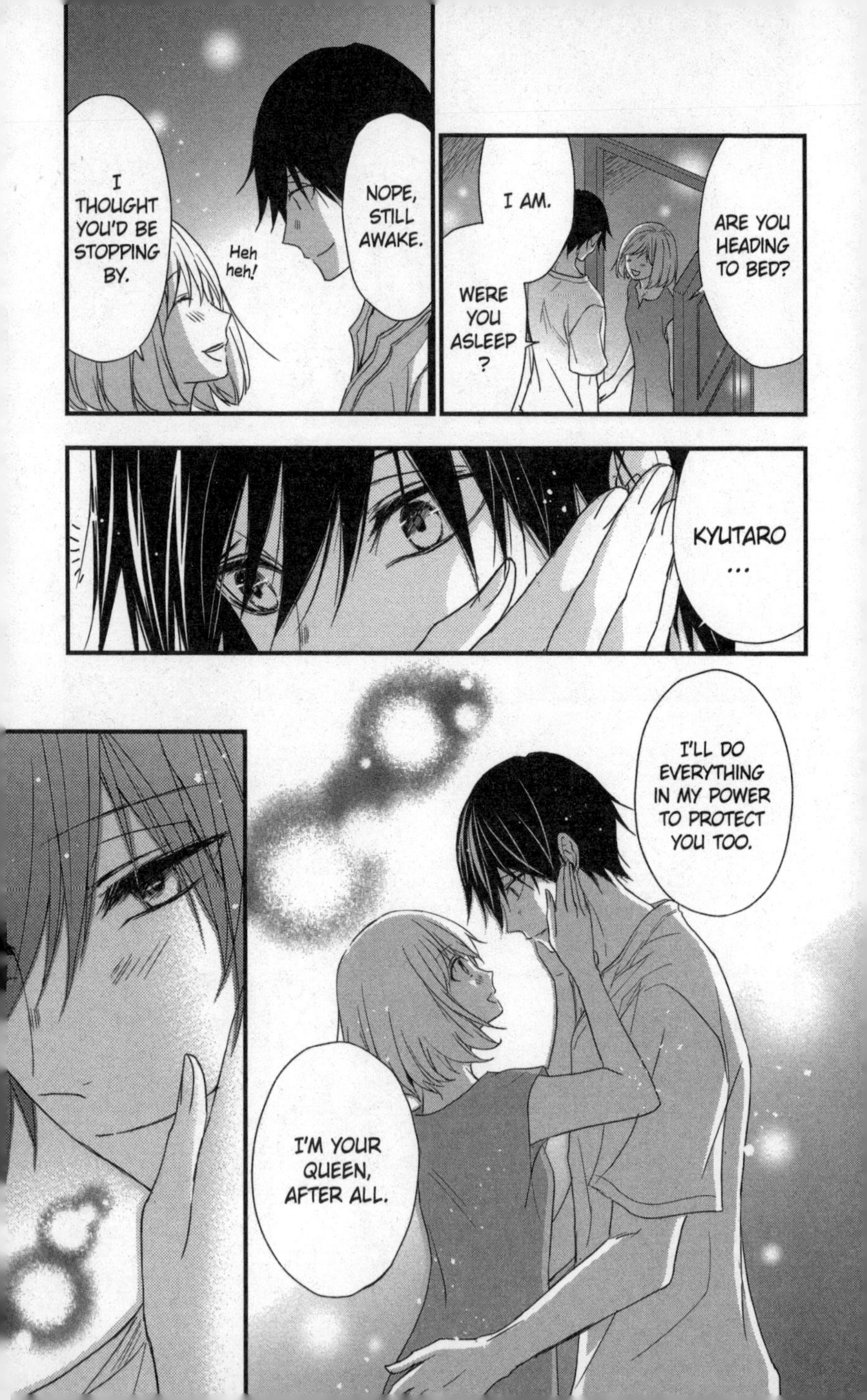
ARE YOU HEADING TO BED?
I AM.
WERE YOU ASLEEP?
NOPE, STILL AWAKE.
Heh heh!
I THOUGHT YOU'D BE STOPPING BY.
KYUTARO...
I'LL DO EVERYTHING IN MY POWER TO PROTECT YOU TOO.
I'M YOUR QUEEN, AFTER ALL.

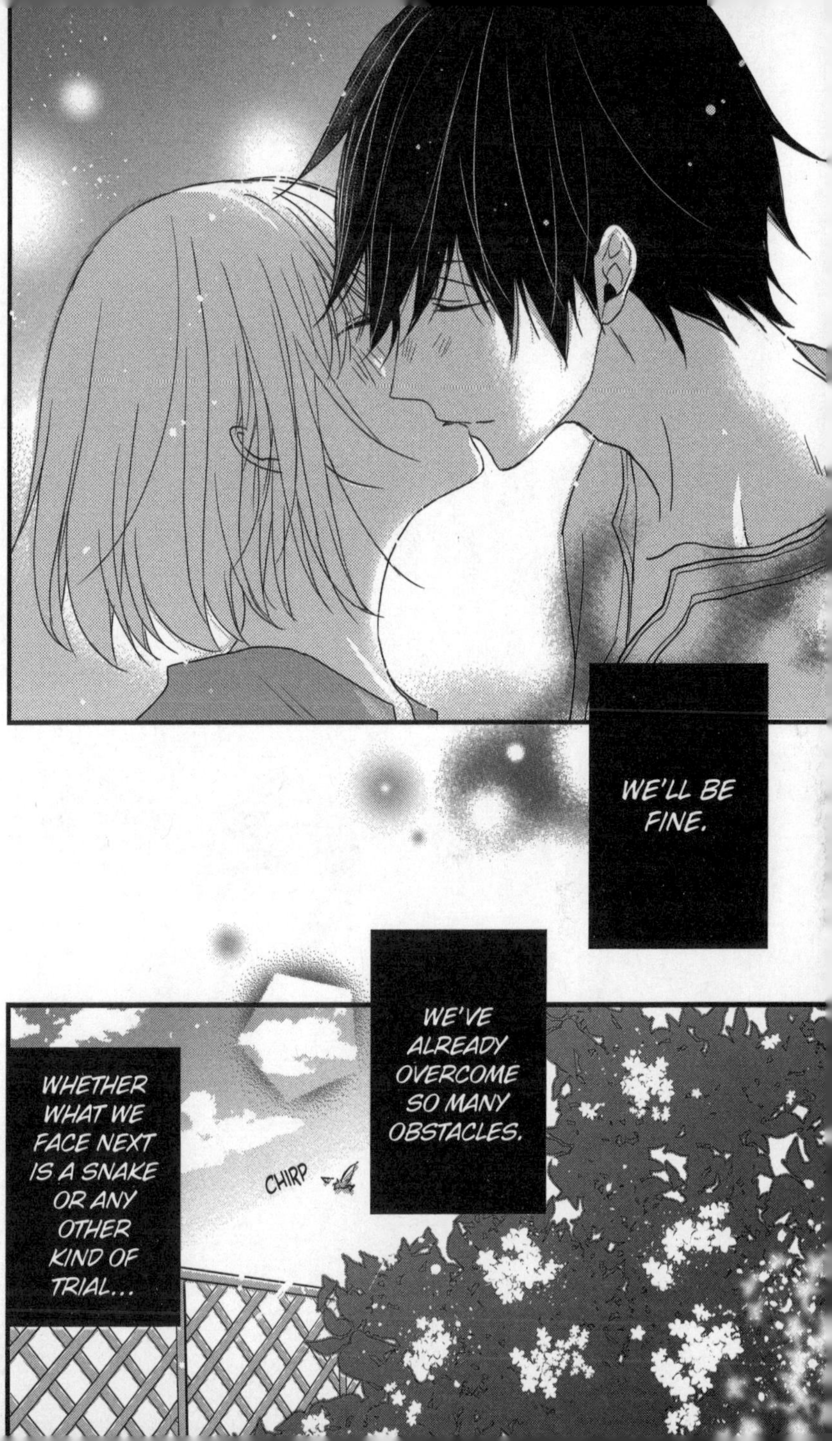
WE'LL BE FINE.
WE'VE ALREADY OVERCOME SO MANY OBSTACLES.
CHIRP
WHETHER WHAT WE FACE NEXT IS A SNAKE OR ANY OTHER KIND OF TRIAL...

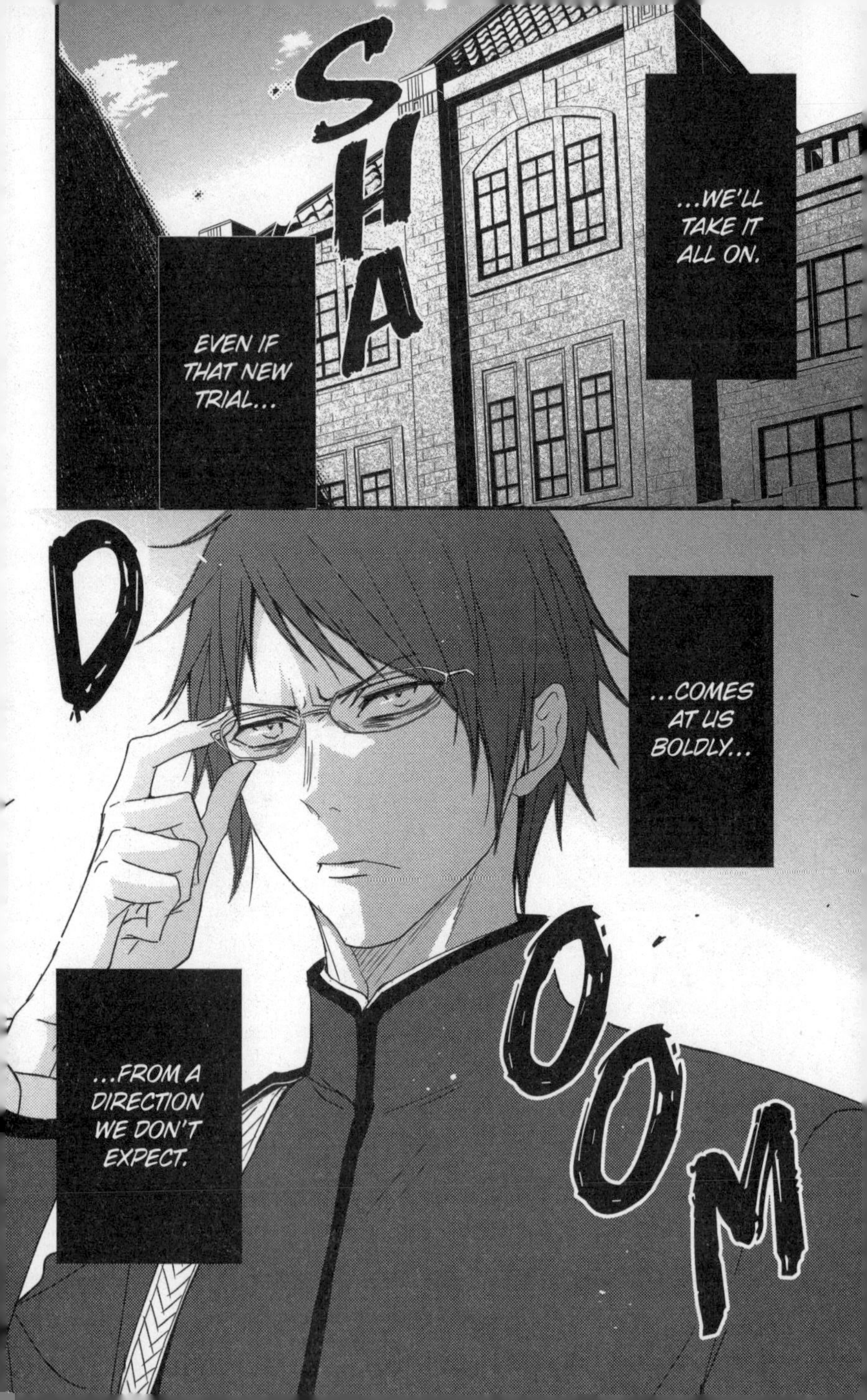
...WE'LL TAKE IT ALL ON.
SHA
EVEN IF THAT NEW TRIAL...
...COMES AT US BOLDLY...
DOOOM
...FROM A DIRECTION WE DON'T EXPECT.

MONTHLY BETSUCOMI SALE DATE NOTICE ON TWITTER

CHAPTER 46

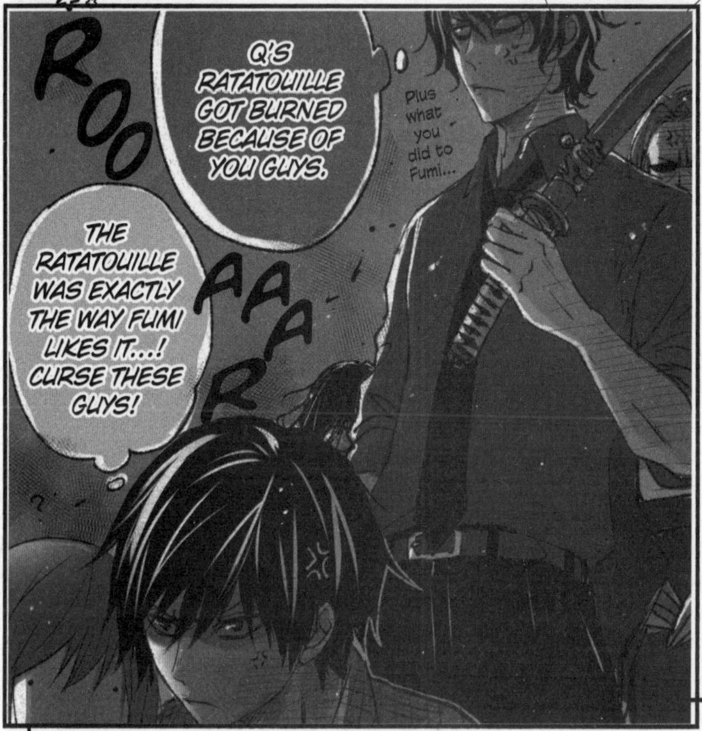
Q'S RATATOUILLE GOT BURNED BECAUSE OF YOU GUYS.
Plus what you did to Fumi...
ROOAAAR
THE RATATOUILLE WAS EXACTLY THE WAY FUMI LIKES IT...! CURSE THESE GUYS!

LET'S SEE... WHAT'S UP IN *QUEEN'S QUALITY* THIS MONTH?
(1) IT SEEMS SHE NOW HAS TWO PAIRS FOR SPECIAL OCCASIONS.
(2) DID YOU NOTICE? (TWO PLACES.)
(3) THERE SEEMS TO BE MULTIPLE REASONS WHY THE GENBU CLAN IS IN A BAD MOOD.

I HOPE CHAPTER 46 WILL BRING BACK YOUR MEMORY OF THE SEIRYU CLAN.

I MADE RATATOUILLE MANY TIMES THIS SUMMER. I LIKE TO ADD CANNED TUNA AND EAT IT OVER RICE.

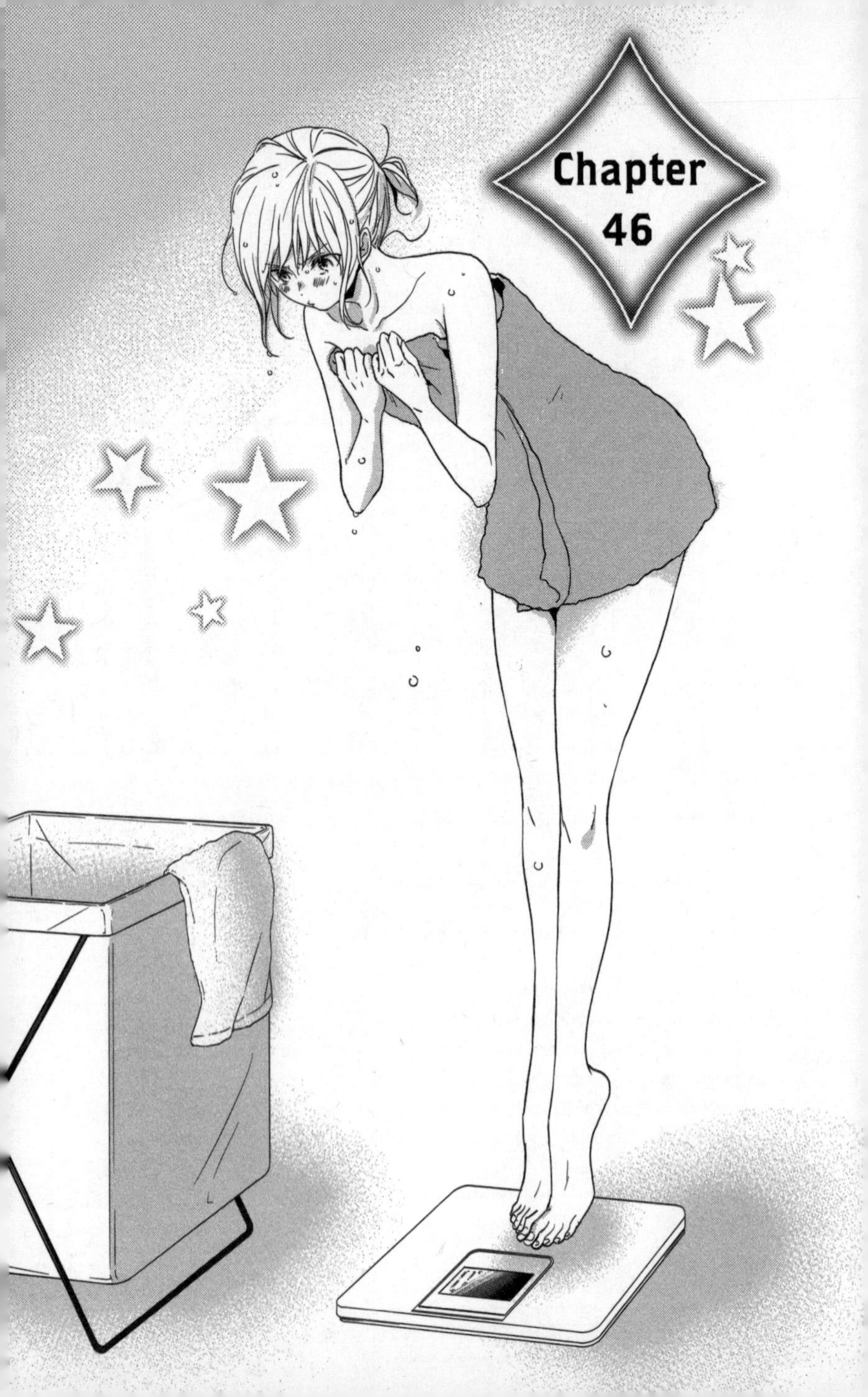
Chapter
46

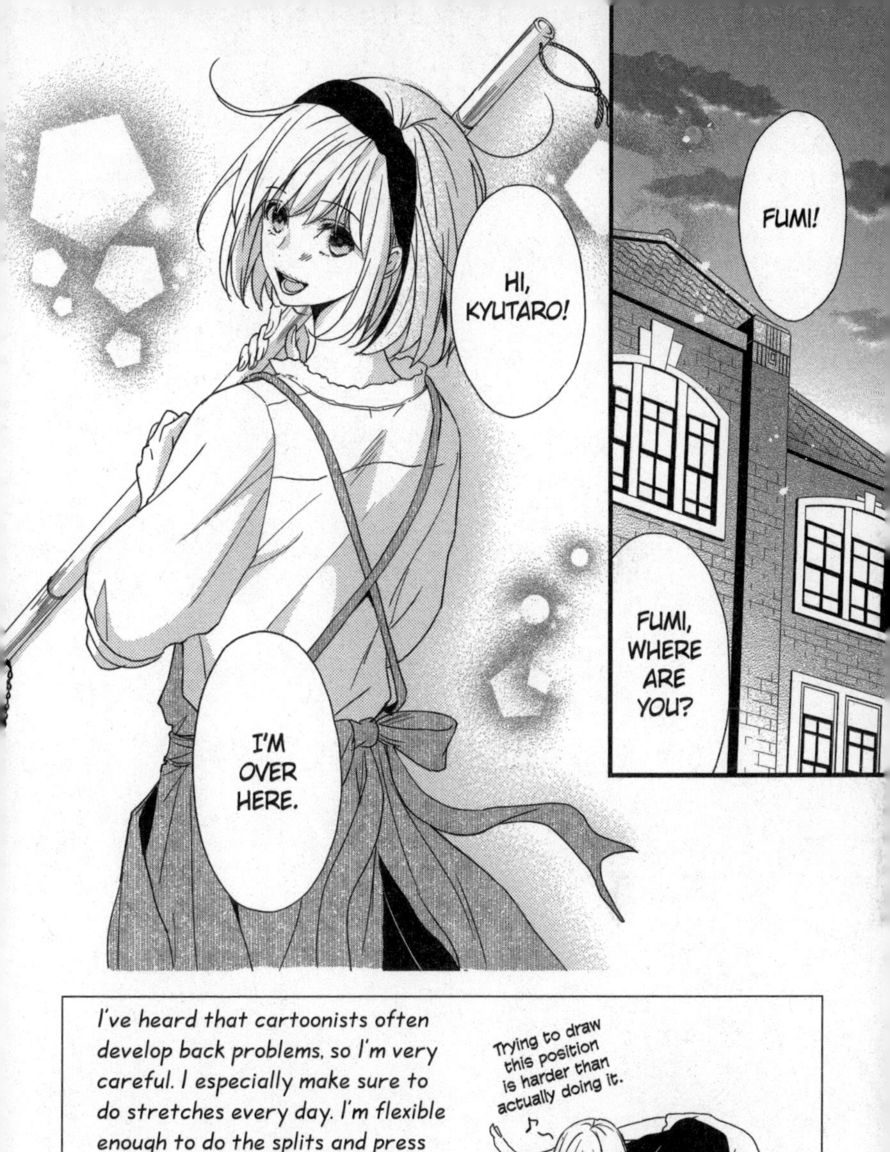
FUMI!
FUMI, WHERE ARE YOU?
HI, KYUTARO!
I'M OVER HERE.

I've heard that cartoonists often develop back problems, so I'm very careful. I especially make sure to do stretches every day. I'm flexible enough to do the splits and press my tummy to the floor. Oddly, when I'm in this position, any tightness in my back and shoulders melts away. If you work on it daily, morning and night, anyone should be able to lie flat like that. I recommend it.

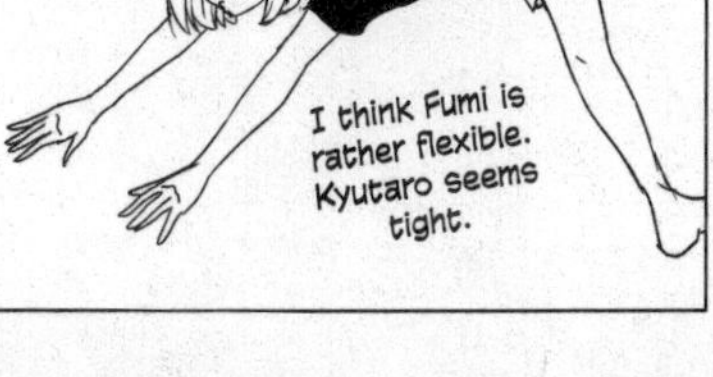
Trying to draw this position is harder than actually doing it.
I think Fumi is rather flexible. Kyutaro seems tight.

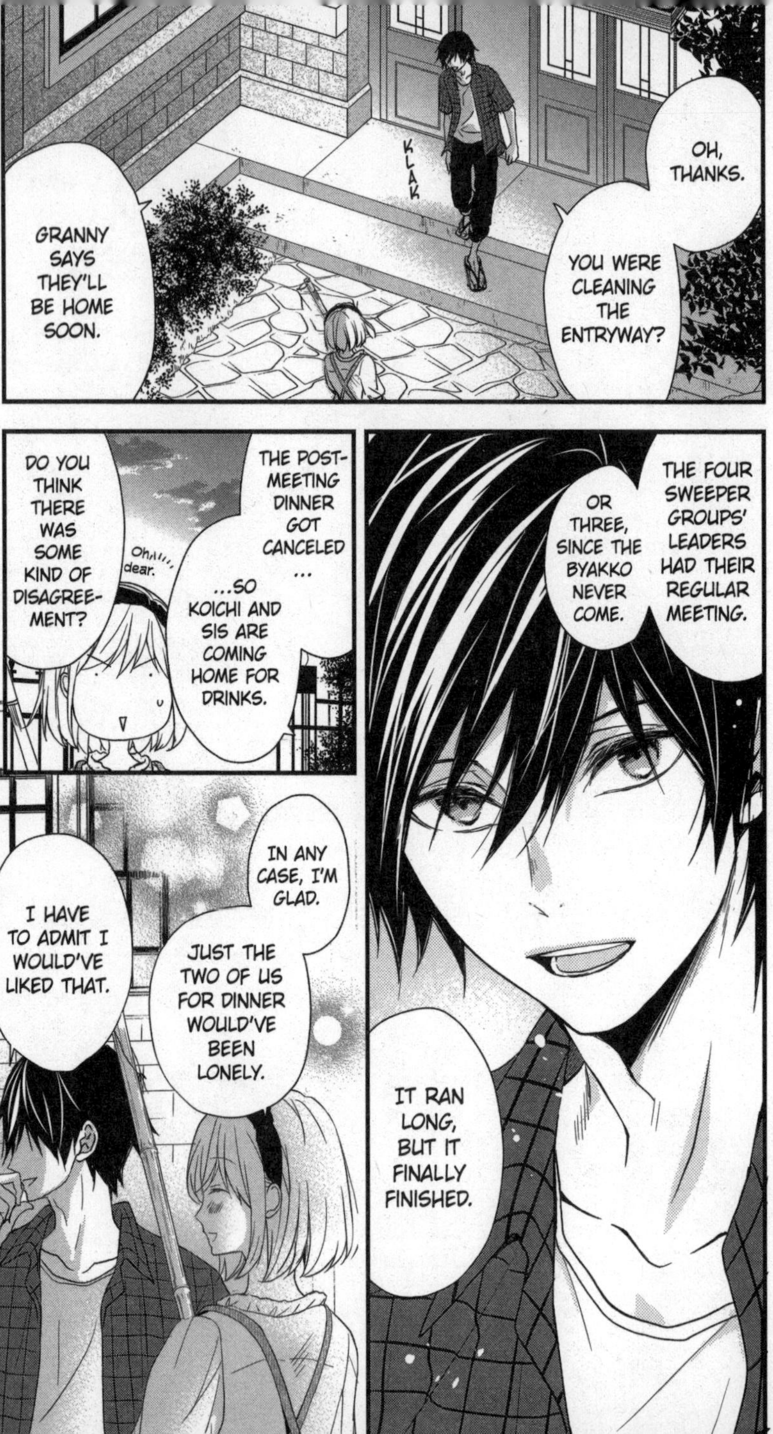
OH, THANKS.
YOU WERE CLEANING THE ENTRYWAY?
KLAK
GRANNY SAYS THEY'LL BE HOME SOON.
THE FOUR SWEEPER GROUPS' LEADERS HAD THEIR REGULAR MEETING.
OR THREE, SINCE THE BYAKKO NEVER COME.
IT RAN LONG, BUT IT FINALLY FINISHED.
THE POST-MEETING DINNER GOT CANCELED...
...SO KOICHI AND SIS ARE COMING HOME FOR DRINKS.
Oh, dear.
DO YOU THINK THERE WAS SOME KIND OF DISAGREE-MENT?
IN ANY CASE, I'M GLAD.
JUST THE TWO OF US FOR DINNER WOULD'VE BEEN LONELY.
I HAVE TO ADMIT I WOULD'VE LIKED THAT.

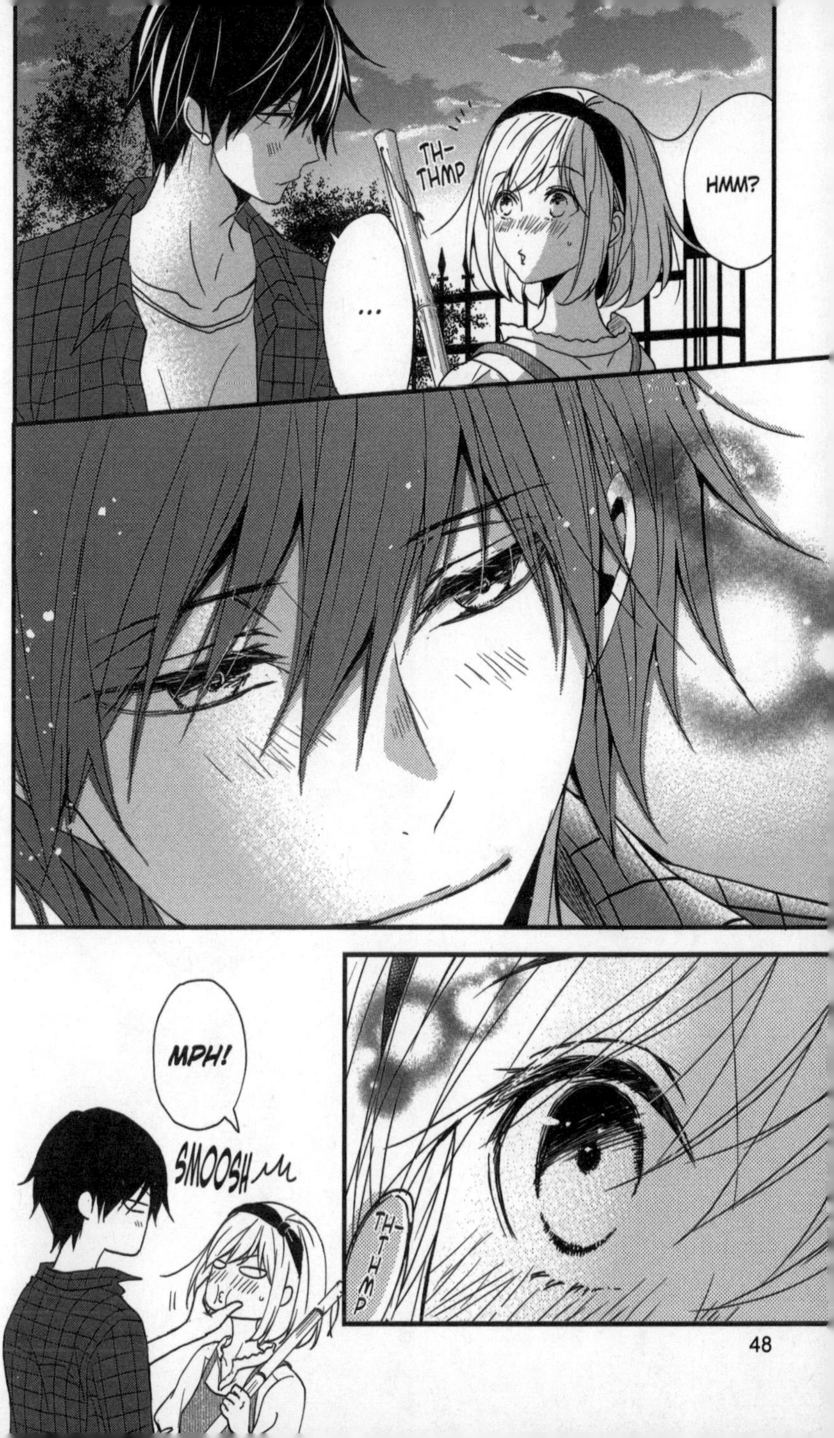
HMM?
TH-THMP
...
TH-THMP
MPH!
SMOOSH

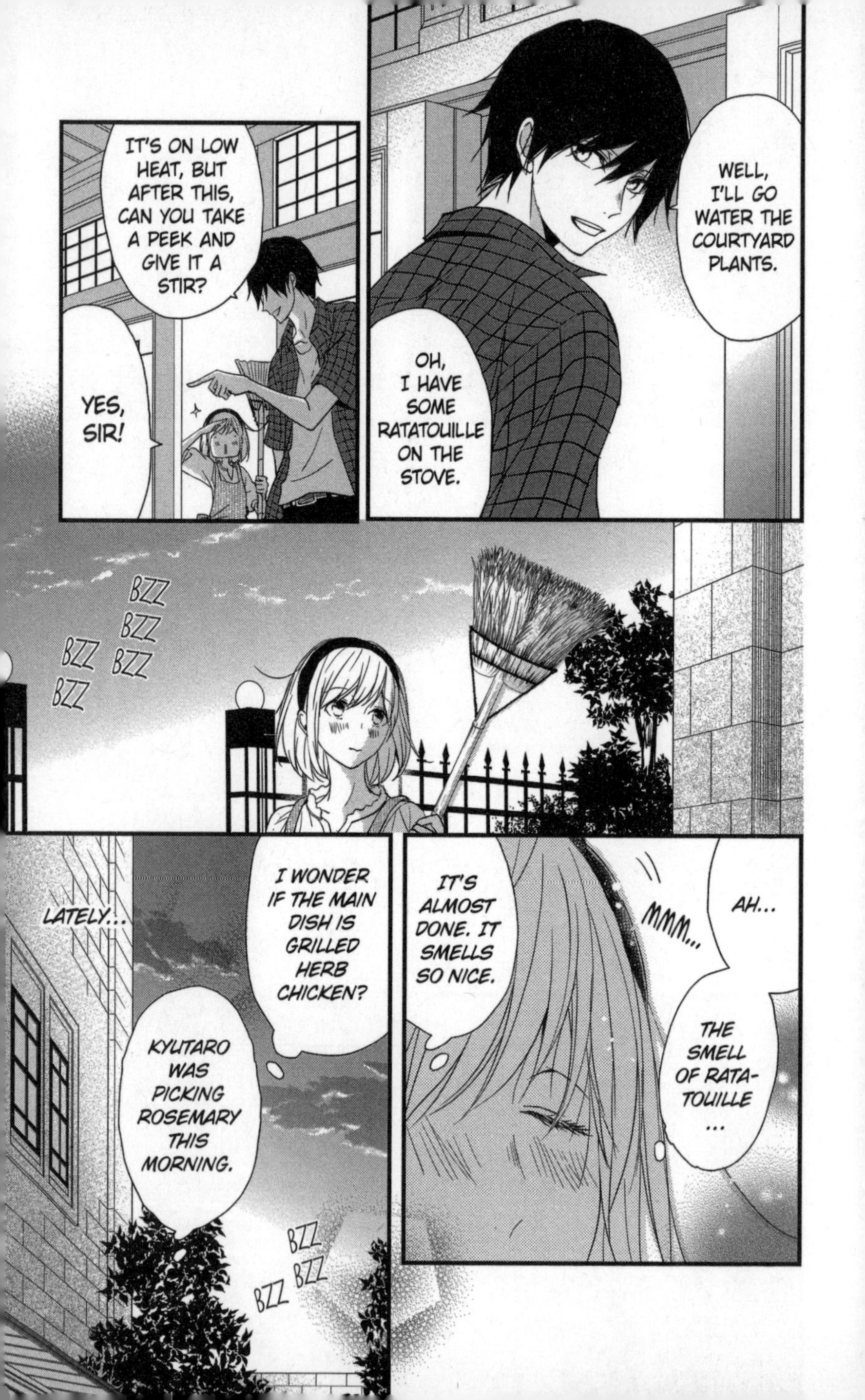
WELL, I'LL GO WATER THE COURTYARD PLANTS.
OH, I HAVE SOME RATATOUILLE ON THE STOVE.
IT'S ON LOW HEAT, BUT AFTER THIS, CAN YOU TAKE A PEEK AND GIVE IT A STIR?
YES, SIR!
BZZ BZZ BZZ BZZ BZZ
AH...
MMM...
THE SMELL OF RATA-TOUILLE ...
IT'S ALMOST DONE. IT SMELLS SO NICE.
I WONDER IF THE MAIN DISH IS GRILLED HERB CHICKEN?
LATELY...
KYUTARO WAS PICKING ROSEMARY THIS MORNING.
BZZ BZZ BZZ

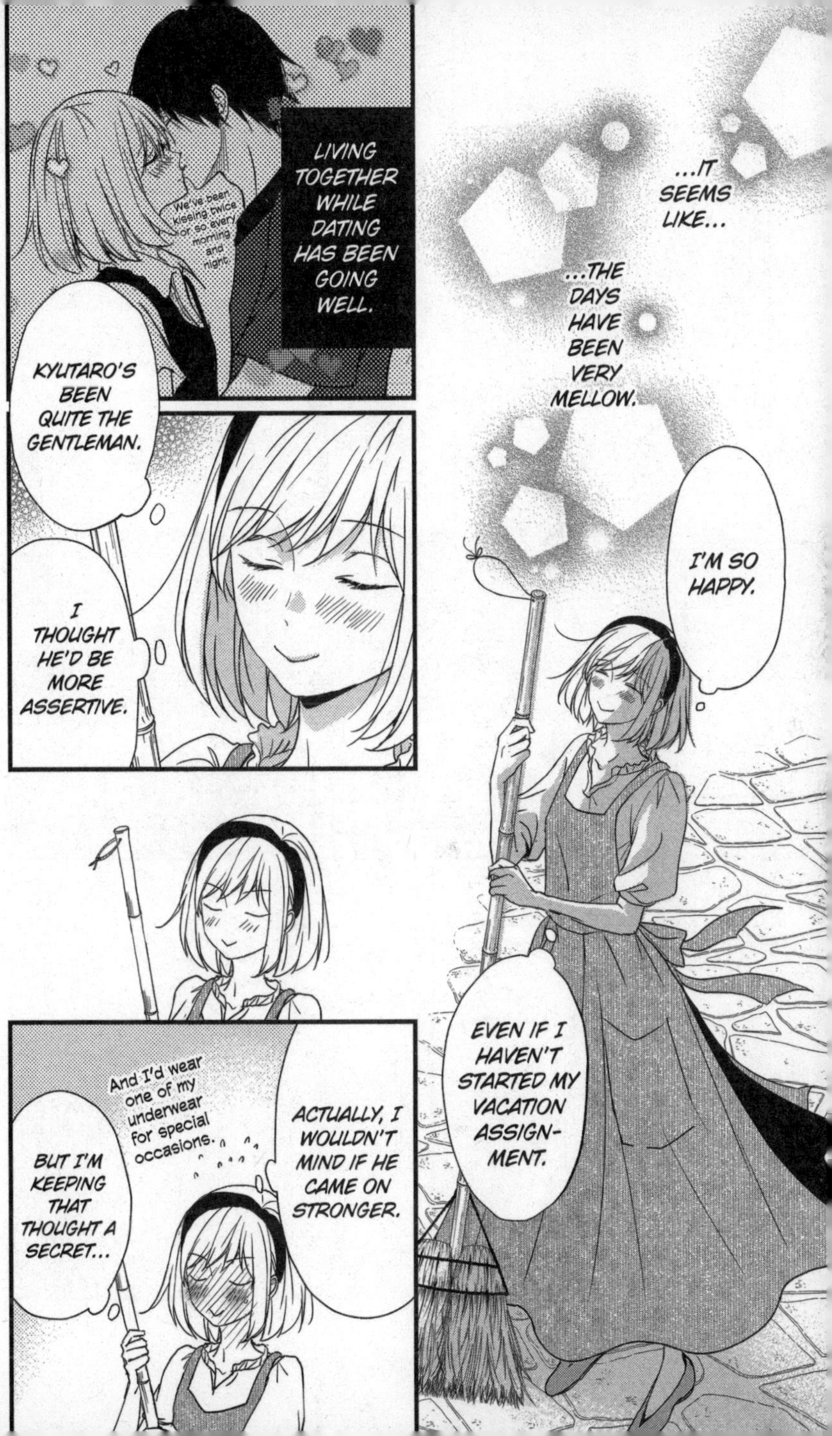
...IT SEEMS LIKE...
...THE DAYS HAVE BEEN VERY MELLOW.
I'M SO HAPPY.
EVEN IF I HAVEN'T STARTED MY VACATION ASSIGN-MENT.
LIVING TOGETHER WHILE DATING HAS BEEN GOING WELL.
We've been kissing twice or so every morning and night.
KYUTARO'S BEEN QUITE THE GENTLEMAN.
I THOUGHT HE'D BE MORE ASSERTIVE.
ACTUALLY, I WOULDN'T MIND IF HE CAME ON STRONGER.
And I'd wear one of my underwear for special occasions.
BUT I'M KEEPING THAT THOUGHT A SECRET...

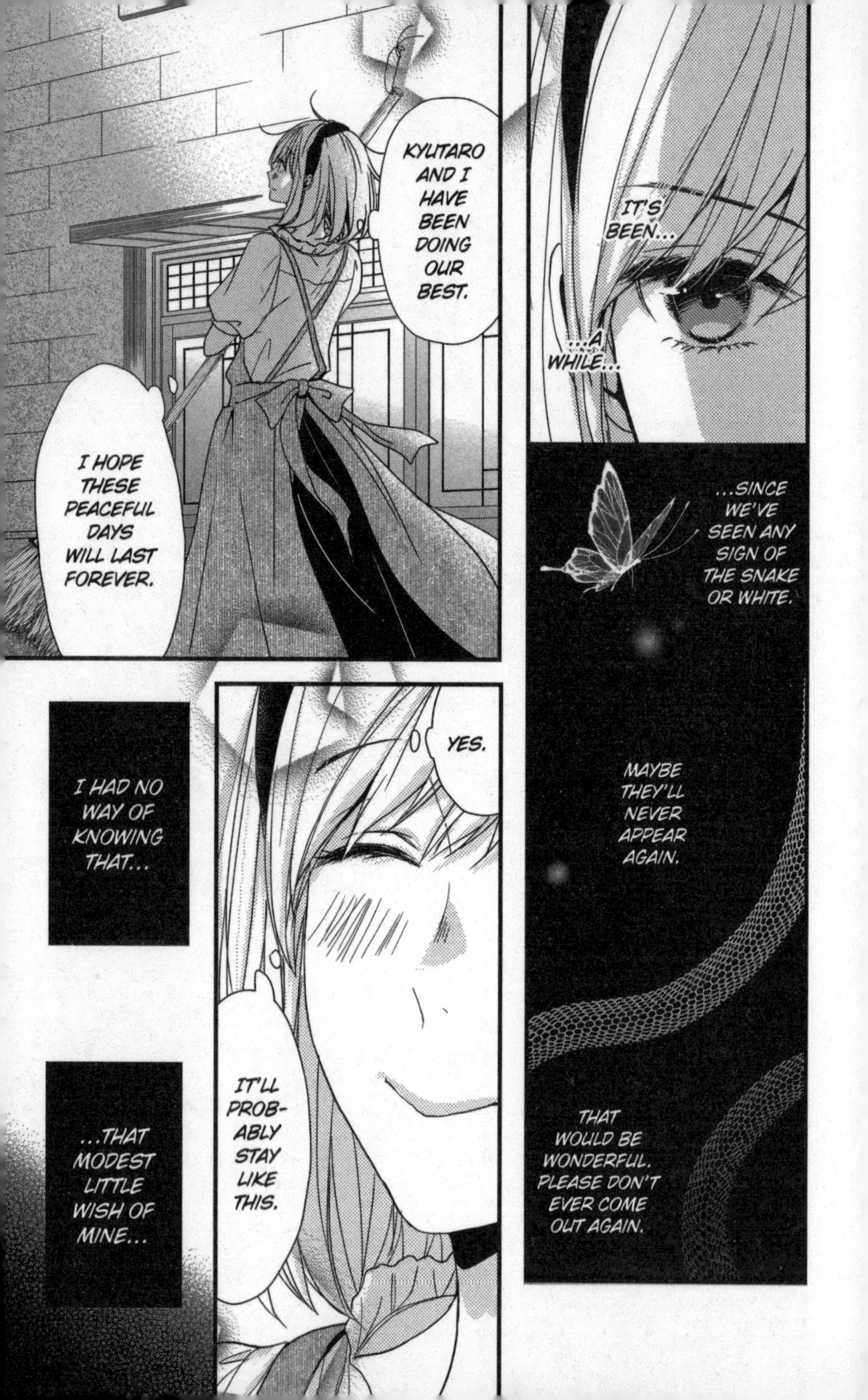
IT'S BEEN...
...A WHILE...
...SINCE WE'VE SEEN ANY SIGN OF THE SNAKE OR WHITE.
MAYBE THEY'LL NEVER APPEAR AGAIN.
THAT WOULD BE WONDERFUL. PLEASE DON'T EVER COME OUT AGAIN.
KYUTARO AND I HAVE BEEN DOING OUR BEST.
I HOPE THESE PEACEFUL DAYS WILL LAST FOREVER.
YES.
IT'LL PROBABLY STAY LIKE THIS.
I HAD NO WAY OF KNOWING THAT...
...THAT MODEST LITTLE WISH OF MINE...

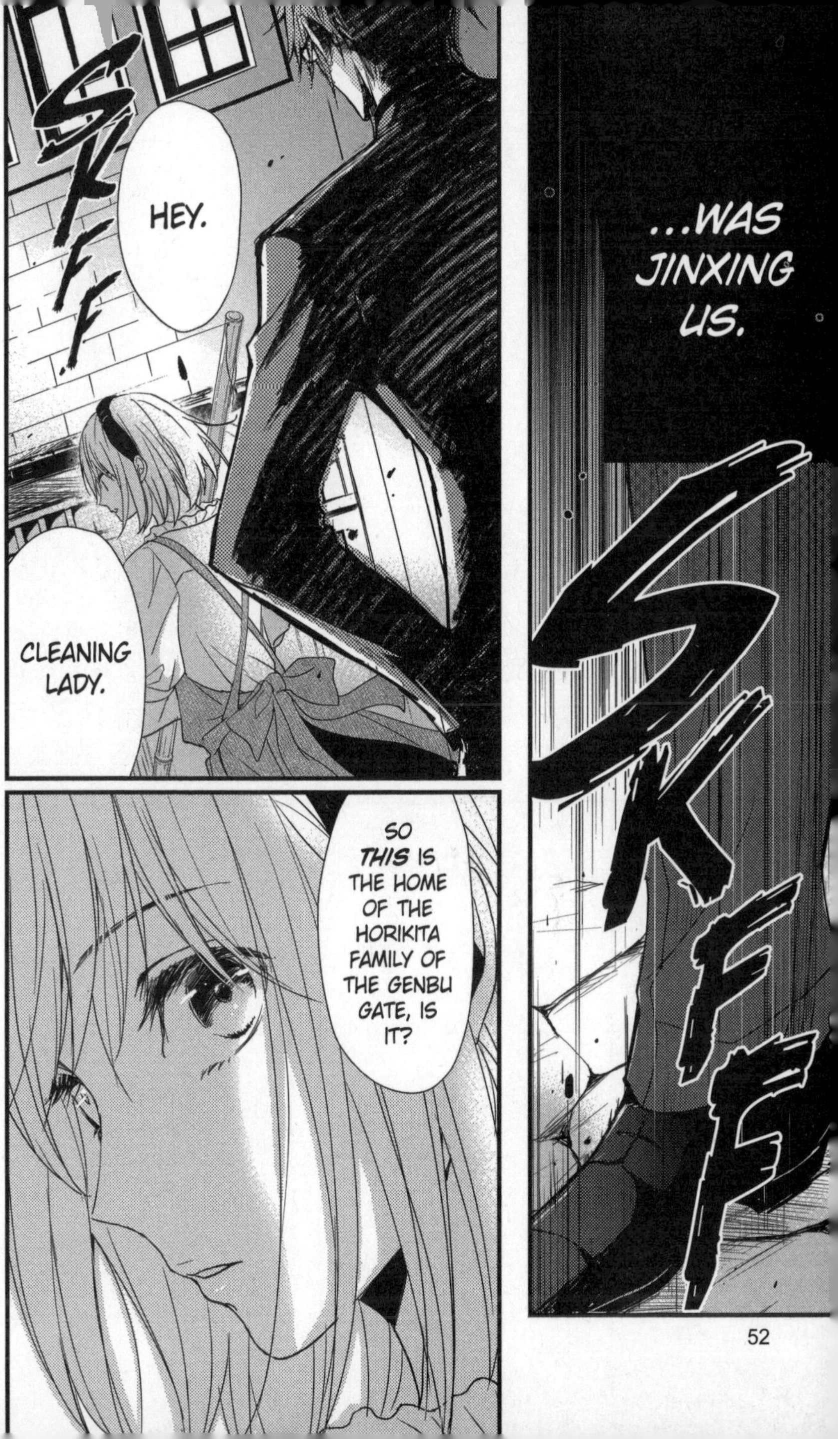
...WAS JINXING US.
SKFFF
SKFFF
HEY.
CLEANING LADY.
SO *THIS* IS THE HOME OF THE HORIKITA FAMILY OF THE GENBU GATE, IS IT?

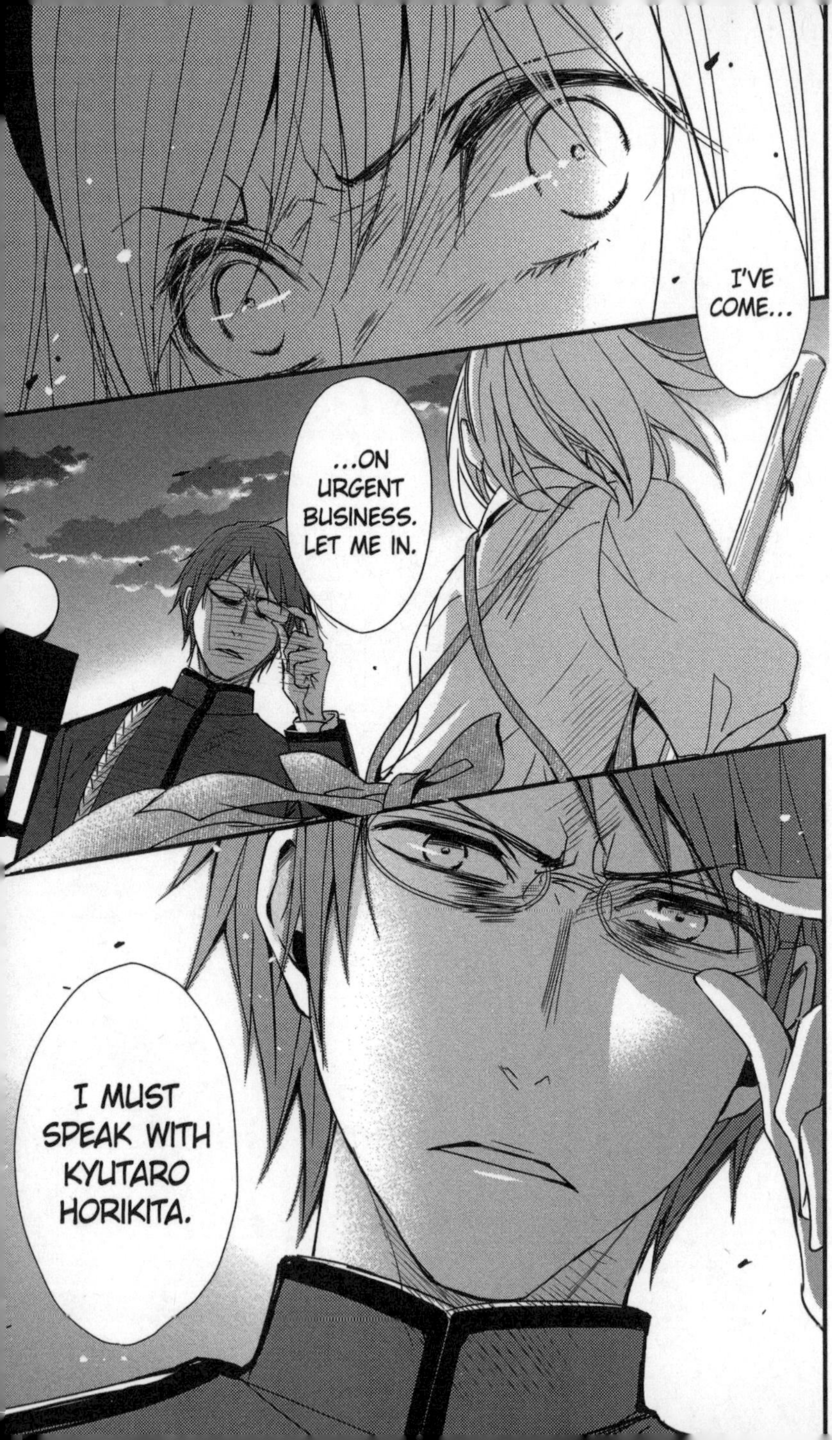
I'VE COME...
...ON URGENT BUSINESS. LET ME IN.
I MUST SPEAK WITH KYUTARO HORIKITA.

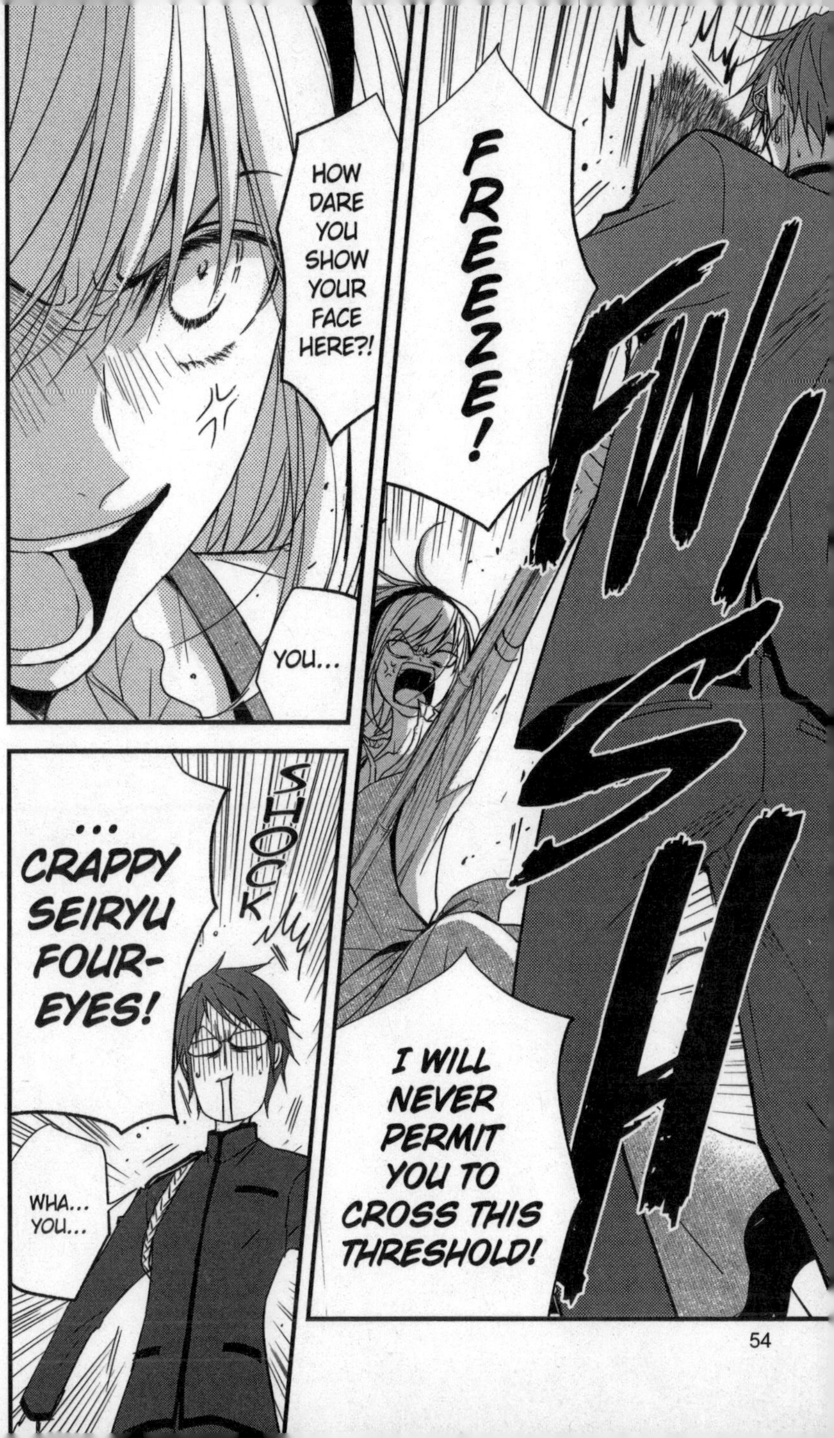
FREEZE!
FWISH
I WILL NEVER PERMIT YOU TO CROSS THIS THRESHOLD!
HOW DARE YOU SHOW YOUR FACE HERE?!
YOU...
SHOCK
...CRAPPY SEIRYU FOUR-EYES!
WHA... YOU...

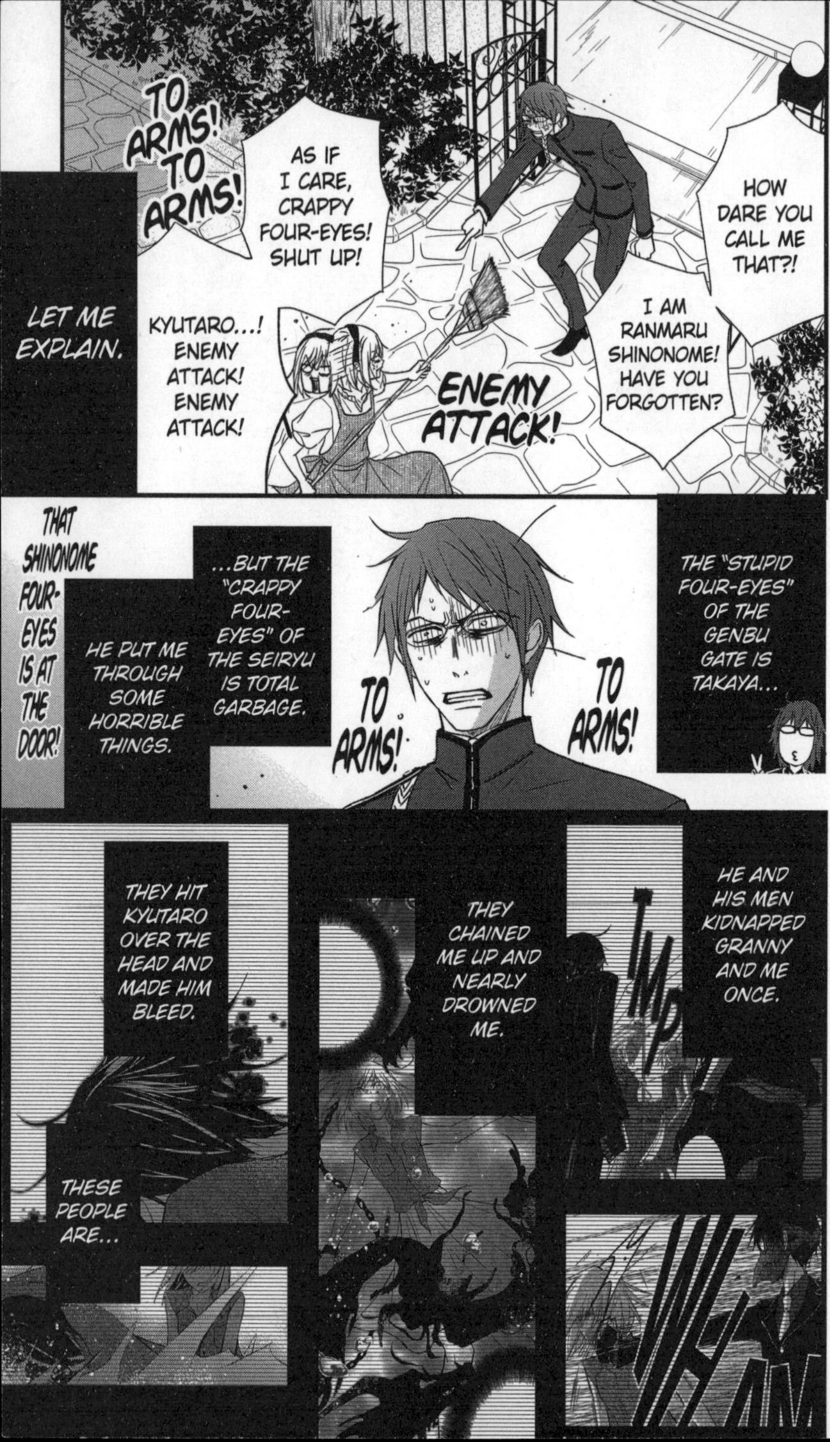
HOW DARE YOU CALL ME THAT?!
I AM RANMARU SHINONOME! HAVE YOU FORGOTTEN?
AS IF I CARE, CRAPPY FOUR-EYES! SHUT UP!
TO ARMS! TO ARMS!
ENEMY ATTACK!
KYUTARO...! ENEMY ATTACK! ENEMY ATTACK!
LET ME EXPLAIN.
THE "STUPID FOUR-EYES" OF THE GENBU GATE IS TAKAYA...
TO ARMS!
TO ARMS!
...BUT THE "CRAPPY FOUR-EYES" OF THE SEIRYU IS TOTAL GARBAGE.
HE PUT ME THROUGH SOME HORRIBLE THINGS.
THAT SHINONOME FOUR-EYES IS AT THE DOOR!
HE AND HIS MEN KIDNAPPED GRANNY AND ME ONCE.
THEY CHAINED ME UP AND NEARLY DROWNED ME.
THEY HIT KYUTARO OVER THE HEAD AND MADE HIM BLEED.
THESE PEOPLE ARE...

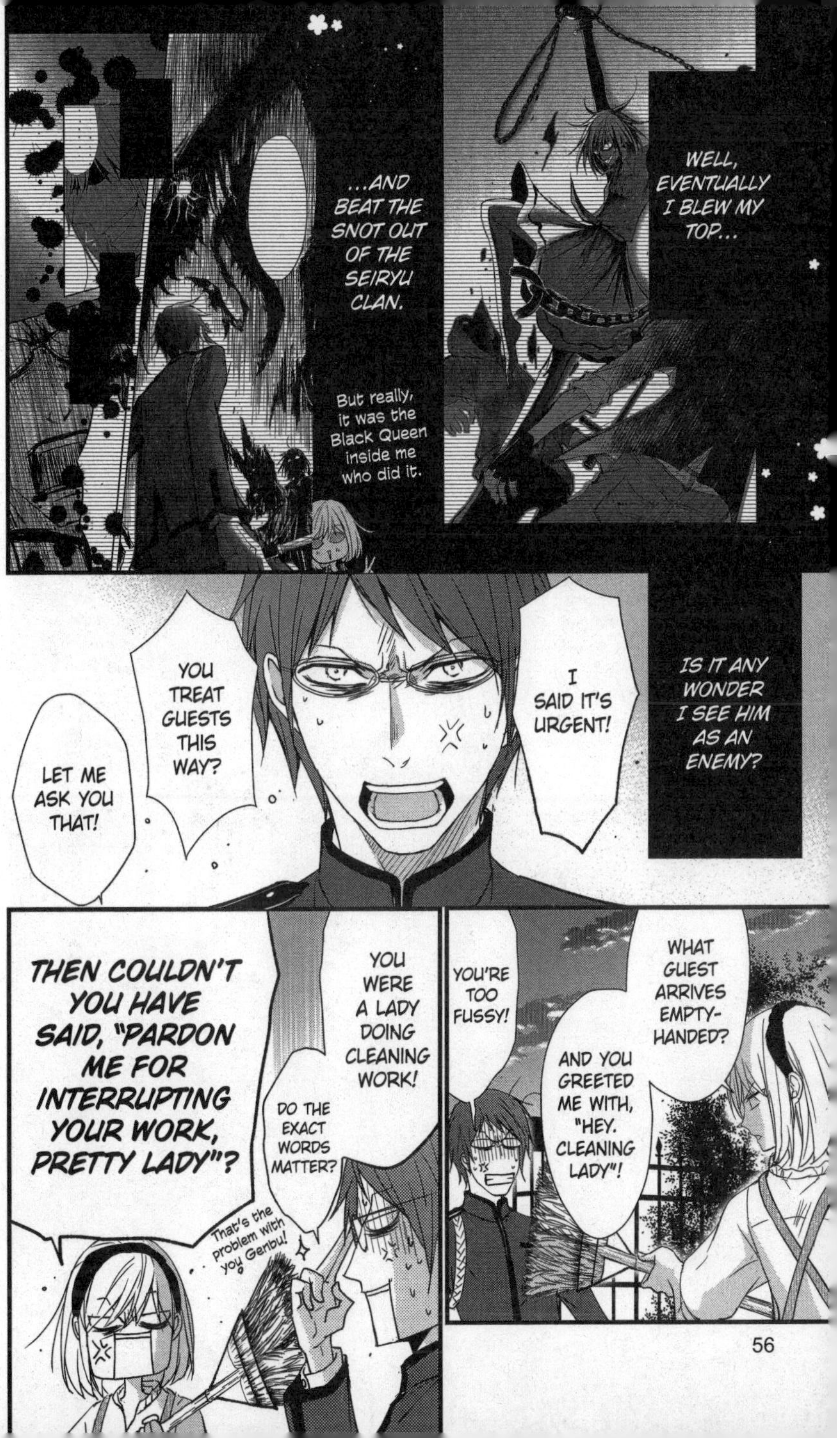
WELL, EVENTUALLY I BLEW MY TOP...
...AND BEAT THE SNOT OUT OF THE SEIRYU CLAN.
But really, it was the Black Queen inside me who did it.
IS IT ANY WONDER I SEE HIM AS AN ENEMY?
I SAID IT'S URGENT!
YOU TREAT GUESTS THIS WAY?
LET ME ASK YOU THAT!
WHAT GUEST ARRIVES EMPTY-HANDED?
AND YOU GREETED ME WITH, "HEY. CLEANING LADY"!
YOU'RE TOO FUSSY!
YOU WERE A LADY DOING CLEANING WORK!
DO THE EXACT WORDS MATTER?
THEN COULDN'T YOU HAVE SAID, "PARDON ME FOR INTERRUPTING YOUR WORK, PRETTY LADY"?
That's the problem with you Genbu!

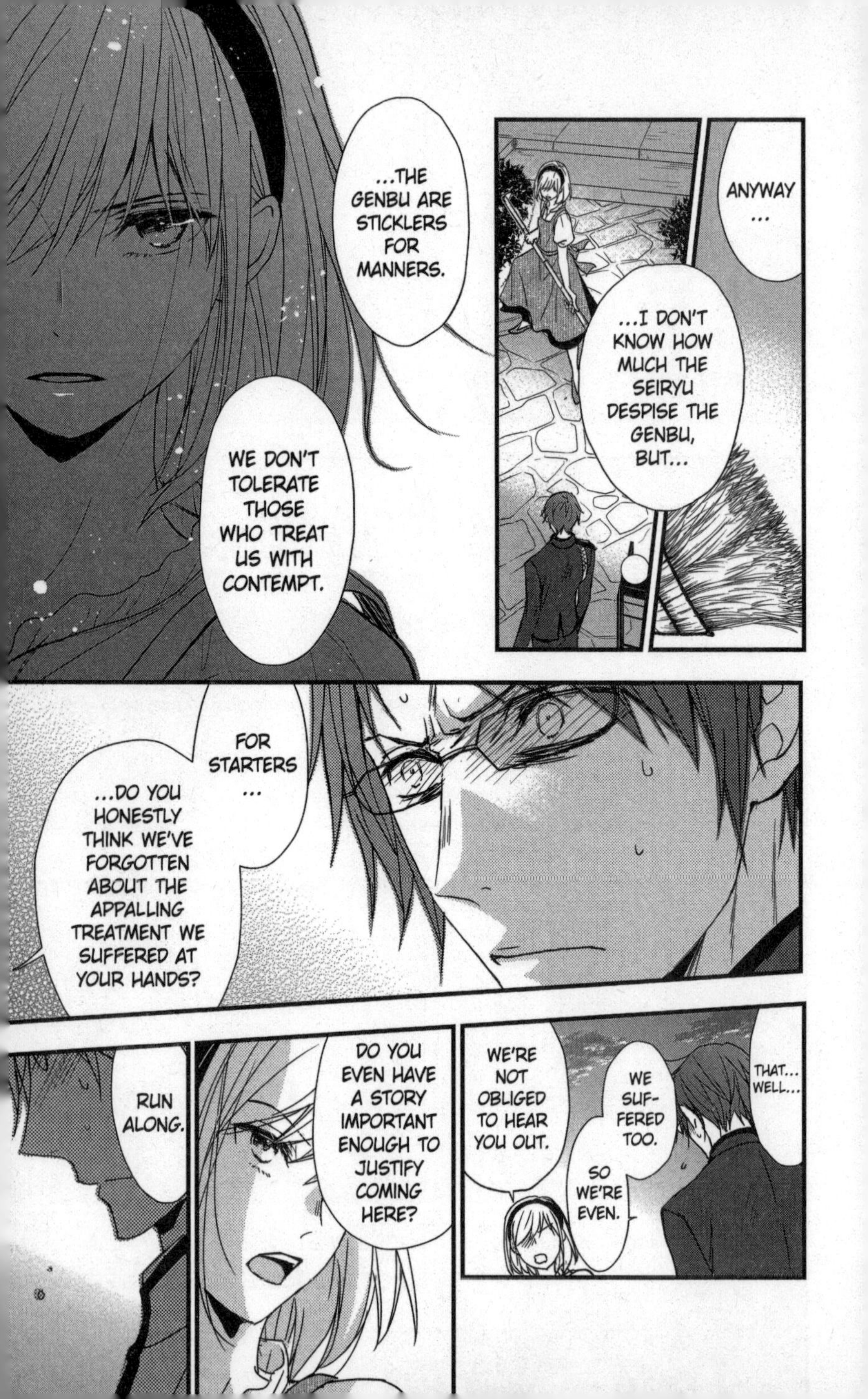
ANYWAY...
...I DON'T KNOW HOW MUCH THE SEIRYU DESPISE THE GENBU, BUT...
...THE GENBU ARE STICKLERS FOR MANNERS.
WE DON'T TOLERATE THOSE WHO TREAT US WITH CONTEMPT.
FOR STARTERS...
...DO YOU HONESTLY THINK WE'VE FORGOTTEN ABOUT THE APPALLING TREATMENT WE SUFFERED AT YOUR HANDS?
THAT... WELL...
WE SUFFERED TOO.
SO WE'RE EVEN.
WE'RE NOT OBLIGED TO HEAR YOU OUT.
DO YOU EVEN HAVE A STORY IMPORTANT ENOUGH TO JUSTIFY COMING HERE?
RUN ALONG.

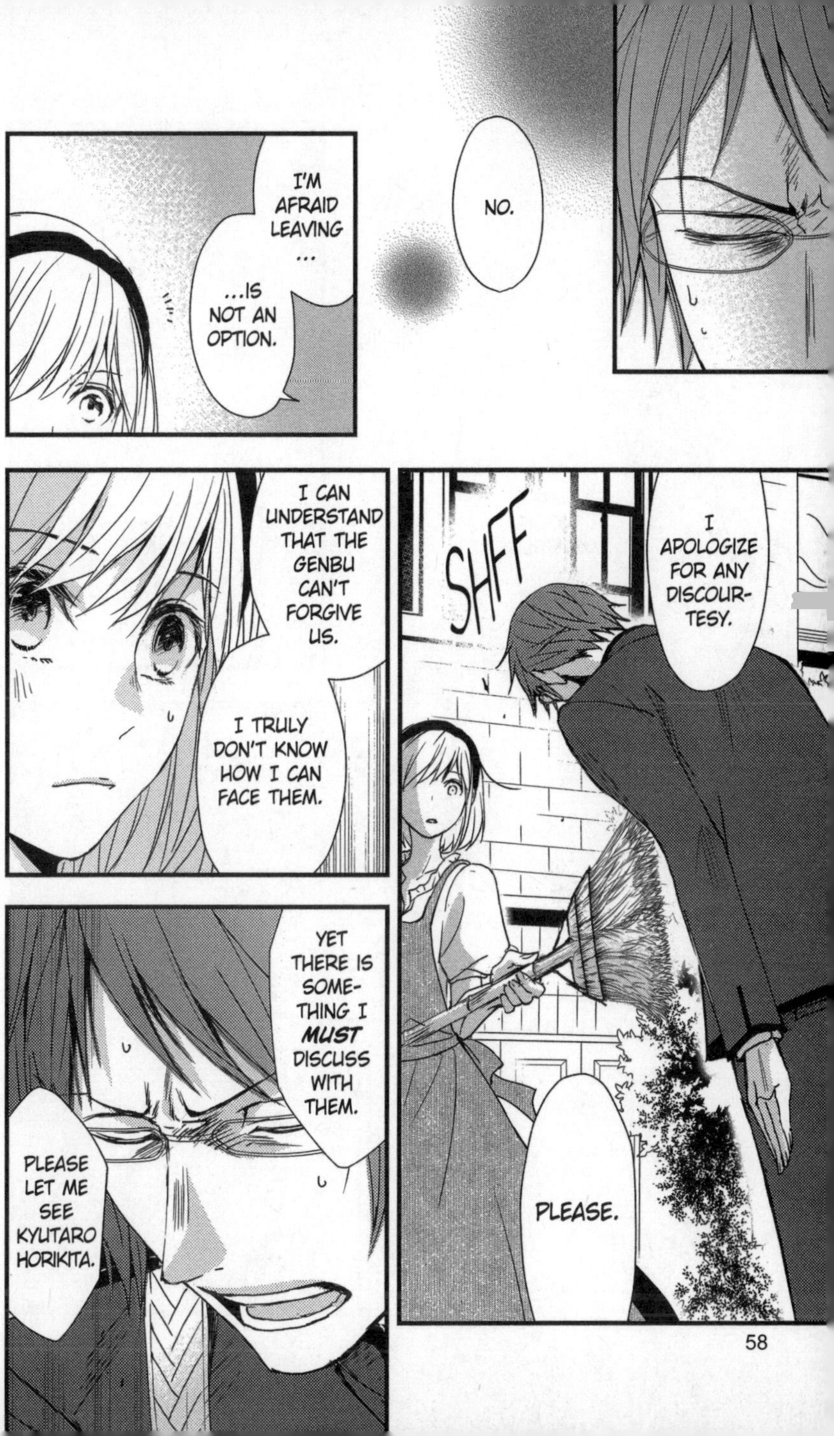
NO.
I'M AFRAID LEAVING ...
...IS NOT AN OPTION.
SHFF
I APOLOGIZE FOR ANY DISCOUR-TESY.
PLEASE.
I CAN UNDERSTAND THAT THE GENBU CAN'T FORGIVE US.
I TRULY DON'T KNOW HOW I CAN FACE THEM.
YET THERE IS SOME-THING I ***MUST*** DISCUSS WITH THEM.
PLEASE LET ME SEE KYUTARO HORIKITA.

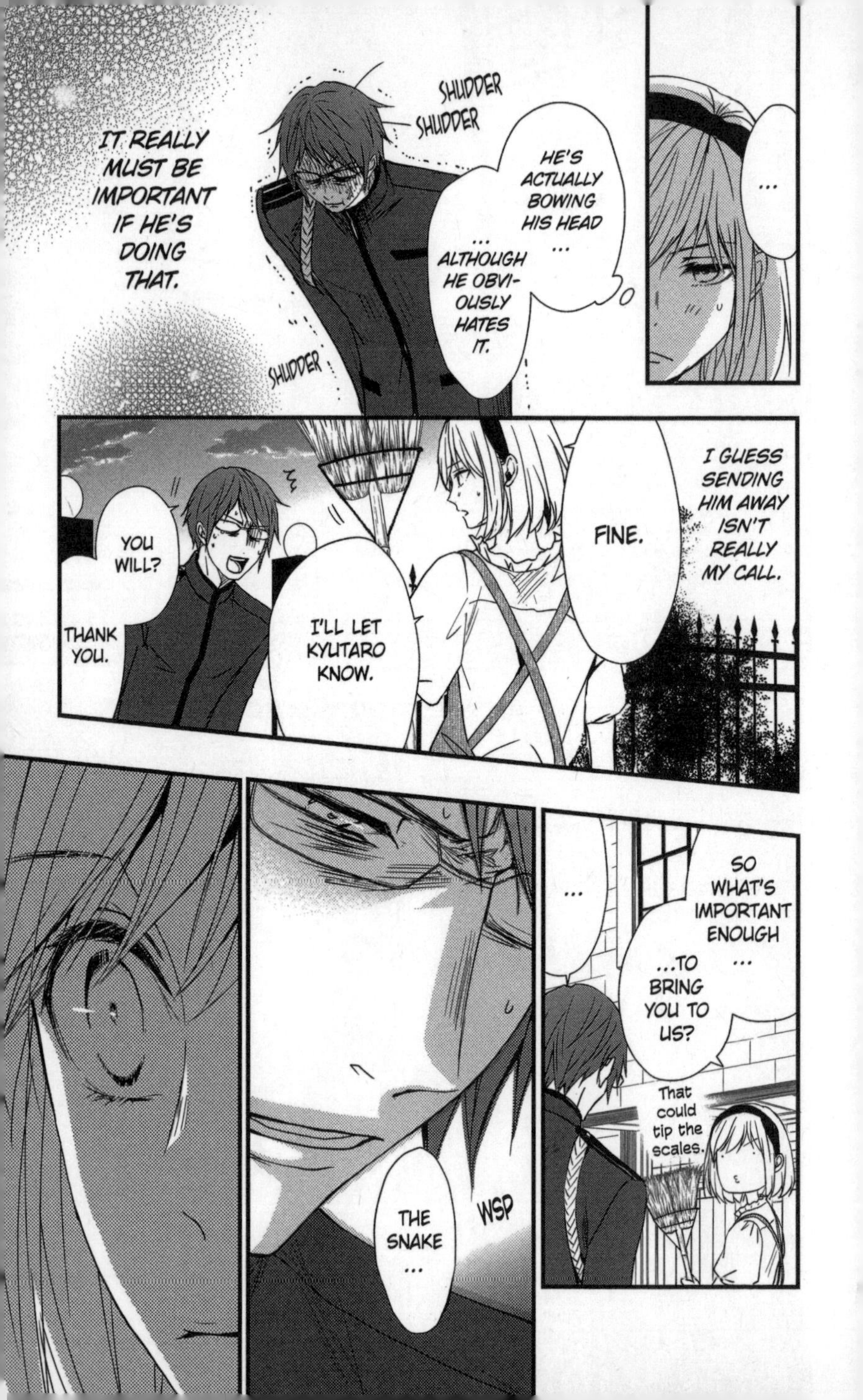
...
HE'S ACTUALLY BOWING HIS HEAD ...
... ALTHOUGH HE OBVIOUSLY HATES IT.
SHUDDER
SHUDDER
IT REALLY MUST BE IMPORTANT IF HE'S DOING THAT.
SHUDDER
I GUESS SENDING HIM AWAY ISN'T REALLY MY CALL.
FINE.
I'LL LET KYUTARO KNOW.
YOU WILL?
THANK YOU.
...
SO WHAT'S IMPORTANT ENOUGH ...
...TO BRING YOU TO US?
That could tip the scales.
WSP
THE SNAKE ...

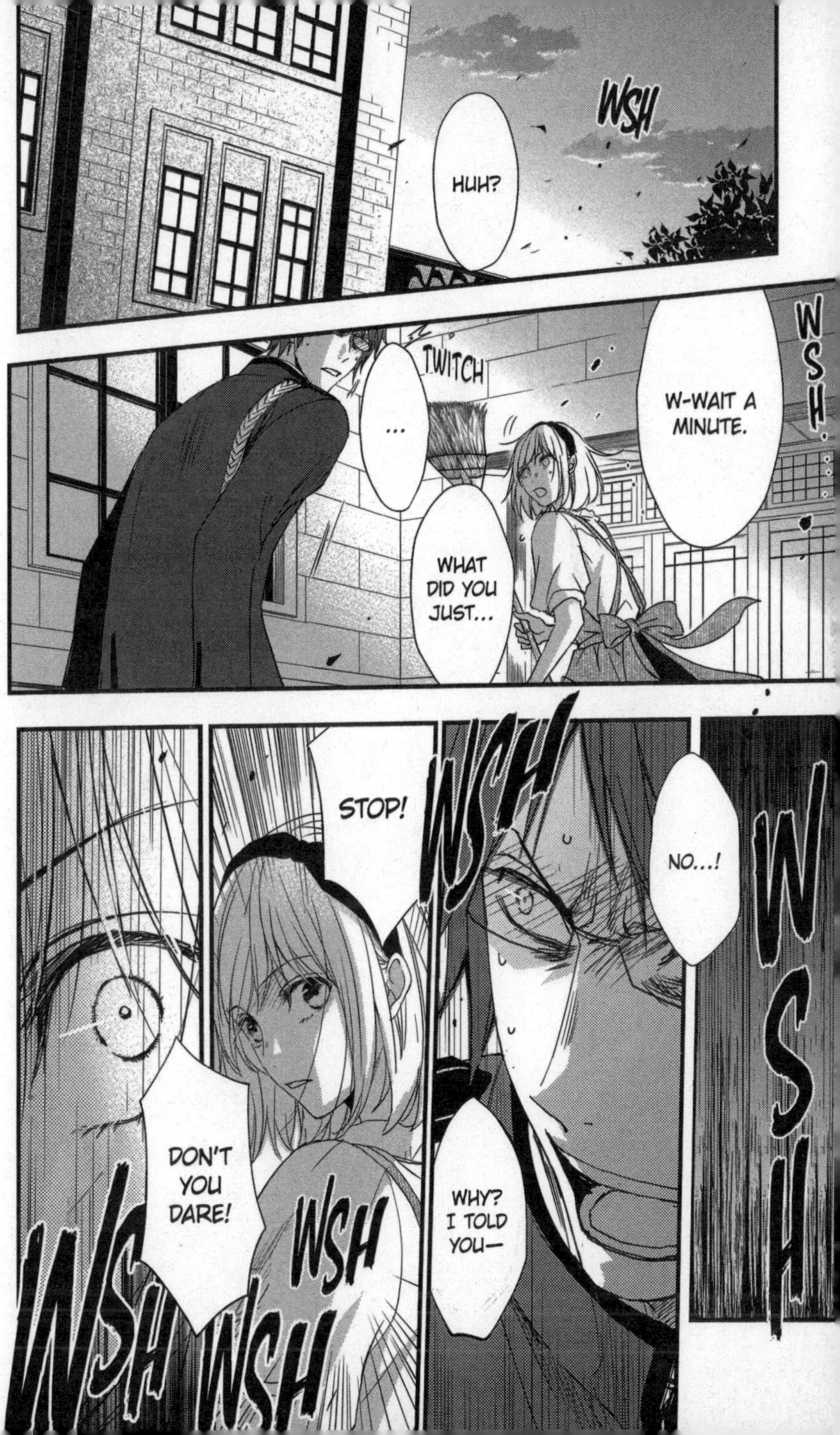
WSH
HUH?
WSH...
W-WAIT A MINUTE.
TWITCH
...
WHAT DID YOU JUST...
WSH
NO...!
WSH
STOP!
WHY? I TOLD YOU—
DON'T YOU DARE!
WSH
WSH WSH

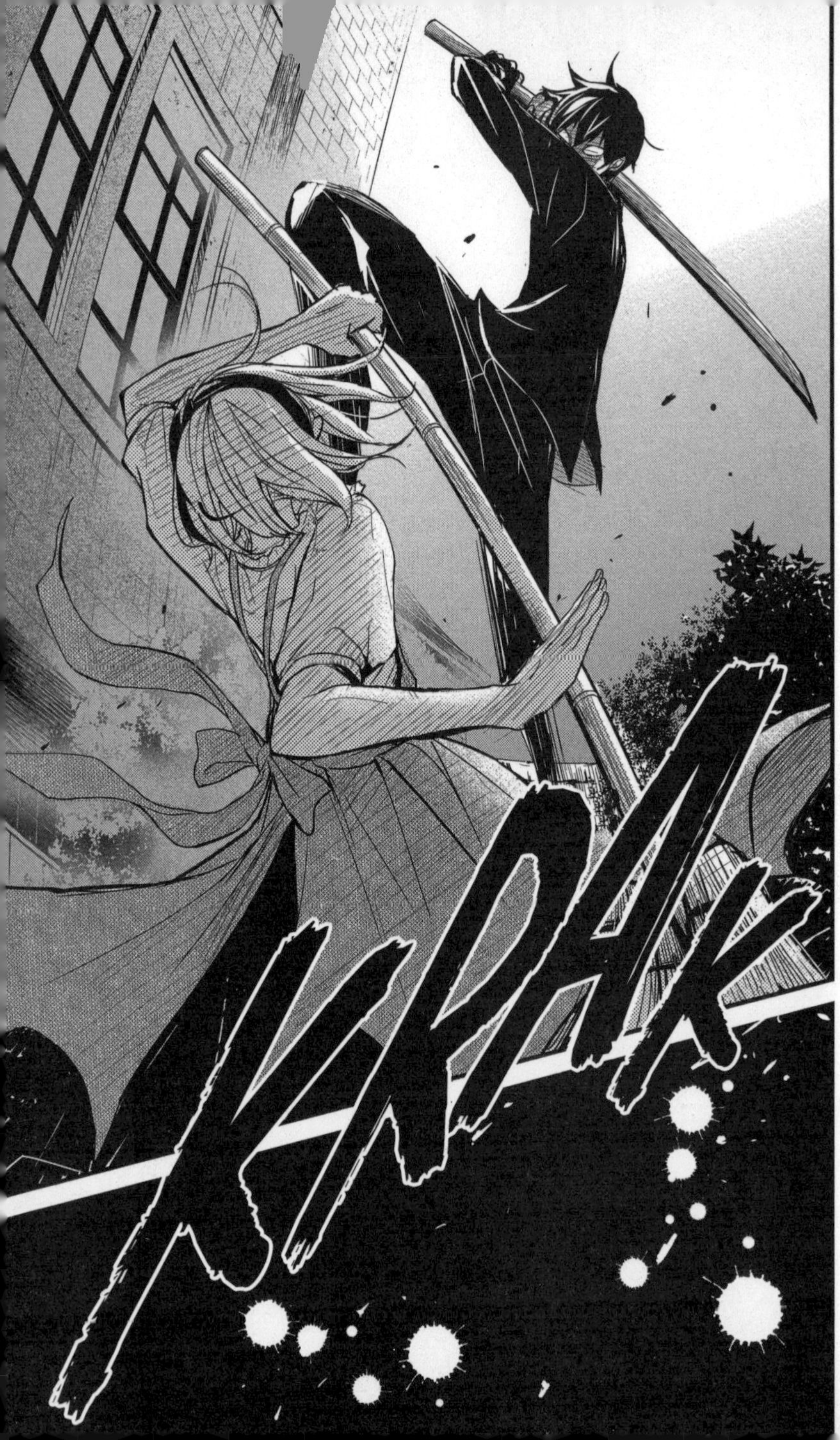
KADAK

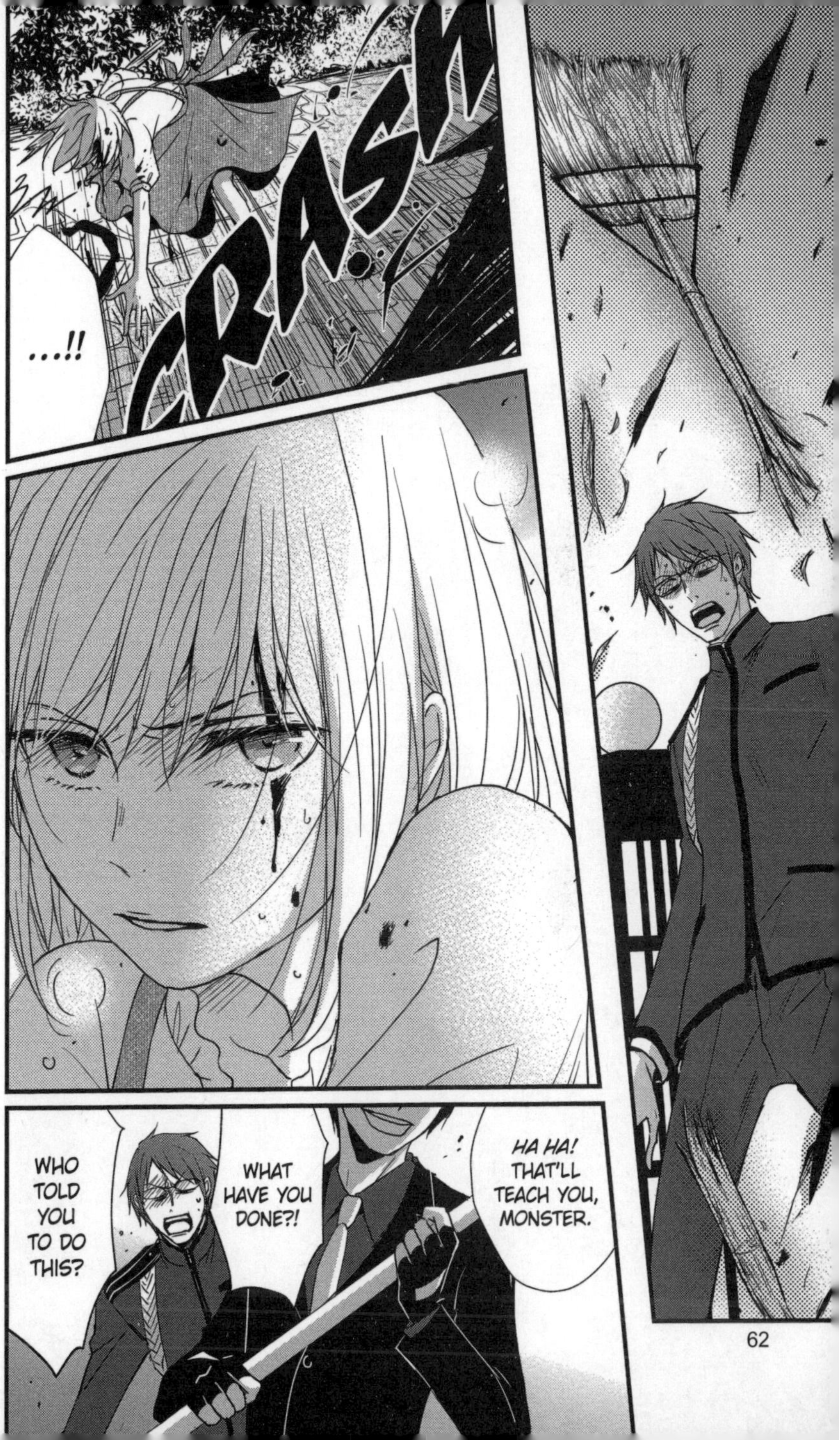
CRASH
...!!
HA HA! THAT'LL TEACH YOU, MONSTER.
WHAT HAVE YOU DONE?!
WHO TOLD YOU TO DO THIS?

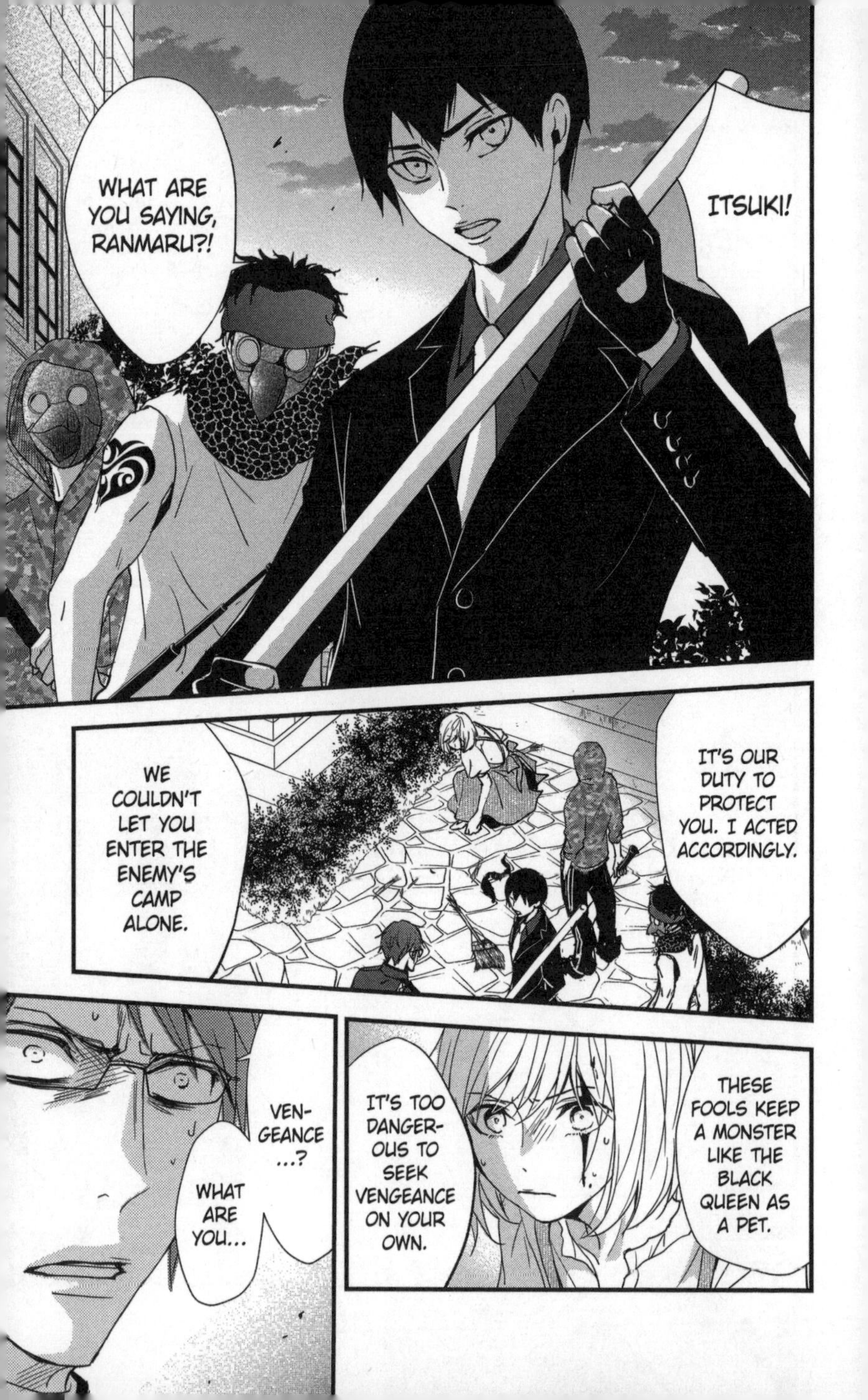
ITSUKI!
WHAT ARE YOU SAYING, RANMARU?!
IT'S OUR DUTY TO PROTECT YOU. I ACTED ACCORDINGLY.
WE COULDN'T LET YOU ENTER THE ENEMY'S CAMP ALONE.
THESE FOOLS KEEP A MONSTER LIKE THE BLACK QUEEN AS A PET.
IT'S TOO DANGER-OUS TO SEEK VENGEANCE ON YOUR OWN.
VEN-GEANCE ...?
WHAT ARE YOU...

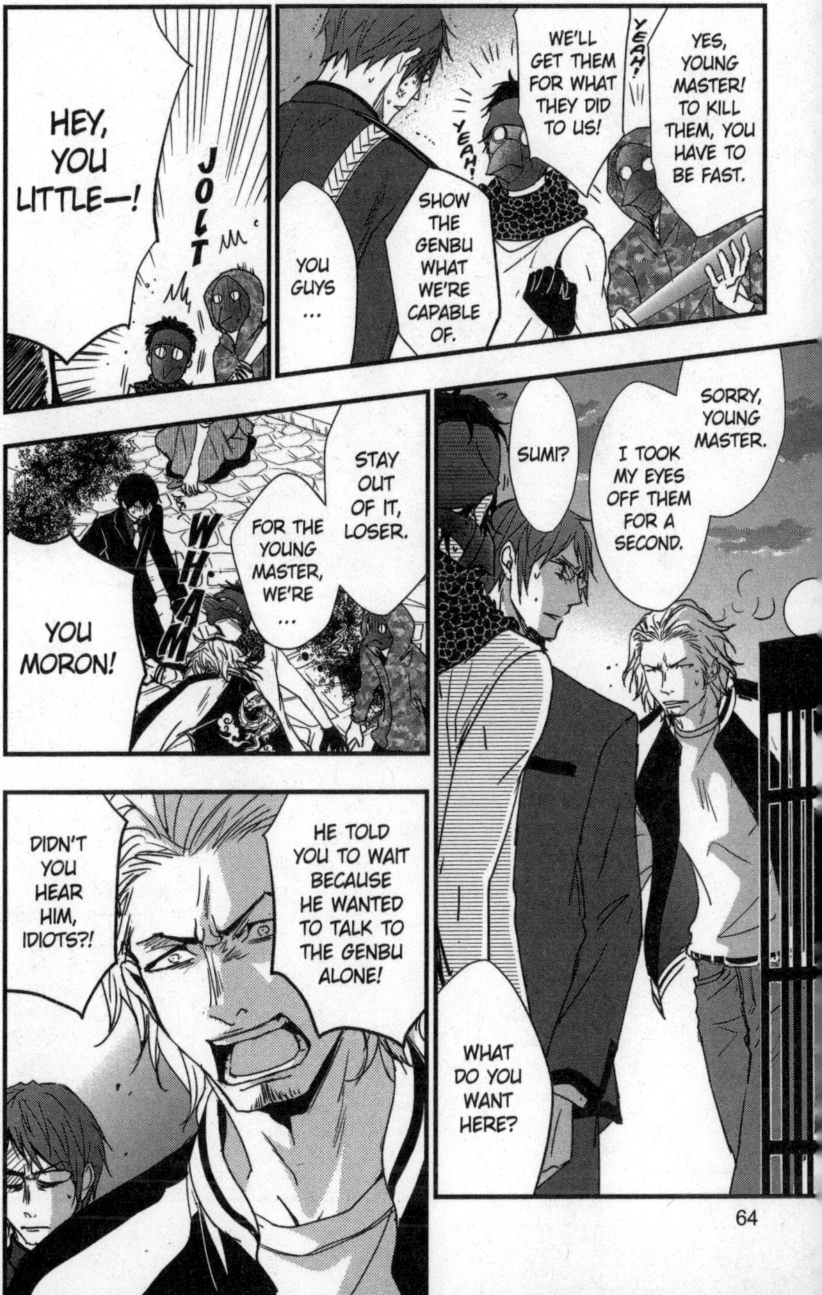
YES, YOUNG MASTER! TO KILL THEM, YOU HAVE TO BE FAST.
YEAH!
WE'LL GET THEM FOR WHAT THEY DID TO US!
YEAH!
SHOW THE GENBU WHAT WE'RE CAPABLE OF.
YOU GUYS ...
HEY, YOU LITTLE—!
JOLT
SORRY, YOUNG MASTER.
I TOOK MY EYES OFF THEM FOR A SECOND.
SUMI?
WHAT DO YOU WANT HERE?
STAY OUT OF IT, LOSER.
FOR THE YOUNG MASTER, WE'RE ...
WHAM
YOU MORON!
HE TOLD YOU TO WAIT BECAUSE HE WANTED TO TALK TO THE GENBU ALONE!
DIDN'T YOU HEAR HIM, IDIOTS?!

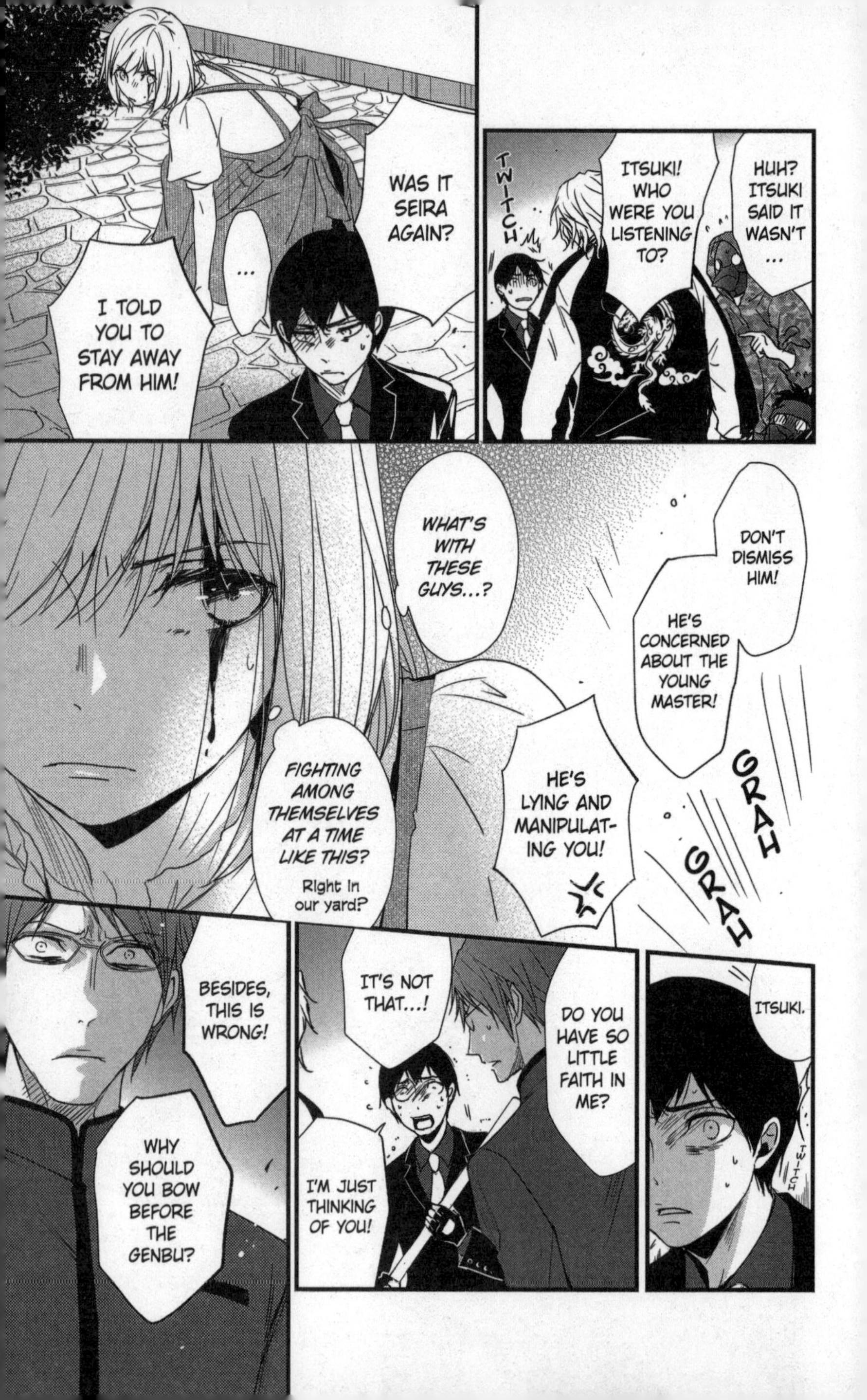
HUH? ITSUKI SAID IT WASN'T ...
ITSUKI! WHO WERE YOU LISTENING TO?
TWITCH
WAS IT SEIRA AGAIN?
...
I TOLD YOU TO STAY AWAY FROM HIM!
DON'T DISMISS HIM!
HE'S CONCERNED ABOUT THE YOUNG MASTER!
GRAH
GRAH
HE'S LYING AND MANIPULATING YOU!
WHAT'S WITH THESE GUYS...?
FIGHTING AMONG THEMSELVES AT A TIME LIKE THIS?
Right in our yard?
ITSUKI.
TWITCH
DO YOU HAVE SO LITTLE FAITH IN ME?
IT'S NOT THAT...!
I'M JUST THINKING OF YOU!
BESIDES, THIS IS WRONG!
WHY SHOULD YOU BOW BEFORE THE GENBU?

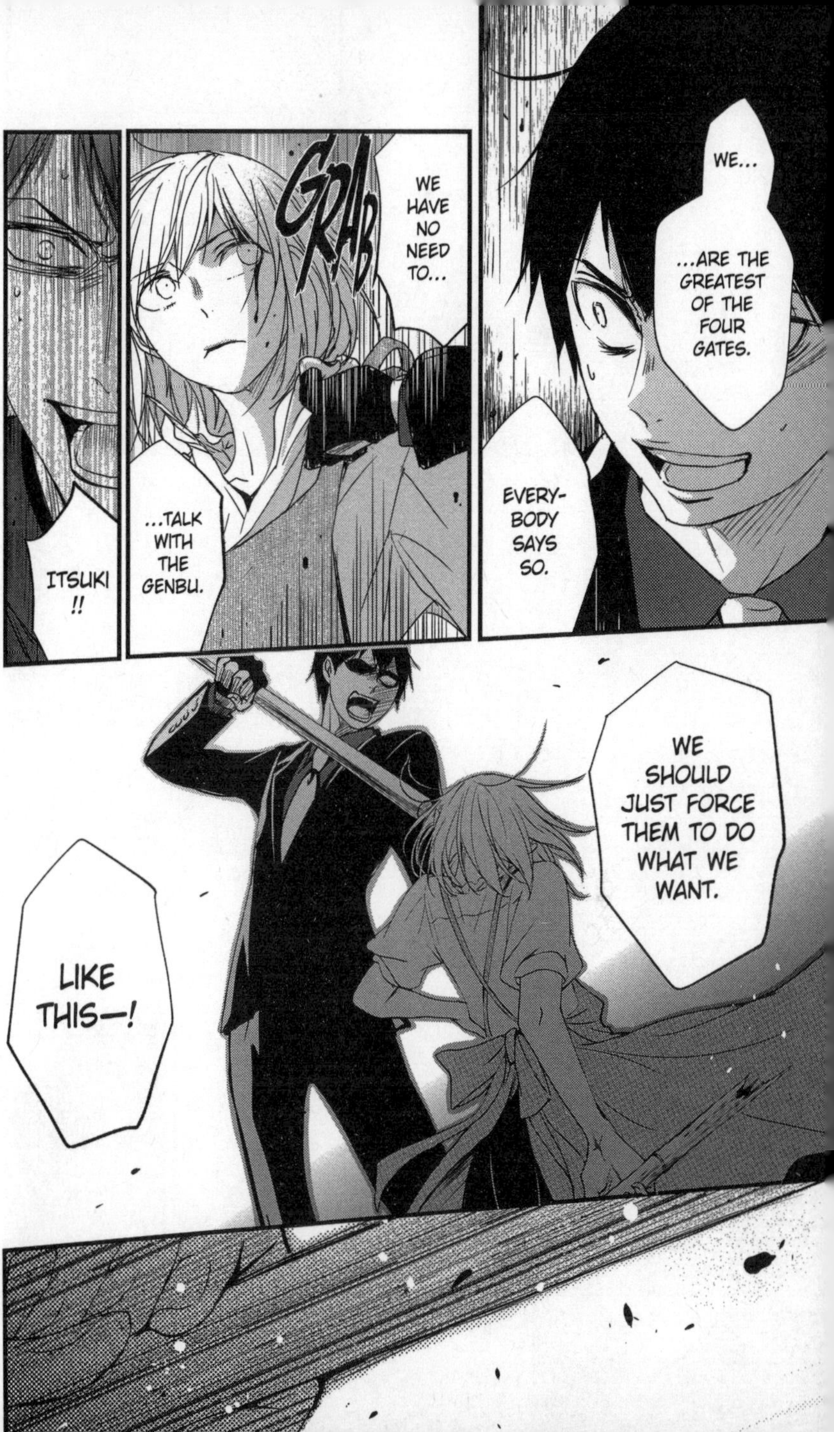
WE...
...ARE THE GREATEST OF THE FOUR GATES.
EVERY-BODY SAYS SO.
GRAB
WE HAVE NO NEED TO...
...TALK WITH THE GENBU.
ITSUKI !!
WE SHOULD JUST FORCE THEM TO DO WHAT WE WANT.
LIKE THIS—!

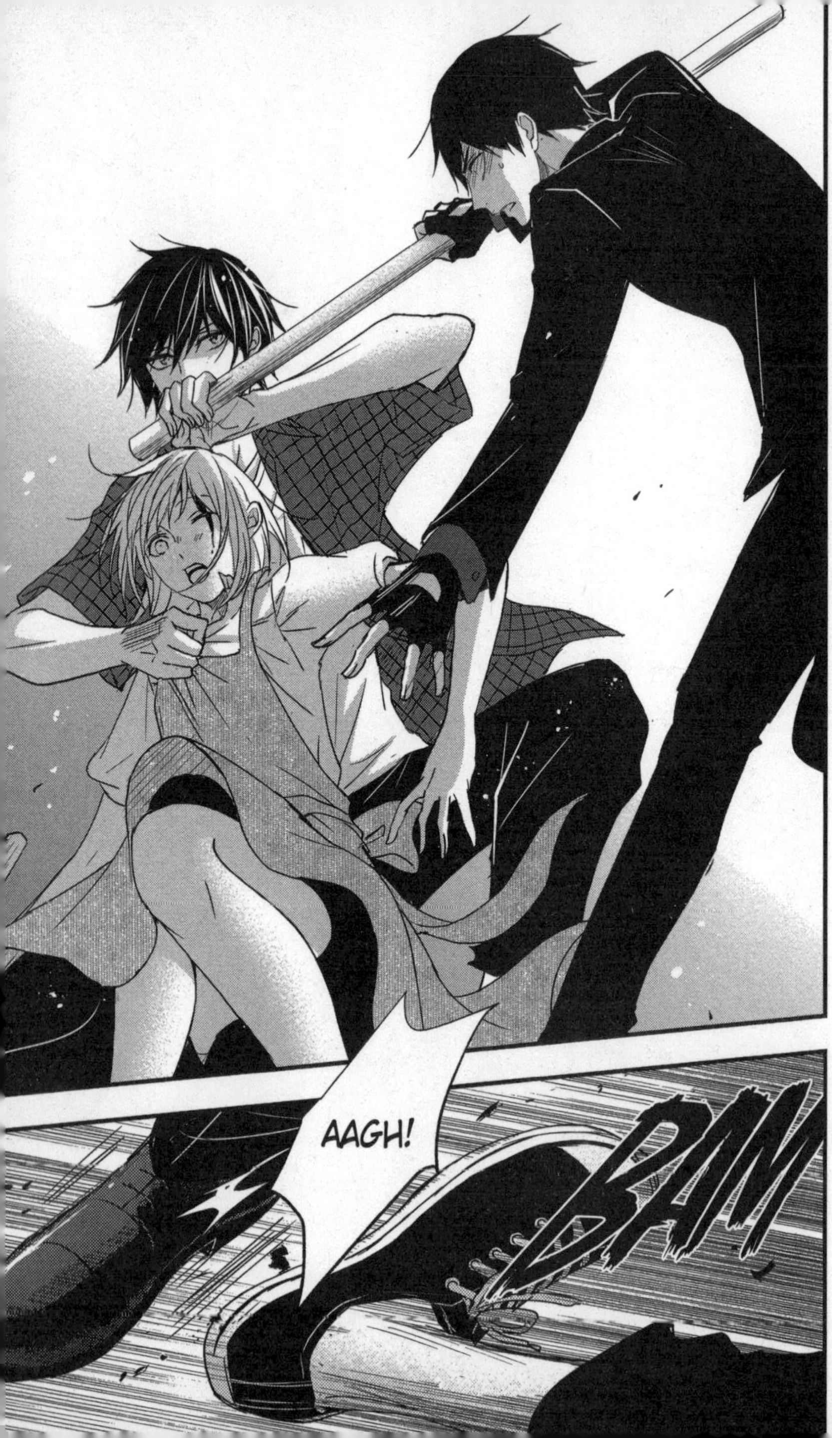
AAGH!
BAM

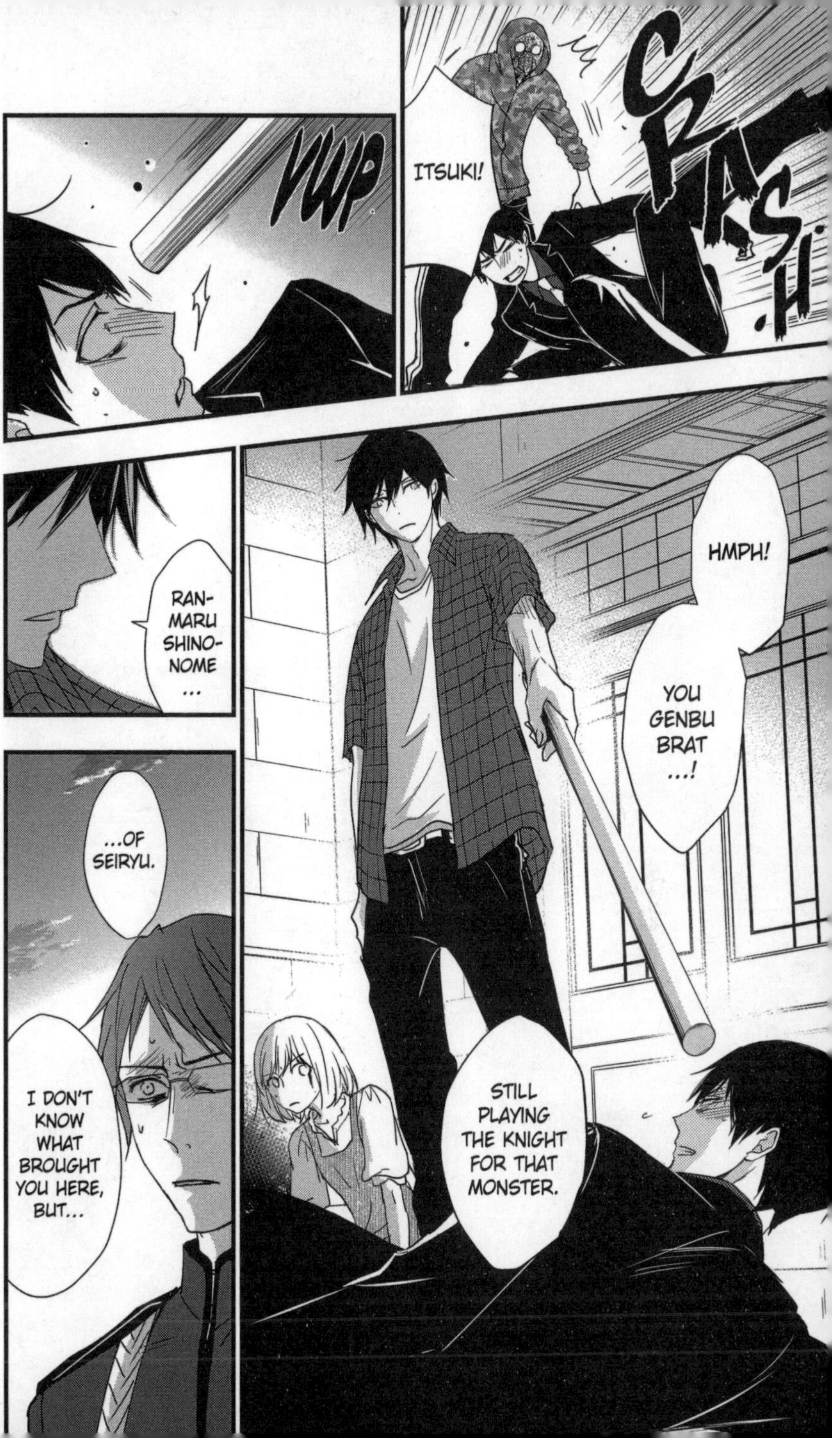
CRASH
ITSUKI!
VUUP
HMPH!
YOU GENBU BRAT ...!
STILL PLAYING THE KNIGHT FOR THAT MONSTER.
RAN-MARU SHINO-NOME ...
...OF SEIRYU.
I DON'T KNOW WHAT BROUGHT YOU HERE, BUT...

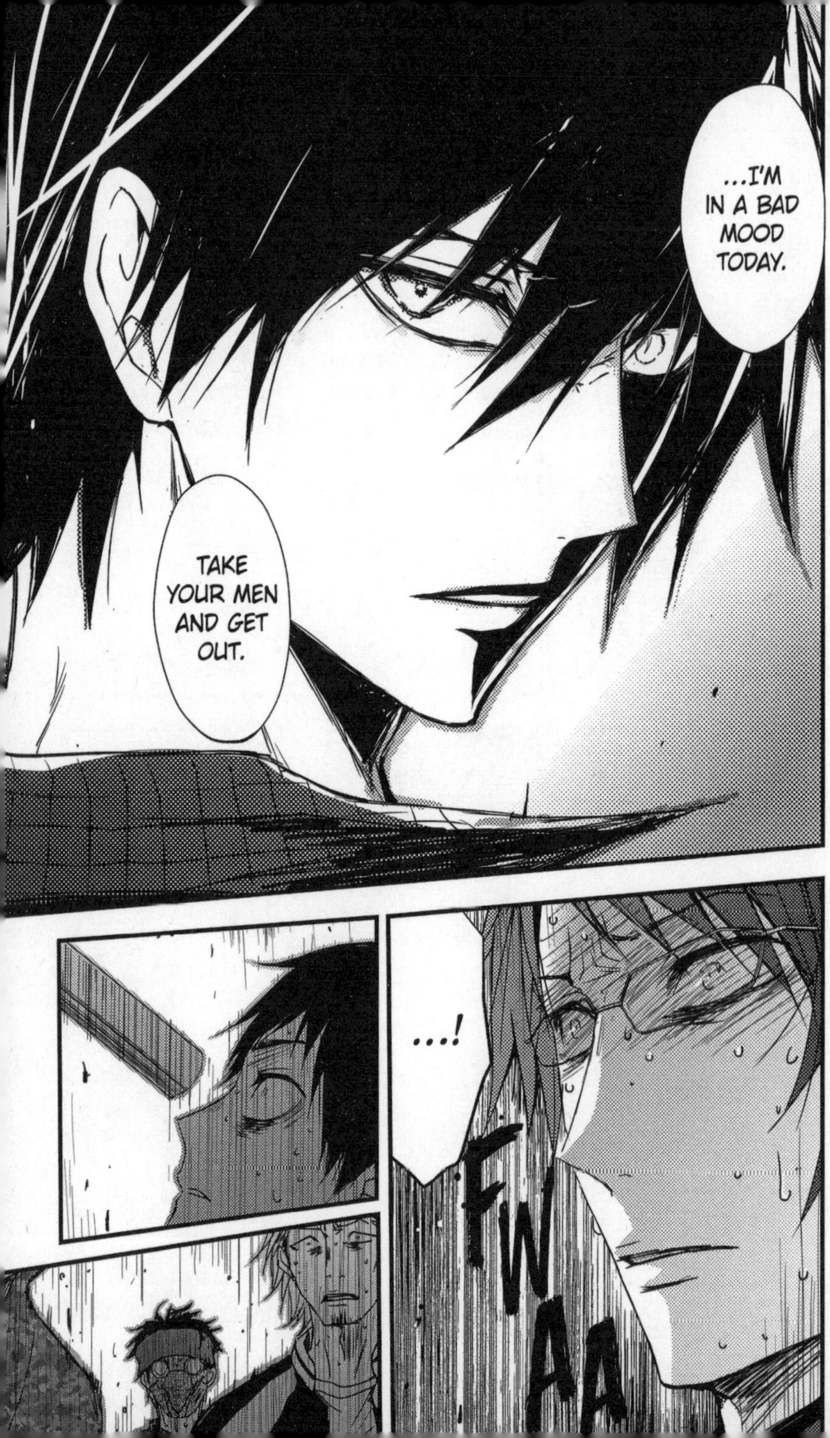
...I'M IN A BAD MOOD TODAY.
TAKE YOUR MEN AND GET OUT.
...!
FWAA

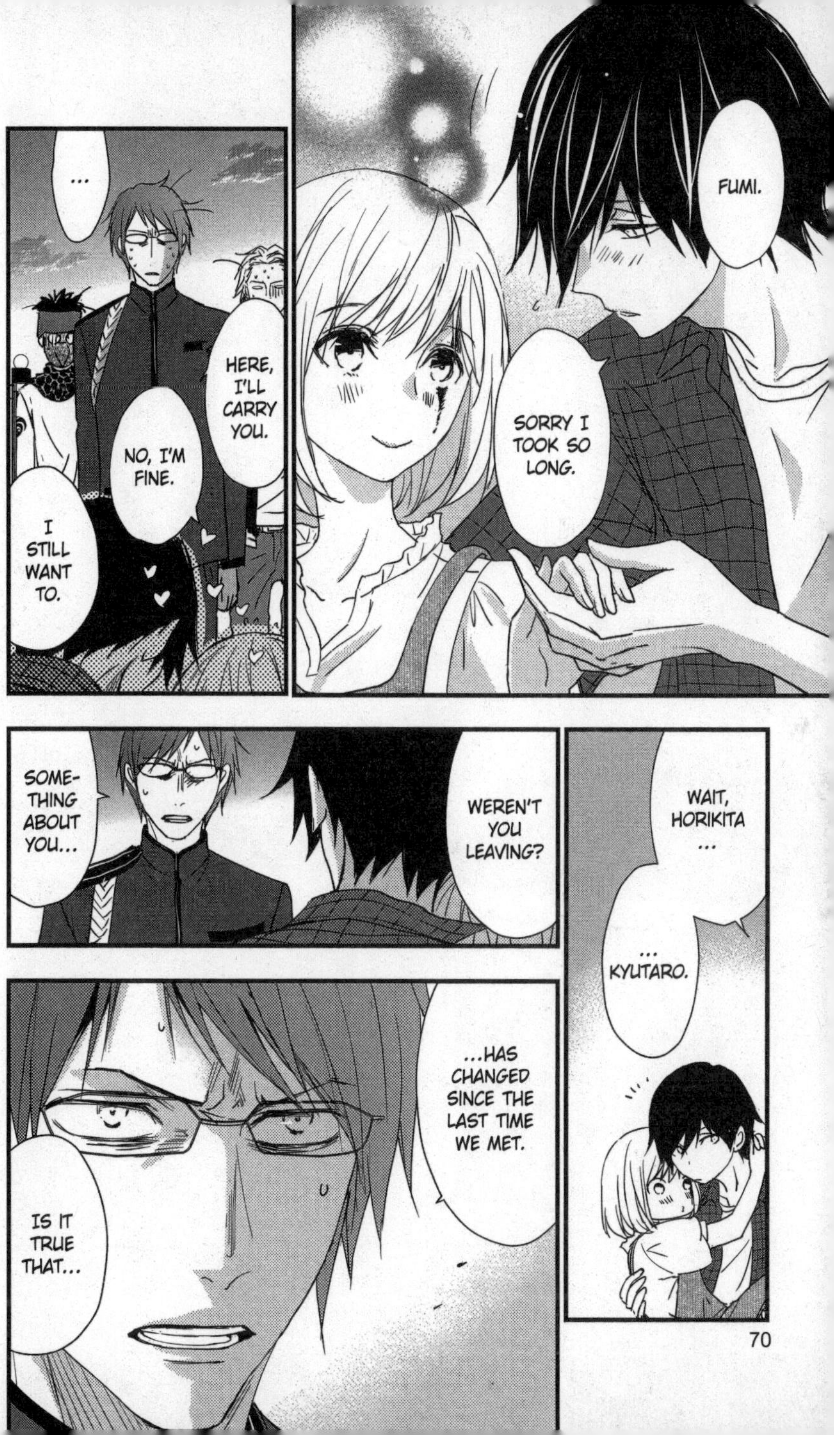
FUMI.
SORRY I TOOK SO LONG.
...
HERE, I'LL CARRY YOU.
NO, I'M FINE.
I STILL WANT TO.
WAIT, HORIKITA ...
... KYUTARO.
WEREN'T YOU LEAVING?
SOME-THING ABOUT YOU...
...HAS CHANGED SINCE THE LAST TIME WE MET.
IS IT TRUE THAT...

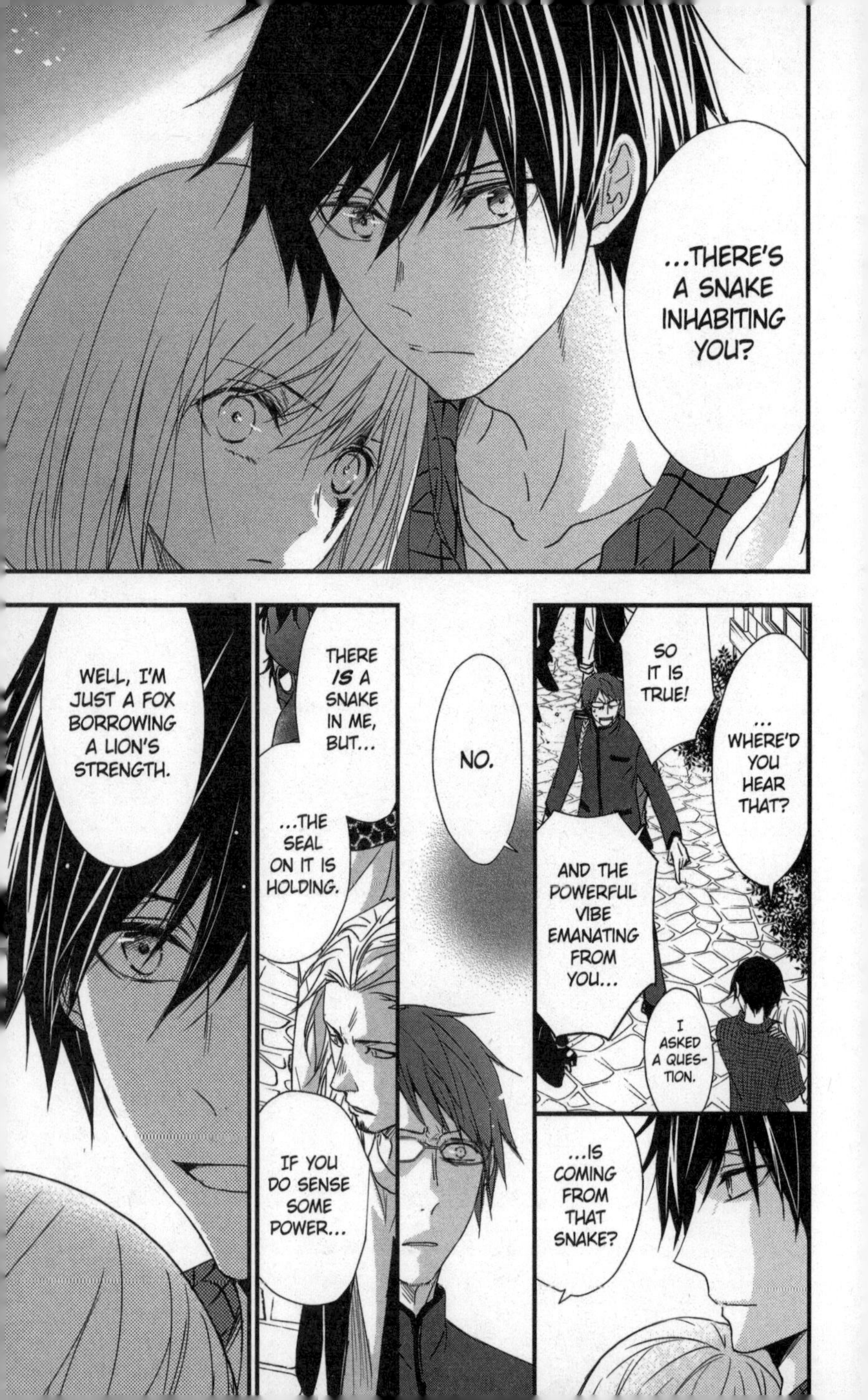
...THERE'S A SNAKE INHABITING YOU?
...WHERE'D YOU HEAR THAT?
SO IT IS TRUE!
AND THE POWERFUL VIBE EMANATING FROM YOU...
I ASKED A QUESTION.
...IS COMING FROM THAT SNAKE?
NO.
THERE *IS* A SNAKE IN ME, BUT...
...THE SEAL ON IT IS HOLDING.
IF YOU DO SENSE SOME POWER...
WELL, I'M JUST A FOX BORROWING A LION'S STRENGTH.

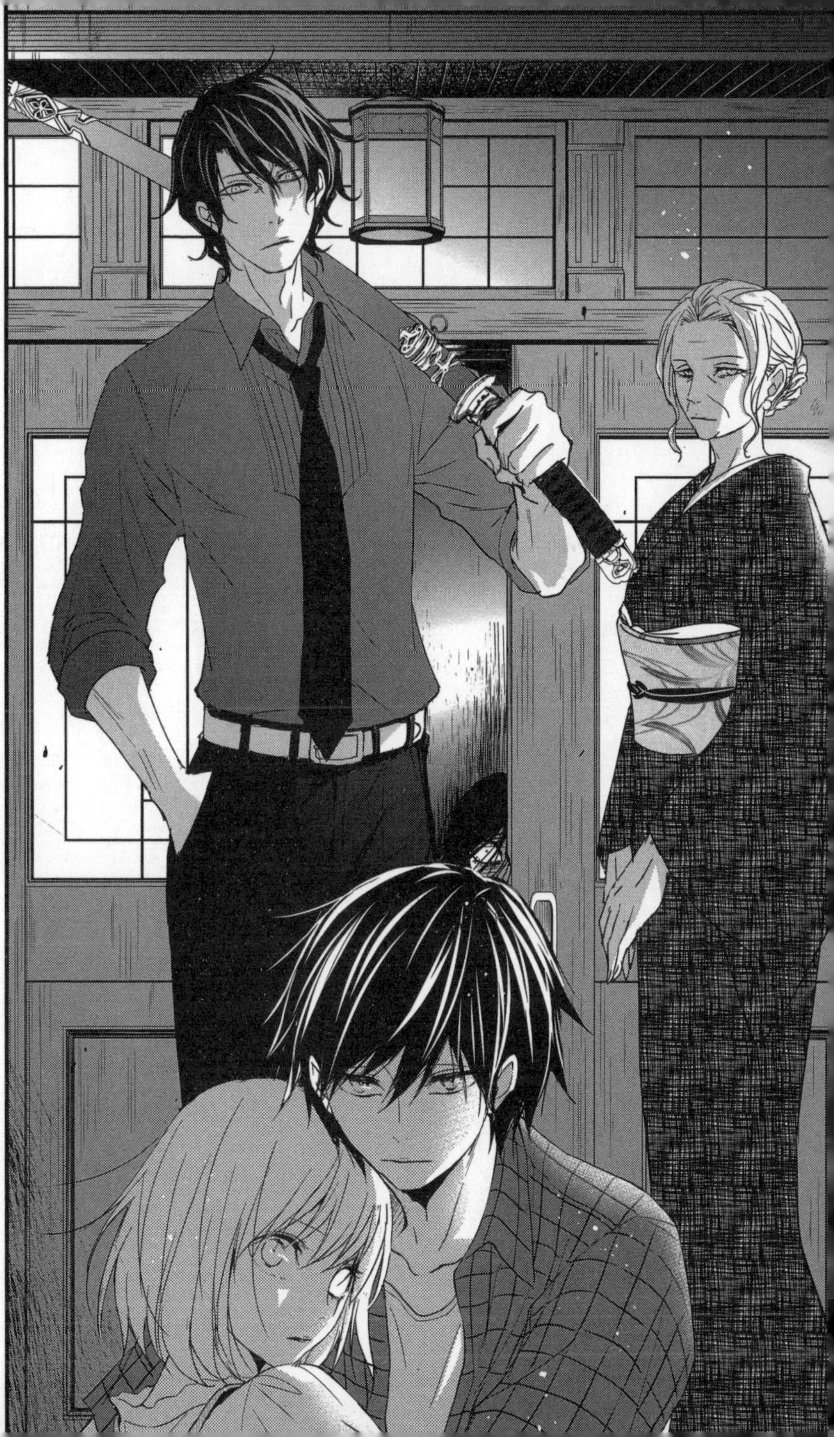

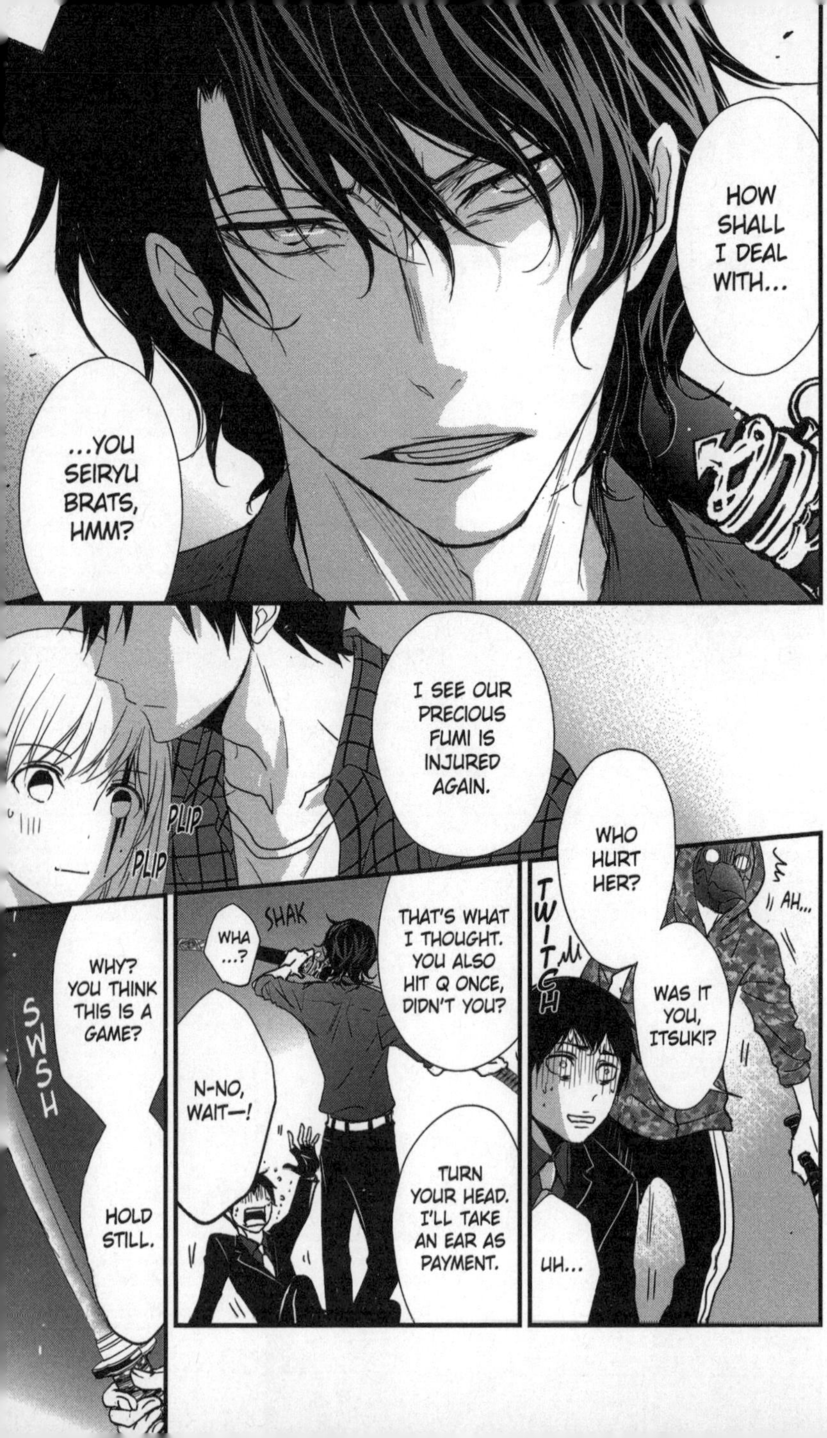
HOW SHALL I DEAL WITH...
...YOU SEIRYU BRATS, HMM?
I SEE OUR PRECIOUS FUMI IS INJURED AGAIN.
PLIP
PLIP
WHO HURT HER?
AH...
TWITCH
WAS IT YOU, ITSUKI?
UH...
THAT'S WHAT I THOUGHT. YOU ALSO HIT Q ONCE, DIDN'T YOU?
SHAK
WHA ...?
TURN YOUR HEAD. I'LL TAKE AN EAR AS PAYMENT.
N-NO, WAIT—!
SWSH
WHY? YOU THINK THIS IS A GAME?
HOLD STILL.

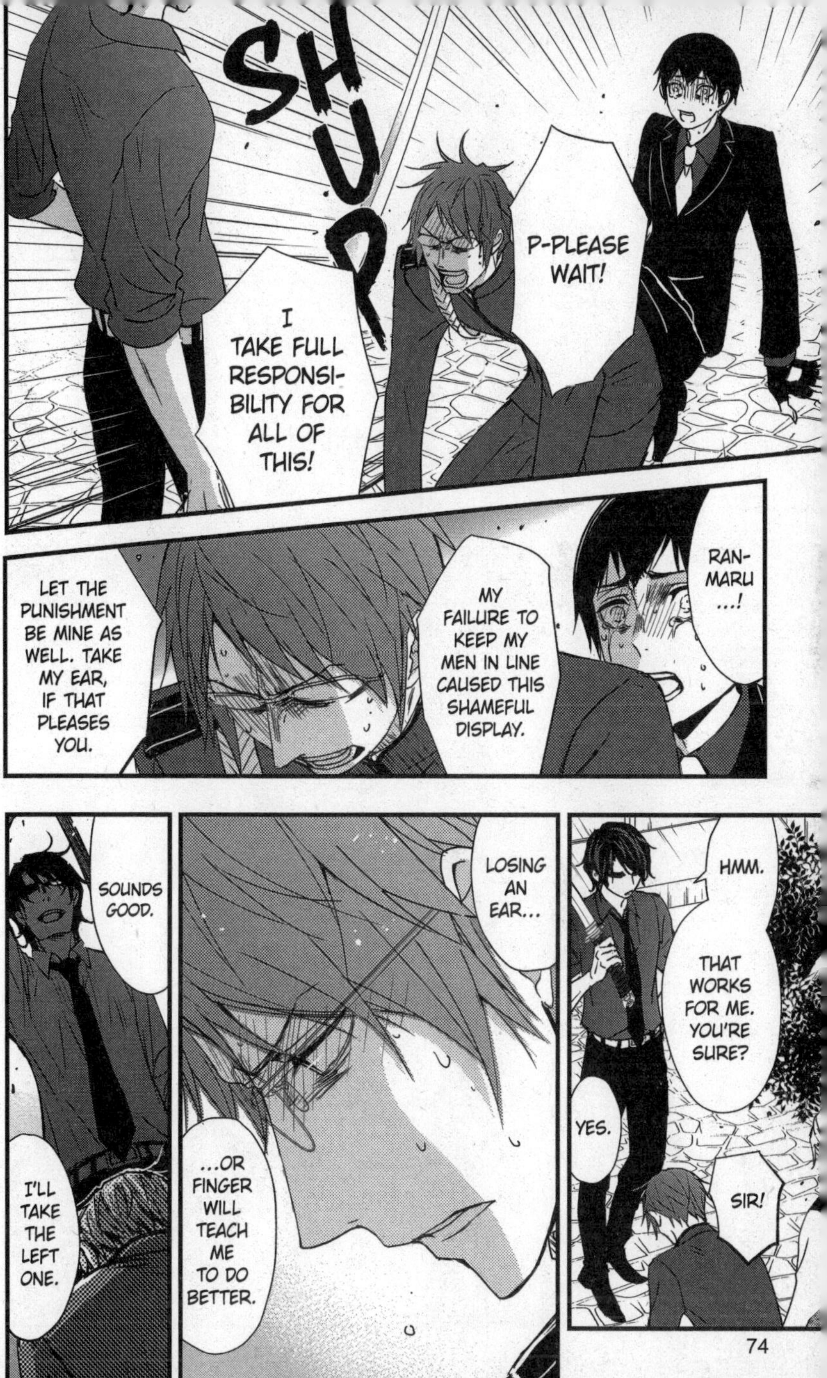
P-PLEASE WAIT!
SHUP
I TAKE FULL RESPONSIBILITY FOR ALL OF THIS!
RAN-MARU ...!
MY FAILURE TO KEEP MY MEN IN LINE CAUSED THIS SHAMEFUL DISPLAY.
LET THE PUNISHMENT BE MINE AS WELL. TAKE MY EAR, IF THAT PLEASES YOU.
HMM.
THAT WORKS FOR ME. YOU'RE SURE?
YES.
SIR!
LOSING AN EAR...
...OR FINGER WILL TEACH ME TO DO BETTER.
SOUNDS GOOD.
I'LL TAKE THE LEFT ONE.

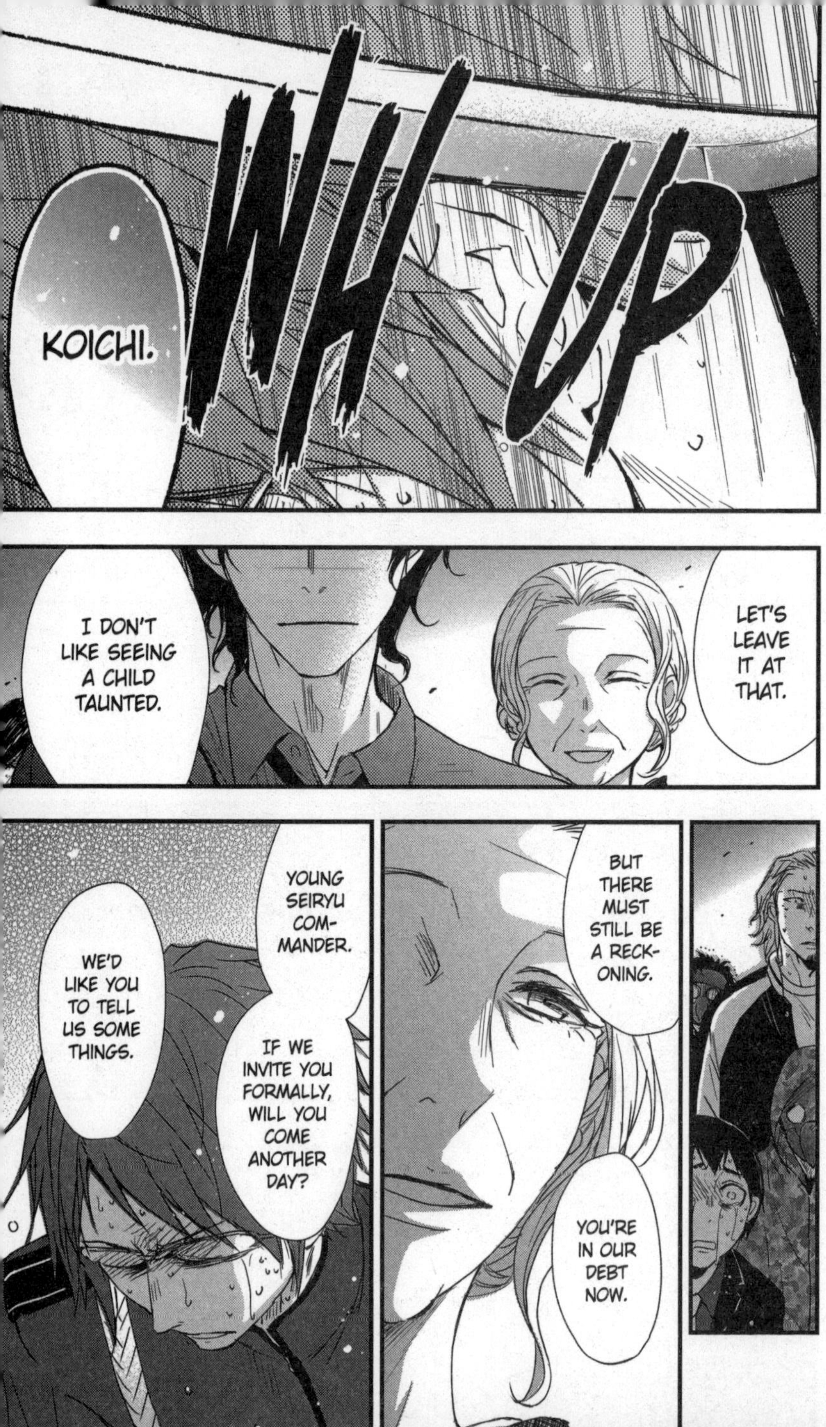
WHUP
KOICHI.
LET'S LEAVE IT AT THAT.
I DON'T LIKE SEEING A CHILD TAUNTED.
BUT THERE MUST STILL BE A RECK-ONING.
YOU'RE IN OUR DEBT NOW.
YOUNG SEIRYU COM-MANDER.
WE'D LIKE YOU TO TELL US SOME THINGS.
IF WE INVITE YOU FORMALLY, WILL YOU COME ANOTHER DAY?

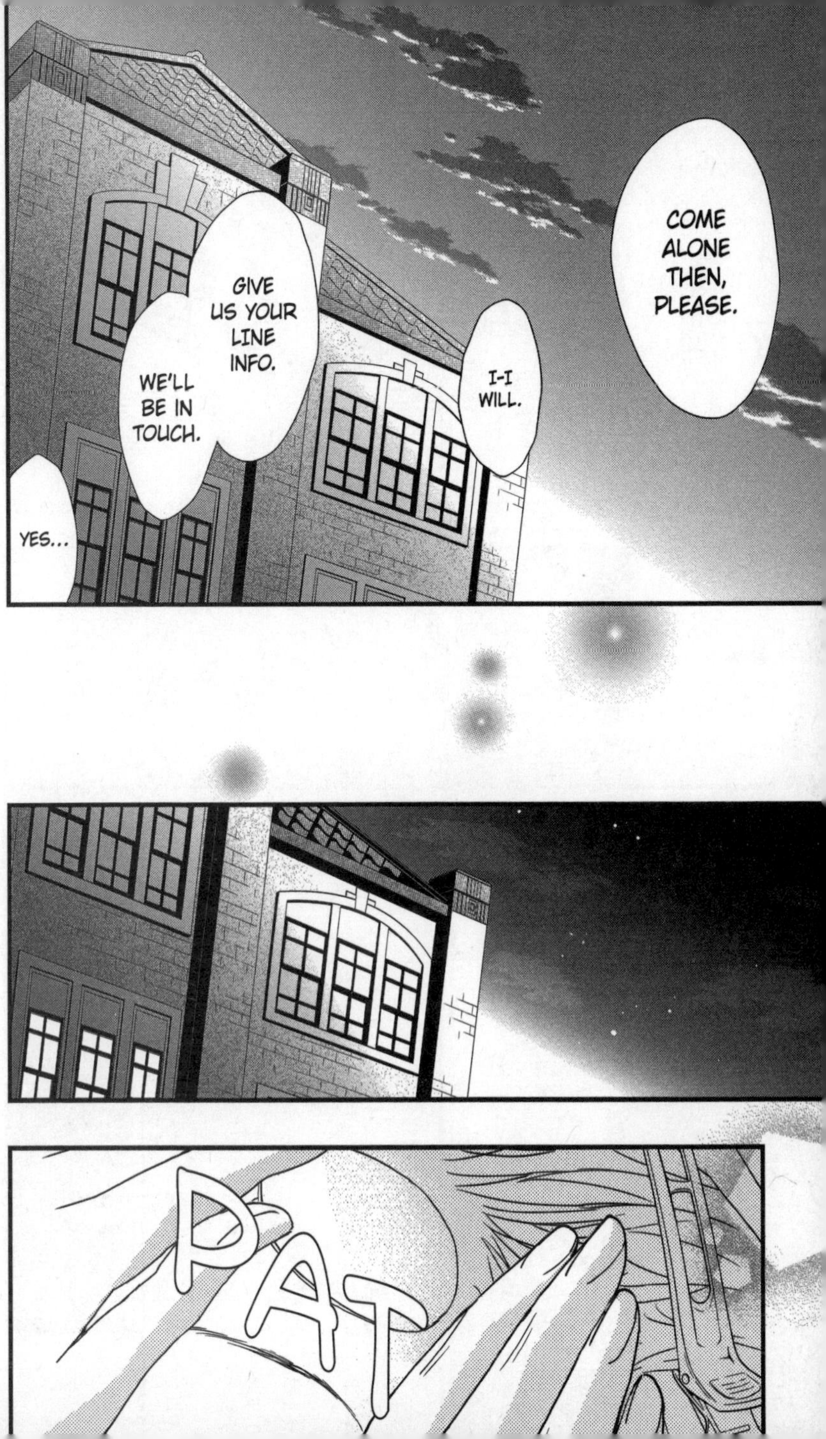
COME ALONE THEN, PLEASE.
I-I WILL.
GIVE US YOUR LINE INFO.
WE'LL BE IN TOUCH.
YES...
PAT

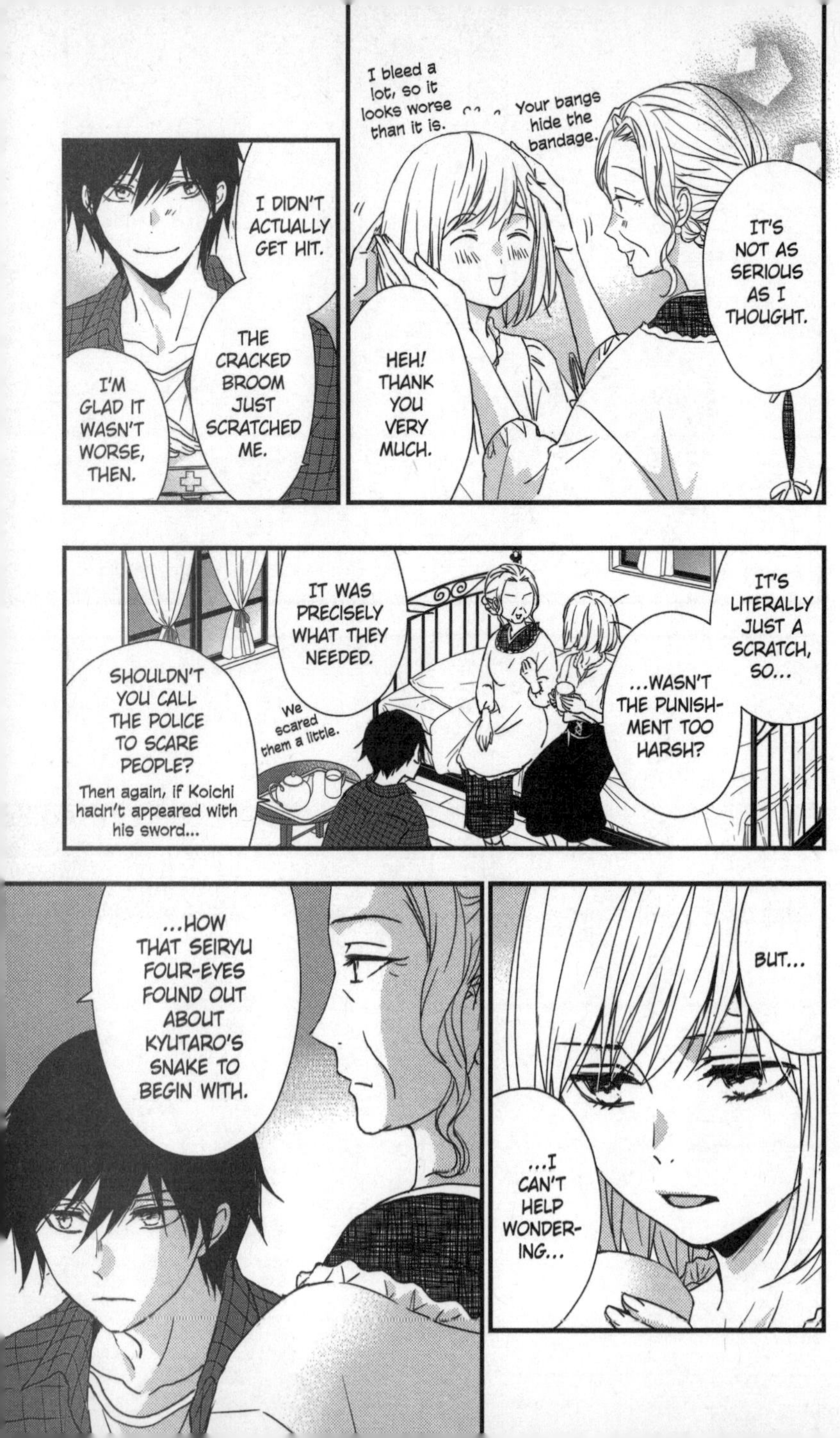
IT'S NOT AS SERIOUS AS I THOUGHT.
HEH! THANK YOU VERY MUCH.
Your bangs hide the bandage.
I bleed a lot, so it looks worse than it is.
I DIDN'T ACTUALLY GET HIT.
THE CRACKED BROOM JUST SCRATCHED ME.
I'M GLAD IT WASN'T WORSE, THEN.
IT'S LITERALLY JUST A SCRATCH, SO...
...WASN'T THE PUNISHMENT TOO HARSH?
IT WAS PRECISELY WHAT THEY NEEDED.
We scared them a little.
SHOULDN'T YOU CALL THE POLICE TO SCARE PEOPLE?
Then again, if Koichi hadn't appeared with his sword...
BUT...
...I CAN'T HELP WONDERING...
...HOW THAT SEIRYU FOUR-EYES FOUND OUT ABOUT KYUTARO'S SNAKE TO BEGIN WITH.

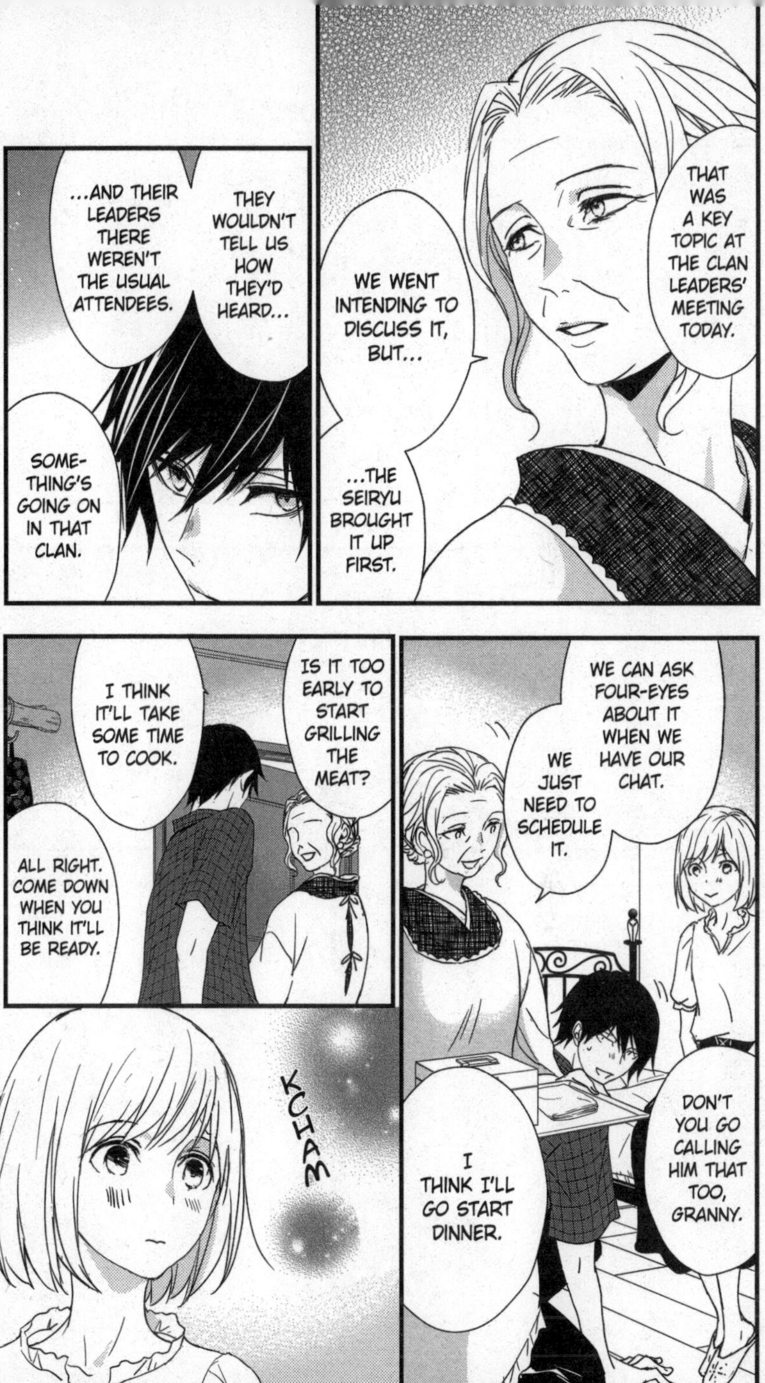
THAT WAS A KEY TOPIC AT THE CLAN LEADERS' MEETING TODAY.
WE WENT INTENDING TO DISCUSS IT, BUT...
...THE SEIRYU BROUGHT IT UP FIRST.
THEY WOULDN'T TELL US HOW THEY'D HEARD...
...AND THEIR LEADERS THERE WEREN'T THE USUAL ATTENDEES.
SOME-THING'S GOING ON IN THAT CLAN.
WE CAN ASK FOUR-EYES ABOUT IT WHEN WE HAVE OUR CHAT.
WE JUST NEED TO SCHEDULE IT.
DON'T YOU GO CALLING HIM THAT TOO, GRANNY.
I THINK I'LL GO START DINNER.
IS IT TOO EARLY TO START GRILLING THE MEAT?
I THINK IT'LL TAKE SOME TIME TO COOK.
ALL RIGHT. COME DOWN WHEN YOU THINK IT'LL BE READY.
KCHAM

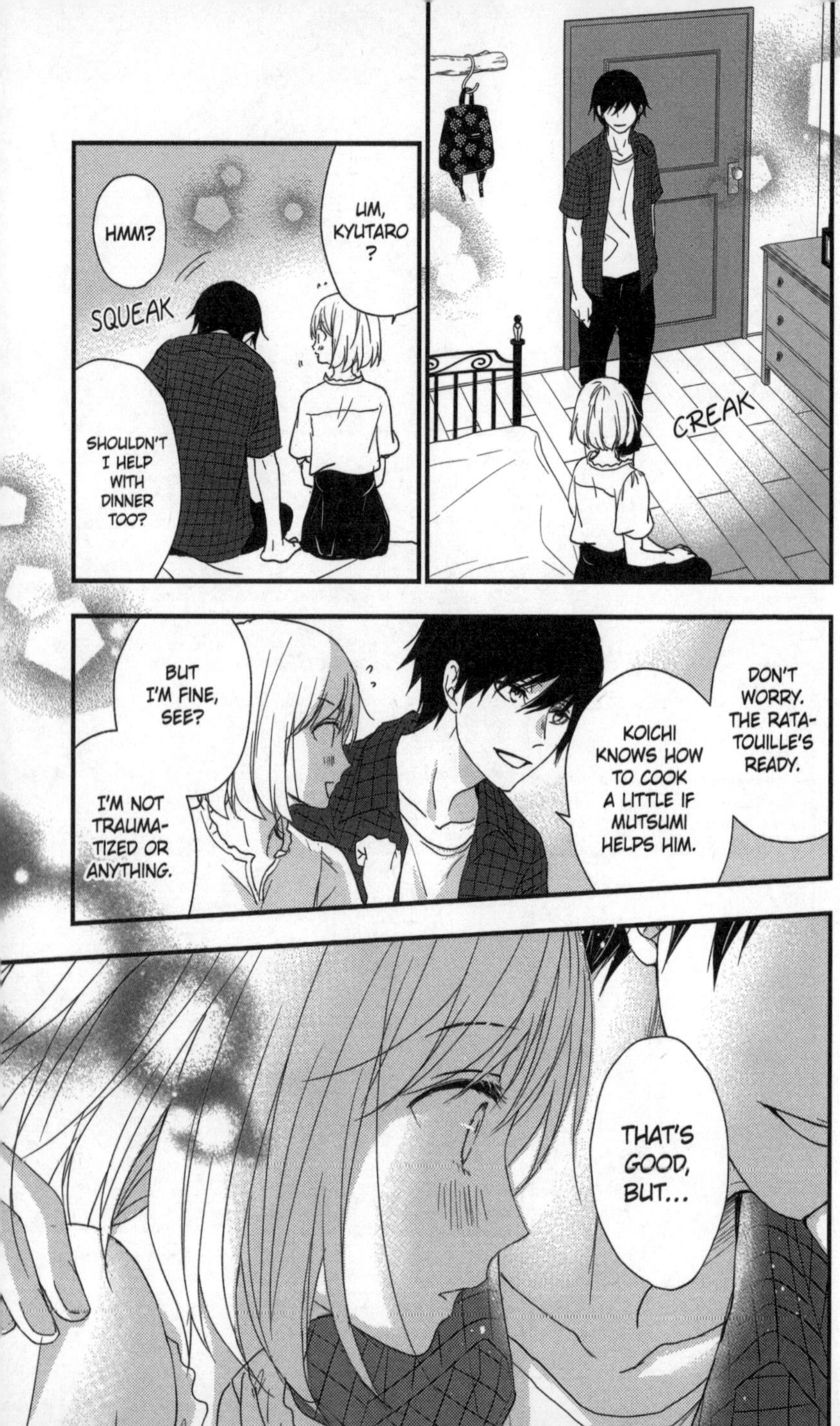
CREAK
UM, KYUTARO?
HMM?
SQUEAK
SHOULDN'T I HELP WITH DINNER TOO?
DON'T WORRY. THE RATA-TOUILLE'S READY.
KOICHI KNOWS HOW TO COOK A LITTLE IF MUTSUMI HELPS HIM.
BUT I'M FINE, SEE?
I'M NOT TRAUMA-TIZED OR ANYTHING.
THAT'S GOOD, BUT...

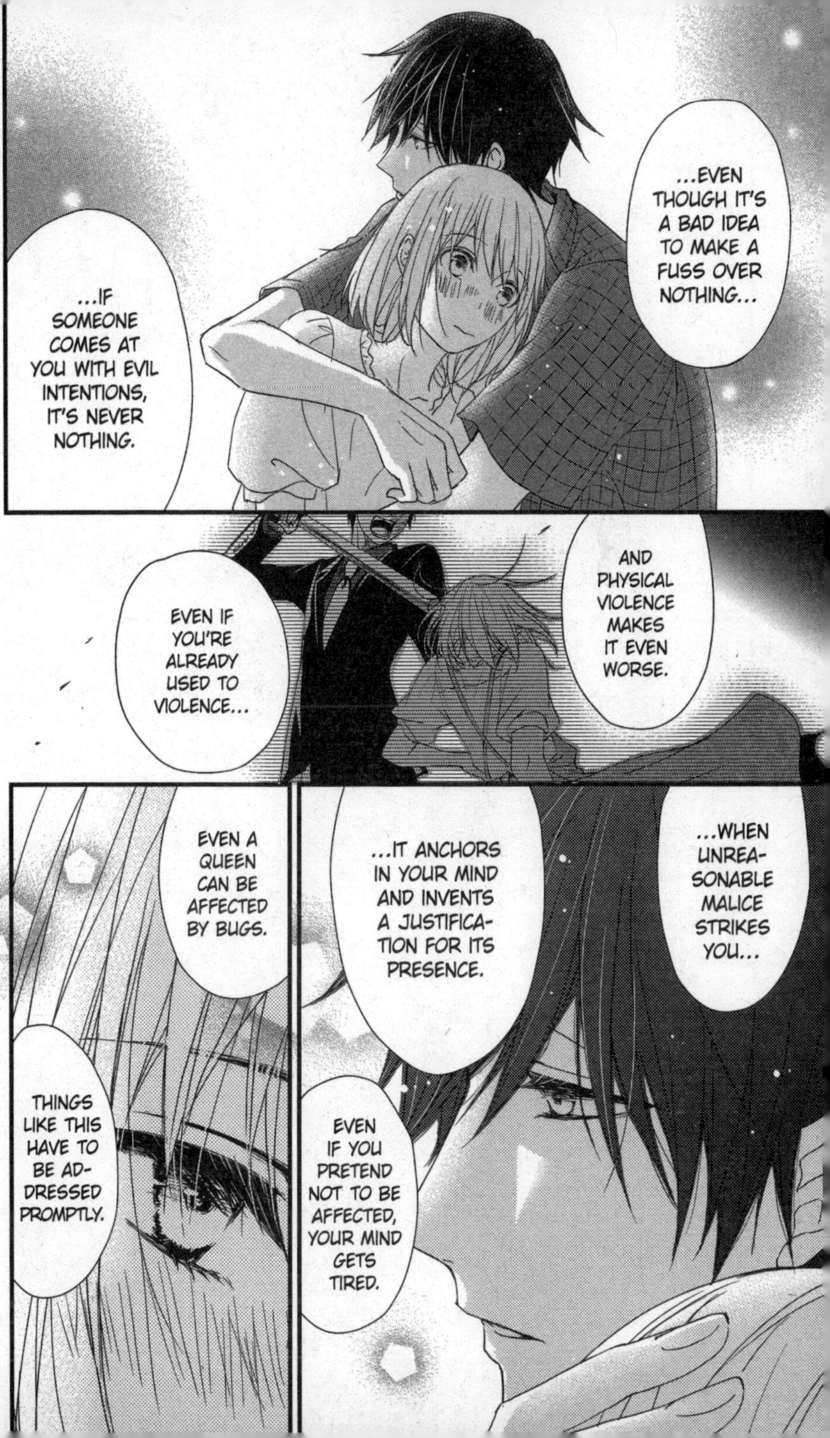

...EVEN THOUGH IT'S A BAD IDEA TO MAKE A FUSS OVER NOTHING...
...IF SOMEONE COMES AT YOU WITH EVIL INTENTIONS, IT'S NEVER NOTHING.
AND PHYSICAL VIOLENCE MAKES IT EVEN WORSE.
EVEN IF YOU'RE ALREADY USED TO VIOLENCE...
...WHEN UNREASONABLE MALICE STRIKES YOU...
...IT ANCHORS IN YOUR MIND AND INVENTS A JUSTIFICATION FOR ITS PRESENCE.
EVEN IF YOU PRETEND NOT TO BE AFFECTED, YOUR MIND GETS TIRED.
EVEN A QUEEN CAN BE AFFECTED BY BUGS.
THINGS LIKE THIS HAVE TO BE ADDRESSED PROMPTLY.

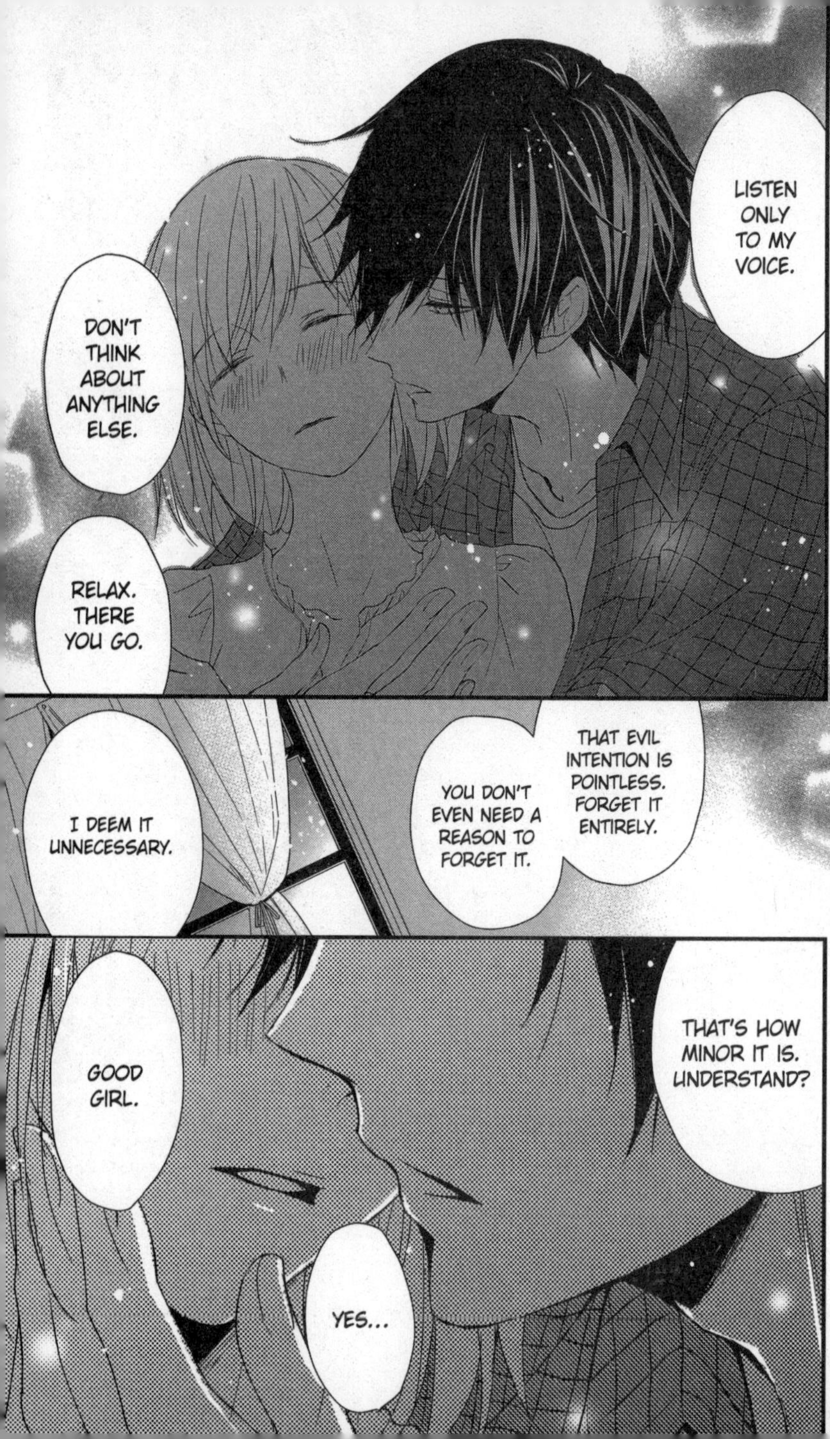
LISTEN ONLY TO MY VOICE.
DON'T THINK ABOUT ANYTHING ELSE.
RELAX. THERE YOU GO.
THAT EVIL INTENTION IS POINTLESS. FORGET IT ENTIRELY.
YOU DON'T EVEN NEED A REASON TO FORGET IT.
I DEEM IT UNNECESSARY.
THAT'S HOW MINOR IT IS. UNDERSTAND?
GOOD GIRL.
YES...

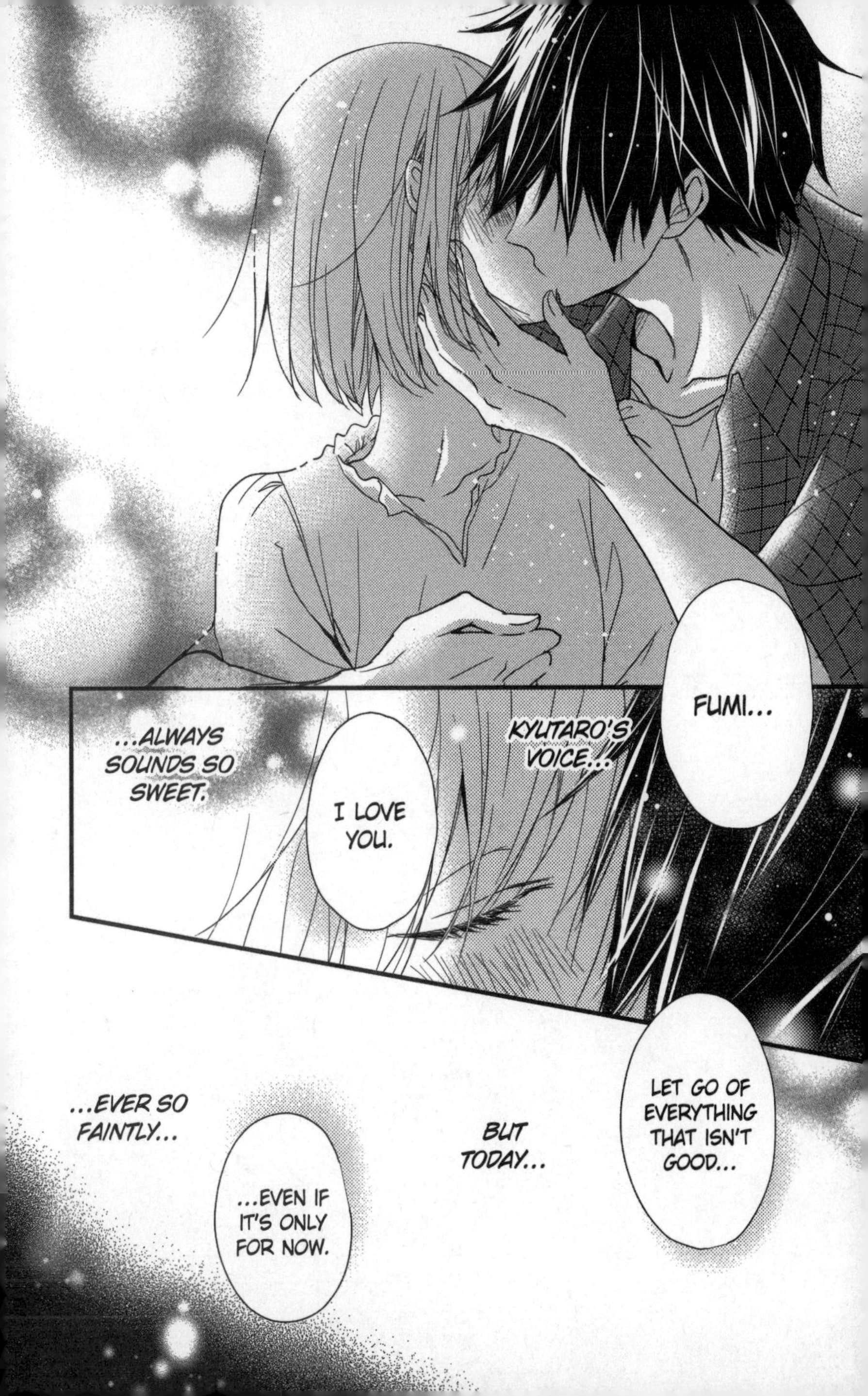
FUMI...
KYUTARO'S VOICE...
I LOVE YOU.
...ALWAYS SOUNDS SO SWEET.
LET GO OF EVERYTHING THAT ISN'T GOOD...
BUT TODAY...
...EVER SO FAINTLY...
...EVEN IF IT'S ONLY FOR NOW.

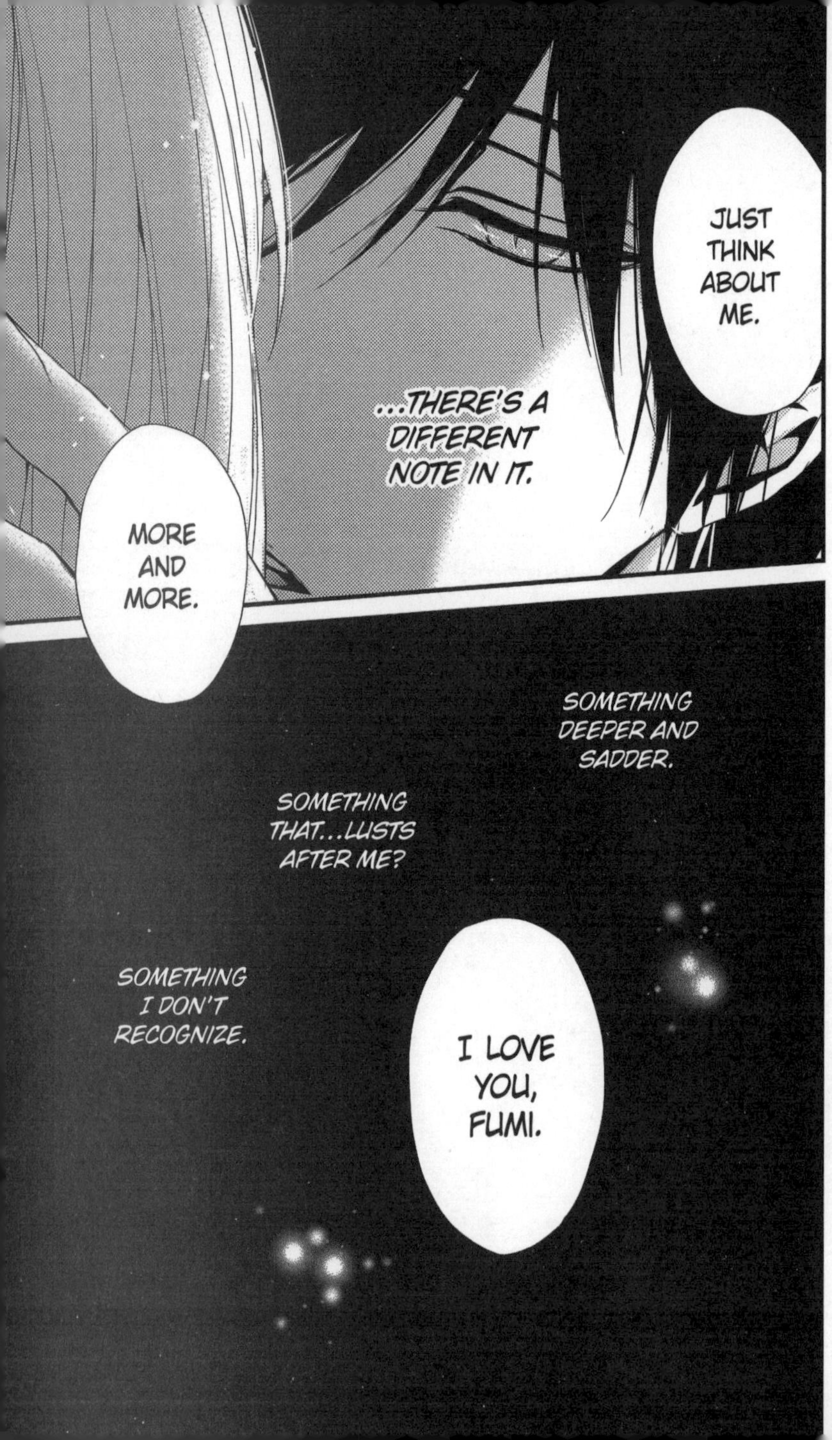
JUST THINK ABOUT ME.
...THERE'S A DIFFERENT NOTE IN IT.
MORE AND MORE.
SOMETHING DEEPER AND SADDER.
SOMETHING THAT...LUSTS AFTER ME?
I LOVE YOU, FUMI.
SOMETHING I DON'T RECOGNIZE.

KYOUSUKE MOTOMI
C/O QUEEN'S QUALITY EDITOR
VIZ MEDIA
P.O. BOX 77010
SAN FRANCISCO, CA 94107

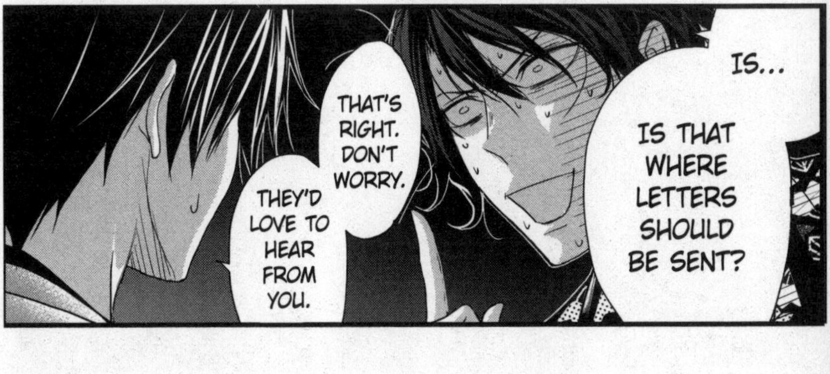
IS...
IS THAT WHERE LETTERS SHOULD BE SENT?
THAT'S RIGHT. DON'T WORRY.
THEY'D LOVE TO HEAR FROM YOU.

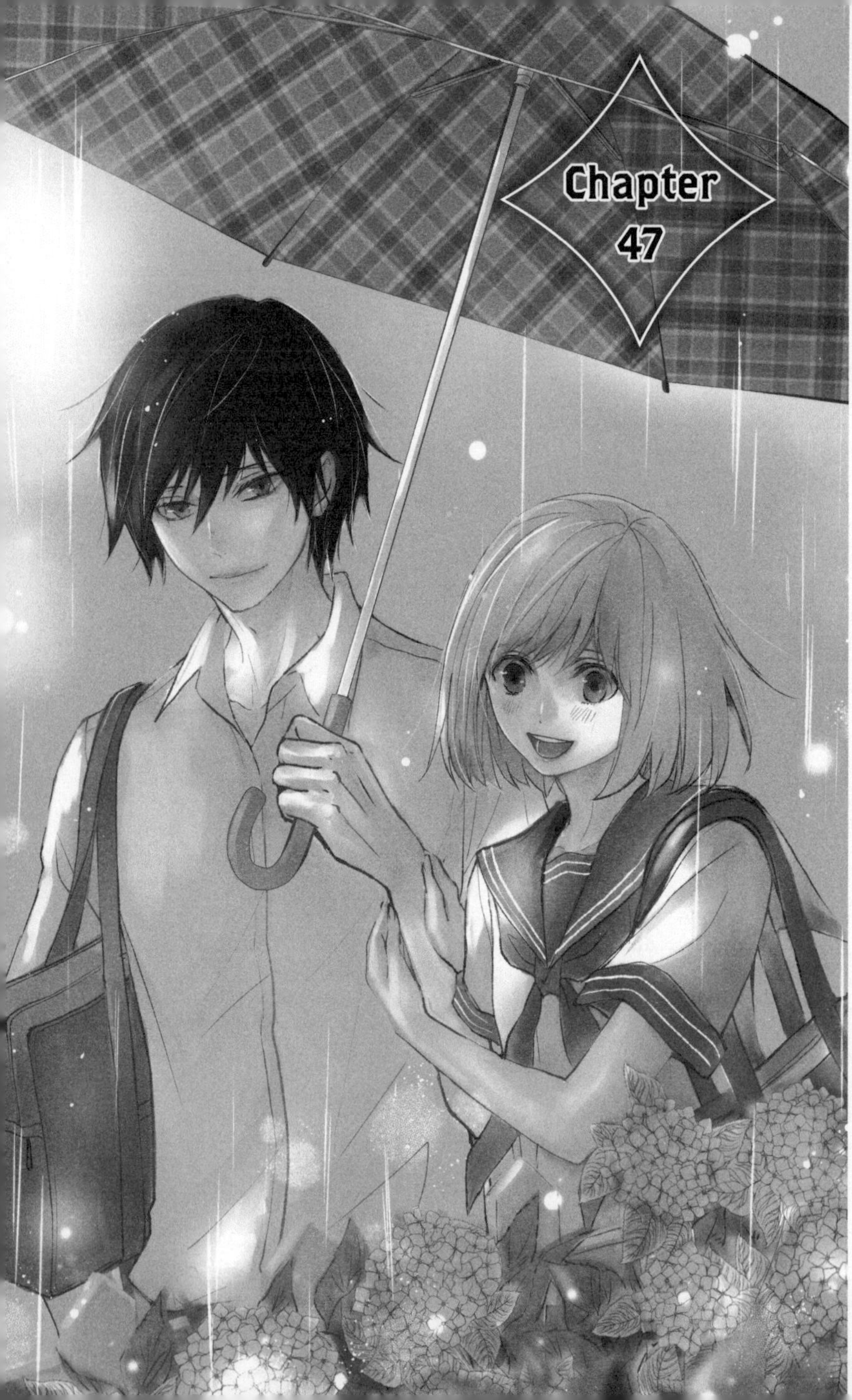
Chapter
47

CHAPTER 47

MONTHLY BETSUCOMI SALE DATE NOTICE ON TWITTER

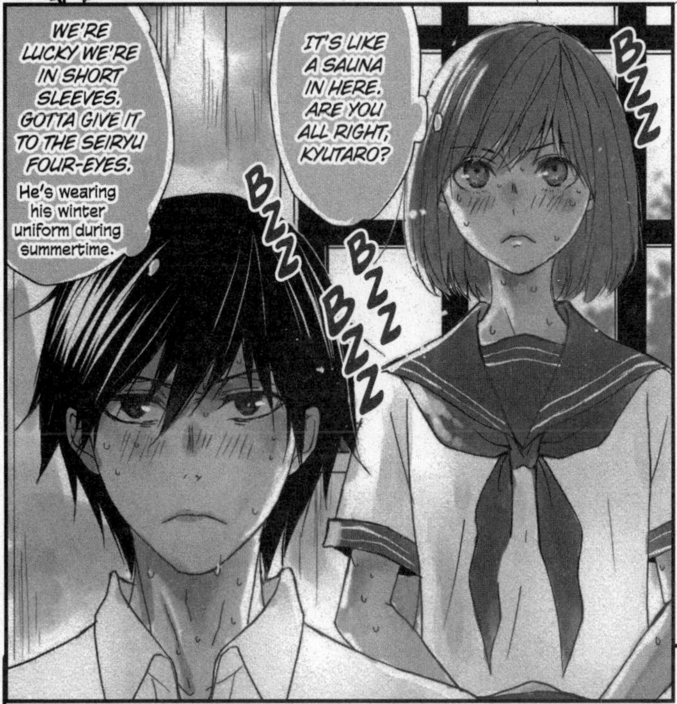
BZZ
IT'S LIKE A SAUNA IN HERE. ARE YOU ALL RIGHT, KYUTARO?
WE'RE LUCKY WE'RE IN SHORT SLEEVES. GOTTA GIVE IT TO THE SEIRYU FOUR-EYES.
He's wearing his winter uniform during summertime.
BZZ
BZZ
BZZ

LET'S SEE... WHAT'S UP IN *QUEEN'S QUALITY* THIS MONTH?
(1) THE GENBU FOUR-EYES VERSUS THE SEIRYU FOUR-EYES.
(2) IT'S SUMMER VACATION, ISN'T IT? IS THE OLD SCHOOL BUILDING AIR-CONDITIONED?
(3) FIVE...?

RANMARU HATED DOING IT, BUT IN THIS CHAPTER HE KEEPS BOWING HIS HEAD. AND THAT THING STARTS MOVING...!

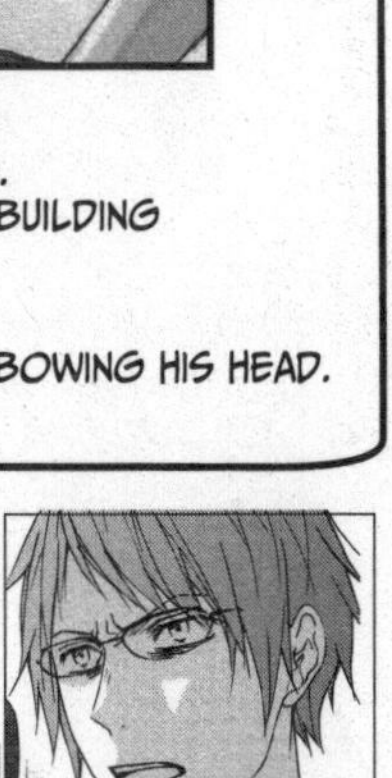

Chapter 47 and on

THE SEIRYU AND GENBU FOUR-EYES CHARACTERS LOOKED SO MUCH ALIKE THAT HAVING THEM SEATED AT THE SAME TABLE MADE THINGS TOO TRICKY, SO AS OF CHAPTER 47, I LIGHTENED RANMARU'S HAIR SIGNIFICANTLY.

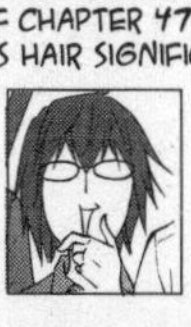

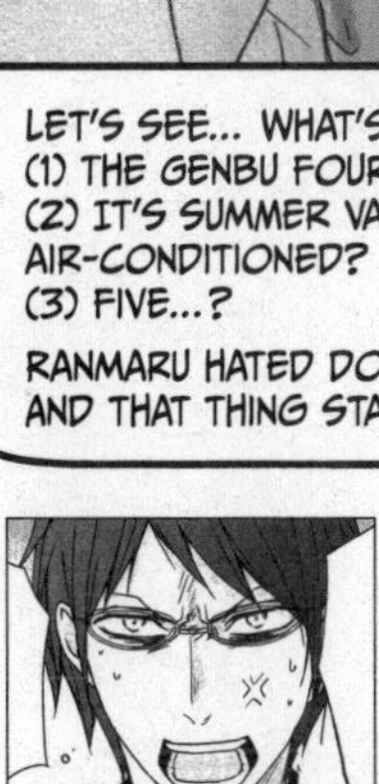

Up to chapter 46

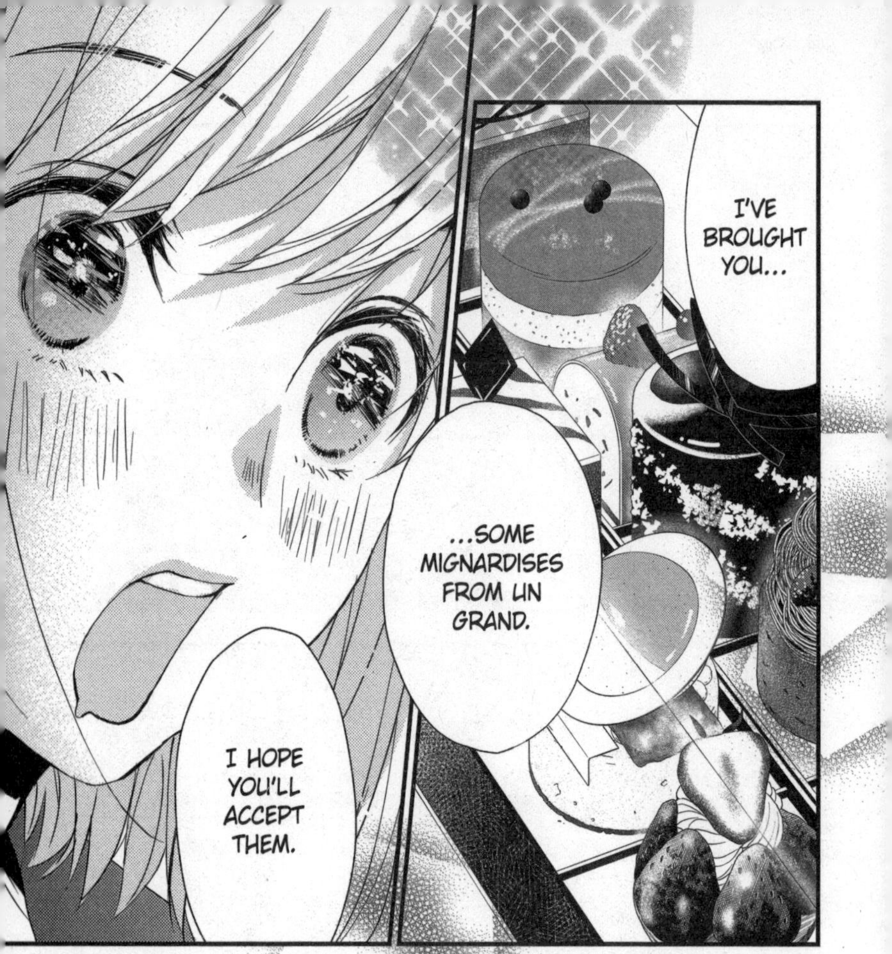
I'VE BROUGHT YOU...
...SOME MIGNARDISES FROM UN GRAND.
I HOPE YOU'LL ACCEPT THEM.

This is another health-related note, but I'm so out of shape that I'm scared I'll collapse in the middle of a series. That thought has motivated me to take up jogging, but I jog so slowly that I suspect people think I'm running in place.
I still enjoy it, though! I can feel the oxygen being pumped to my brain through my body. I hope I'm still at it when I reach volume 11. I'm going for it!

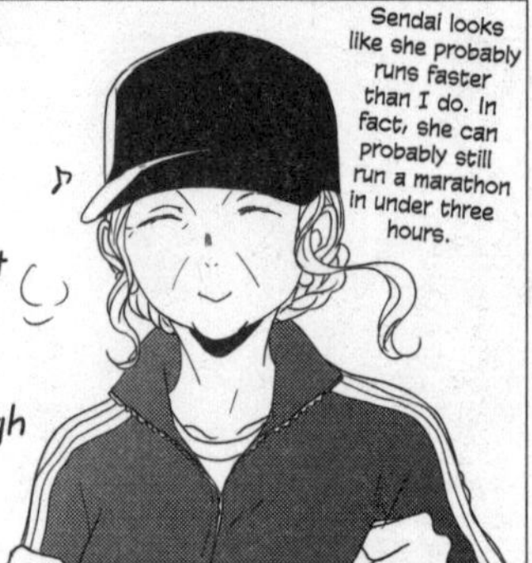
Sendai looks like she probably runs faster than I do. In fact, she can probably still run a marathon in under three hours.

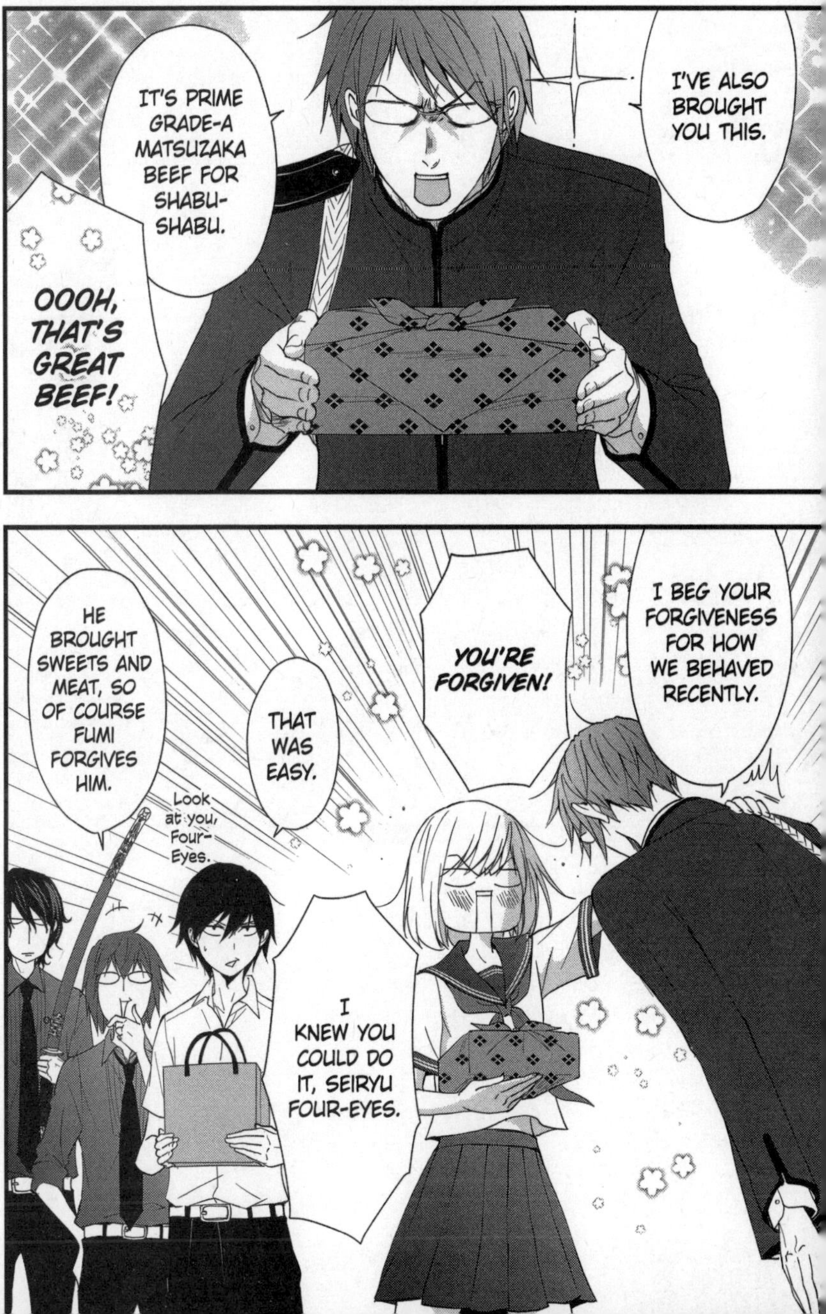
I'VE ALSO BROUGHT YOU THIS.
IT'S PRIME GRADE-A MATSUZAKA BEEF FOR SHABU-SHABU.
OOOH, THAT'S GREAT BEEF!
I BEG YOUR FORGIVENESS FOR HOW WE BEHAVED RECENTLY.
YOU'RE FORGIVEN!
THAT WAS EASY.
HE BROUGHT SWEETS AND MEAT, SO OF COURSE FUMI FORGIVES HIM.
Look at you, Four-Eyes.
I KNEW YOU COULD DO IT, SEIRYU FOUR-EYES.

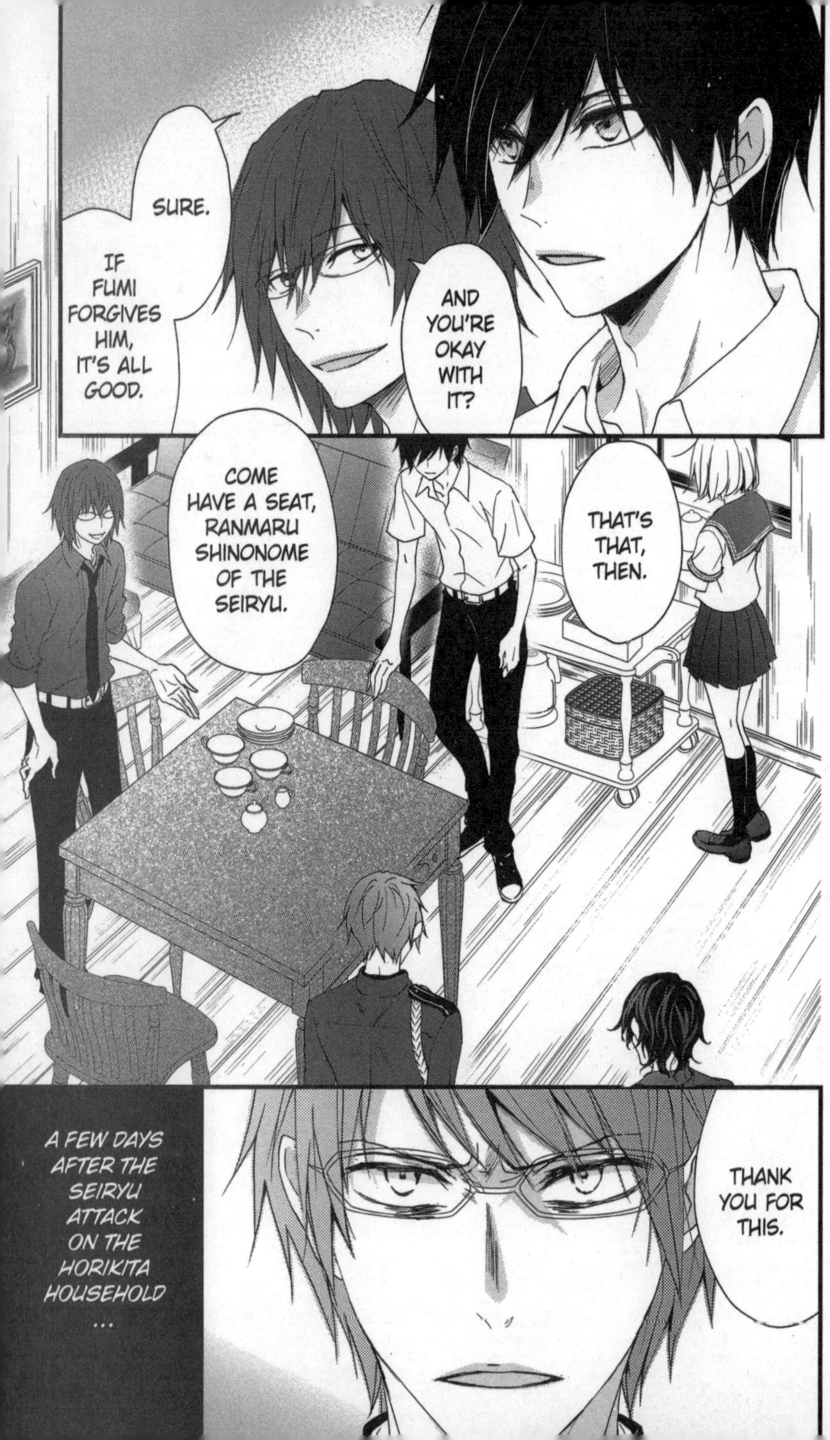
AND YOU'RE OKAY WITH IT?
SURE.
IF FUMI FORGIVES HIM, IT'S ALL GOOD.
THAT'S THAT, THEN.
COME HAVE A SEAT, RANMARU SHINONOME OF THE SEIRYU.
THANK YOU FOR THIS.
A FEW DAYS AFTER THE SEIRYU ATTACK ON THE HORIKITA HOUSEHOLD ...

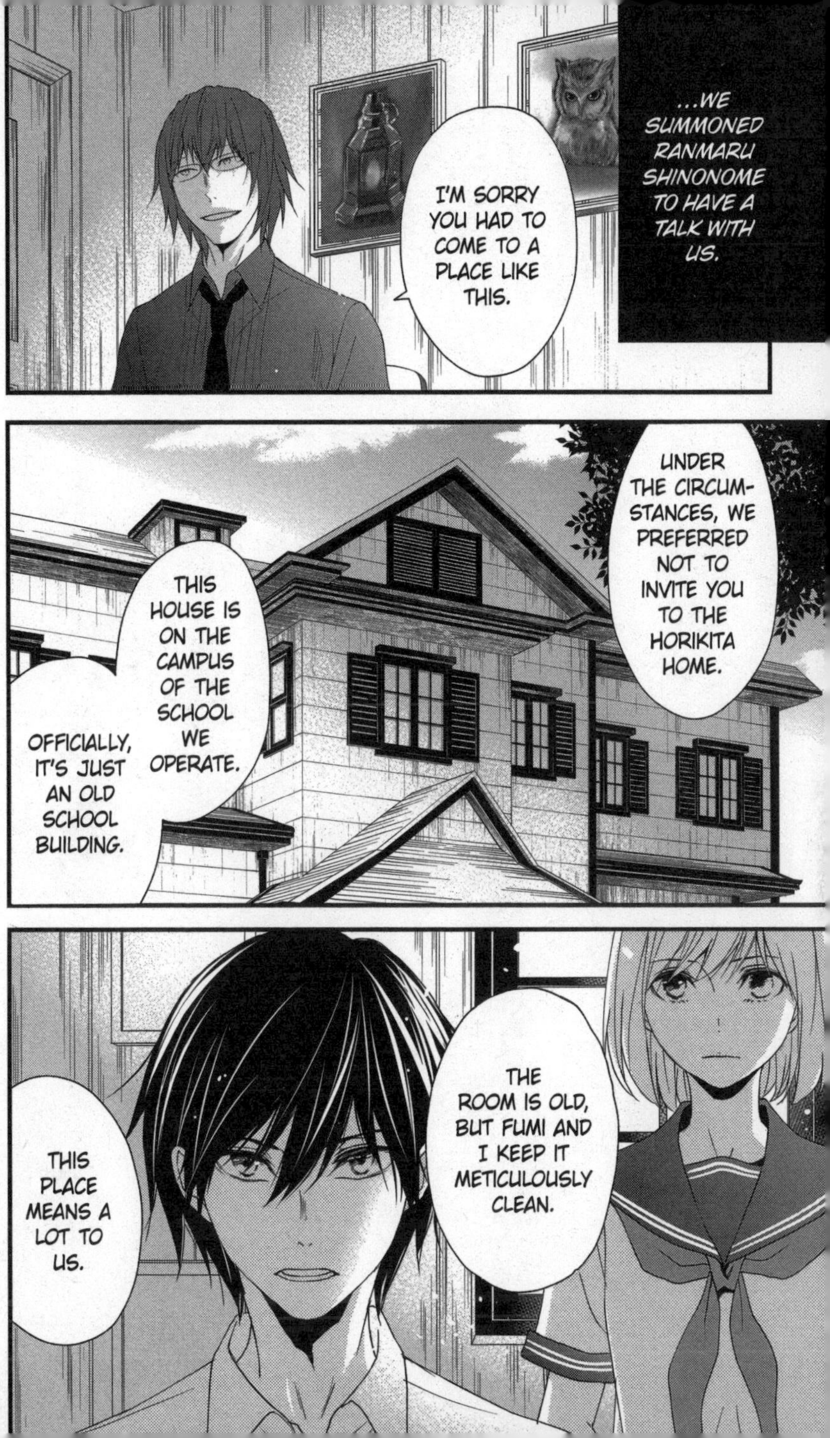
...WE SUMMONED RANMARU SHINONOME TO HAVE A TALK WITH US.
I'M SORRY YOU HAD TO COME TO A PLACE LIKE THIS.
UNDER THE CIRCUM-STANCES, WE PREFERRED NOT TO INVITE YOU TO THE HORIKITA HOME.
THIS HOUSE IS ON THE CAMPUS OF THE SCHOOL WE OPERATE.
OFFICIALLY, IT'S JUST AN OLD SCHOOL BUILDING.
THE ROOM IS OLD, BUT FUMI AND I KEEP IT METICULOUSLY CLEAN.
THIS PLACE MEANS A LOT TO US.

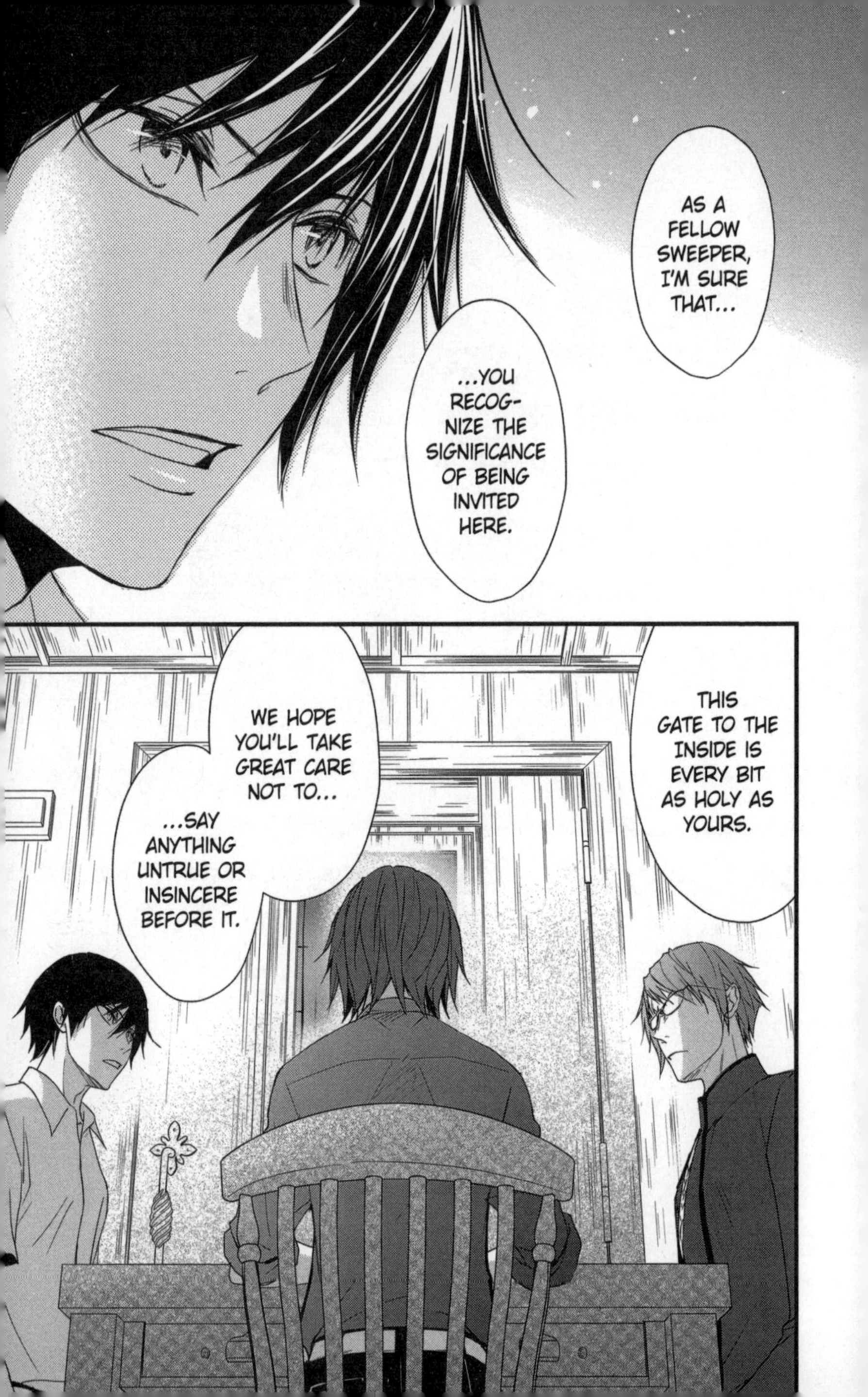
AS A FELLOW SWEEPER, I'M SURE THAT...
...YOU RECOG-NIZE THE SIGNIFICANCE OF BEING INVITED HERE.
THIS GATE TO THE INSIDE IS EVERY BIT AS HOLY AS YOURS.
WE HOPE YOU'LL TAKE GREAT CARE NOT TO...
...SAY ANYTHING UNTRUE OR INSINCERE BEFORE IT.

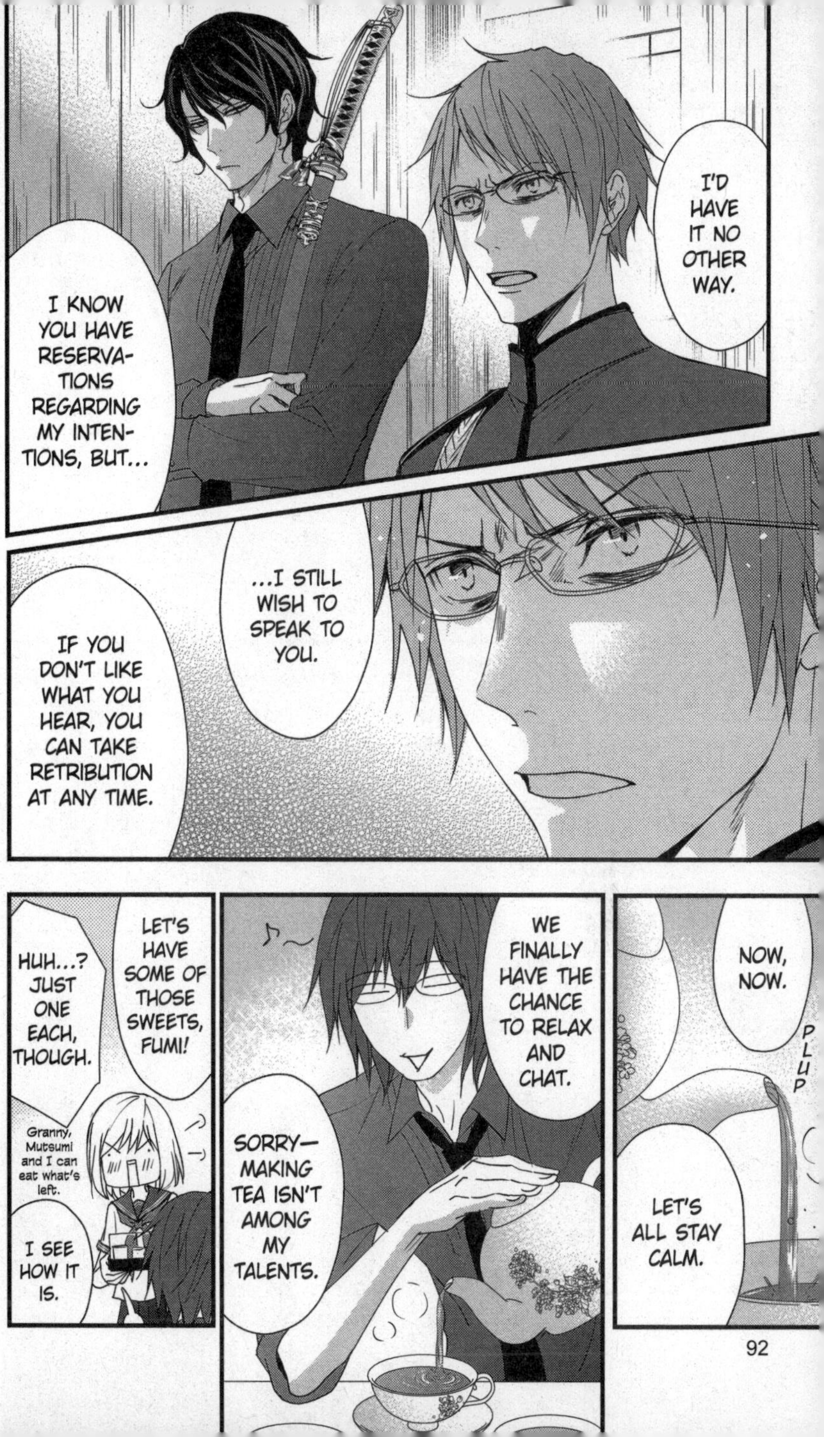

I'D HAVE IT NO OTHER WAY.
I KNOW YOU HAVE RESERVATIONS REGARDING MY INTENTIONS, BUT...
...I STILL WISH TO SPEAK TO YOU.
IF YOU DON'T LIKE WHAT YOU HEAR, YOU CAN TAKE RETRIBUTION AT ANY TIME.
NOW, NOW.
PLUP
LET'S ALL STAY CALM.
WE FINALLY HAVE THE CHANCE TO RELAX AND CHAT.
SORRY—MAKING TEA ISN'T AMONG MY TALENTS.
LET'S HAVE SOME OF THOSE SWEETS, FUMI!
HUH...? JUST ONE EACH, THOUGH.
Granny, Mutsumi and I can eat what's left.
I SEE HOW IT IS.

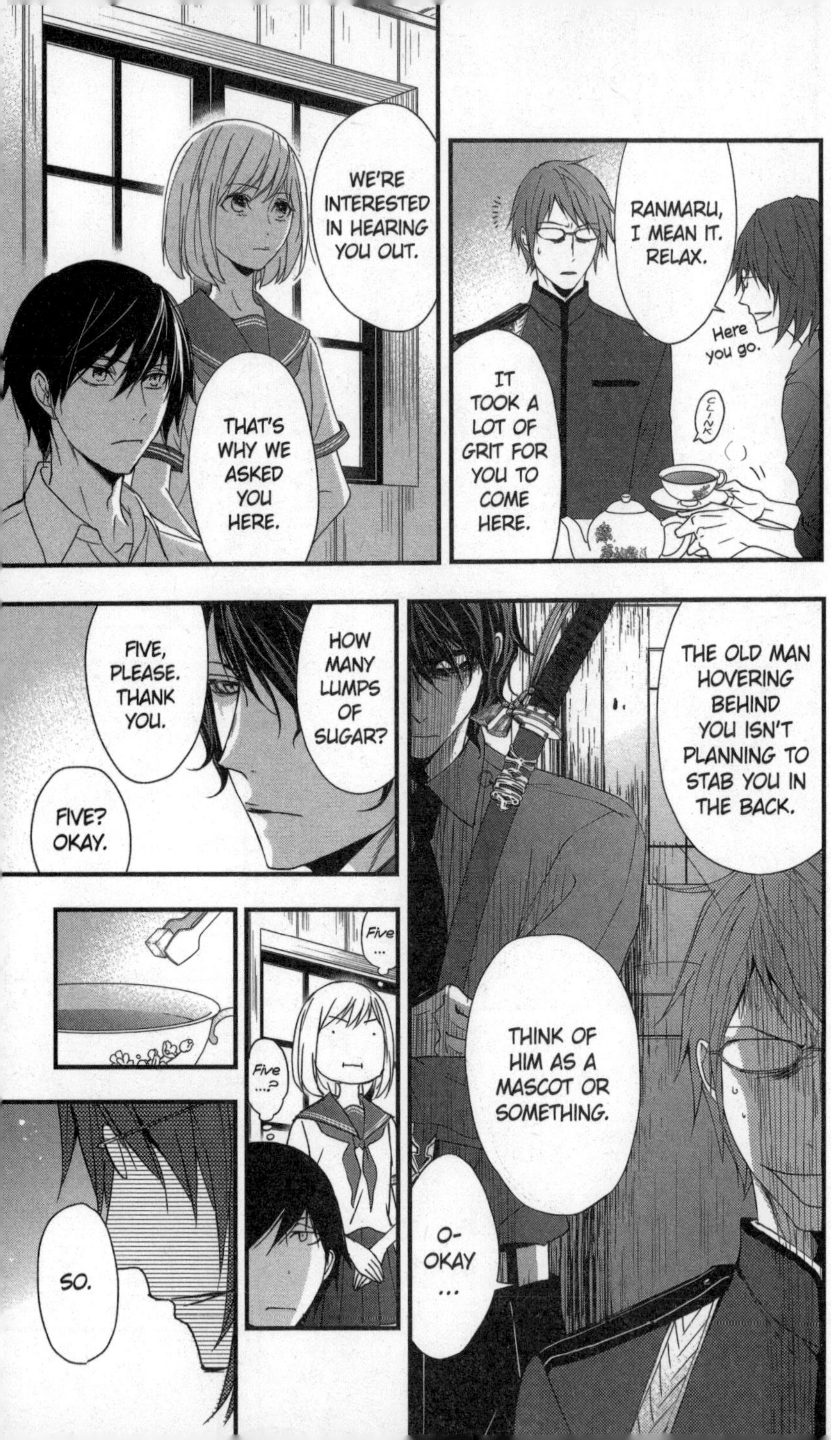
RANMARU, I MEAN IT. RELAX.
Here you go.
CLINK
IT TOOK A LOT OF GRIT FOR YOU TO COME HERE.
WE'RE INTERESTED IN HEARING YOU OUT.
THAT'S WHY WE ASKED YOU HERE.
THE OLD MAN HOVERING BEHIND YOU ISN'T PLANNING TO STAB YOU IN THE BACK.
THINK OF HIM AS A MASCOT OR SOMETHING.
O-OKAY...
HOW MANY LUMPS OF SUGAR?
FIVE, PLEASE. THANK YOU.
FIVE? OKAY.
Five...
Five...?
SO.

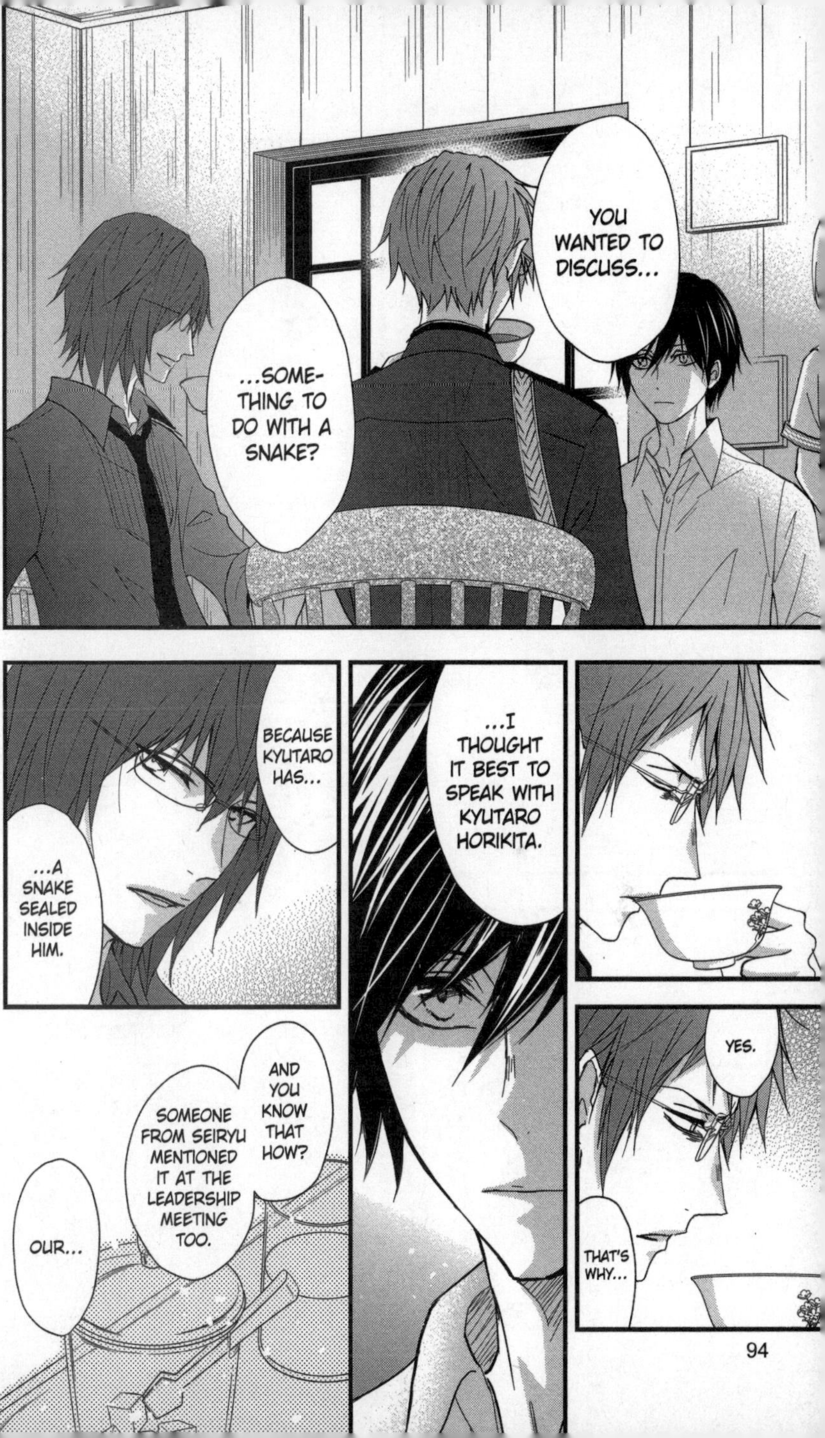
YOU WANTED TO DISCUSS...
...SOME-THING TO DO WITH A SNAKE?
YES.
THAT'S WHY...
...I THOUGHT IT BEST TO SPEAK WITH KYUTARO HORIKITA.
BECAUSE KYUTARO HAS...
...A SNAKE SEALED INSIDE HIM.
AND YOU KNOW THAT HOW?
SOMEONE FROM SEIRYU MENTIONED IT AT THE LEADERSHIP MEETING TOO.
OUR...

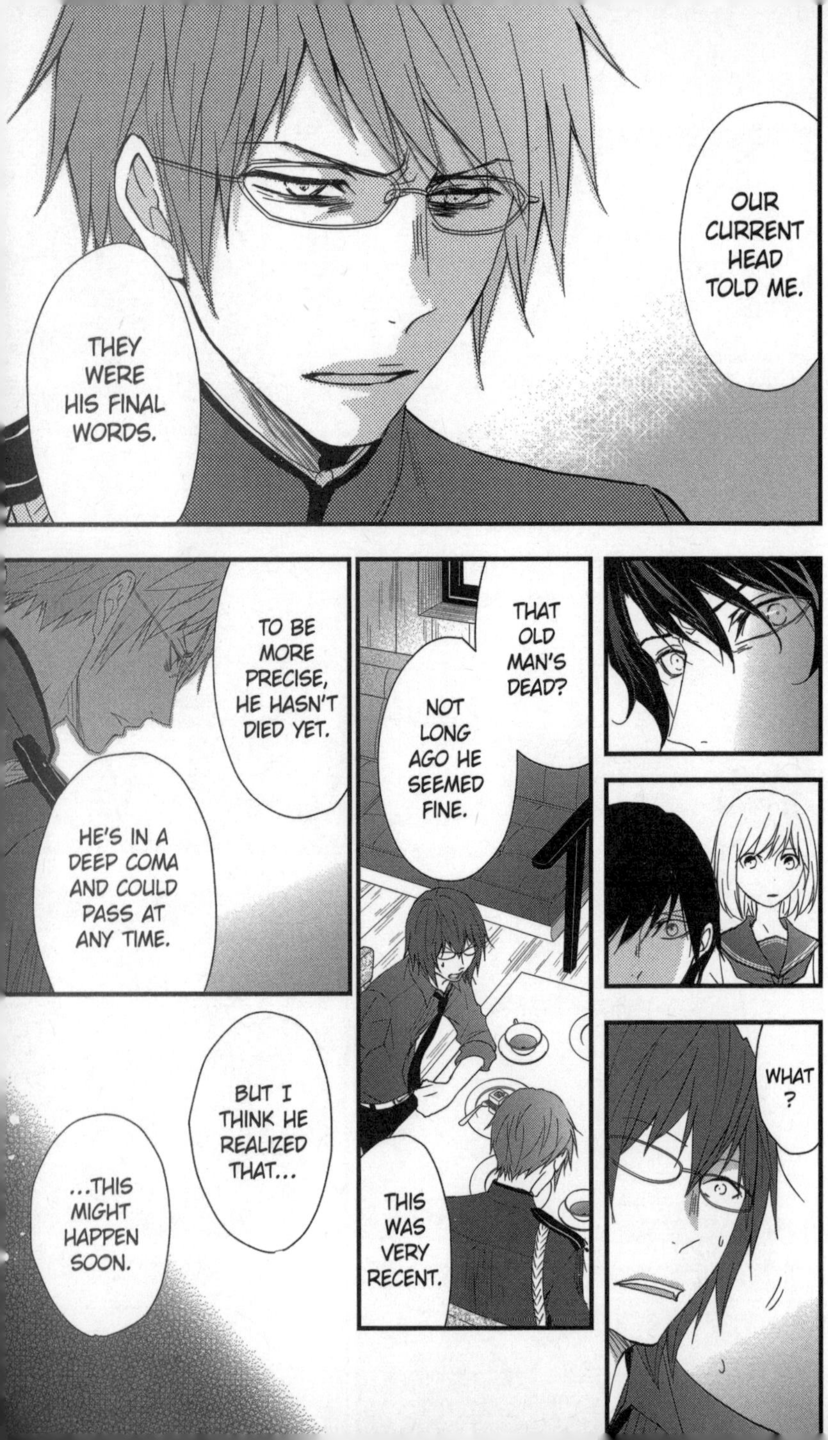
OUR CURRENT HEAD TOLD ME.
THEY WERE HIS FINAL WORDS.
WHAT?
THAT OLD MAN'S DEAD?
NOT LONG AGO HE SEEMED FINE.
THIS WAS VERY RECENT.
TO BE MORE PRECISE, HE HASN'T DIED YET.
HE'S IN A DEEP COMA AND COULD PASS AT ANY TIME.
BUT I THINK HE REALIZED THAT...
...THIS MIGHT HAPPEN SOON.

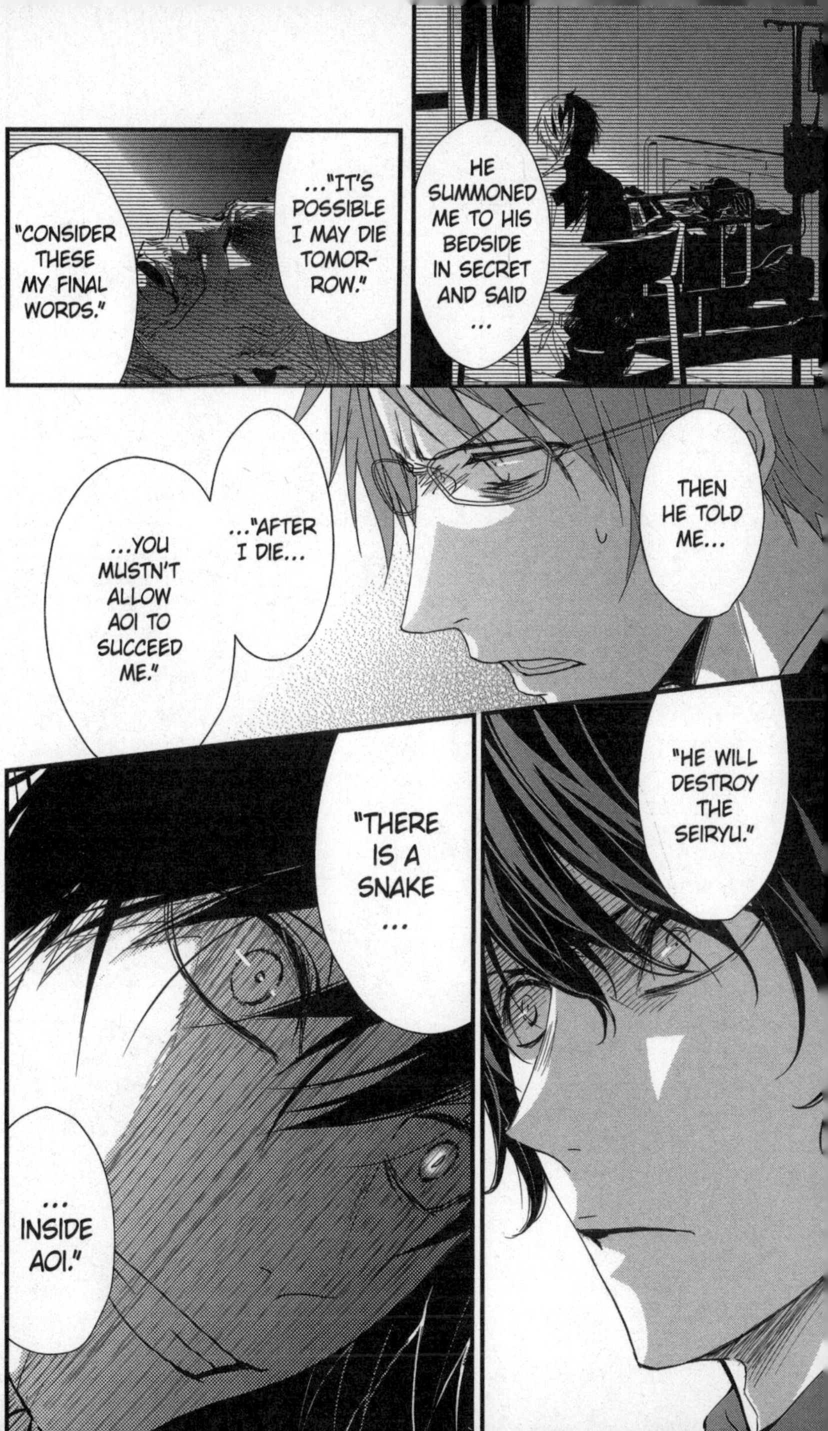
HE SUMMONED ME TO HIS BEDSIDE IN SECRET AND SAID ...
..."IT'S POSSIBLE I MAY DIE TOMOR-ROW."
"CONSIDER THESE MY FINAL WORDS."
THEN HE TOLD ME...
..."AFTER I DIE...
...YOU MUSTN'T ALLOW AOI TO SUCCEED ME."
"HE WILL DESTROY THE SEIRYU."
"THERE IS A SNAKE ...
... INSIDE AOI."

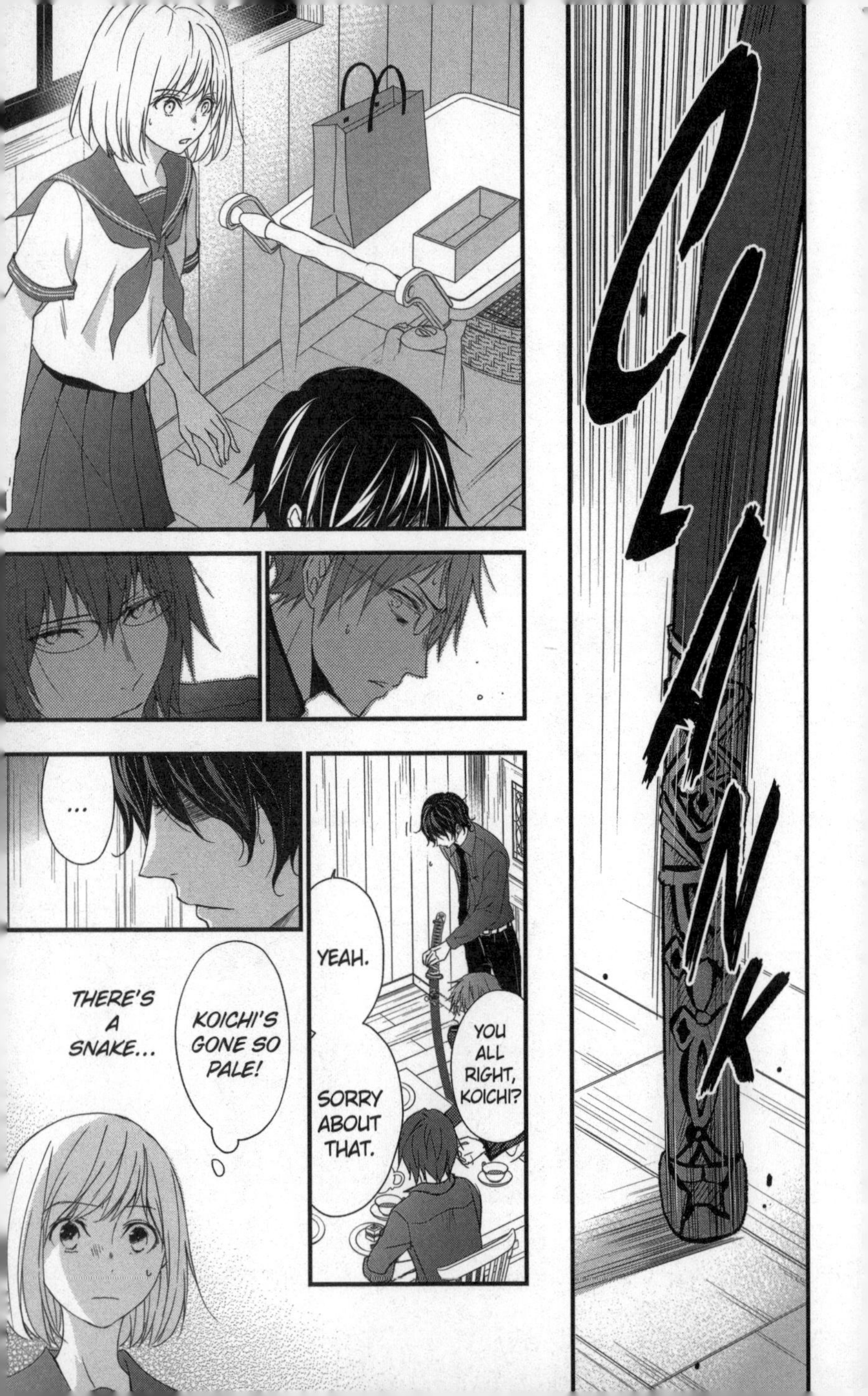
CLANK
YOU ALL RIGHT, KOICHI?
YEAH.
SORRY ABOUT THAT.
...
KOICHI'S GONE SO PALE!
THERE'S A SNAKE...

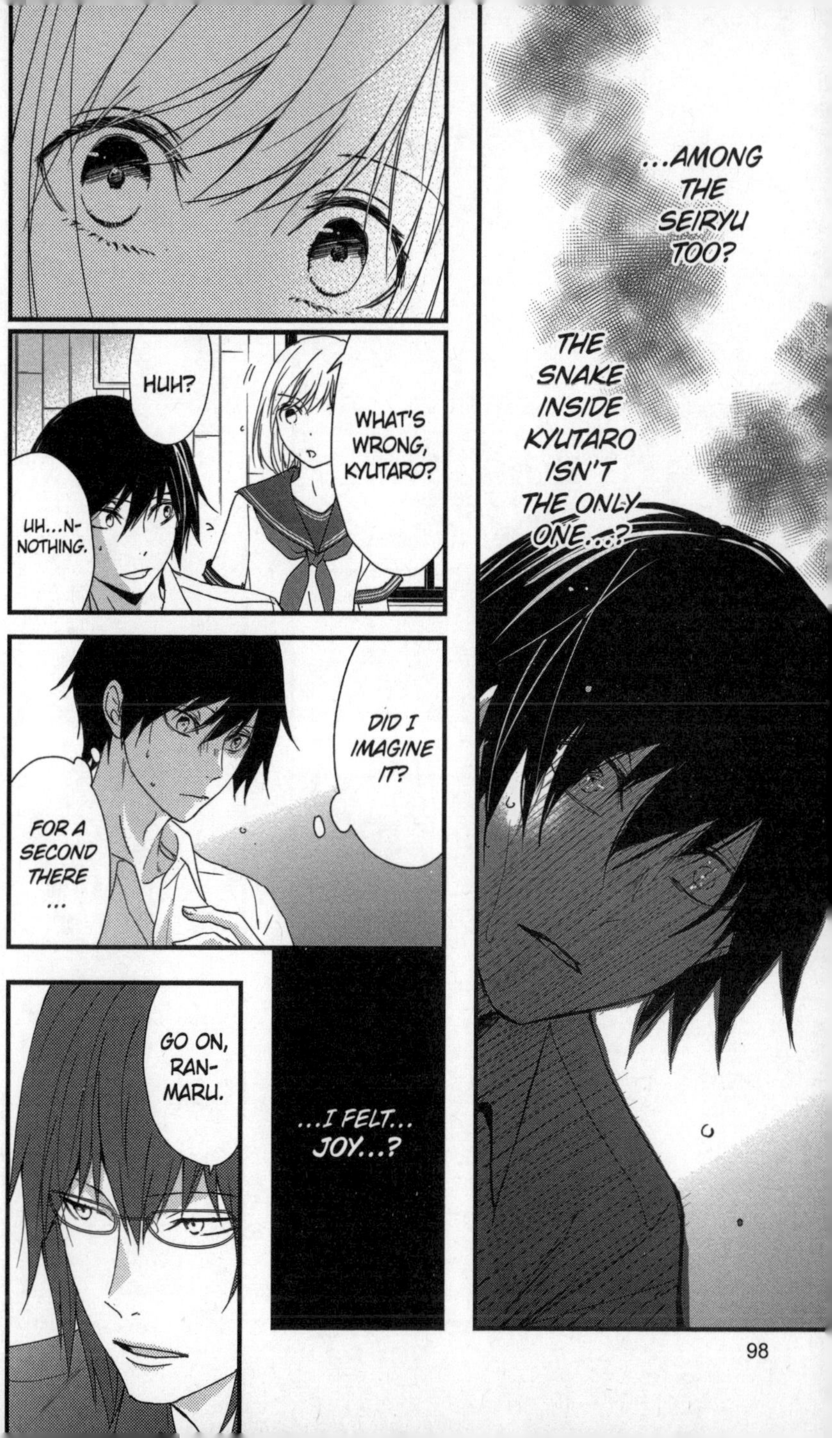
...AMONG THE SEIRYU TOO?
THE SNAKE INSIDE KYUTARO ISN'T THE ONLY ONE...?
WHAT'S WRONG, KYUTARO?
HUH?
UH...N-NOTHING.
DID I IMAGINE IT?
FOR A SECOND THERE ...
...I FELT... JOY...?
GO ON, RAN-MARU.

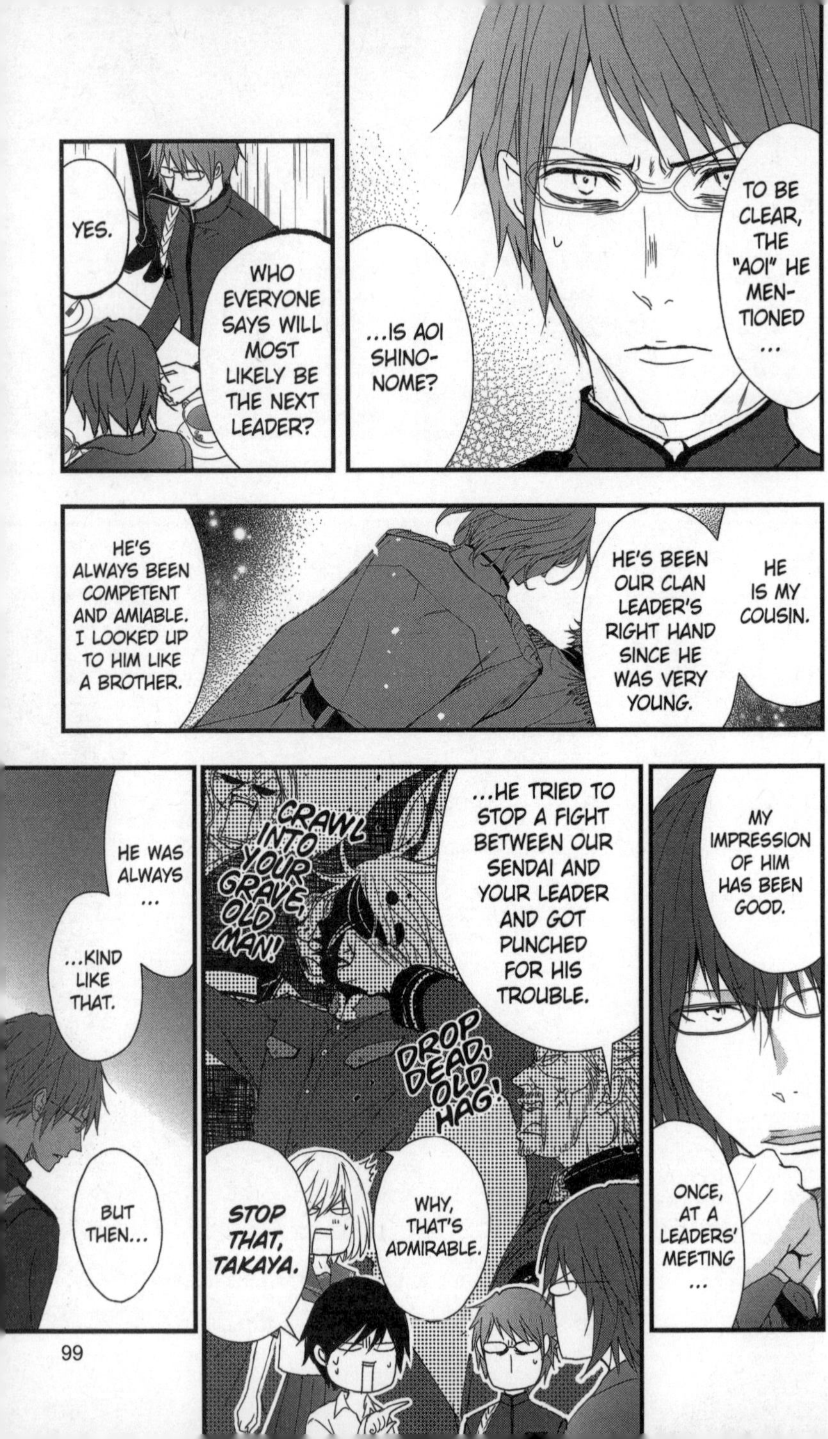

TO BE CLEAR, THE "AOI" HE MEN-TIONED...
...IS AOI SHINO-NOME?
WHO EVERYONE SAYS WILL MOST LIKELY BE THE NEXT LEADER?
YES.
HE IS MY COUSIN.
HE'S BEEN OUR CLAN LEADER'S RIGHT HAND SINCE HE WAS VERY YOUNG.
HE'S ALWAYS BEEN COMPETENT AND AMIABLE. I LOOKED UP TO HIM LIKE A BROTHER.
MY IMPRESSION OF HIM HAS BEEN GOOD.
ONCE, AT A LEADERS' MEETING...
...HE TRIED TO STOP A FIGHT BETWEEN OUR SENDAI AND YOUR LEADER AND GOT PUNCHED FOR HIS TROUBLE.
CRAWL INTO YOUR GRAVE, OLD MAN!
DROP DEAD, OLD HAG!
WHY, THAT'S ADMIRABLE.
STOP THAT, TAKAYA.
HE WAS ALWAYS...
...KIND LIKE THAT.
BUT THEN...

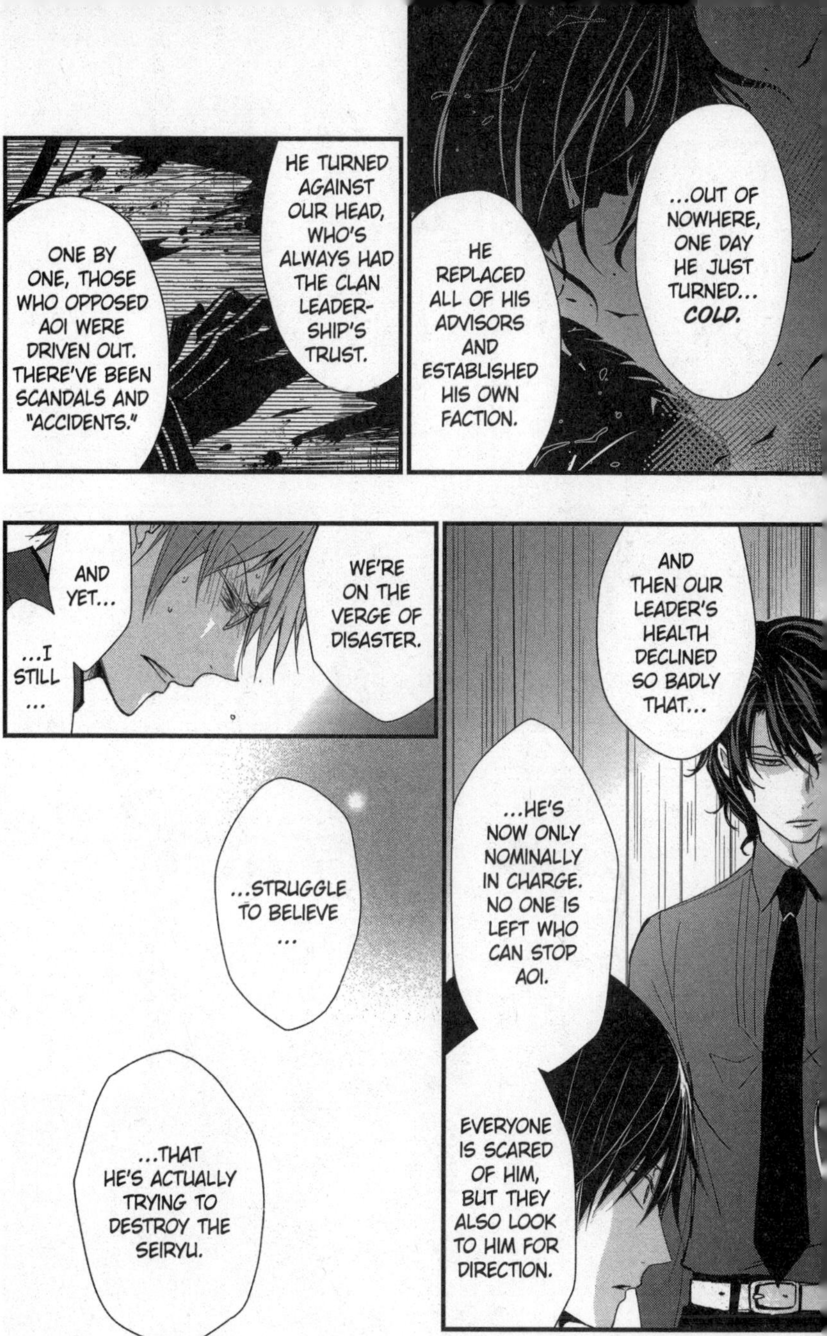
...OUT OF NOWHERE, ONE DAY HE JUST TURNED... COLD.
HE REPLACED ALL OF HIS ADVISORS AND ESTABLISHED HIS OWN FACTION.
HE TURNED AGAINST OUR HEAD, WHO'S ALWAYS HAD THE CLAN LEADER-SHIP'S TRUST.
ONE BY ONE, THOSE WHO OPPOSED AOI WERE DRIVEN OUT. THERE'VE BEEN SCANDALS AND "ACCIDENTS."
AND THEN OUR LEADER'S HEALTH DECLINED SO BADLY THAT...
...HE'S NOW ONLY NOMINALLY IN CHARGE. NO ONE IS LEFT WHO CAN STOP AOI.
EVERYONE IS SCARED OF HIM, BUT THEY ALSO LOOK TO HIM FOR DIRECTION.
WE'RE ON THE VERGE OF DISASTER.
AND YET...
...I STILL...
...STRUGGLE TO BELIEVE...
...THAT HE'S ACTUALLY TRYING TO DESTROY THE SEIRYU.

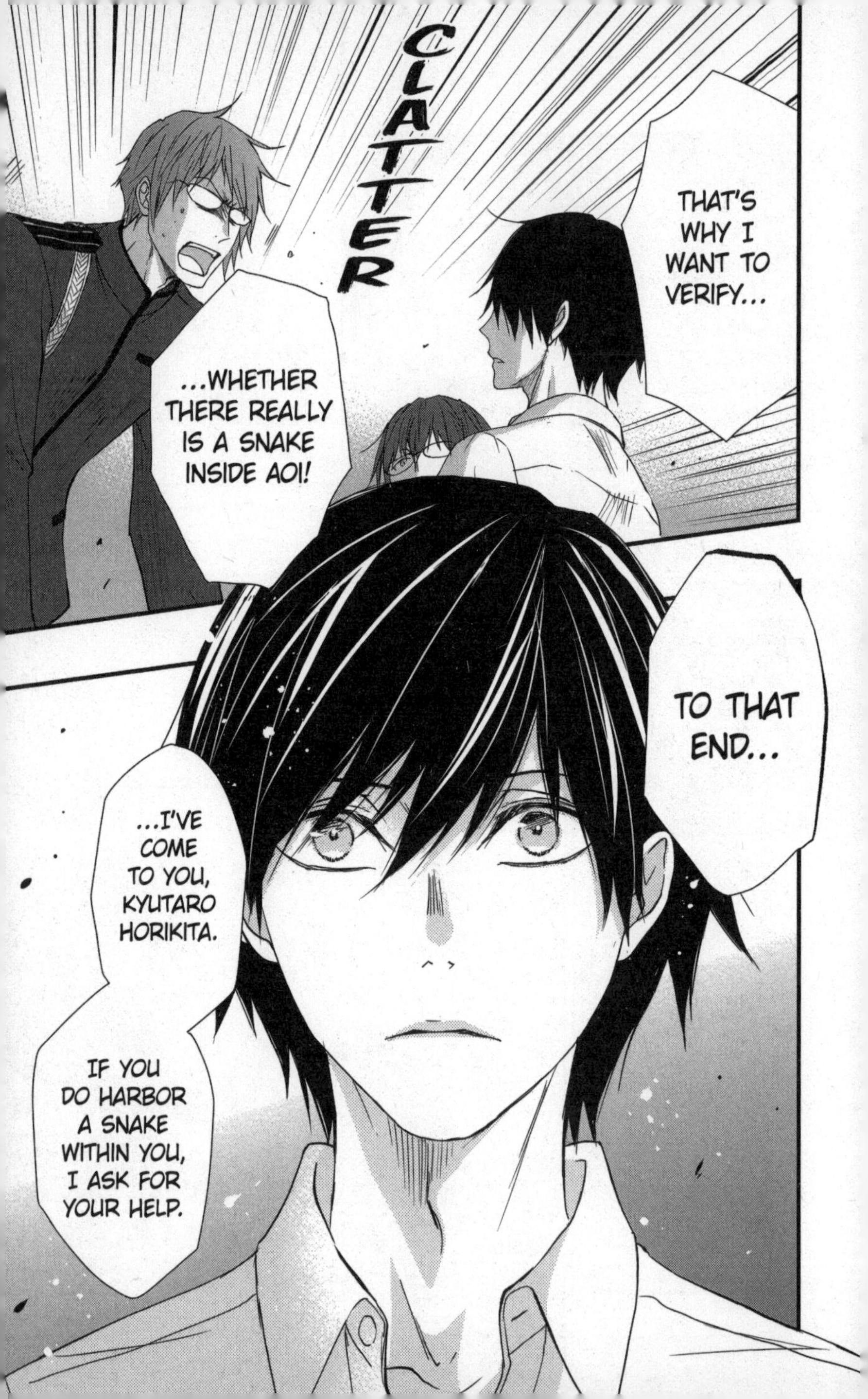
THAT'S WHY I WANT TO VERIFY...
CLATTER
...WHETHER THERE REALLY IS A SNAKE INSIDE AOI!
TO THAT END...
...I'VE COME TO YOU, KYUTARO HORIKITA.
IF YOU DO HARBOR A SNAKE WITHIN YOU, I ASK FOR YOUR HELP.

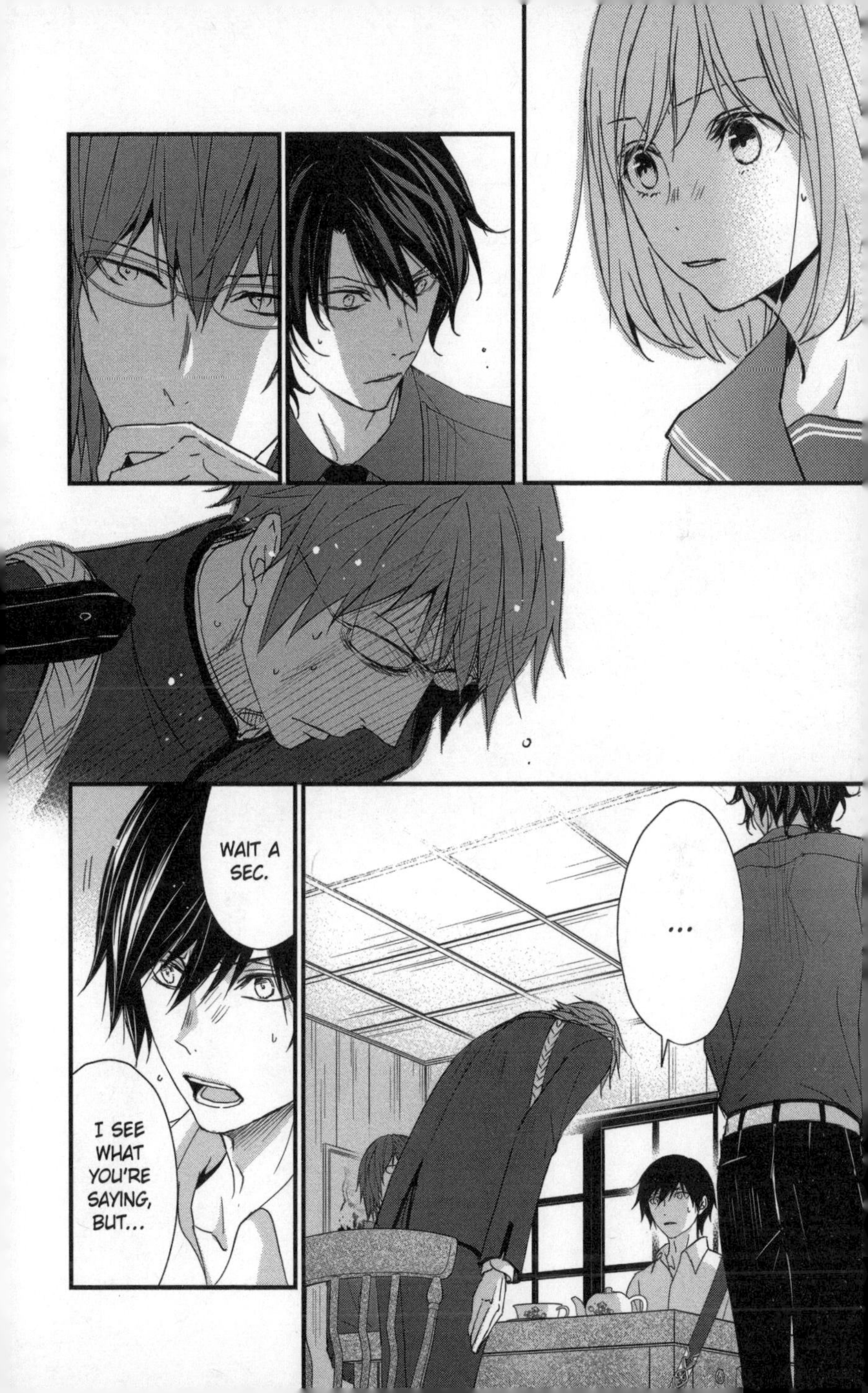
...
WAIT A SEC.
I SEE WHAT YOU'RE SAYING, BUT...

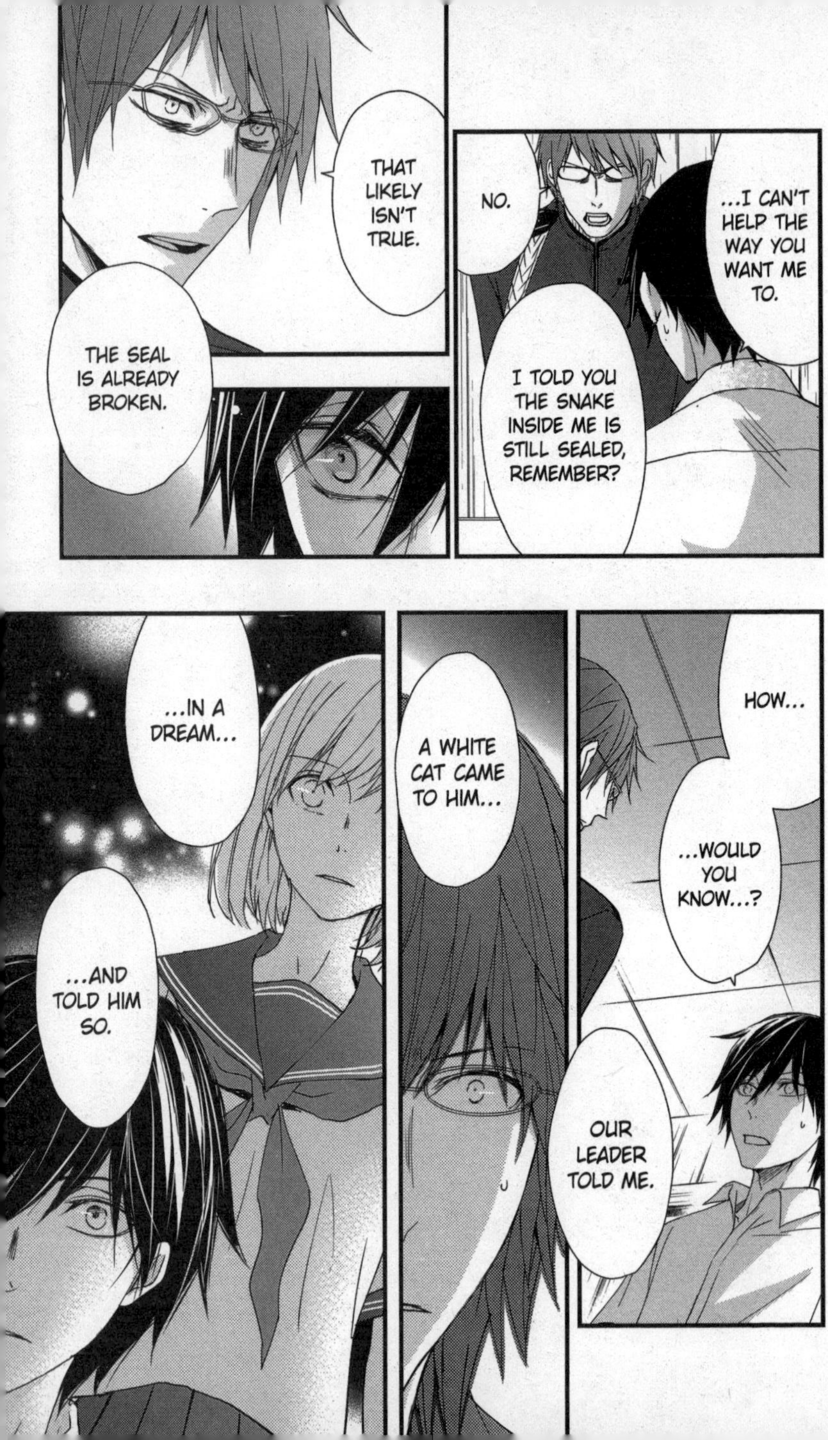
...I CAN'T HELP THE WAY YOU WANT ME TO.
NO.
I TOLD YOU THE SNAKE INSIDE ME IS STILL SEALED, REMEMBER?
THAT LIKELY ISN'T TRUE.
THE SEAL IS ALREADY BROKEN.
HOW...
...WOULD YOU KNOW...?
OUR LEADER TOLD ME.
A WHITE CAT CAME TO HIM...
...IN A DREAM...
...AND TOLD HIM SO.

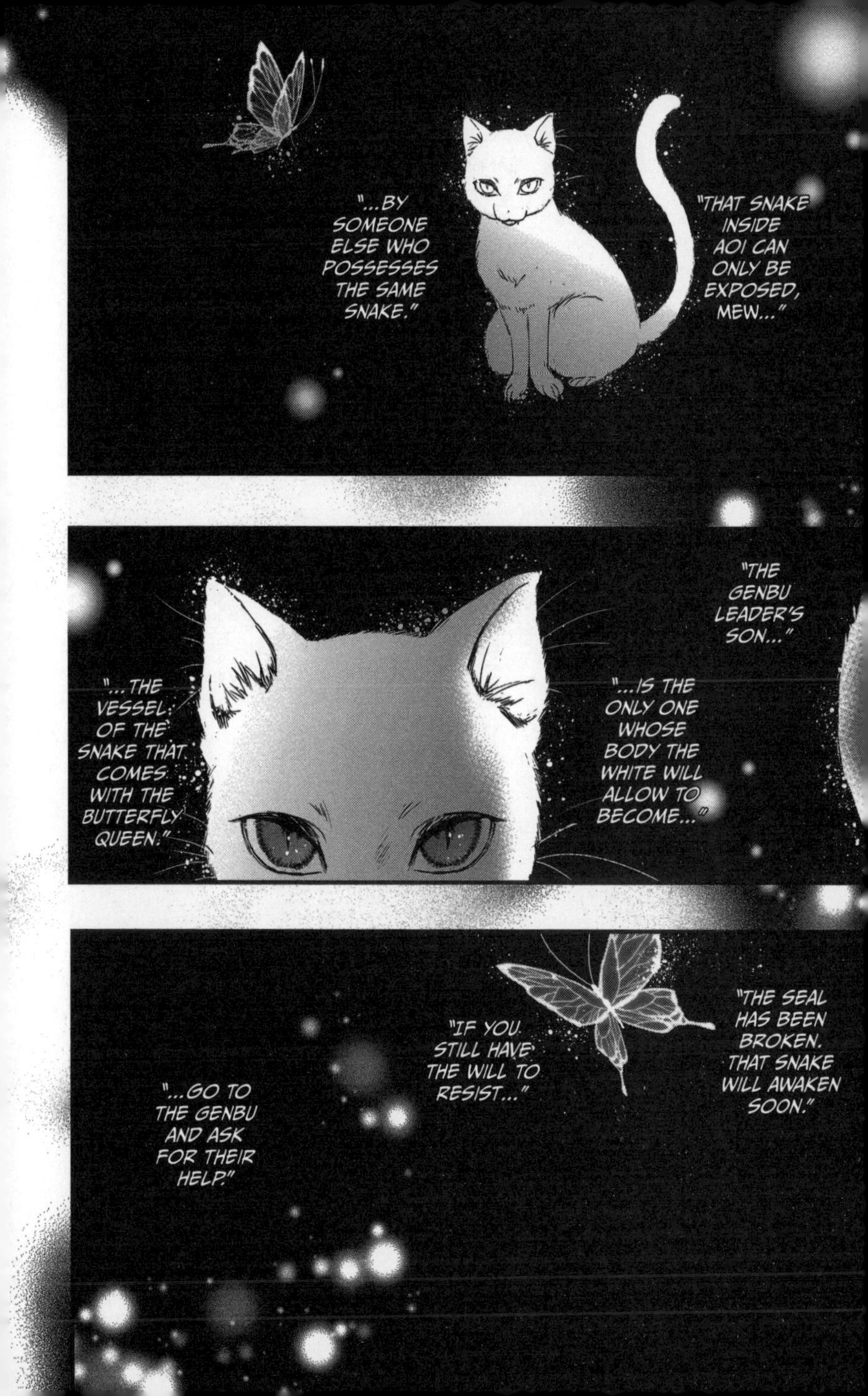
"THAT SNAKE INSIDE AOI CAN ONLY BE EXPOSED, MEW..."
"...BY SOMEONE ELSE WHO POSSESSES THE SAME SNAKE."
"THE GENBU LEADER'S SON..."
"...IS THE ONLY ONE WHOSE BODY THE WHITE WILL ALLOW TO BECOME..."
"...THE VESSEL OF THE SNAKE THAT COMES WITH THE BUTTERFLY QUEEN."
"THE SEAL HAS BEEN BROKEN. THAT SNAKE WILL AWAKEN SOON."
"IF YOU STILL HAVE THE WILL TO RESIST..."
"...GO TO THE GENBU AND ASK FOR THEIR HELP."

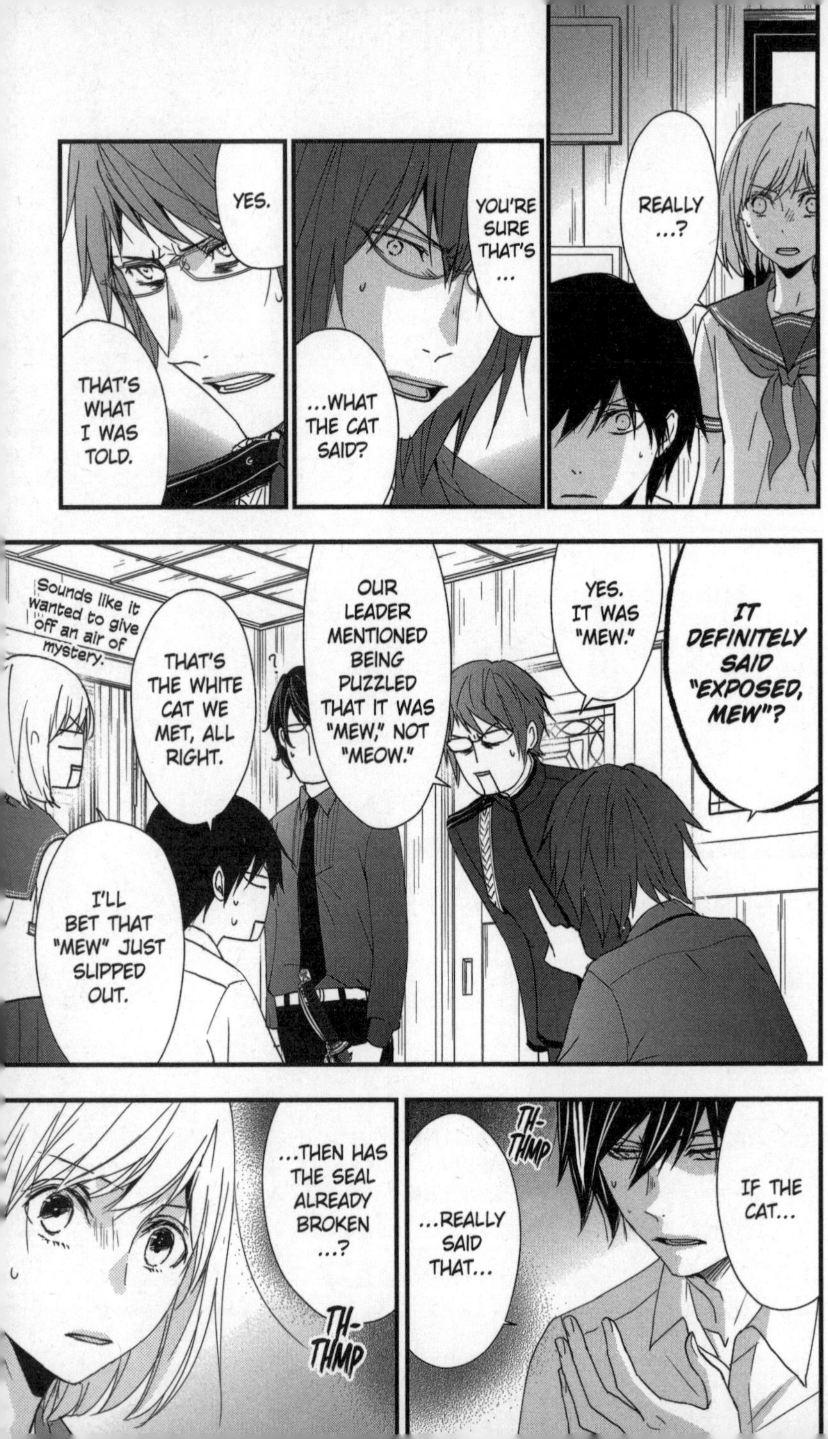
REALLY ...?
YOU'RE SURE THAT'S ...
...WHAT THE CAT SAID?
YES.
THAT'S WHAT I WAS TOLD.
IT DEFINITELY SAID "EXPOSED, MEW"?
YES. IT WAS "MEW."
OUR LEADER MENTIONED BEING PUZZLED THAT IT WAS "MEW," NOT "MEOW."
THAT'S THE WHITE CAT WE MET, ALL RIGHT.
Sounds like it wanted to give off an air of mystery.
I'LL BET THAT "MEW" JUST SLIPPED OUT.
TH-THMP
IF THE CAT...
...REALLY SAID THAT...
...THEN HAS THE SEAL ALREADY BROKEN ...?
TH-THMP

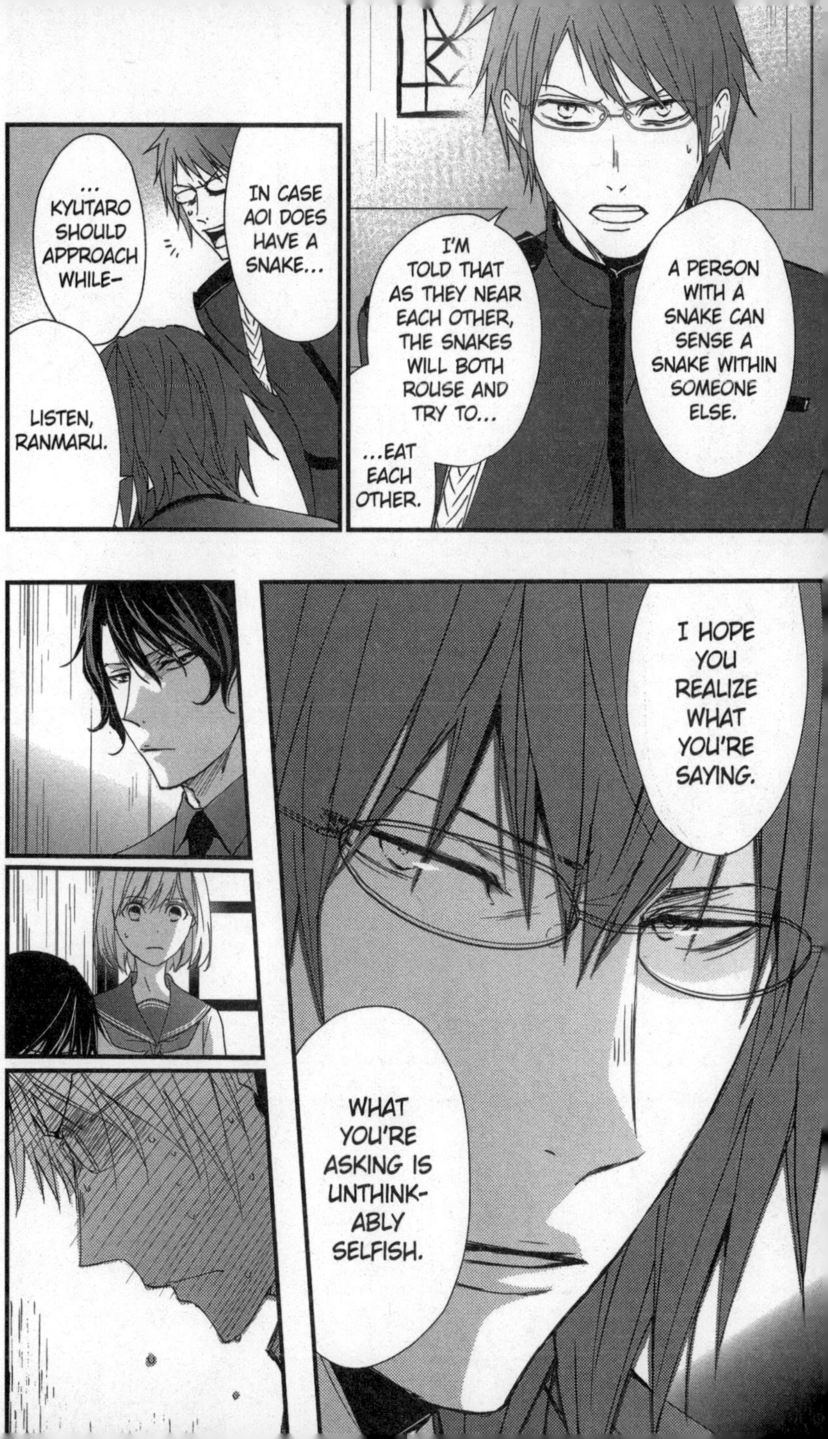
A PERSON WITH A SNAKE CAN SENSE A SNAKE WITHIN SOMEONE ELSE.
I'M TOLD THAT AS THEY NEAR EACH OTHER, THE SNAKES WILL BOTH ROUSE AND TRY TO...
...EAT EACH OTHER.
IN CASE AOI DOES HAVE A SNAKE...
...KYUTARO SHOULD APPROACH WHILE-
LISTEN, RANMARU.
I HOPE YOU REALIZE WHAT YOU'RE SAYING.
WHAT YOU'RE ASKING IS UNTHINK-ABLY SELFISH.

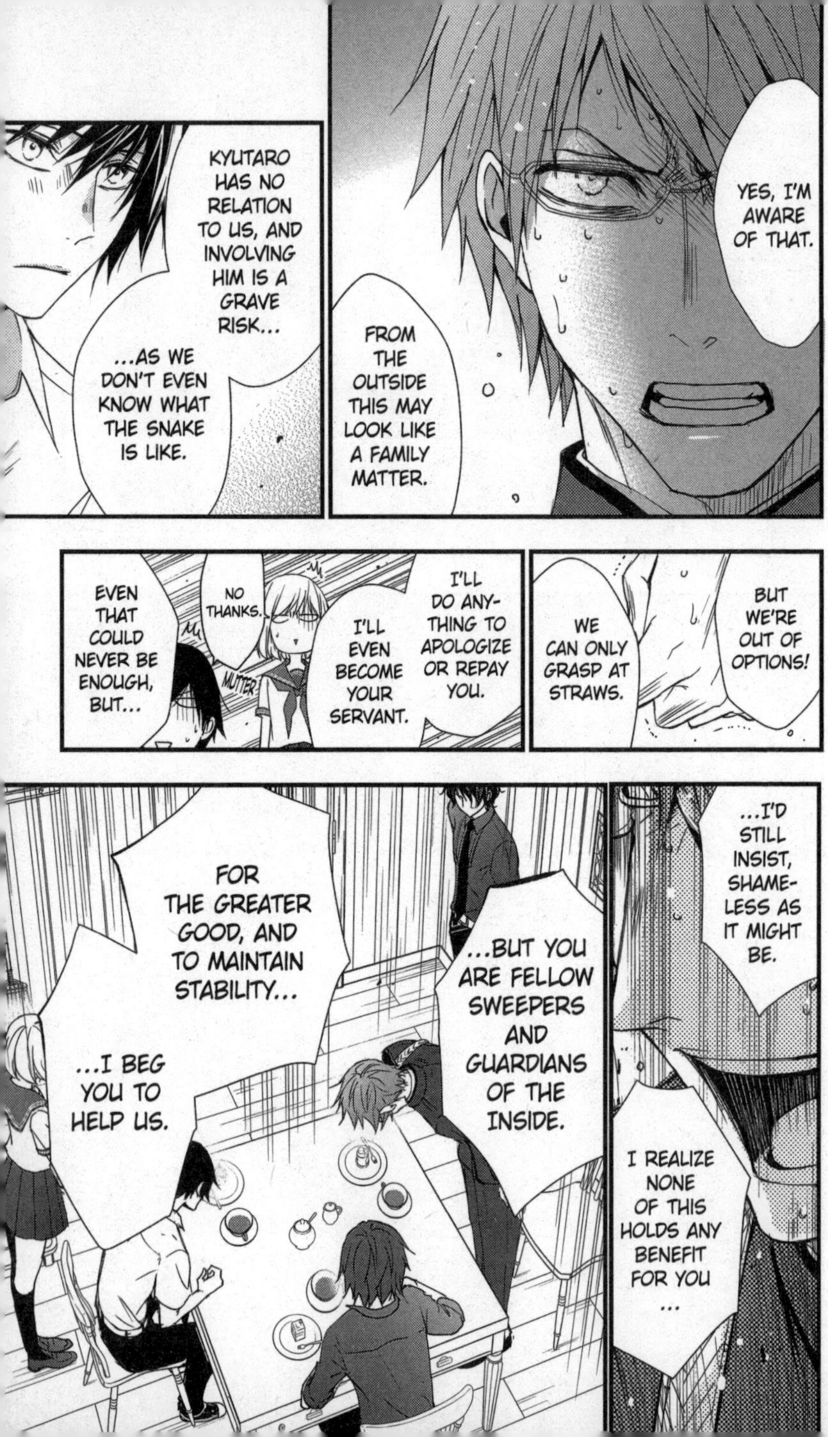
YES, I'M AWARE OF THAT.
FROM THE OUTSIDE THIS MAY LOOK LIKE A FAMILY MATTER.
KYUTARO HAS NO RELATION TO US, AND INVOLVING HIM IS A GRAVE RISK...
...AS WE DON'T EVEN KNOW WHAT THE SNAKE IS LIKE.
BUT WE'RE OUT OF OPTIONS!
WE CAN ONLY GRASP AT STRAWS.
I'LL DO ANYTHING TO APOLOGIZE OR REPAY YOU.
I'LL EVEN BECOME YOUR SERVANT.
NO THANKS.
MUTTER
EVEN THAT COULD NEVER BE ENOUGH, BUT...
...I'D STILL INSIST, SHAMELESS AS IT MIGHT BE.
I REALIZE NONE OF THIS HOLDS ANY BENEFIT FOR YOU...
...BUT YOU ARE FELLOW SWEEPERS AND GUARDIANS OF THE INSIDE.
FOR THE GREATER GOOD, AND TO MAINTAIN STABILITY...
...I BEG YOU TO HELP US.

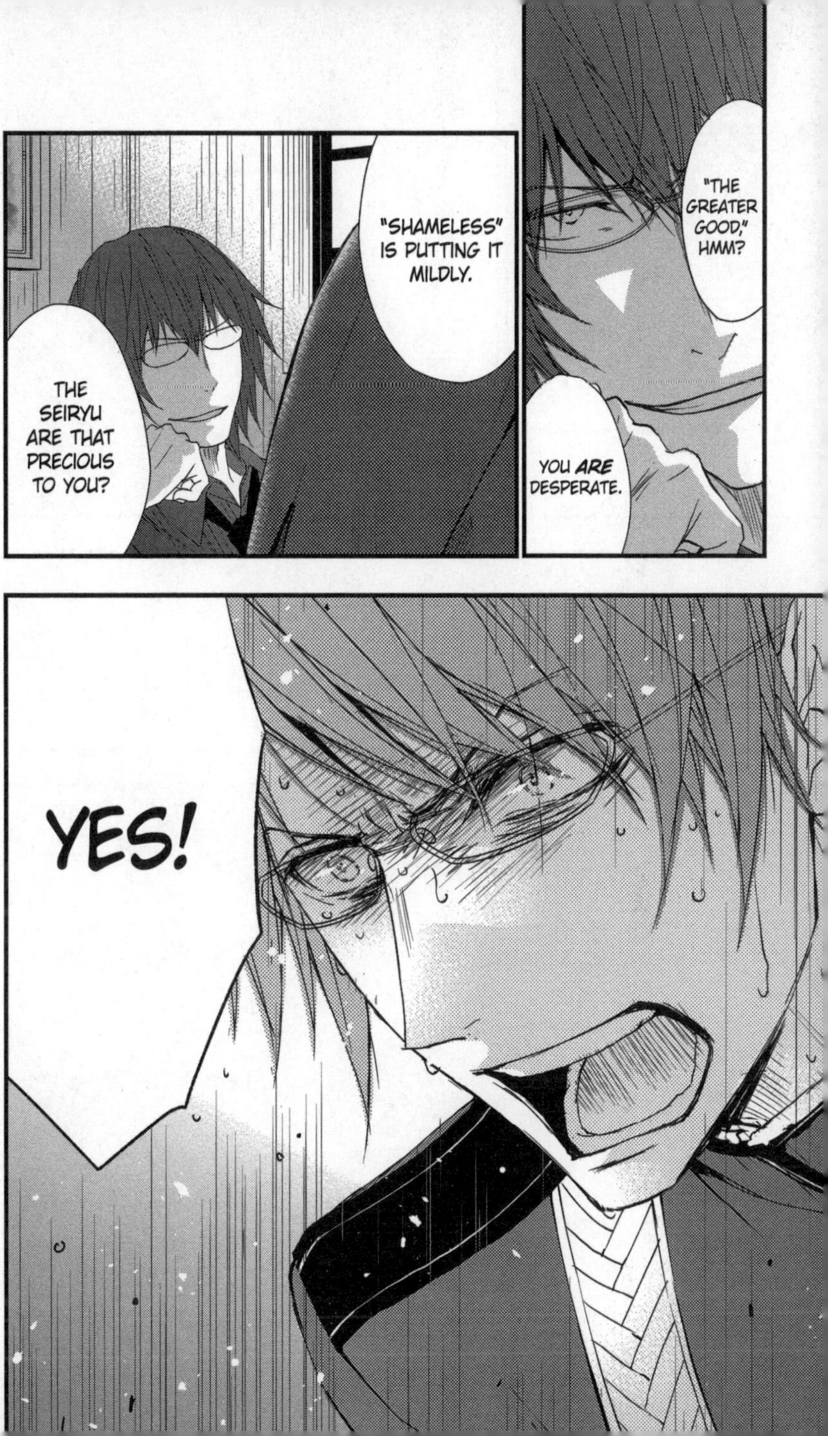
"THE GREATER GOOD," HMM?
YOU **ARE** DESPERATE.
"SHAMELESS" IS PUTTING IT MILDLY.
THE SEIRYU ARE THAT PRECIOUS TO YOU?
YES!

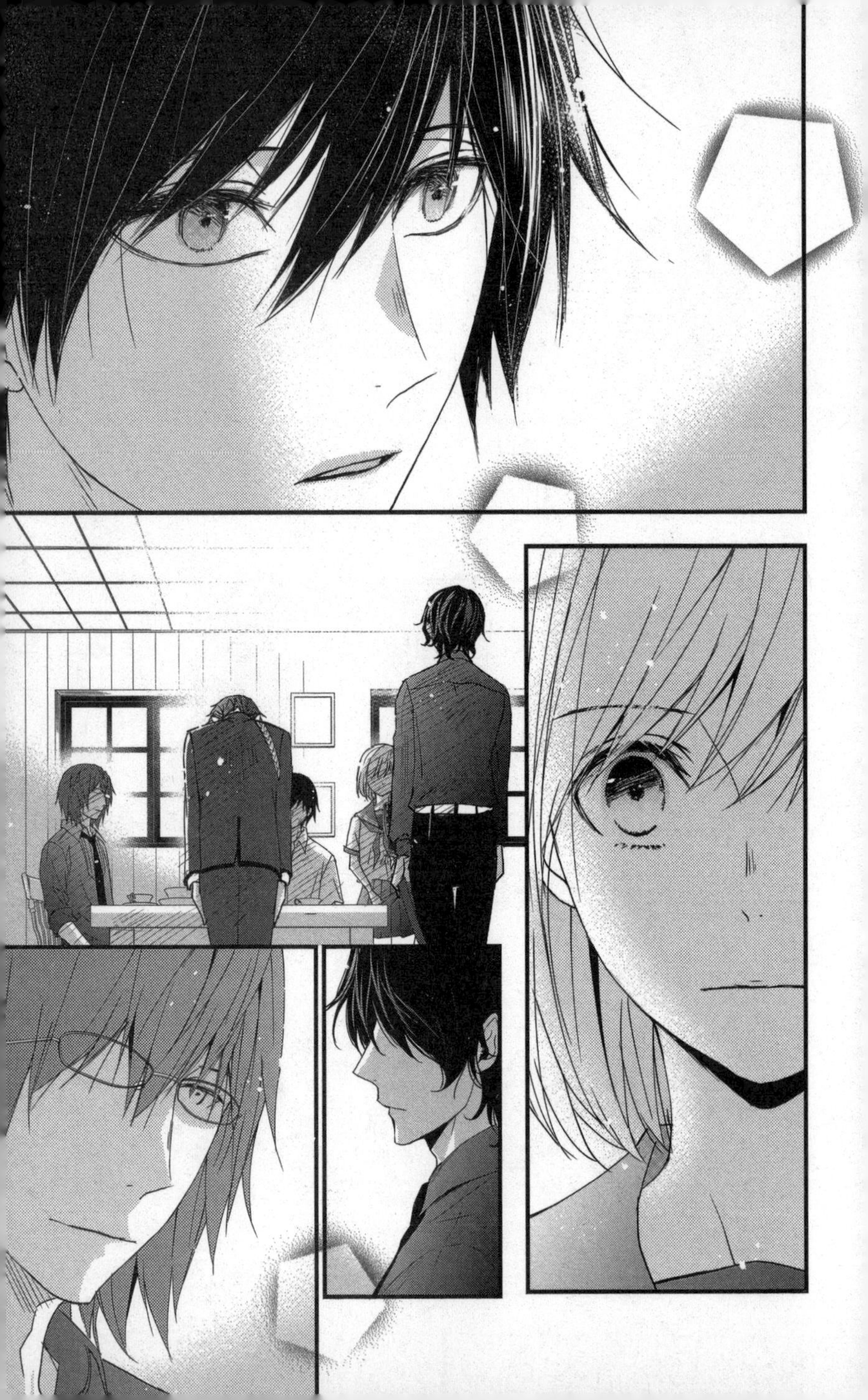

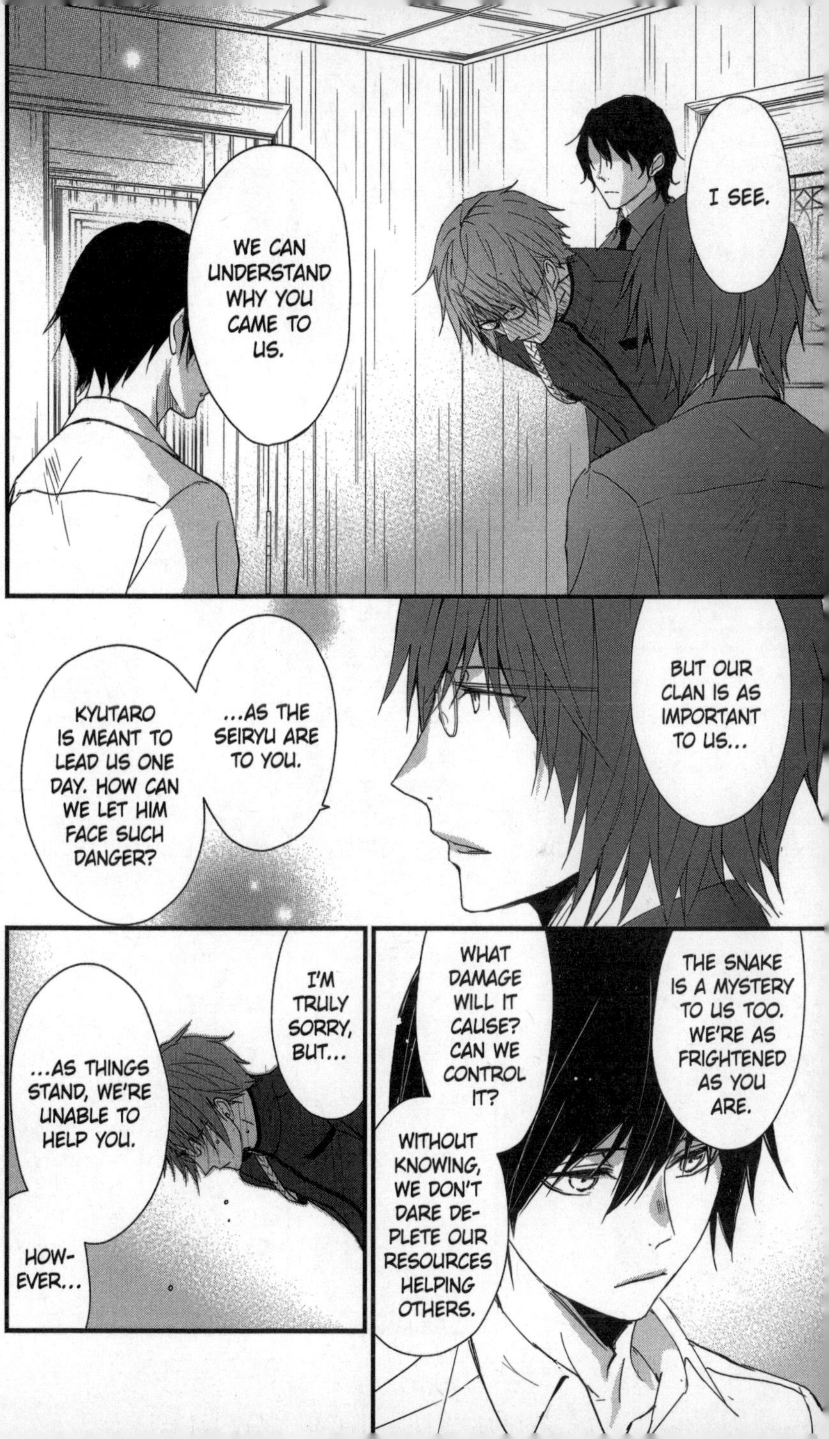
I SEE.
WE CAN UNDERSTAND WHY YOU CAME TO US.
BUT OUR CLAN IS AS IMPORTANT TO US...
...AS THE SEIRYU ARE TO YOU.
KYUTARO IS MEANT TO LEAD US ONE DAY. HOW CAN WE LET HIM FACE SUCH DANGER?
THE SNAKE IS A MYSTERY TO US TOO. WE'RE AS FRIGHTENED AS YOU ARE.
WHAT DAMAGE WILL IT CAUSE? CAN WE CONTROL IT?
WITHOUT KNOWING, WE DON'T DARE DE-PLETE OUR RESOURCES HELPING OTHERS.
I'M TRULY SORRY, BUT...
...AS THINGS STAND, WE'RE UNABLE TO HELP YOU.
HOW-EVER...

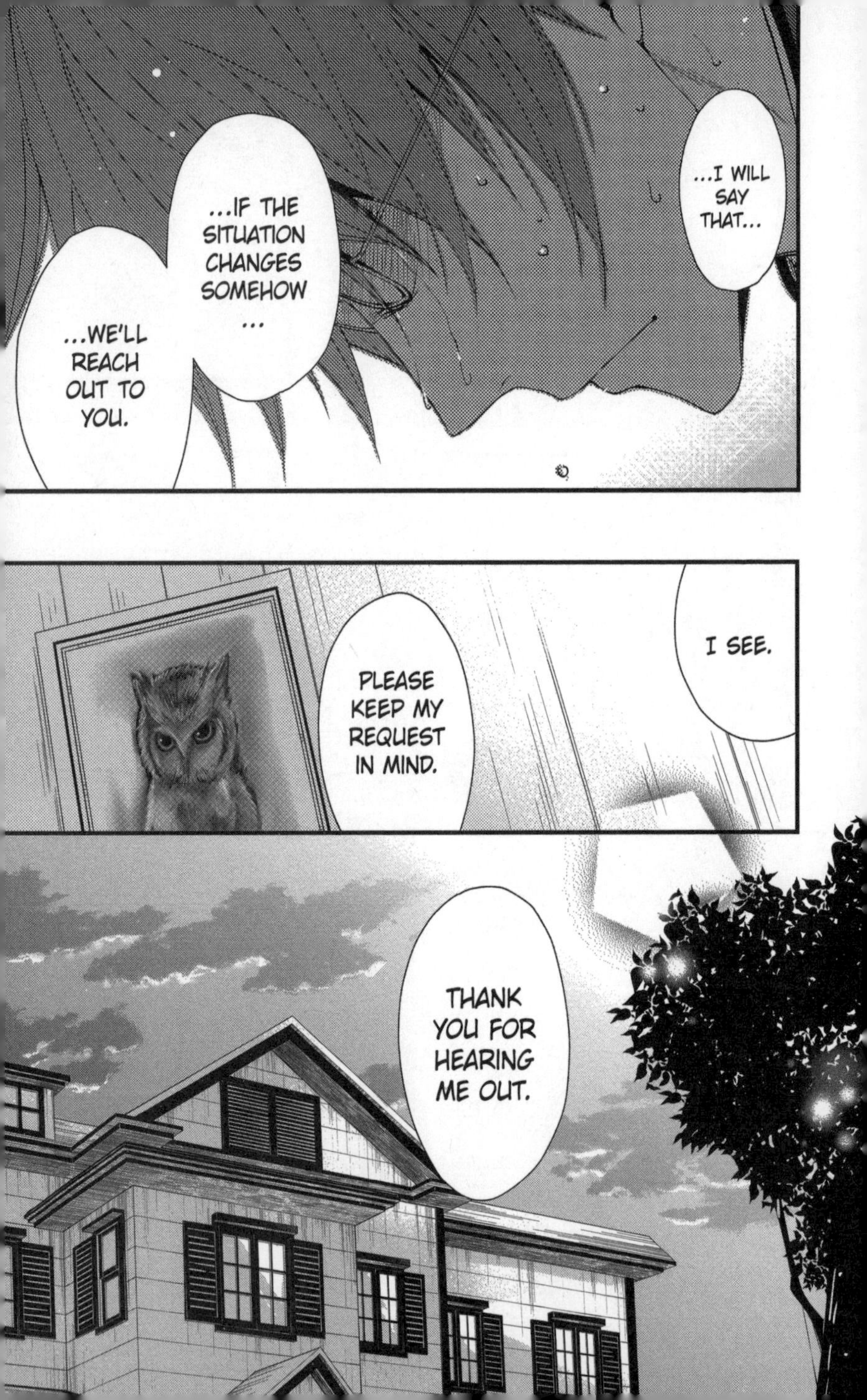
...I WILL SAY THAT...
...IF THE SITUATION CHANGES SOMEHOW...
...WE'LL REACH OUT TO YOU.
I SEE.
PLEASE KEEP MY REQUEST IN MIND.
THANK YOU FOR HEARING ME OUT.

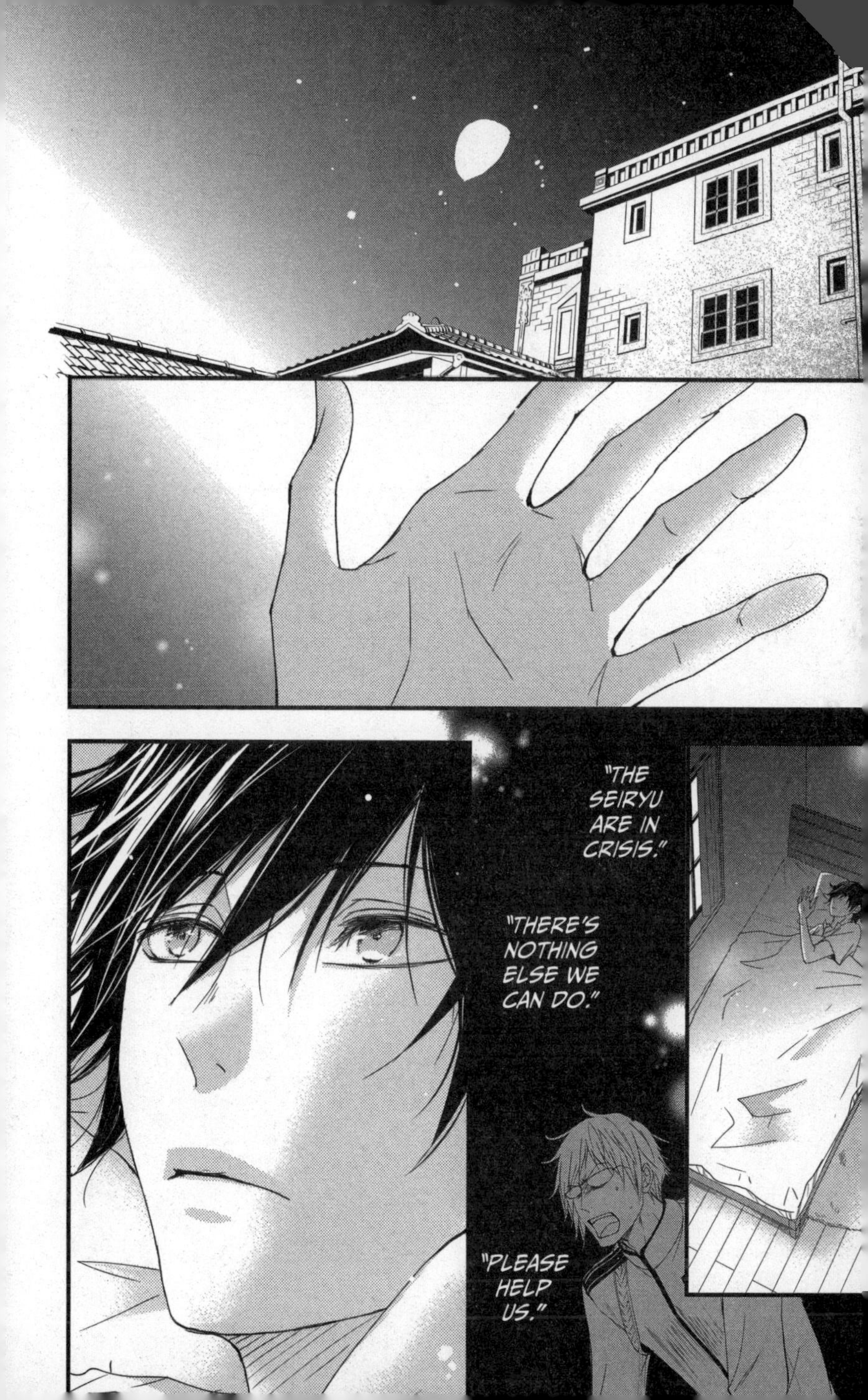
"THE SEIRYU ARE IN CRISIS."
"THERE'S NOTHING ELSE WE CAN DO."
"PLEASE HELP US."

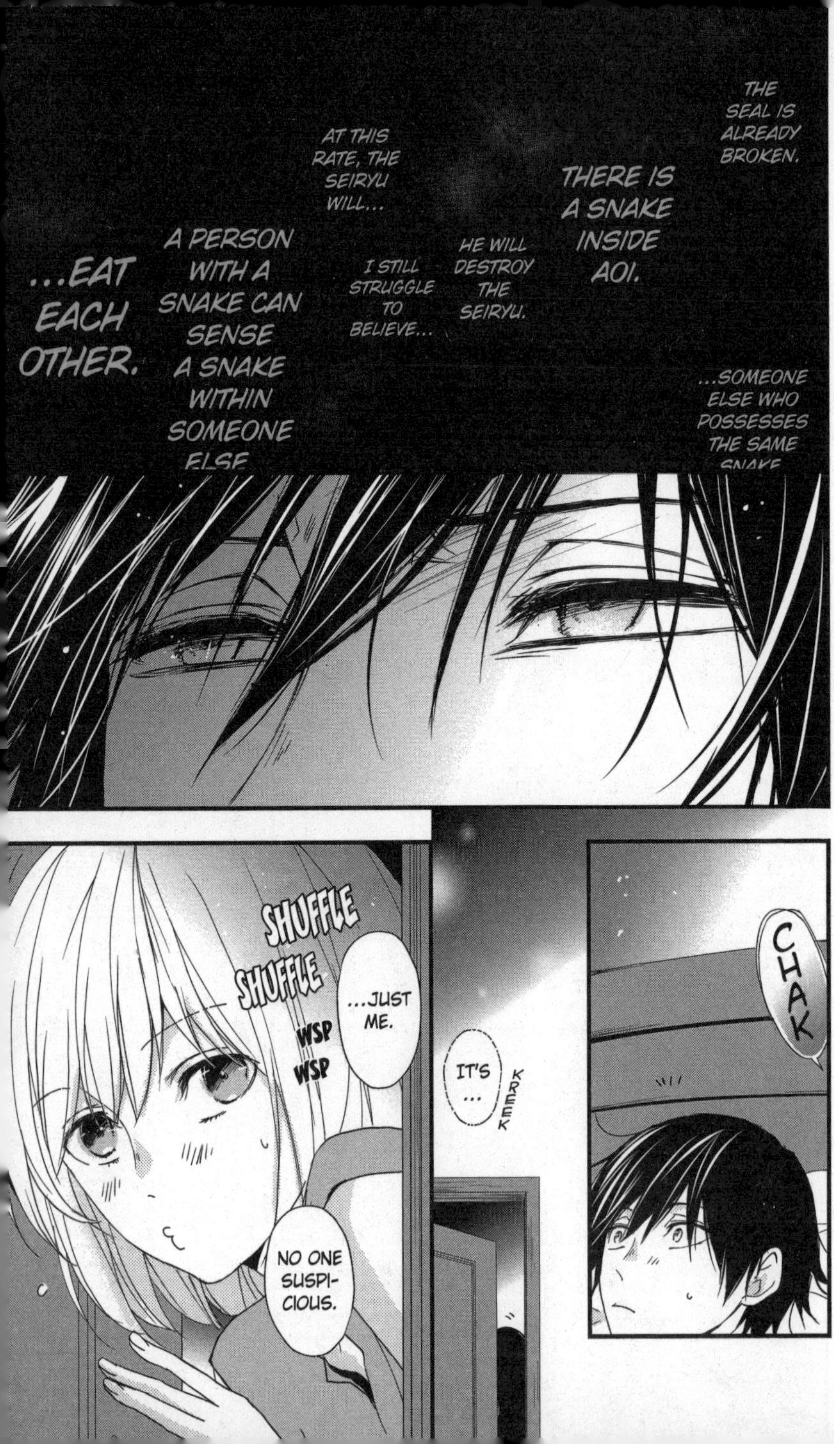
THE SEAL IS ALREADY BROKEN.
...SOMEONE ELSE WHO POSSESSES THE SAME SNAKE
THERE IS A SNAKE INSIDE AOI.
HE WILL DESTROY THE SEIRYU.
AT THIS RATE, THE SEIRYU WILL...
I STILL STRUGGLE TO BELIEVE...
A PERSON WITH A SNAKE CAN SENSE A SNAKE WITHIN SOMEONE ELSE
...EAT EACH OTHER.
CHAK
KREEK
IT'S ...
SHUFFLE
SHUFFLE
WSP
WSP
...JUST ME.
NO ONE SUSPICIOUS.

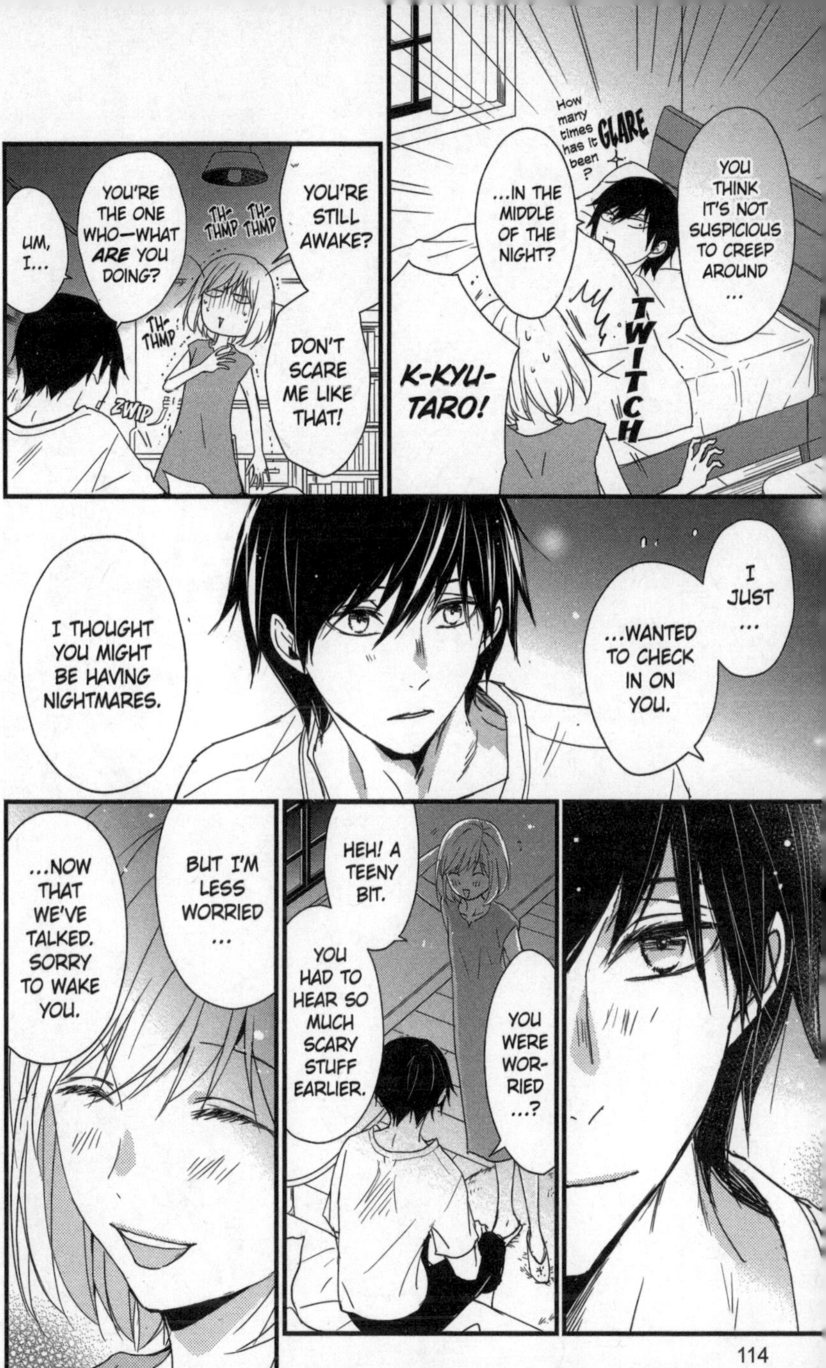
YOU THINK IT'S NOT SUSPICIOUS TO CREEP AROUND ...
GLARE
How many times has it been ?
...IN THE MIDDLE OF THE NIGHT?
TWITCH
K-KYU-TARO!
YOU'RE STILL AWAKE?
DON'T SCARE ME LIKE THAT!
TH-THMP TH-THMP
YOU'RE THE ONE WHO—WHAT ***ARE*** YOU DOING?
TH-THMP
UM, I...
ZWIP
I JUST ...
...WANTED TO CHECK IN ON YOU.
I THOUGHT YOU MIGHT BE HAVING NIGHTMARES.
YOU WERE WOR-RIED ...?
HEH! A TEENY BIT.
YOU HAD TO HEAR SO MUCH SCARY STUFF EARLIER.
BUT I'M LESS WORRIED ...
...NOW THAT WE'VE TALKED. SORRY TO WAKE YOU.

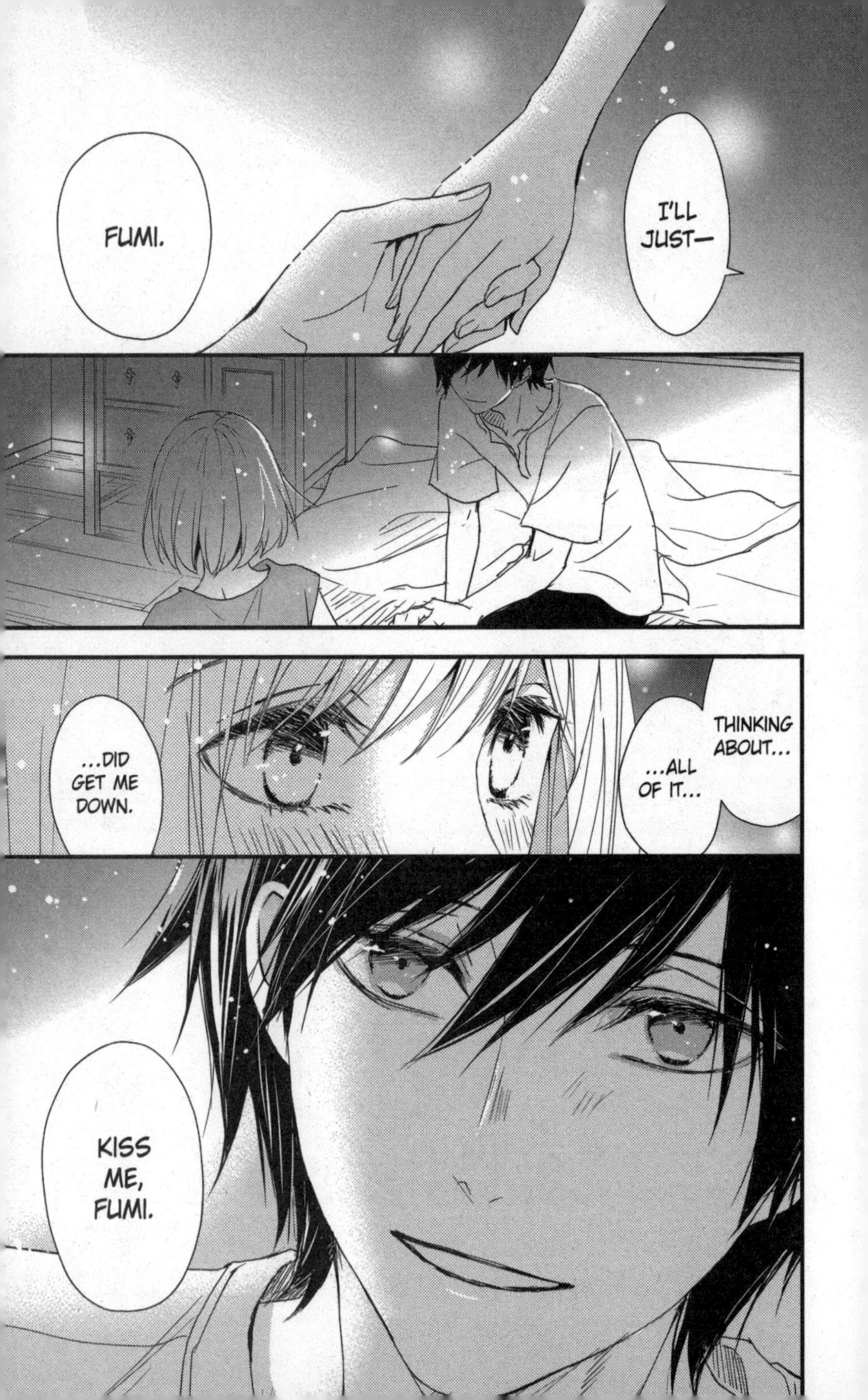
I'LL JUST—
FUMI.
THINKING ABOUT... ...ALL OF IT...
...DID GET ME DOWN.
KISS ME, FUMI.

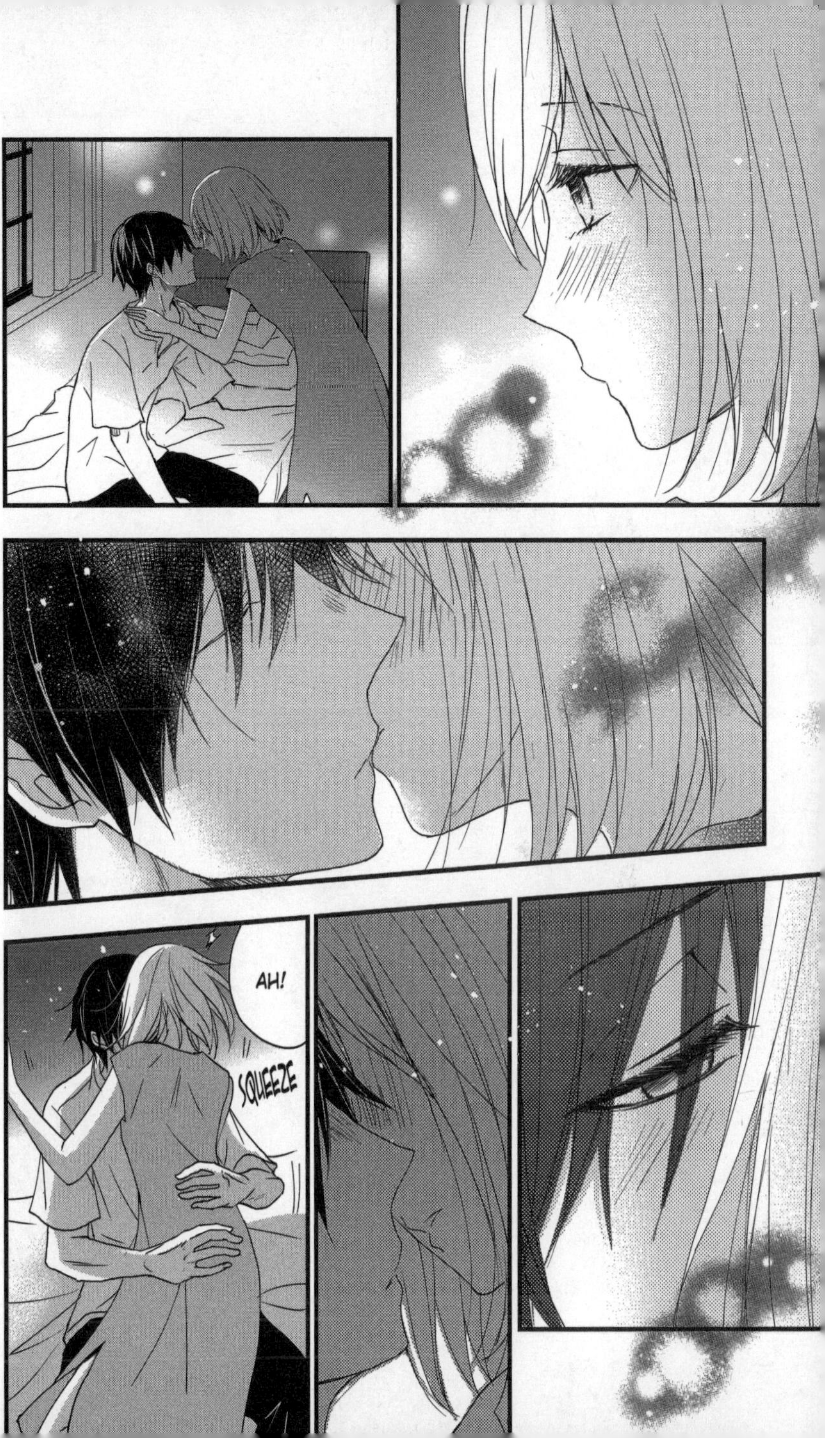
AH!
SQUEEZE

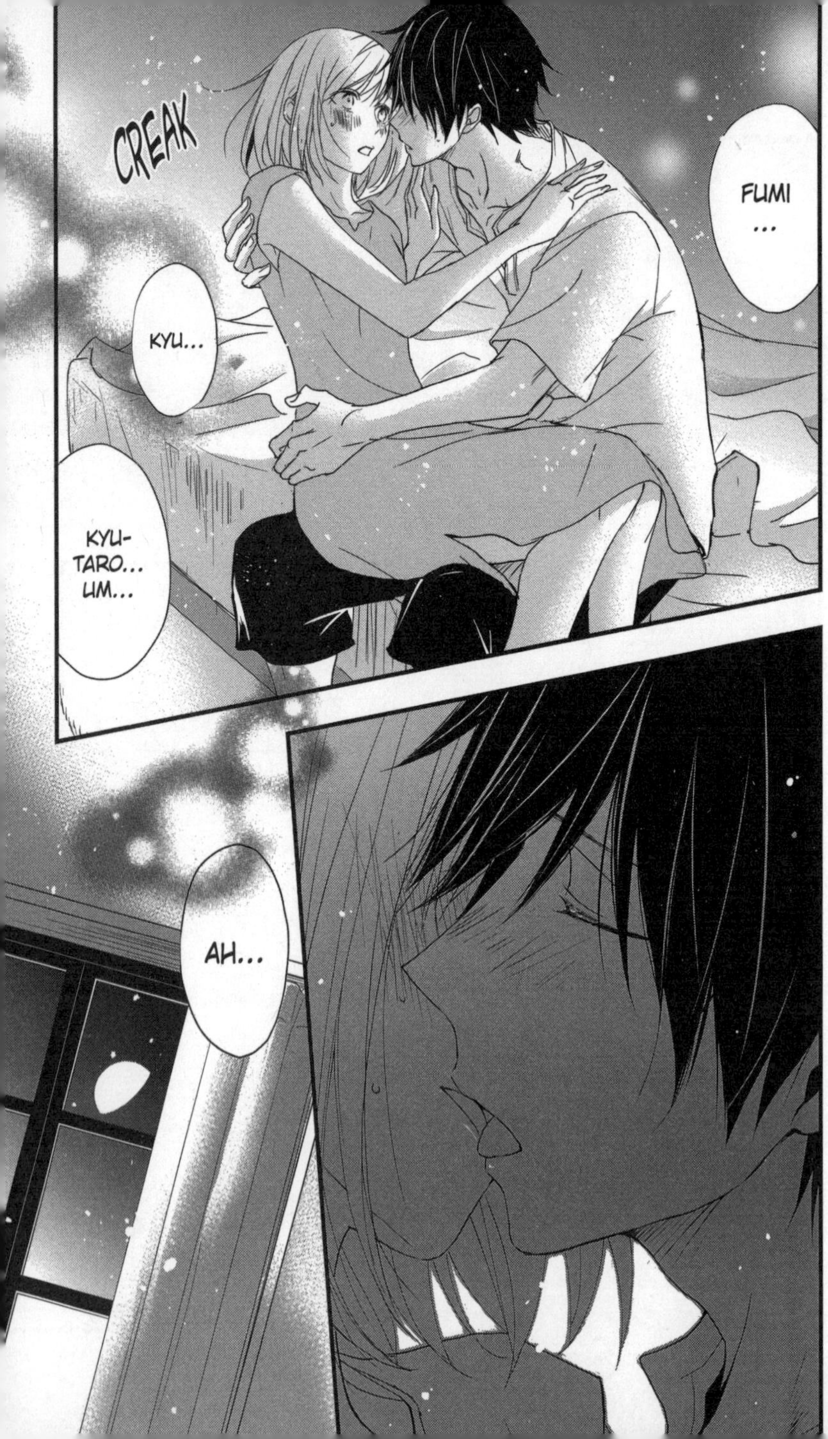
FUMI
...
CREAK
KYU...
KYU-
TARO...
UM...
AH...

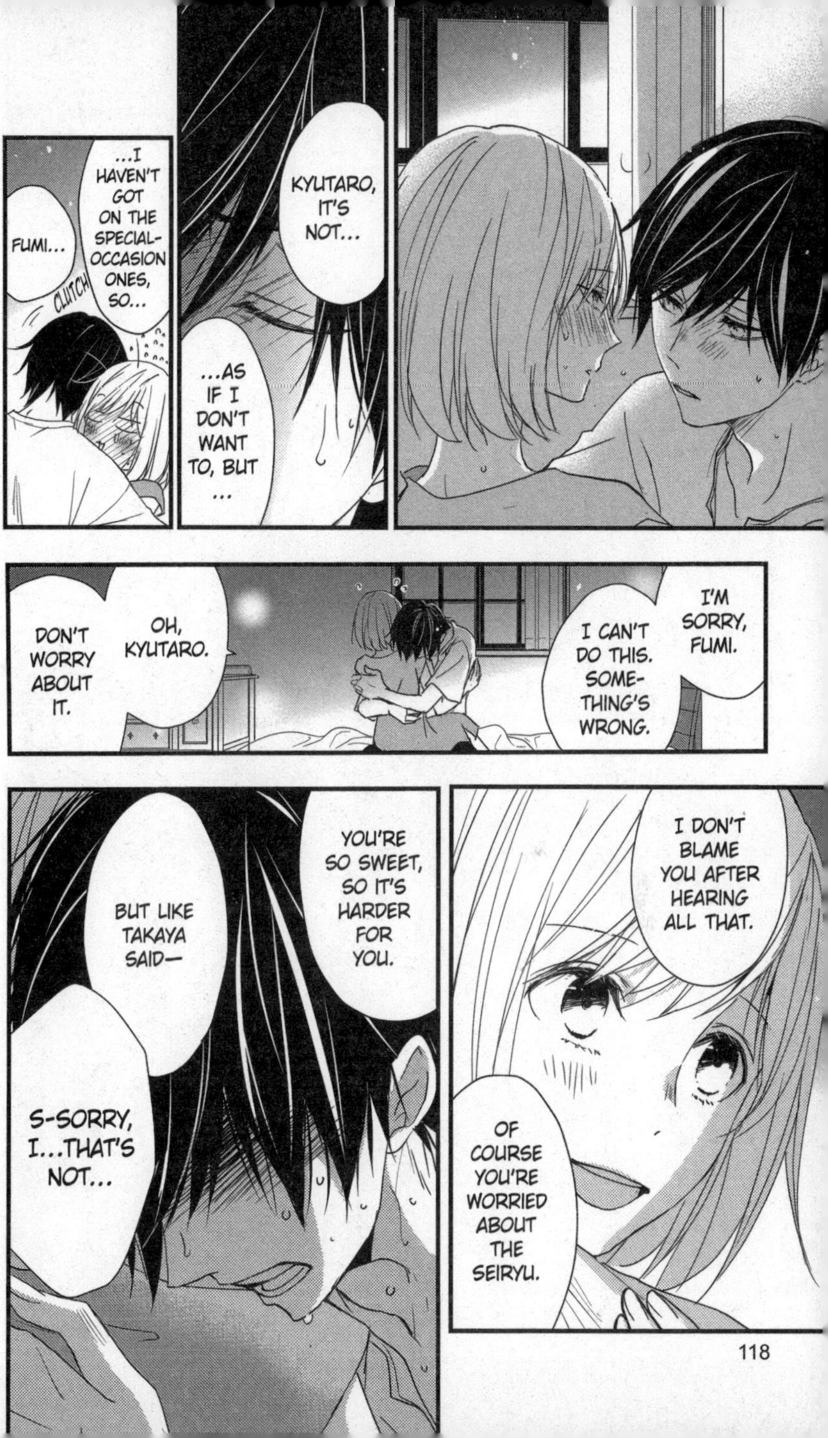
KYUTARO, IT'S NOT...
...AS IF I DON'T WANT TO, BUT...
...I HAVEN'T GOT ON THE SPECIAL-OCCASION ONES, SO...
FUMI...
CLUTCH
I'M SORRY, FUMI.
I CAN'T DO THIS. SOME-THING'S WRONG.
OH, KYUTARO.
DON'T WORRY ABOUT IT.
I DON'T BLAME YOU AFTER HEARING ALL THAT.
OF COURSE YOU'RE WORRIED ABOUT THE SEIRYU.
YOU'RE SO SWEET, SO IT'S HARDER FOR YOU.
BUT LIKE TAKAYA SAID—
S-SORRY, I...THAT'S NOT...

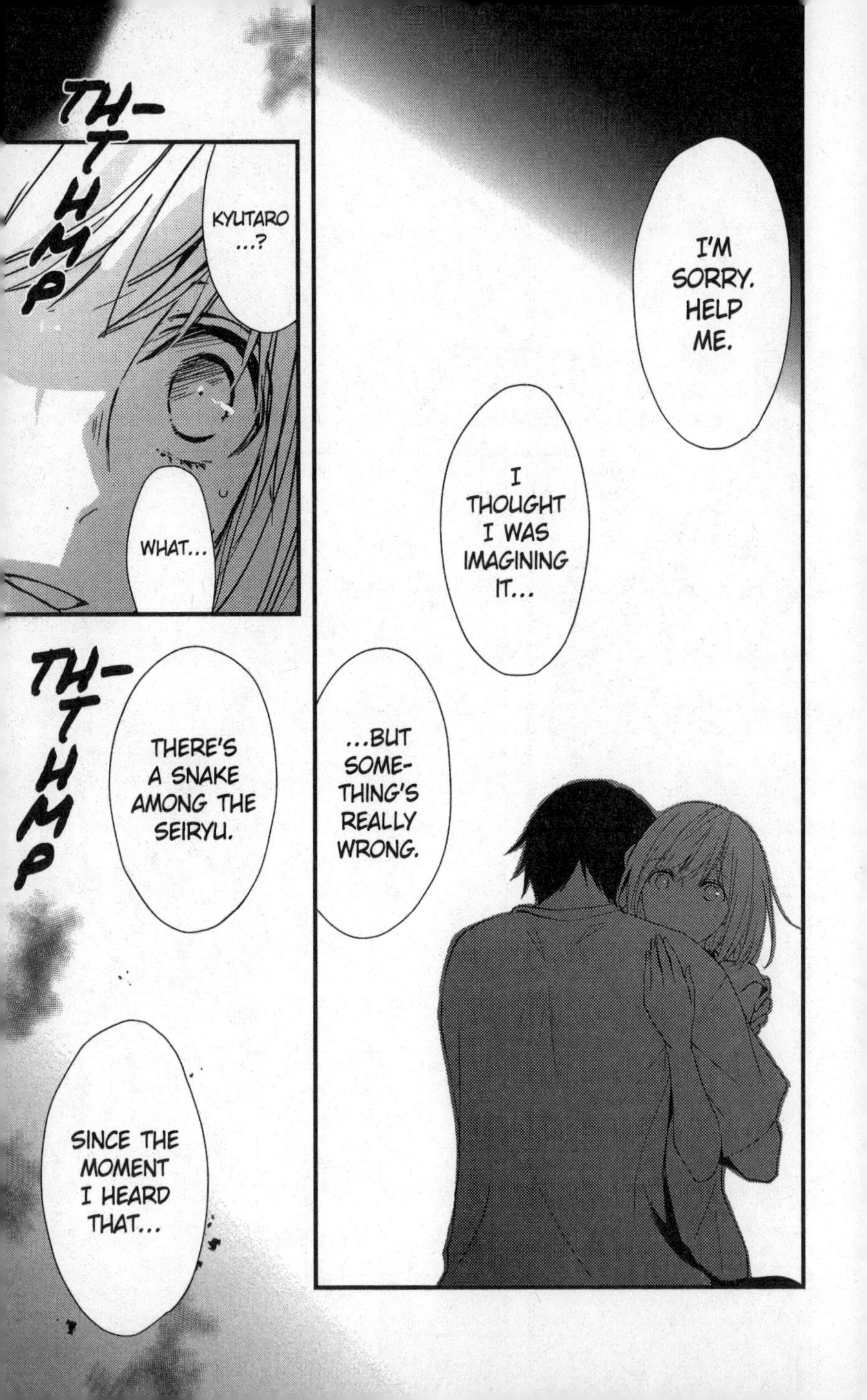
I'M SORRY. HELP ME.
I THOUGHT I WAS IMAGINING IT...
...BUT SOME-THING'S REALLY WRONG.
TH-THUMP
KYUTARO ...?
WHAT...
TH-THUMP
THERE'S A SNAKE AMONG THE SEIRYU.
SINCE THE MOMENT I HEARD THAT...

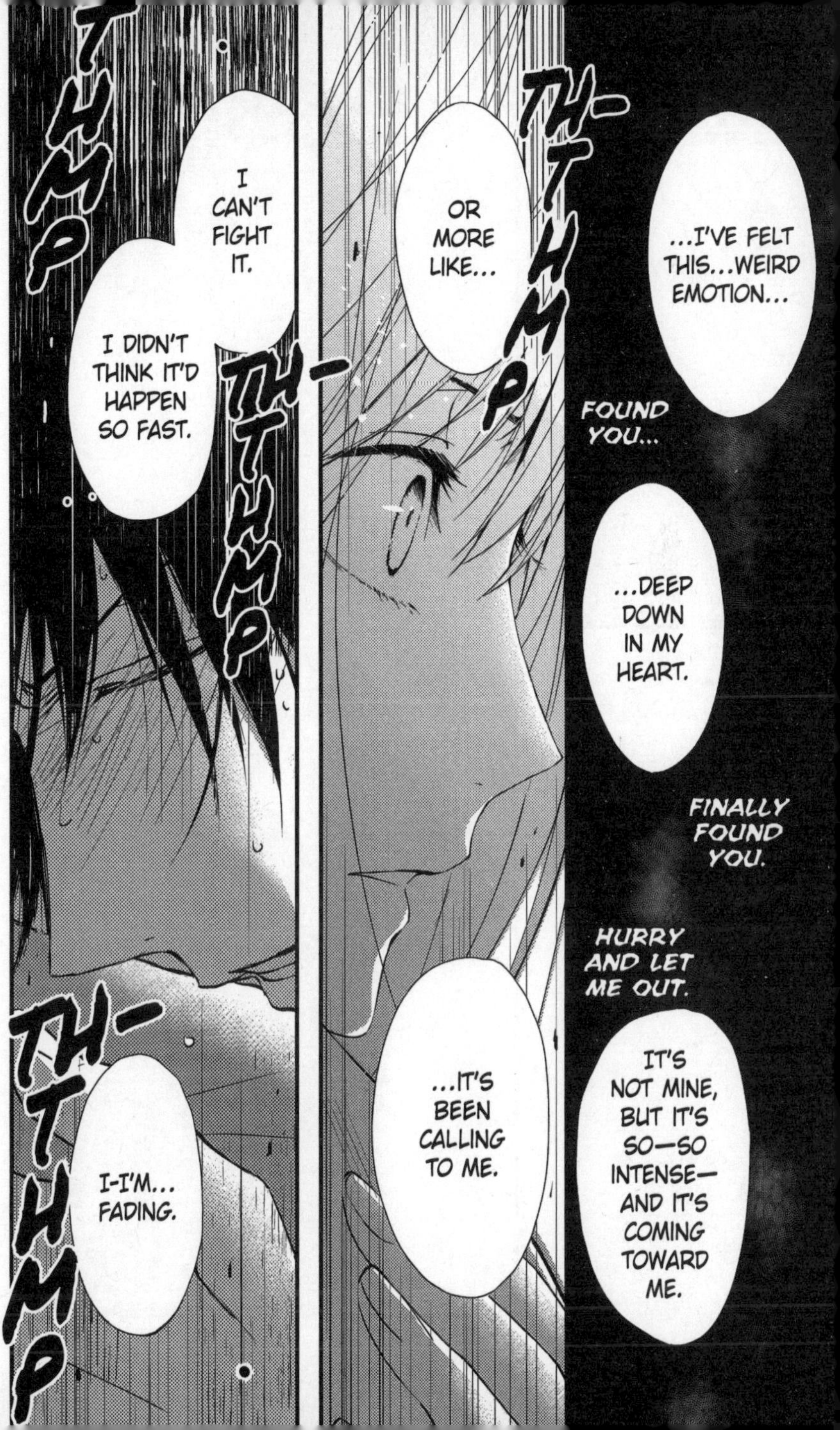
...I'VE FELT THIS...WEIRD EMOTION...
FOUND YOU...
...DEEP DOWN IN MY HEART.
FINALLY FOUND YOU.
HURRY AND LET ME OUT.
IT'S NOT MINE, BUT IT'S SO—SO INTENSE— AND IT'S COMING TOWARD ME.
TH-THUMP
OR MORE LIKE...
...IT'S BEEN CALLING TO ME.
THUMP
I CAN'T FIGHT IT.
TH-THUMP
I DIDN'T THINK IT'D HAPPEN SO FAST.
TH-THUMP
I-I'M... FADING.

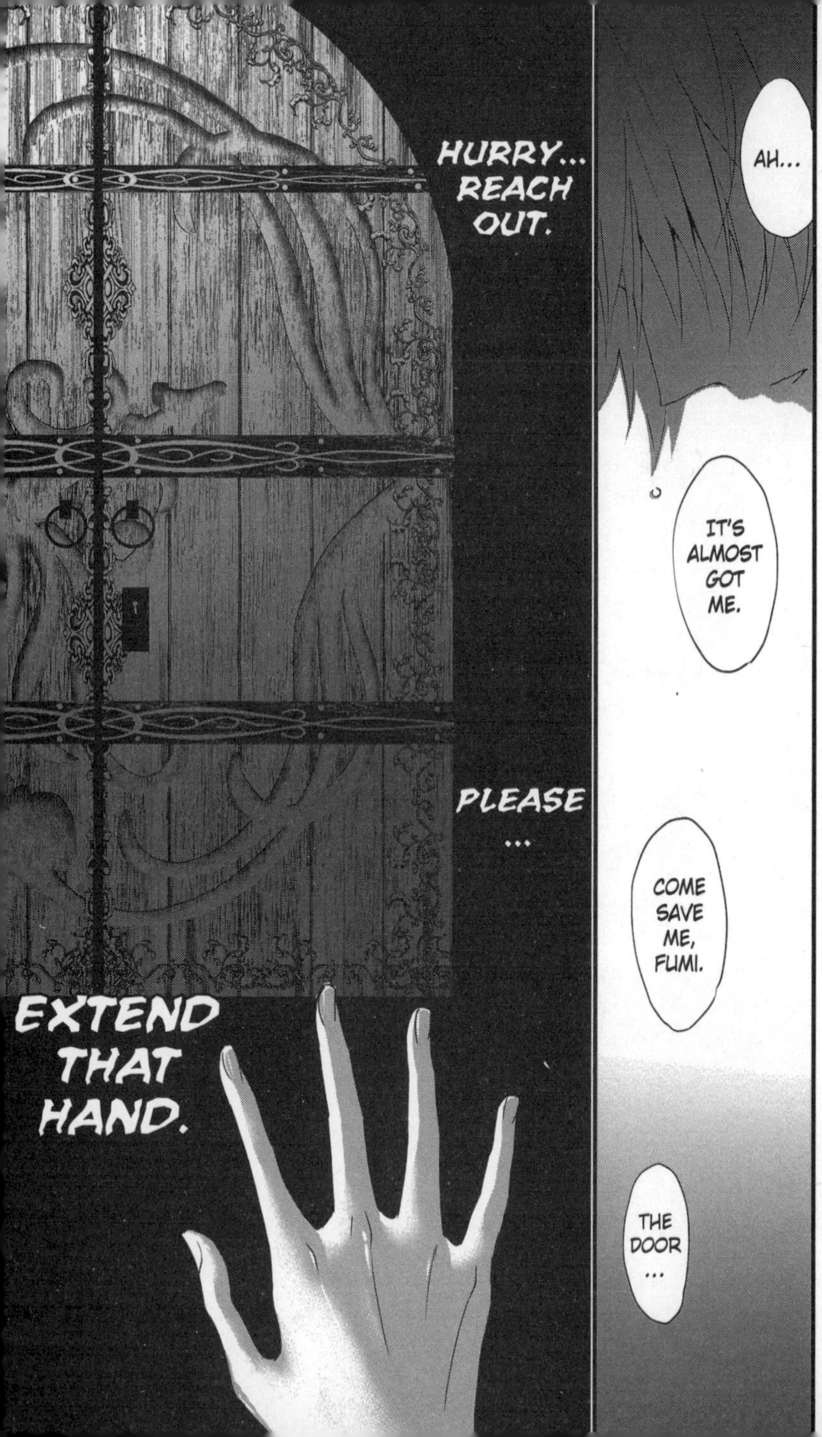
AH...
IT'S ALMOST GOT ME.
COME SAVE ME, FUMI.
THE DOOR ...
HURRY... REACH OUT.
PLEASE ...
EXTEND THAT HAND.

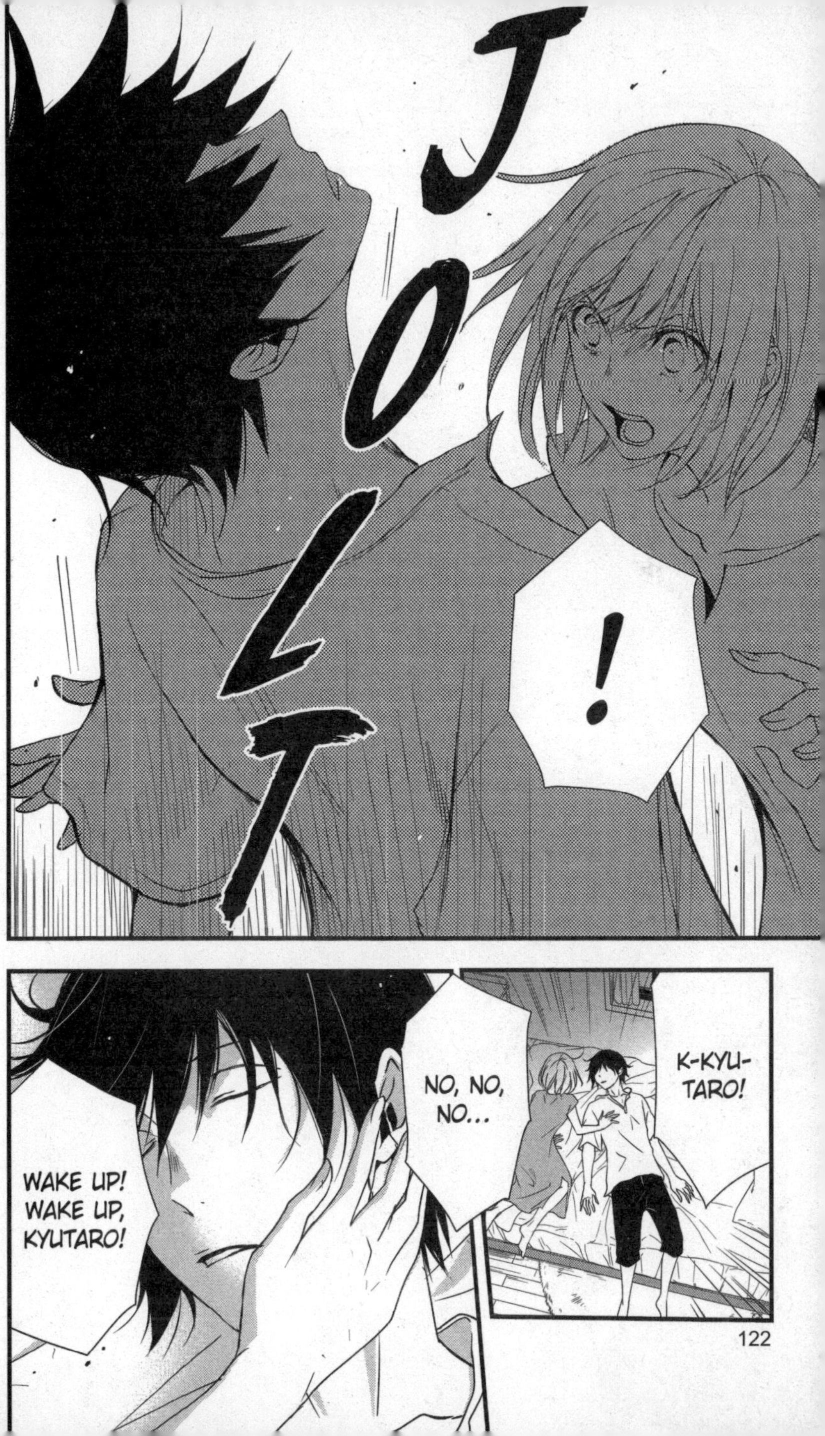
JOLT
!
K-KYU-TARO!
NO, NO, NO...
WAKE UP! WAKE UP, KYUTARO!

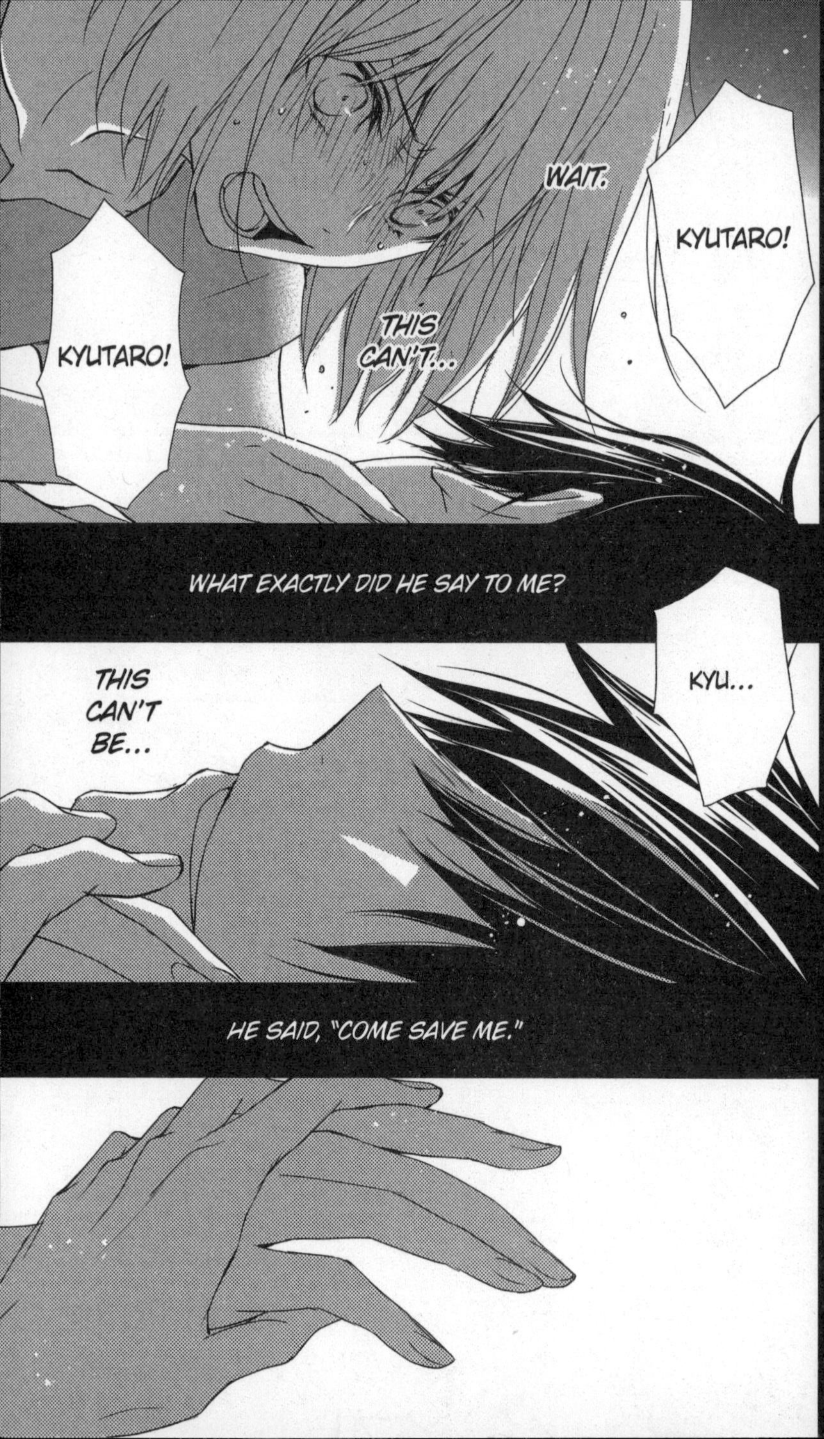
KYUTARO!
WAIT.
THIS CAN'T...
KYUTARO!
WHAT EXACTLY DID HE SAY TO ME?
KYU...
THIS CAN'T BE...
HE SAID, "COME SAVE ME."

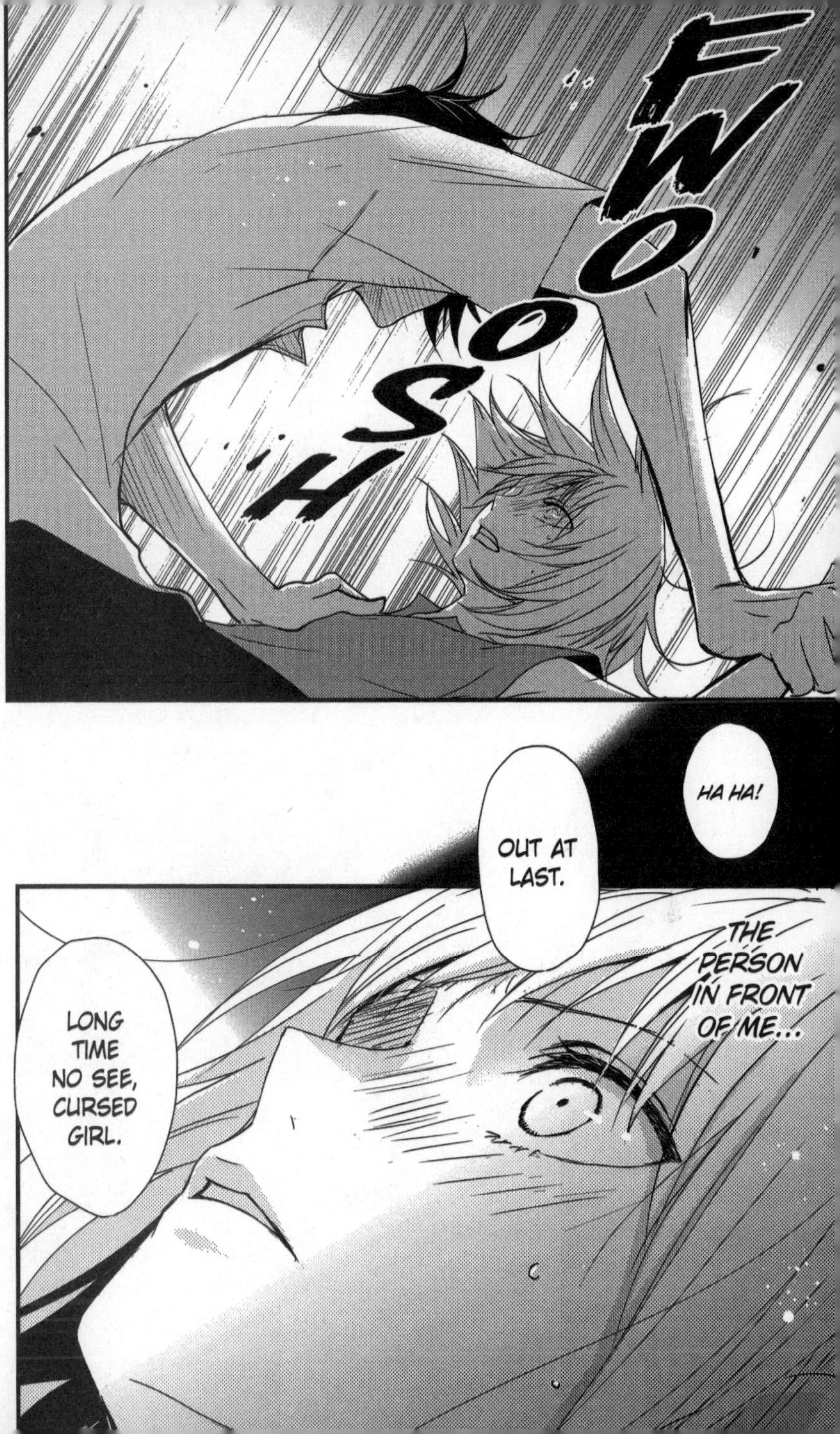
FWOOSH
HA HA!
OUT AT LAST.
THE PERSON IN FRONT OF ME...
LONG TIME NO SEE, CURSED GIRL.

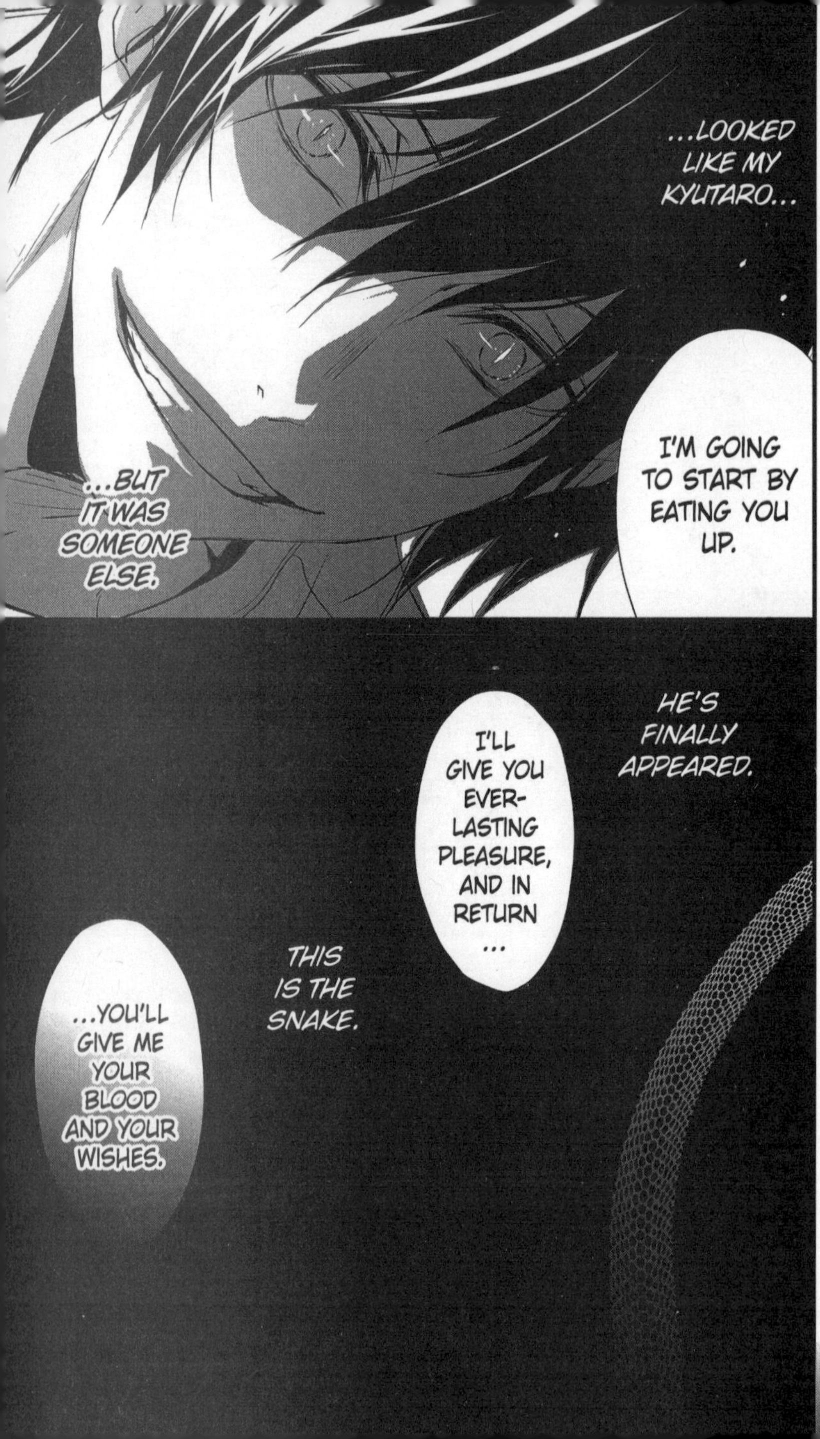
...LOOKED LIKE MY KYUTARO...
I'M GOING TO START BY EATING YOU UP.
...BUT IT WAS SOMEONE ELSE.
HE'S FINALLY APPEARED.
I'LL GIVE YOU EVER-LASTING PLEASURE, AND IN RETURN...
THIS IS THE SNAKE.
...YOU'LL GIVE ME YOUR BLOOD AND YOUR WISHES.

MONTHLY BETSUCOMI SALE DATE NOTICE ON TWITTER

CHAPTER 48

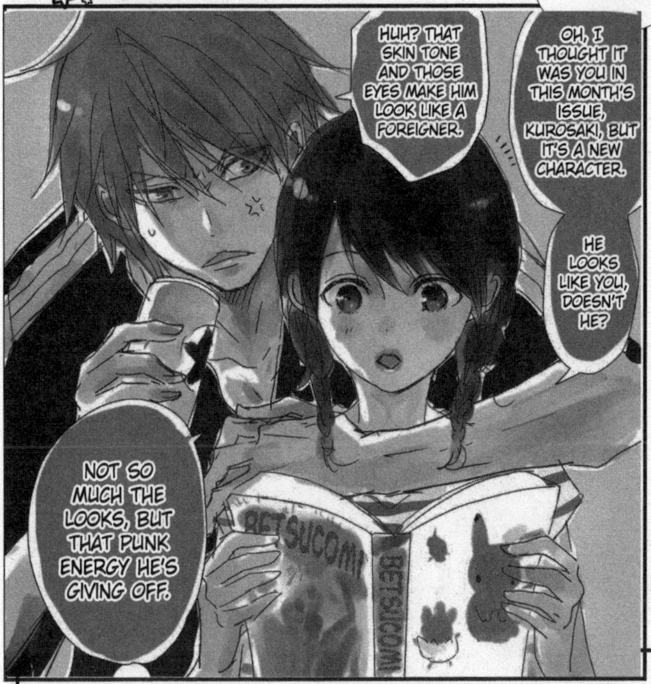
OH, I THOUGHT IT WAS YOU IN THIS MONTH'S ISSUE, KUROSAKI, BUT IT'S A NEW CHARACTER.
HUH? THAT SKIN TONE AND THOSE EYES MAKE HIM LOOK LIKE A FOREIGNER.
HE LOOKS LIKE YOU, DOESN'T HE?
NOT SO MUCH THE LOOKS, BUT THAT PUNK ENERGY HE'S GIVING OFF.
BETSUCOMI
BETSUCOMI
BETSUCOMI

LET'S SEE... WHAT'S UP IN *QUEEN'S QUALITY* THIS MONTH?
(1) THE STORY IS PRETTY SERIOUS, SO I HAD KOICHI PUT ON REGULAR LOUNGEWEAR.
(2) BUT I PUT TAKAYA IN THAT CHARACTER T-SHIRT.
(3) THIS GUY SEEMS TO BE THE TYPE WHO CARRIES A TRUCKLOAD OF "BEAT ME UP" FLAGS.
THERE WAS SUPPOSED TO BE A TURNING POINT FOR KYUTARO, BUT INSTEAD, THERE'S A NEW CHARACTER IN CHAPTER 48!

THE PEOPLE IN THE ILLUSTRATION ABOVE ARE KUROSAKI AND TERU FROM MY PREVIOUS SERIES *DENGEKI DAISY*. I SOMETIMES STILL POST PICTURES OF THEM ON TWITTER. IT'S SO STRANGE, BUT THAT GUY—I CAN'T REALLY TELL YOU WHICH—REALLY DOES LOOK LIKE KUROSAKI. THE MORE I DRAW HIM, THE MORE THE RESEMBLANCE GROWS...

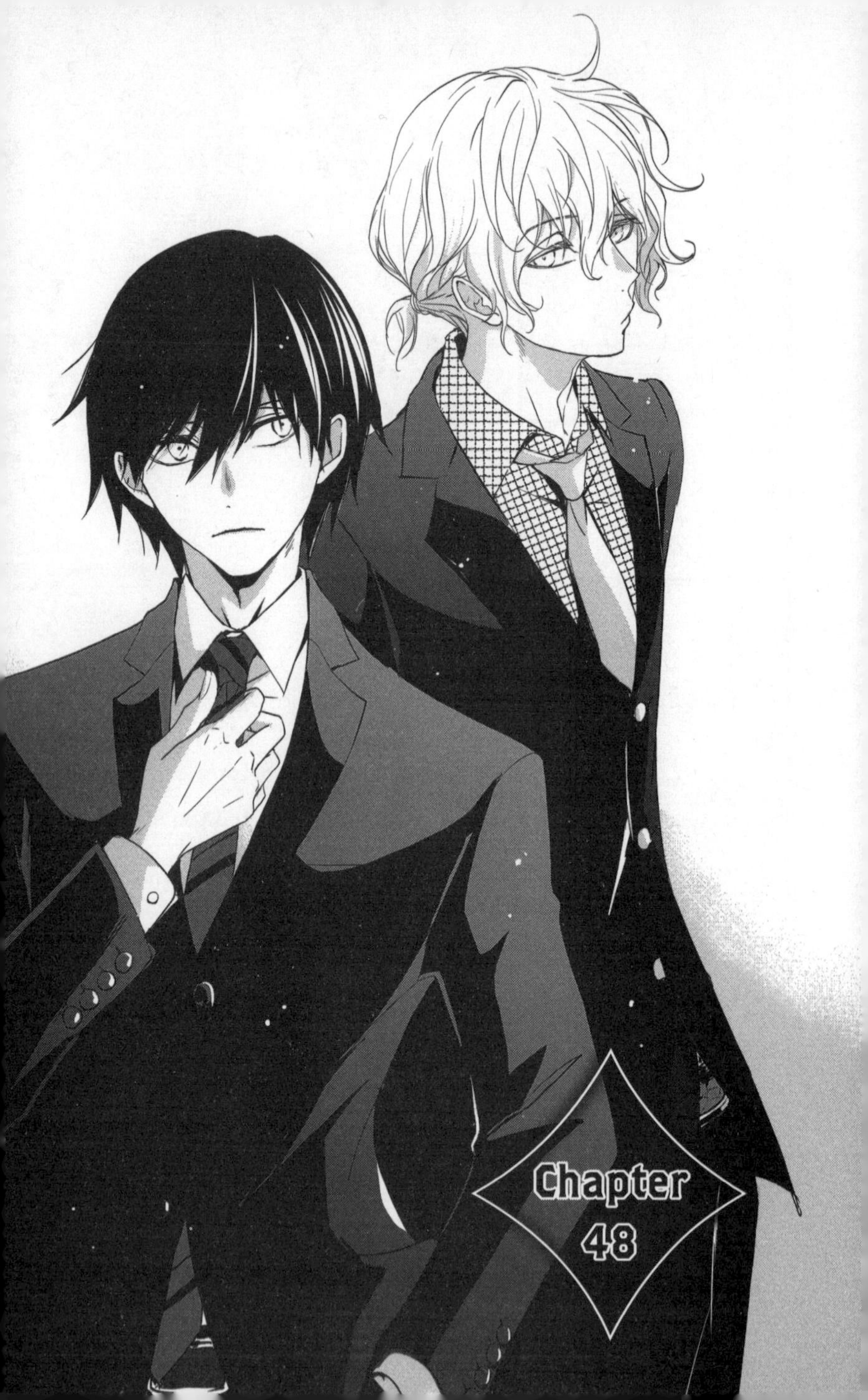
Chapter
48

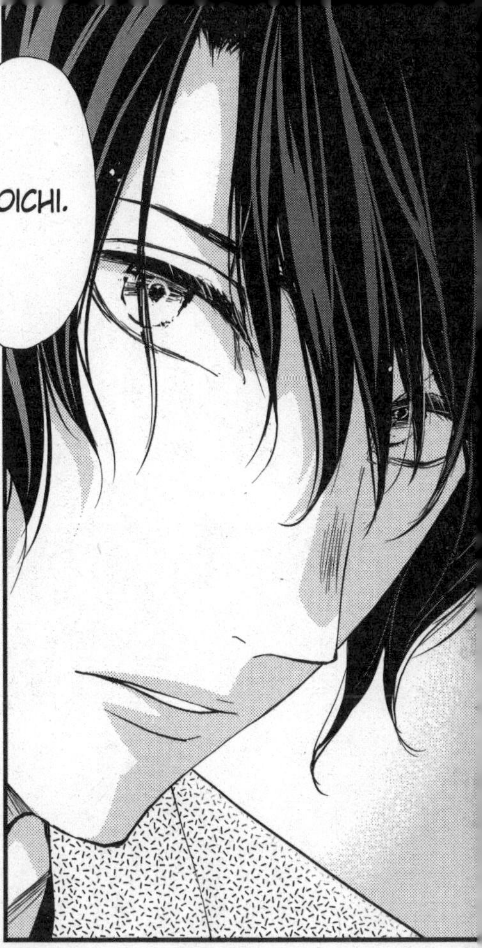
KOICHI.

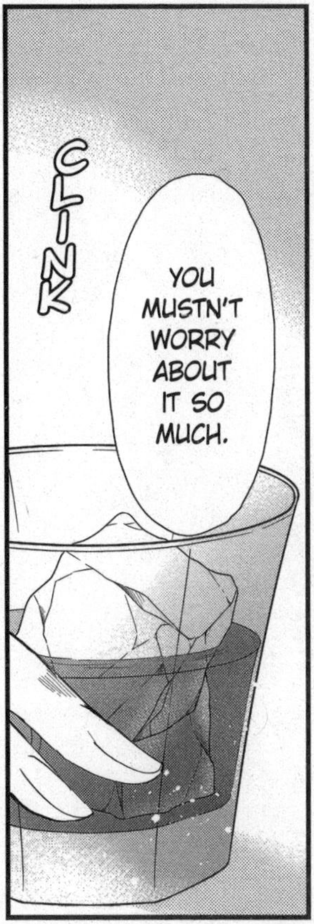
CLINK
YOU MUSTN'T WORRY ABOUT IT SO MUCH.

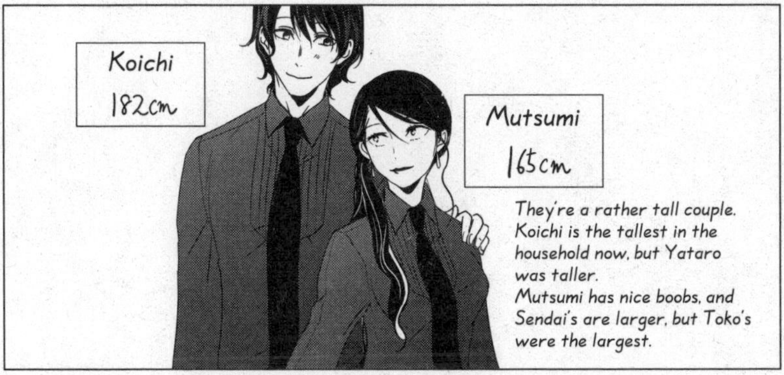
Koichi
182cm
Mutsumi
165cm
They're a rather tall couple. Koichi is the tallest in the household now, but Yataro was taller.
Mutsumi has nice boobs, and Sendai's are larger, but Toko's were the largest.

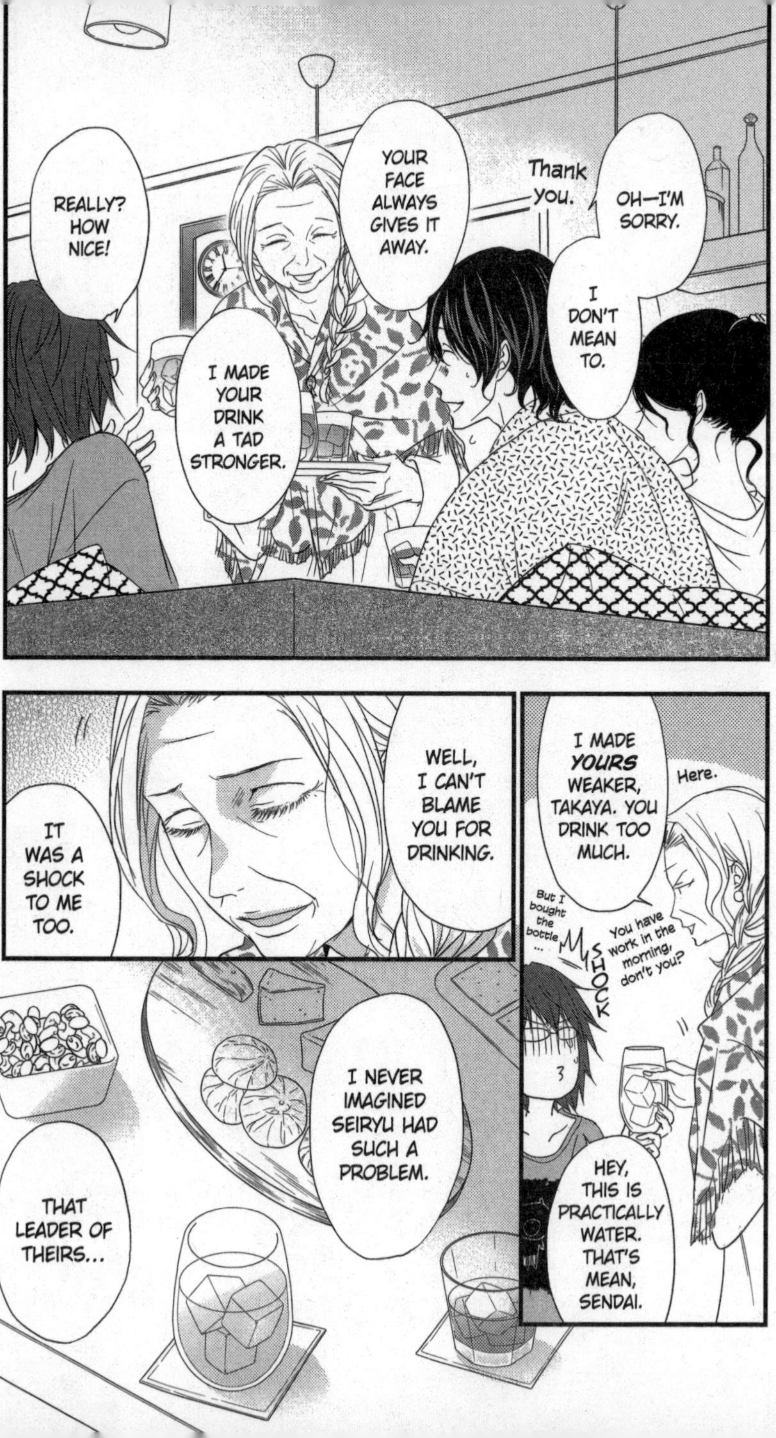
Thank you.
OH—I'M SORRY.
I DON'T MEAN TO.
YOUR FACE ALWAYS GIVES IT AWAY.
I MADE YOUR DRINK A TAD STRONGER.
REALLY? HOW NICE!
Here.
I MADE *YOURS* WEAKER, TAKAYA. YOU DRINK TOO MUCH.
You have work in the morning, don't you?
But I bought the bottle...
SHOCK
HEY, THIS IS PRACTICALLY WATER. THAT'S MEAN, SENDAI.
WELL, I CAN'T BLAME YOU FOR DRINKING.
IT WAS A SHOCK TO ME TOO.
I NEVER IMAGINED SEIRYU HAD SUCH A PROBLEM.
THAT LEADER OF THEIRS...

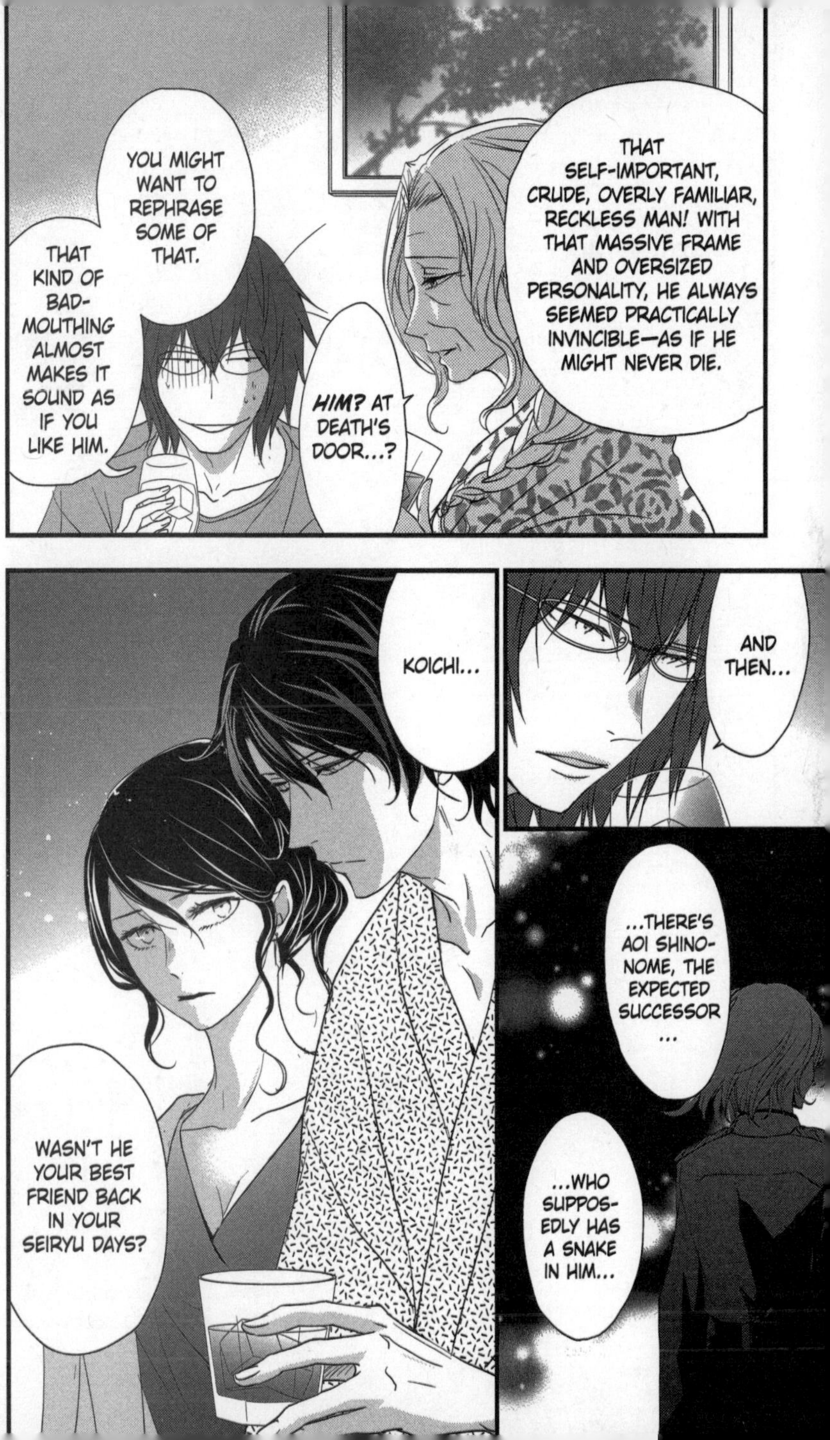
THAT SELF-IMPORTANT, CRUDE, OVERLY FAMILIAR, RECKLESS MAN! WITH THAT MASSIVE FRAME AND OVERSIZED PERSONALITY, HE ALWAYS SEEMED PRACTICALLY INVINCIBLE—AS IF HE MIGHT NEVER DIE.
HIM? AT DEATH'S DOOR...?
YOU MIGHT WANT TO REPHRASE SOME OF THAT.
THAT KIND OF BAD-MOUTHING ALMOST MAKES IT SOUND AS IF YOU LIKE HIM.
AND THEN...
...THERE'S AOI SHINONOME, THE EXPECTED SUCCESSOR...
...WHO SUPPOSEDLY HAS A SNAKE IN HIM...
KOICHI...
WASN'T HE YOUR BEST FRIEND BACK IN YOUR SEIRYU DAYS?

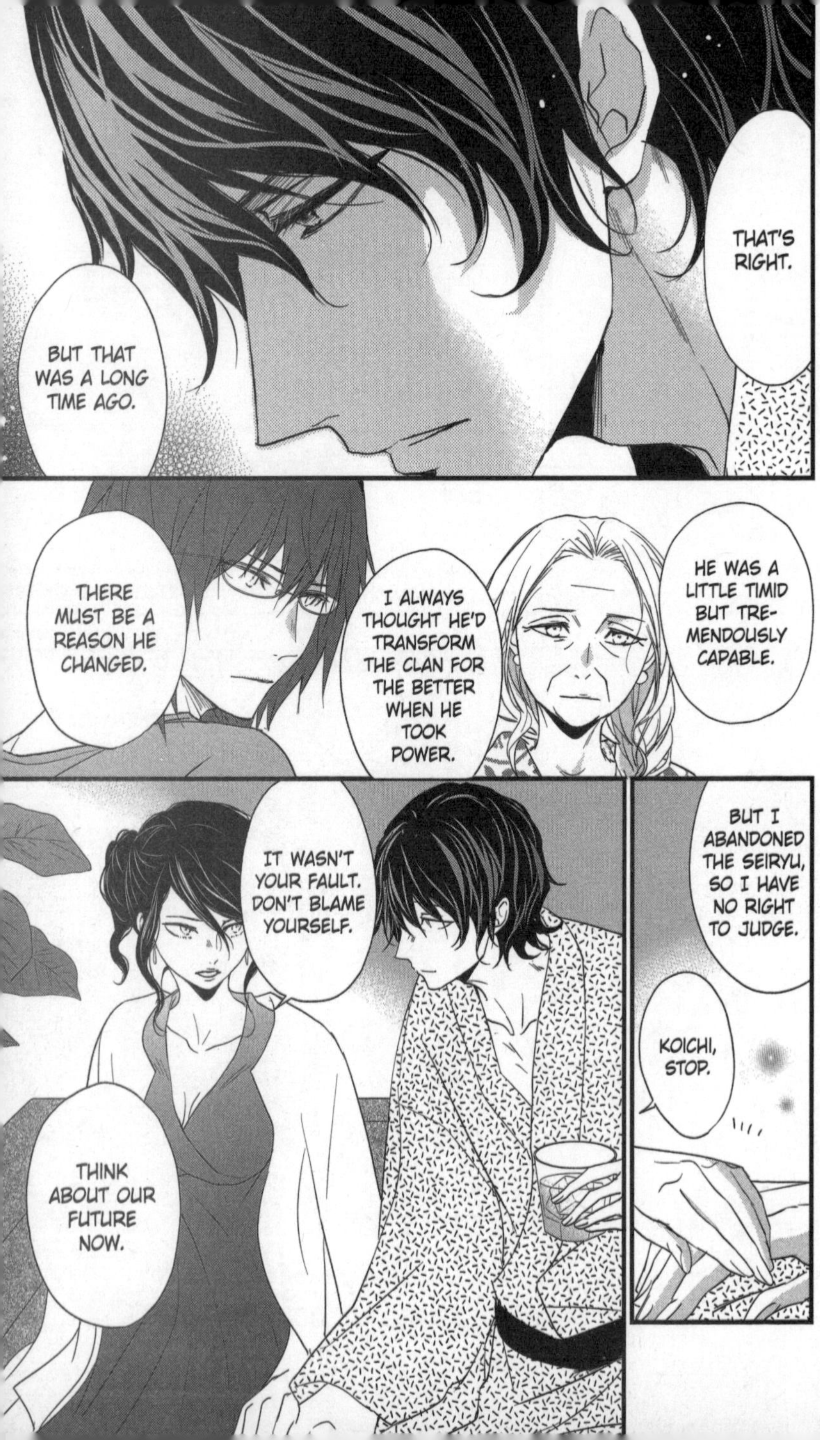
THAT'S RIGHT.
BUT THAT WAS A LONG TIME AGO.
HE WAS A LITTLE TIMID BUT TRE-MENDOUSLY CAPABLE.
I ALWAYS THOUGHT HE'D TRANSFORM THE CLAN FOR THE BETTER WHEN HE TOOK POWER.
THERE MUST BE A REASON HE CHANGED.
BUT I ABANDONED THE SEIRYU, SO I HAVE NO RIGHT TO JUDGE.
KOICHI, STOP.
IT WASN'T YOUR FAULT. DON'T BLAME YOURSELF.
THINK ABOUT OUR FUTURE NOW.

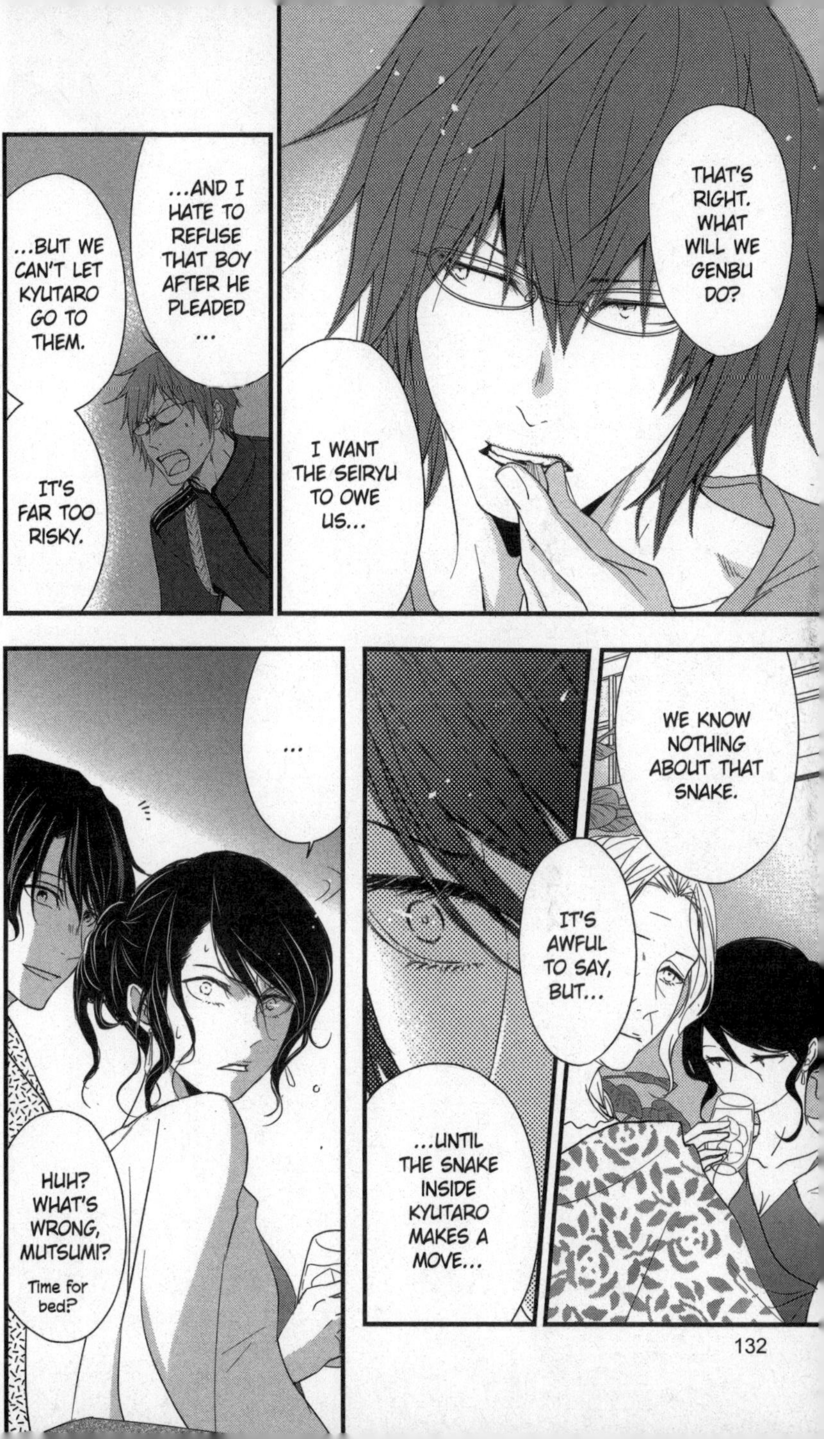
THAT'S RIGHT. WHAT WILL WE GENBU DO?
I WANT THE SEIRYU TO OWE US...
...AND I HATE TO REFUSE THAT BOY AFTER HE PLEADED ...
...BUT WE CAN'T LET KYUTARO GO TO THEM.
IT'S FAR TOO RISKY.
WE KNOW NOTHING ABOUT THAT SNAKE.
IT'S AWFUL TO SAY, BUT...
...UNTIL THE SNAKE INSIDE KYUTARO MAKES A MOVE...
...
HUH? WHAT'S WRONG, MUTSUMI?
Time for bed?

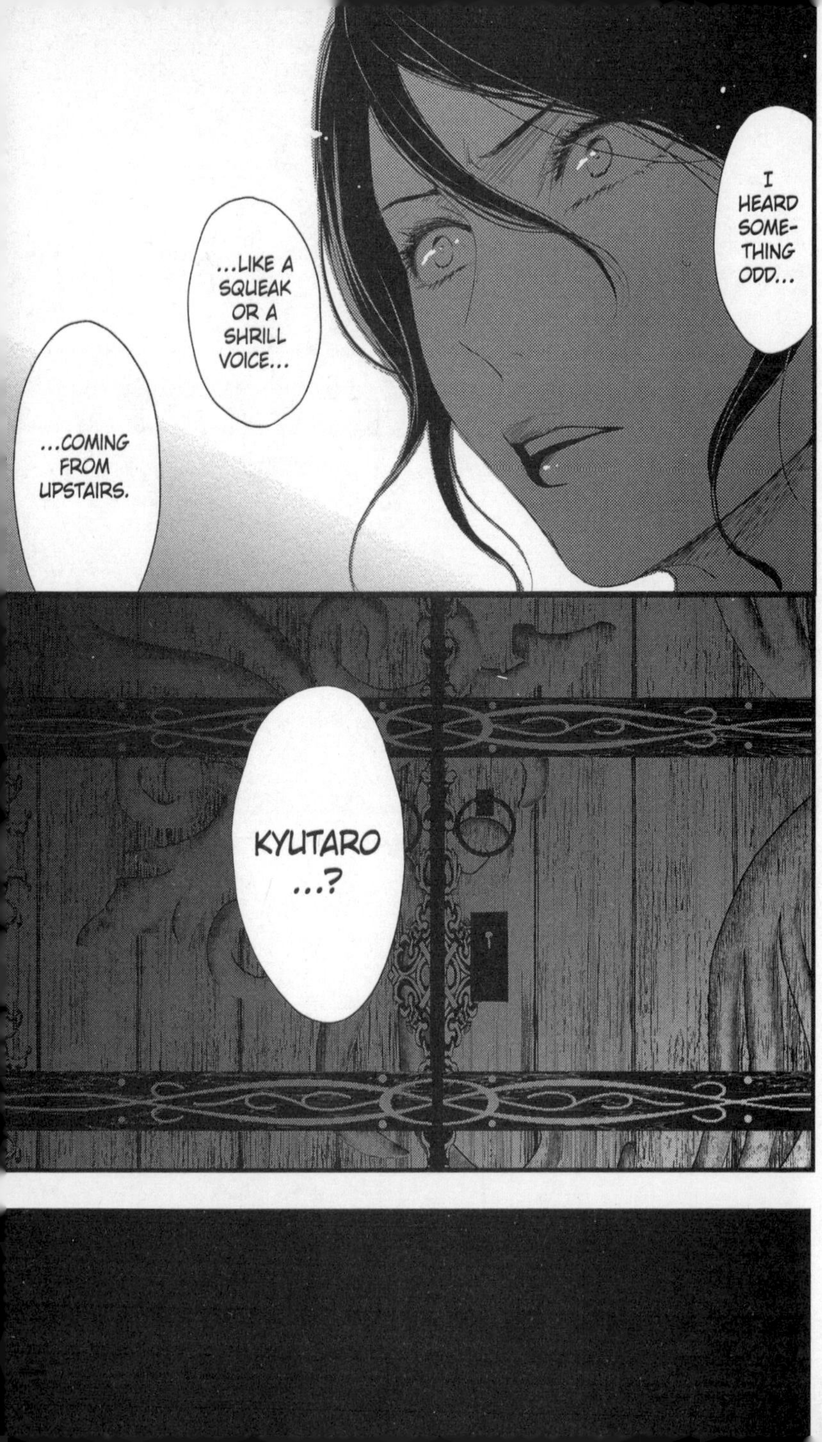
I HEARD SOMETHING ODD...
...LIKE A SQUEAK OR A SHRILL VOICE...
...COMING FROM UPSTAIRS.
KYUTARO ...?

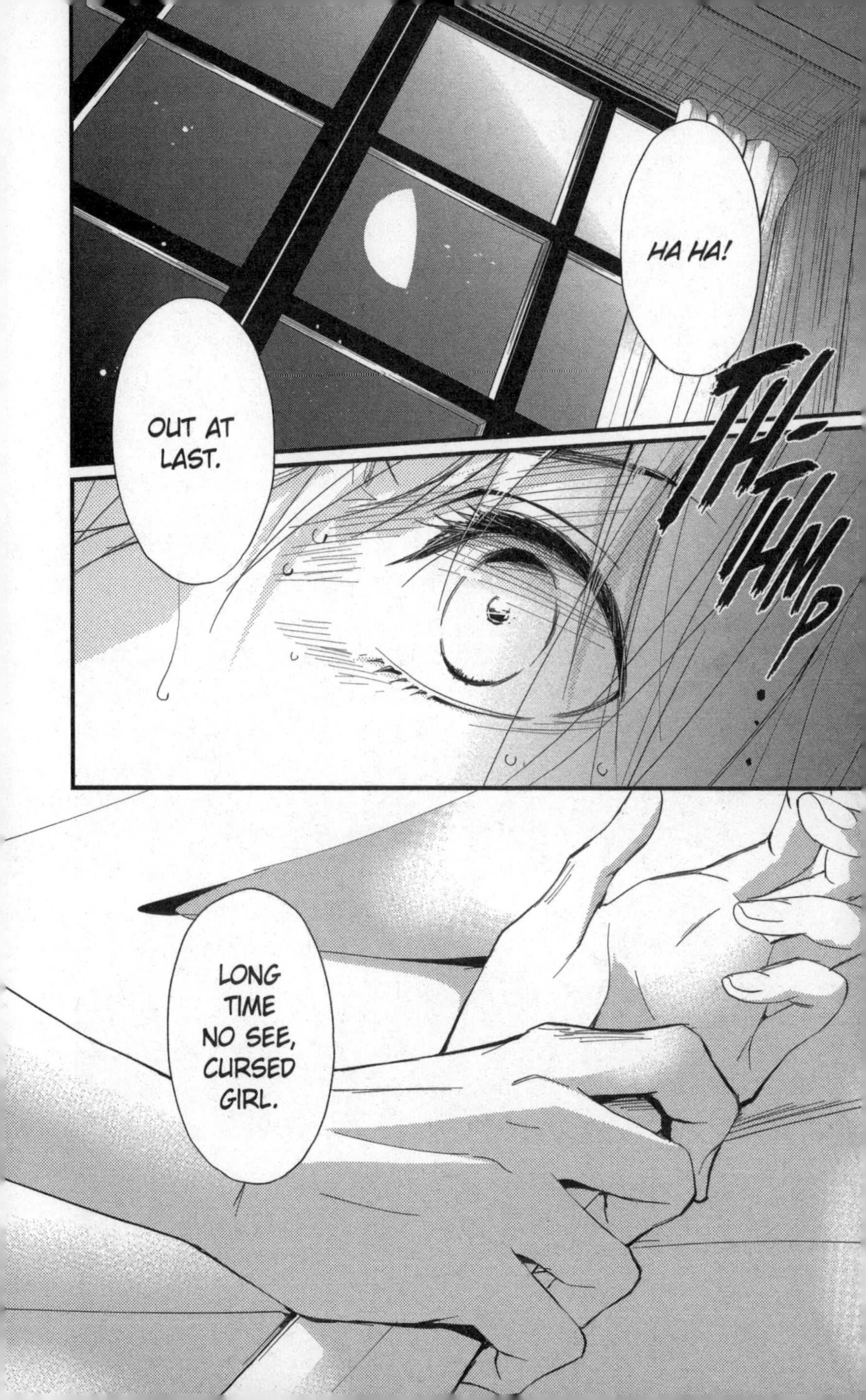
HA HA!
OUT AT LAST.
TH-THUMP...
LONG TIME NO SEE, CURSED GIRL.

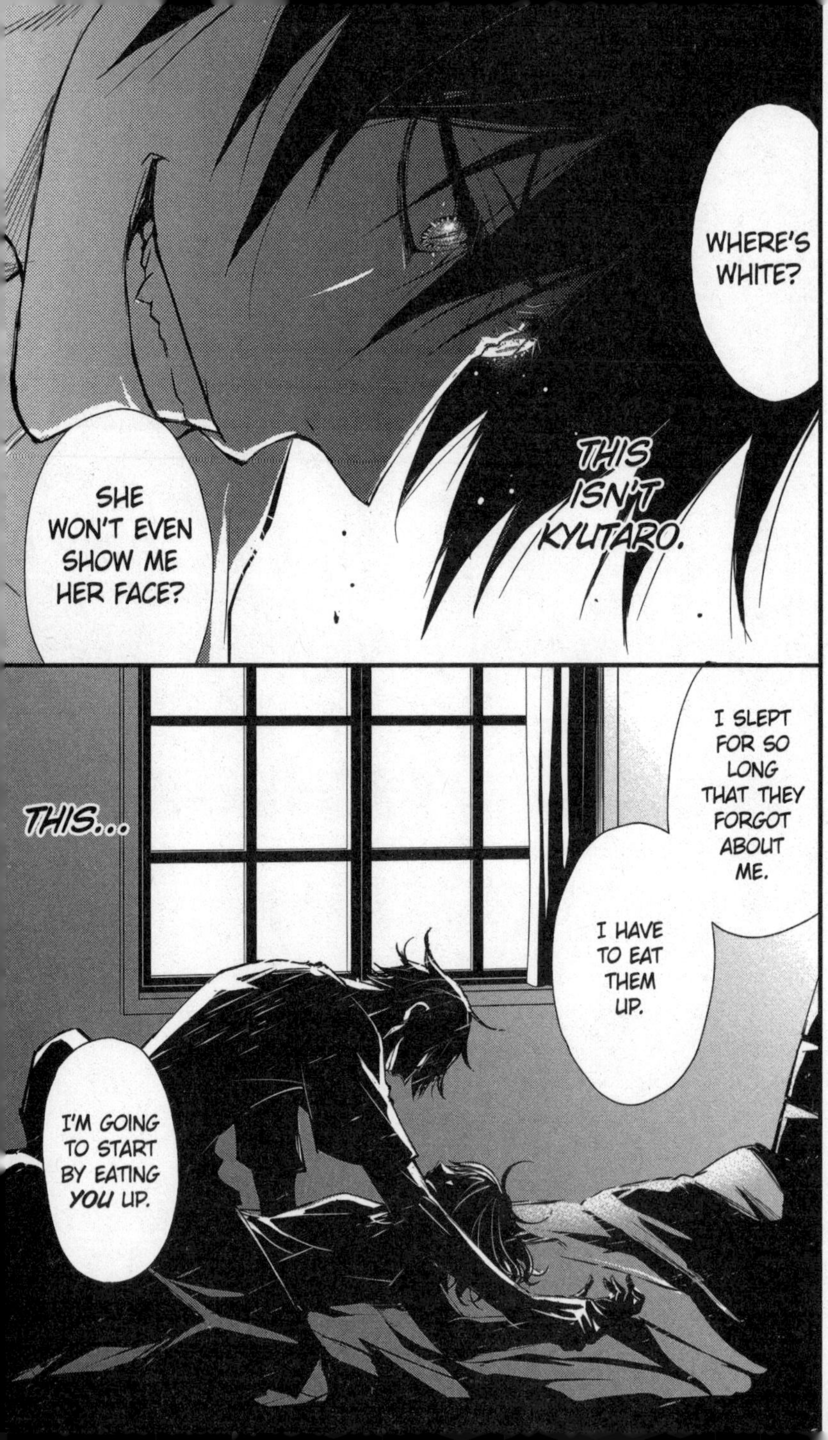
WHERE'S WHITE?
THIS ISN'T KYUTARO.
SHE WON'T EVEN SHOW ME HER FACE?
I SLEPT FOR SO LONG THAT THEY FORGOT ABOUT ME.
I HAVE TO EAT THEM UP.
THIS...
I'M GOING TO START BY EATING *YOU* UP.

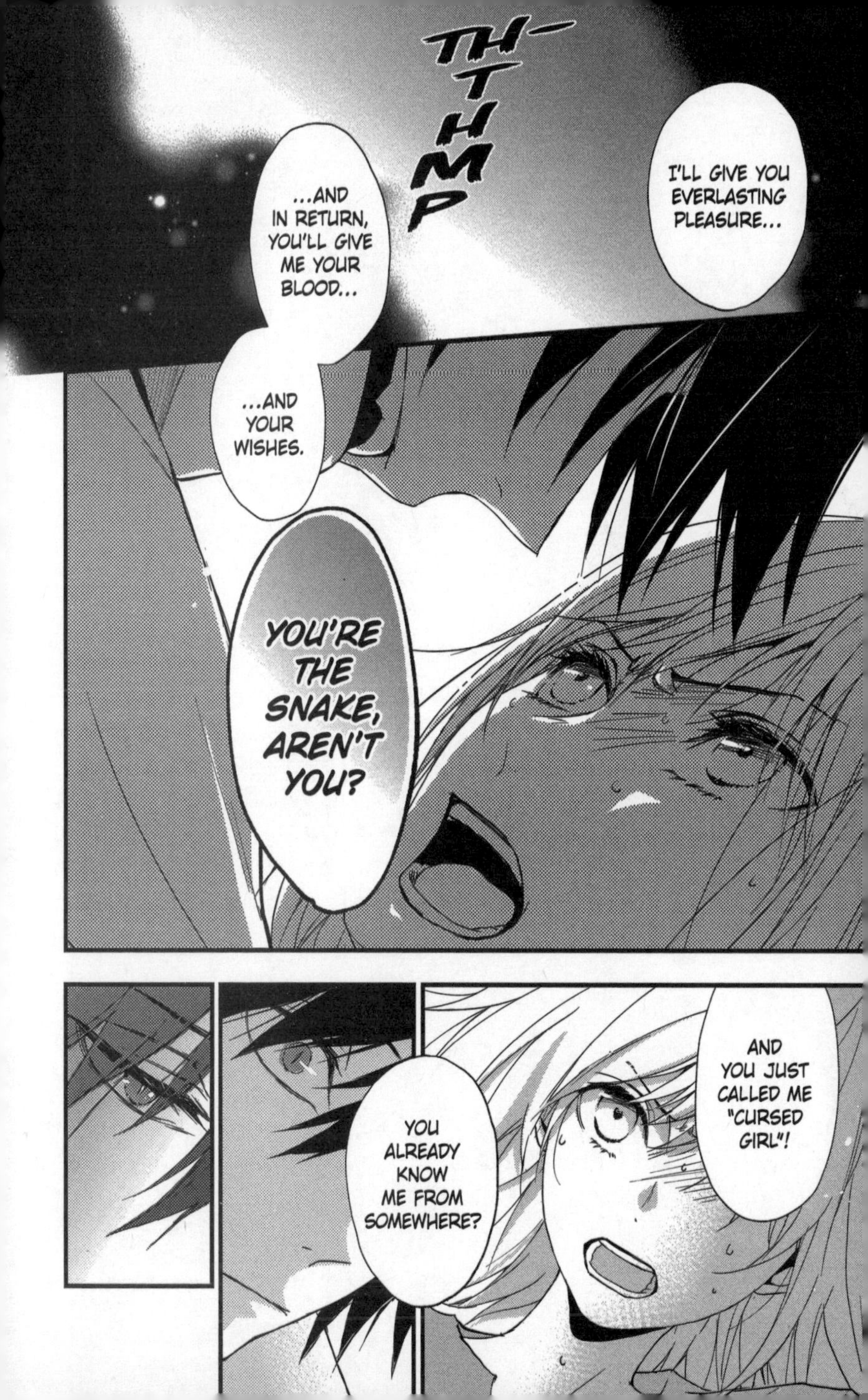
I'LL GIVE YOU EVERLASTING PLEASURE...
TH-THMP
...AND IN RETURN, YOU'LL GIVE ME YOUR BLOOD...
...AND YOUR WISHES.
YOU'RE THE SNAKE, AREN'T YOU?
AND YOU JUST CALLED ME "CURSED GIRL"!
YOU ALREADY KNOW ME FROM SOMEWHERE?

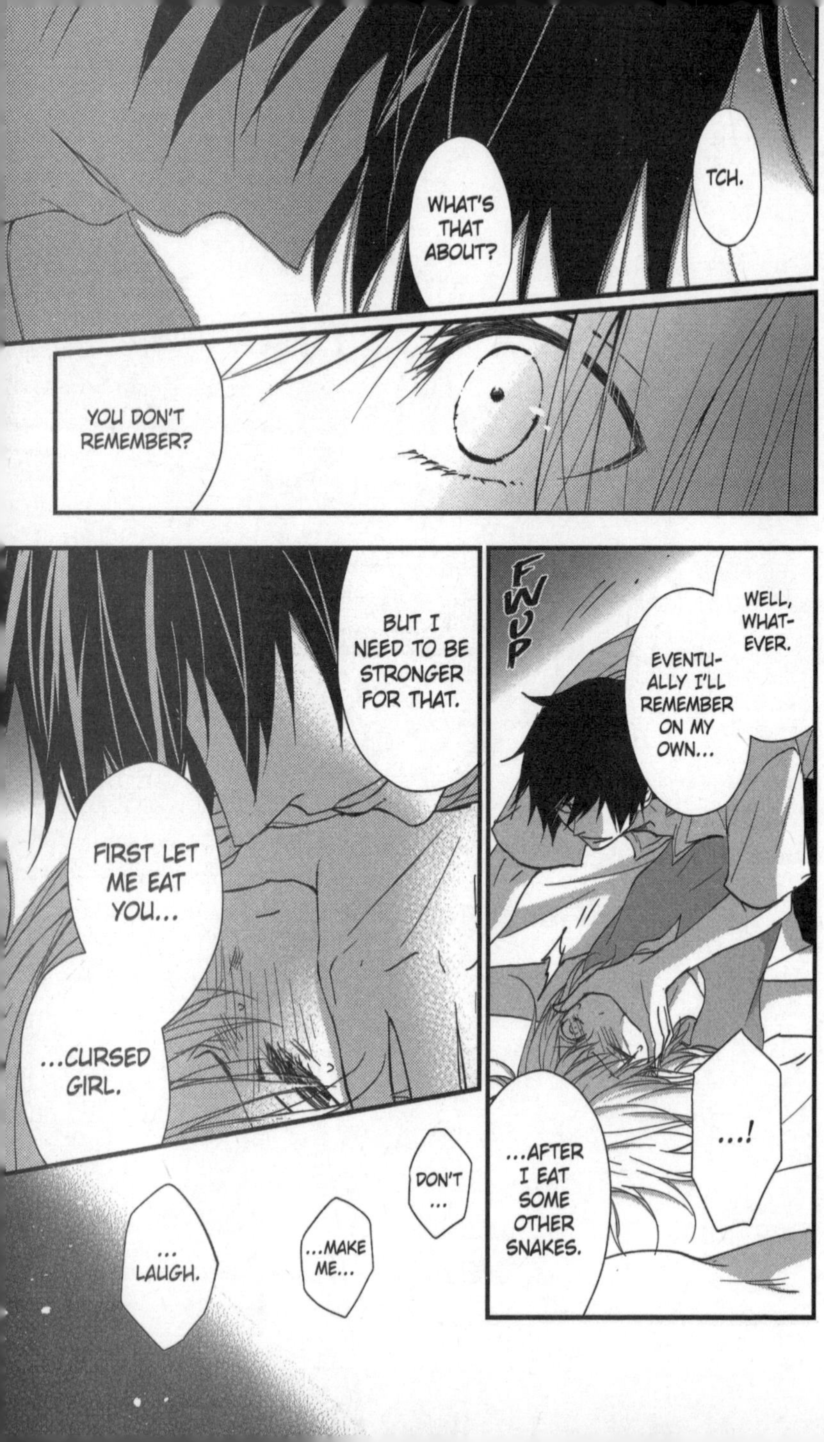
TCH.
WHAT'S THAT ABOUT?
YOU DON'T REMEMBER?
FWUP
WELL, WHAT-EVER.
EVENTU-ALLY I'LL REMEMBER ON MY OWN...
...!
...AFTER I EAT SOME OTHER SNAKES.
BUT I NEED TO BE STRONGER FOR THAT.
FIRST LET ME EAT YOU...
...CURSED GIRL.
DON'T ...
...MAKE ME...
... LAUGH.

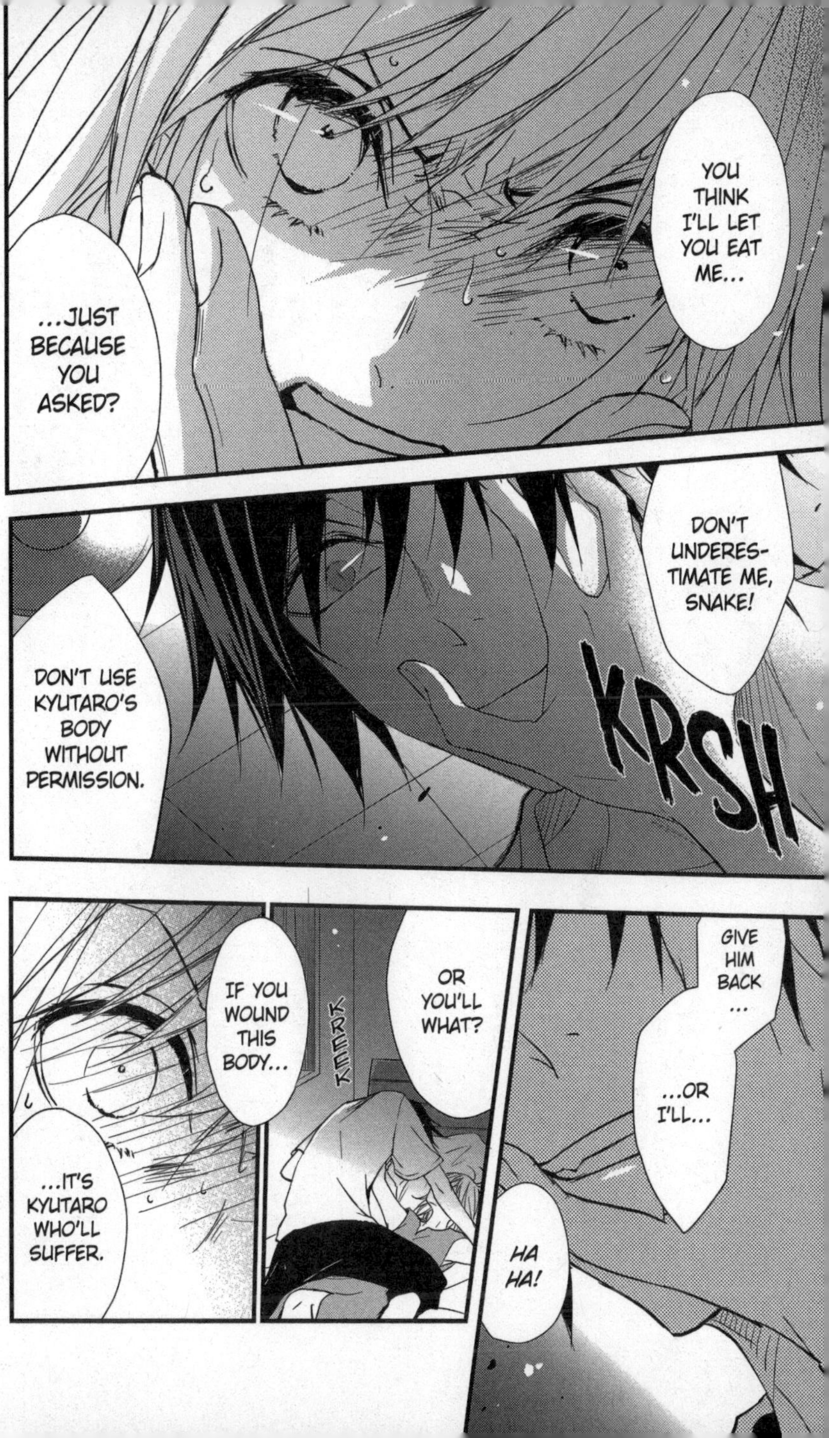
YOU THINK I'LL LET YOU EAT ME...
...JUST BECAUSE YOU ASKED?
DON'T UNDERES-TIMATE ME, SNAKE!
KRSH
DON'T USE KYUTARO'S BODY WITHOUT PERMISSION.
GIVE HIM BACK...
...OR I'LL...
HA HA!
OR YOU'LL WHAT?
KREEK
IF YOU WOUND THIS BODY...
...IT'S KYUTARO WHO'LL SUFFER.

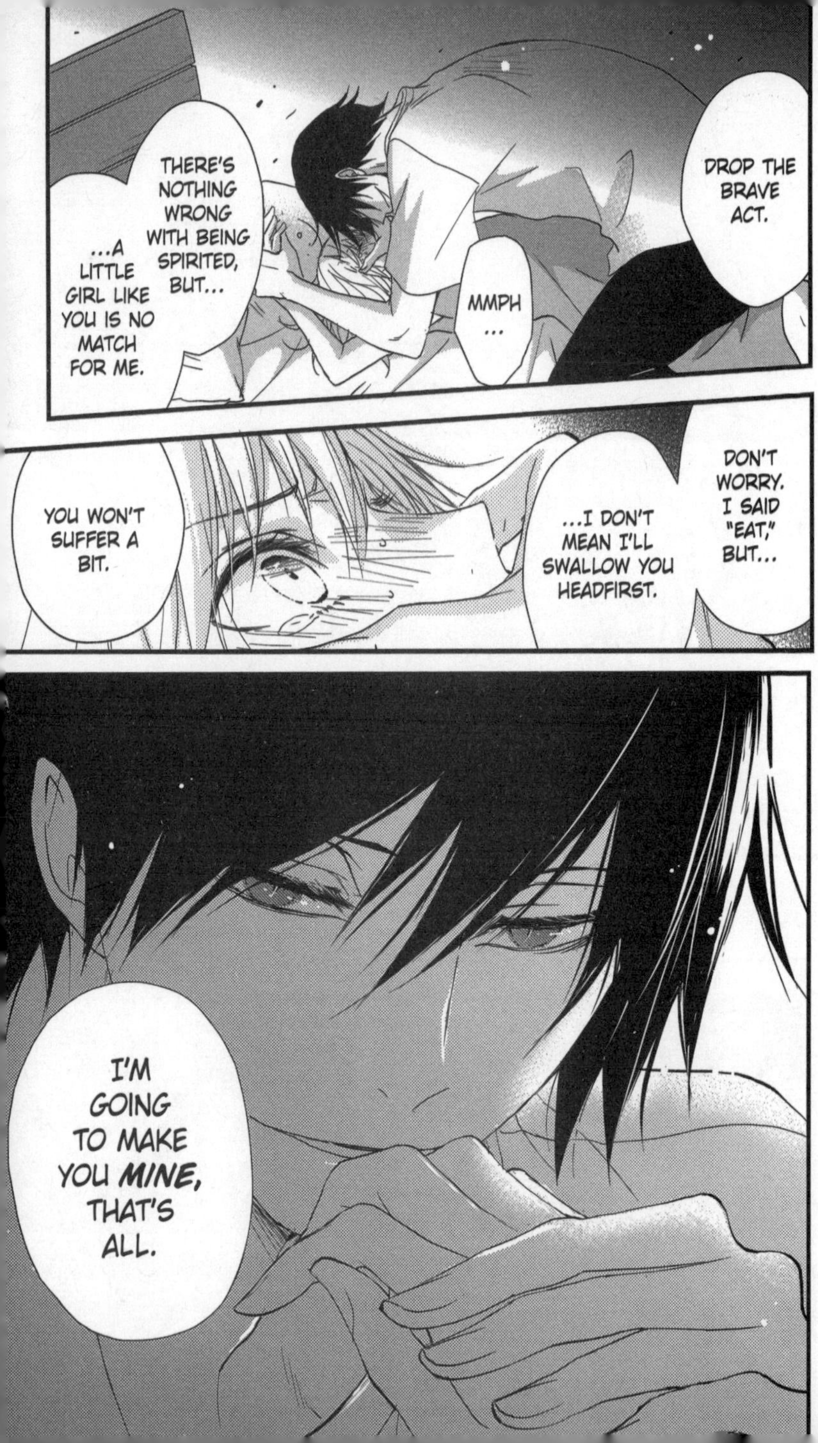
DROP THE BRAVE ACT.
MMPH...
THERE'S NOTHING WRONG WITH BEING SPIRITED, BUT...
...A LITTLE GIRL LIKE YOU IS NO MATCH FOR ME.
DON'T WORRY. I SAID "EAT," BUT...
...I DON'T MEAN I'LL SWALLOW YOU HEADFIRST.
YOU WON'T SUFFER A BIT.
I'M GOING TO MAKE YOU *MINE,* THAT'S ALL.

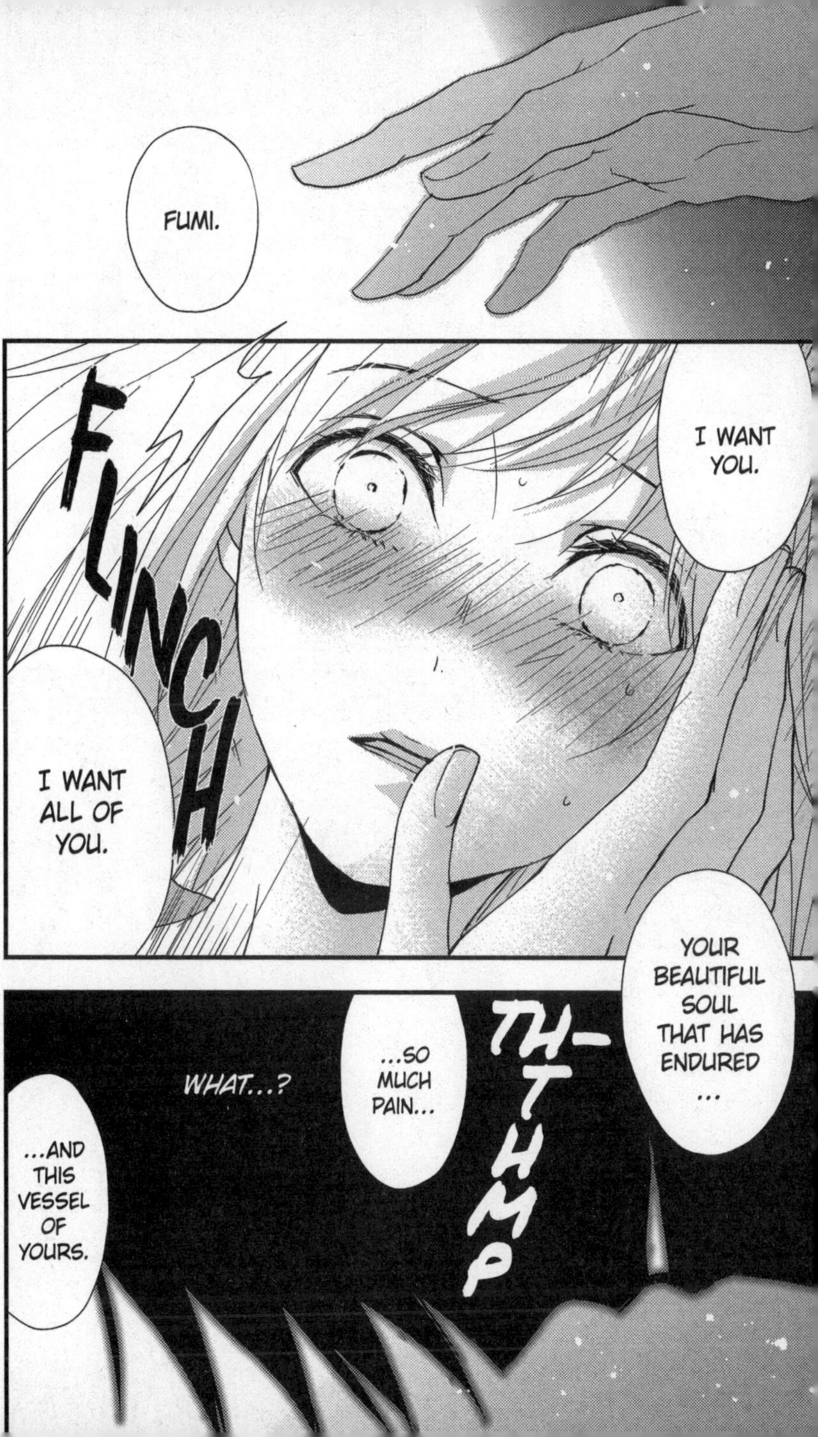
FUMI.
I WANT YOU.
FLINCH
I WANT ALL OF YOU.
YOUR BEAUTIFUL SOUL THAT HAS ENDURED...
TH-THUMP
...SO MUCH PAIN...
WHAT...?
...AND THIS VESSEL OF YOURS.

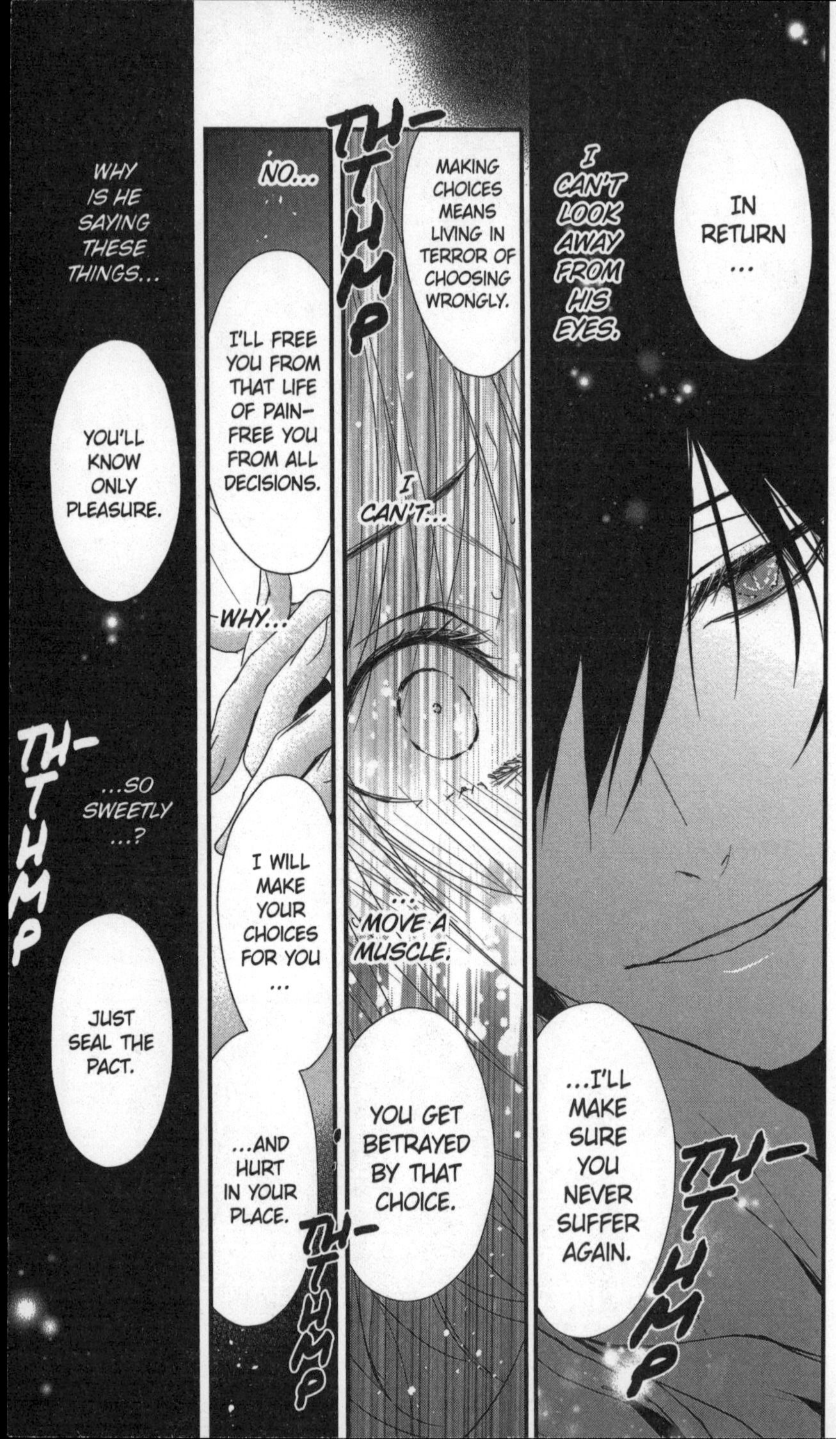
IN RETURN ...
I CAN'T LOOK AWAY FROM HIS EYES.
...I'LL MAKE SURE YOU NEVER SUFFER AGAIN.
TH-THUMP
TH-THUMP
MAKING CHOICES MEANS LIVING IN TERROR OF CHOOSING WRONGLY.
I CAN'T...
...MOVE A MUSCLE.
YOU GET BETRAYED BY THAT CHOICE.
NO...
I'LL FREE YOU FROM THAT LIFE OF PAIN—FREE YOU FROM ALL DECISIONS.
WHY...
I WILL MAKE YOUR CHOICES FOR YOU ...
...AND HURT IN YOUR PLACE.
TH-THUMP
WHY IS HE SAYING THESE THINGS...
YOU'LL KNOW ONLY PLEASURE.
TH-THUMP
...SO SWEETLY ...?
JUST SEAL THE PACT.

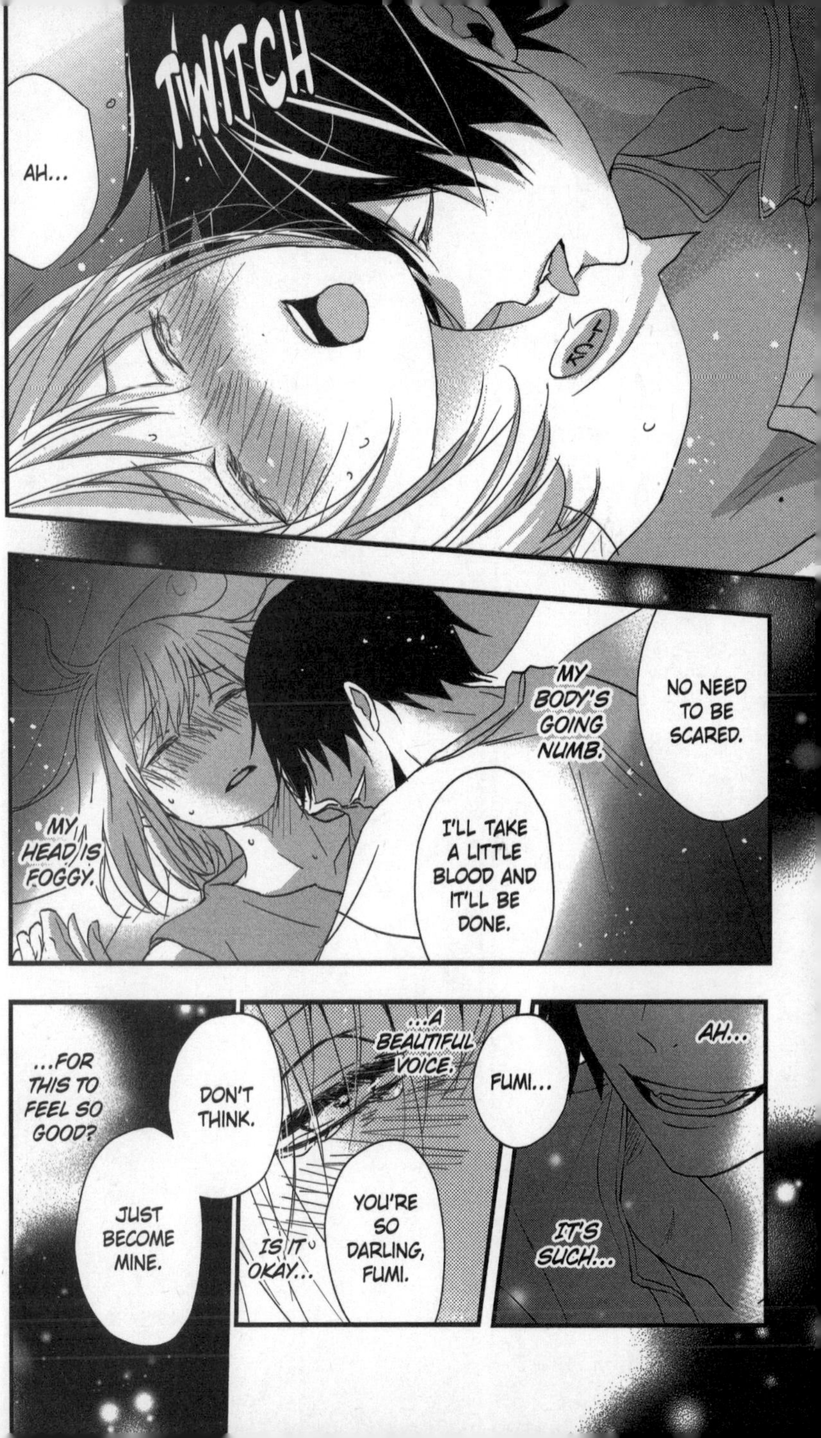
TWITCH
LICK
AH...
NO NEED TO BE SCARED.
MY BODY'S GOING NUMB.
I'LL TAKE A LITTLE BLOOD AND IT'LL BE DONE.
MY HEAD IS FOGGY.
AH...
FUMI...
IT'S SUCH...
...A BEAUTIFUL VOICE.
YOU'RE SO DARLING, FUMI.
IS IT OKAY...
...FOR THIS TO FEEL SO GOOD?
DON'T THINK.
JUST BECOME MINE.

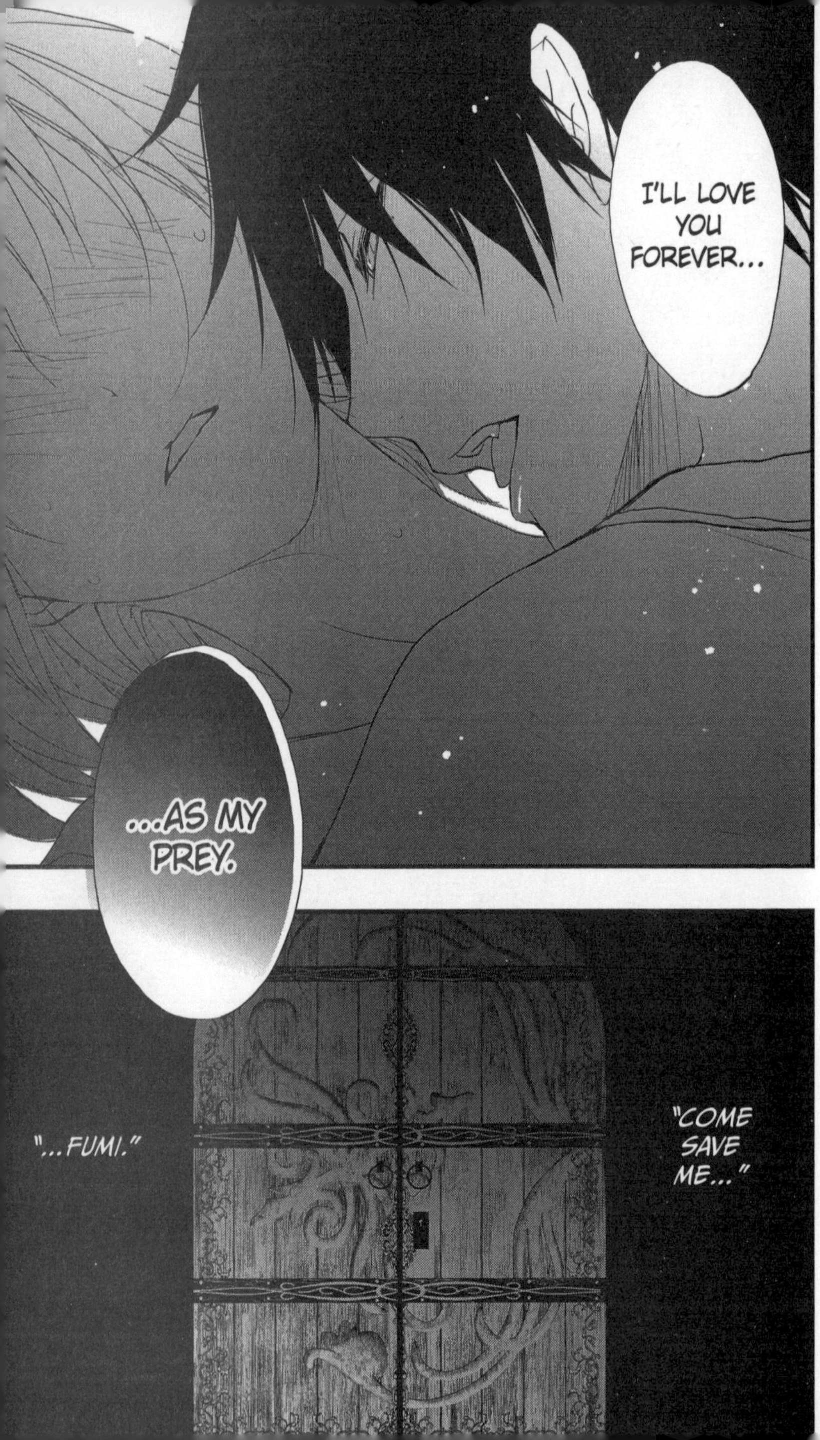
I'LL LOVE YOU FOREVER...
...AS MY PREY.
"COME SAVE ME..."
"...FUMI."

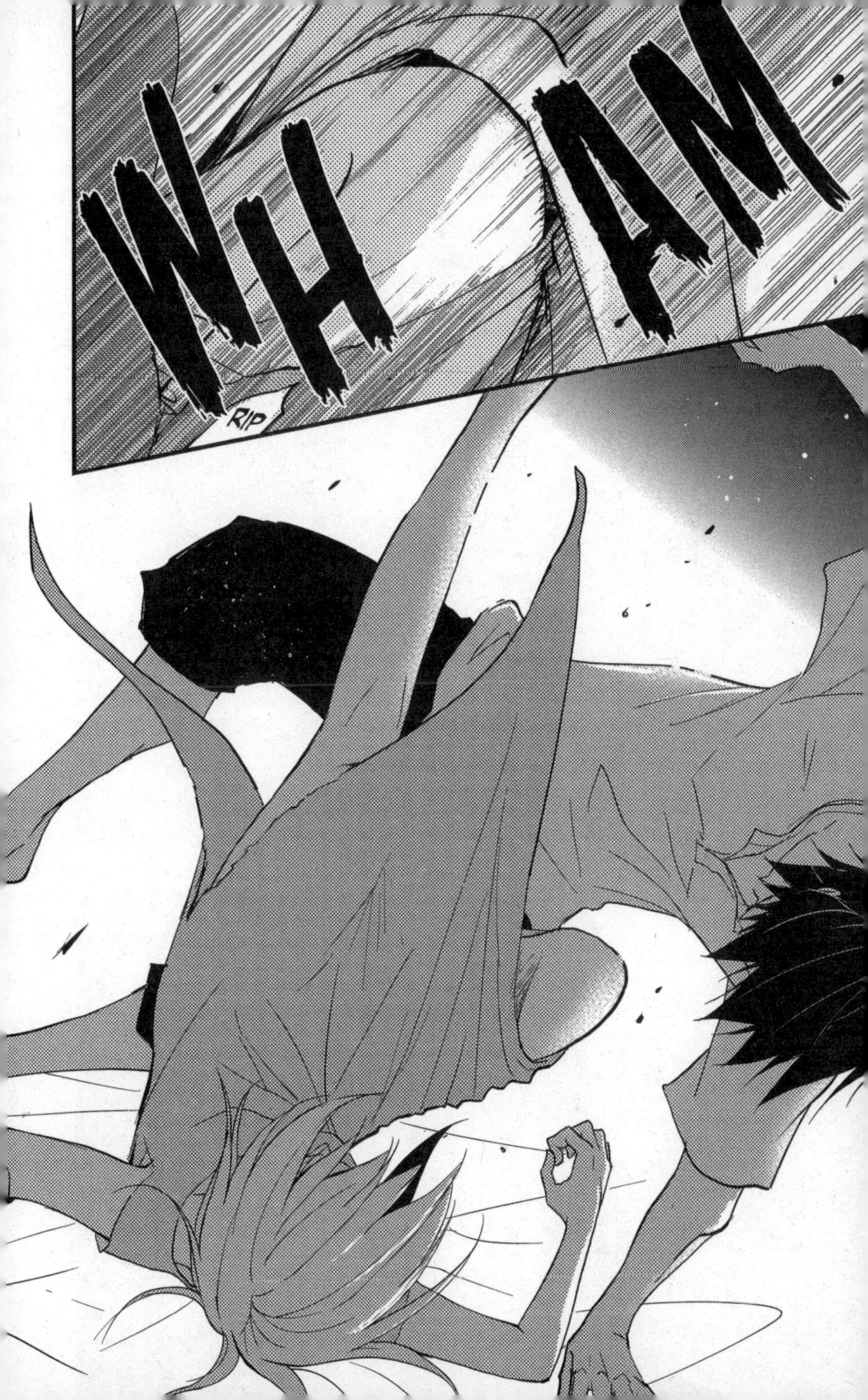
WHAM
RIP

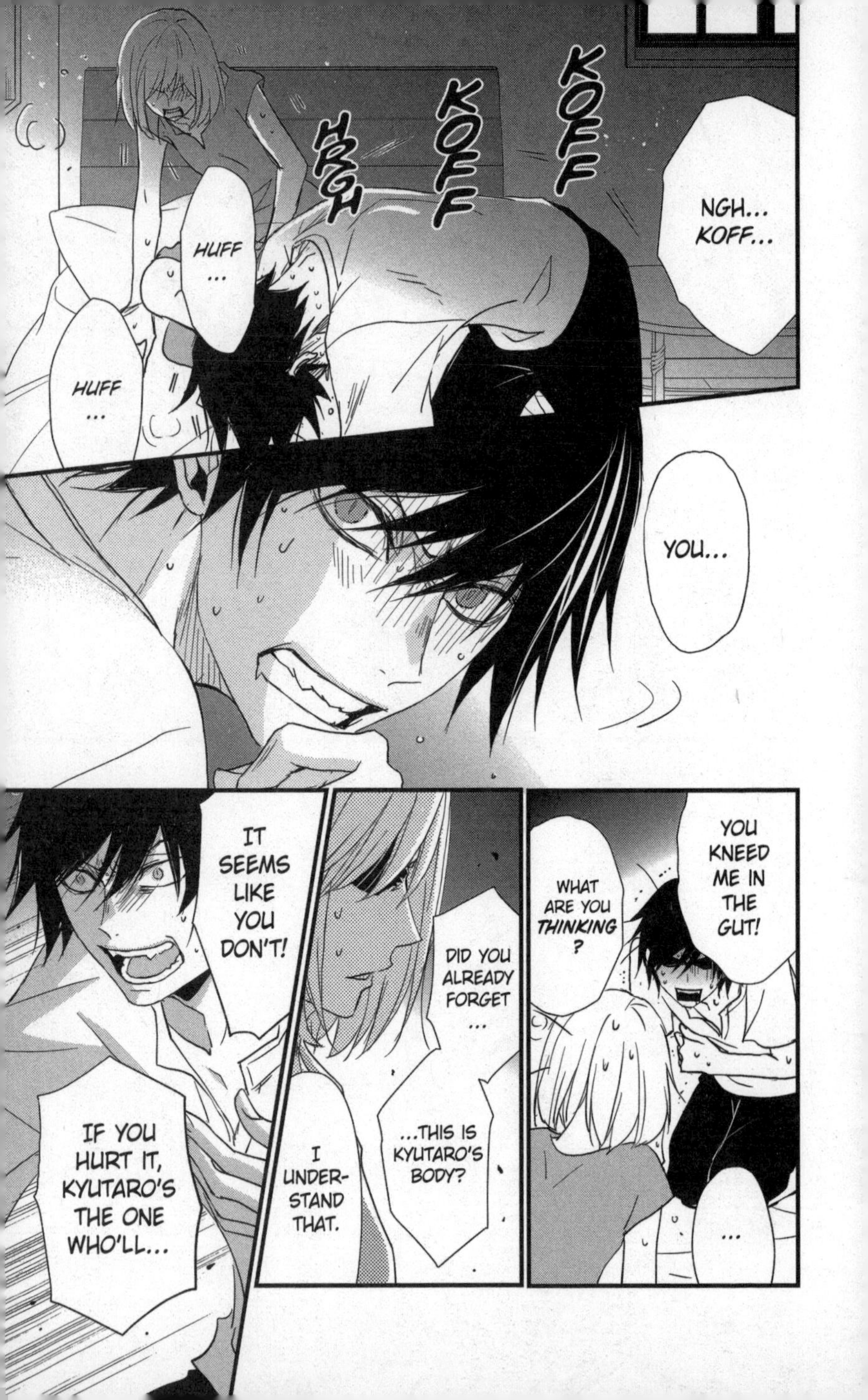
NGH... KOFF...
KOFF
KOFF
HNGH
HUFF...
HUFF...
YOU...
YOU KNEED ME IN THE GUT!
WHAT ARE YOU *THINKING*?
...
DID YOU ALREADY FORGET...
...THIS IS KYUTARO'S BODY?
I UNDER-STAND THAT.
IT SEEMS LIKE YOU DON'T!
IF YOU HURT IT, KYUTARO'S THE ONE WHO'LL...

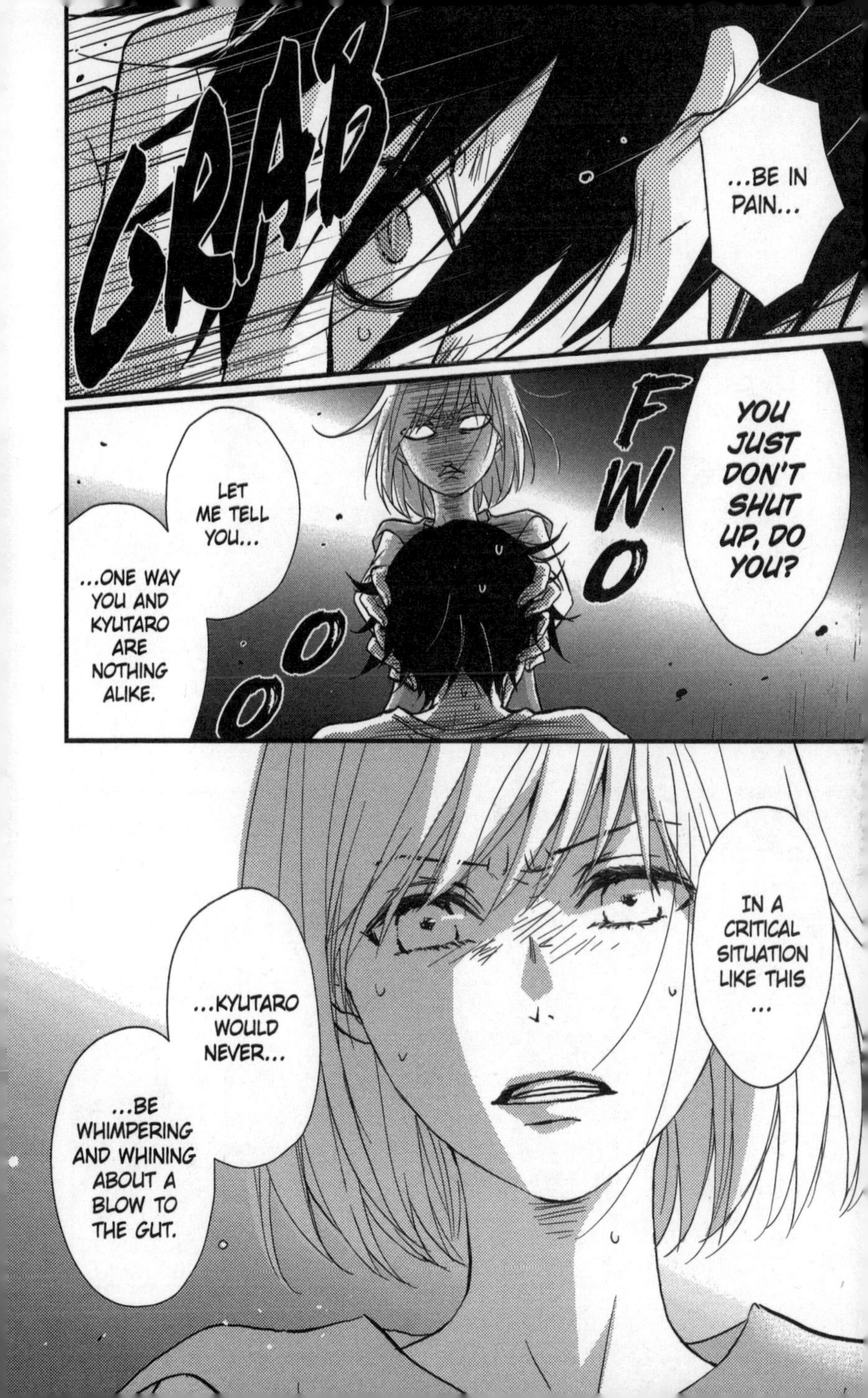
...BE IN PAIN...
GRAB
YOU JUST DON'T SHUT UP, DO YOU?
FWOOO
LET ME TELL YOU...
...ONE WAY YOU AND KYUTARO ARE NOTHING ALIKE.
IN A CRITICAL SITUATION LIKE THIS ...
...KYUTARO WOULD NEVER...
...BE WHIMPERING AND WHINING ABOUT A BLOW TO THE GUT.

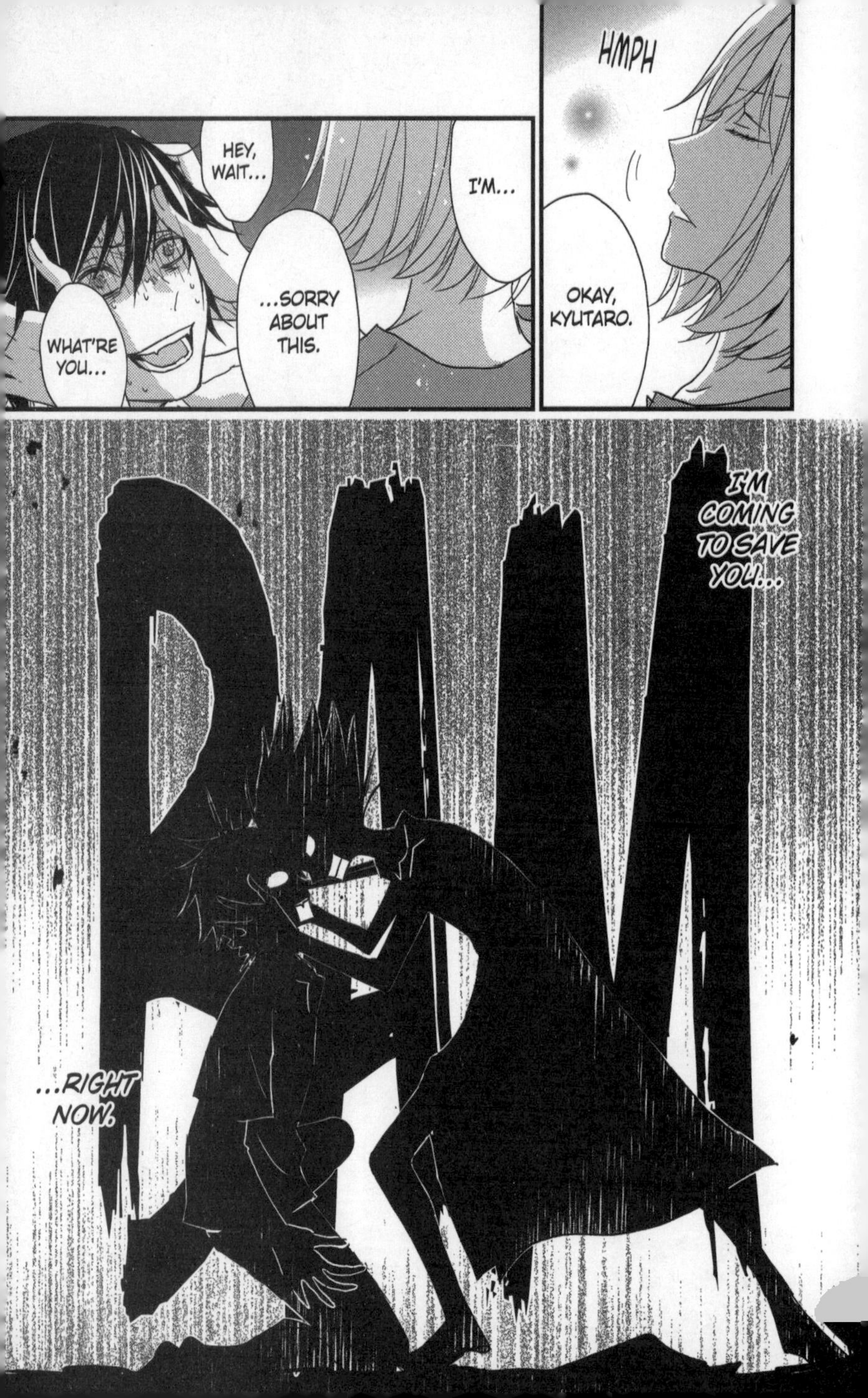
HMPH
OKAY, KYUTARO.
I'M...
HEY, WAIT...
...SORRY ABOUT THIS.
WHAT'RE YOU...
I'M COMING TO SAVE YOU...
...RIGHT NOW.

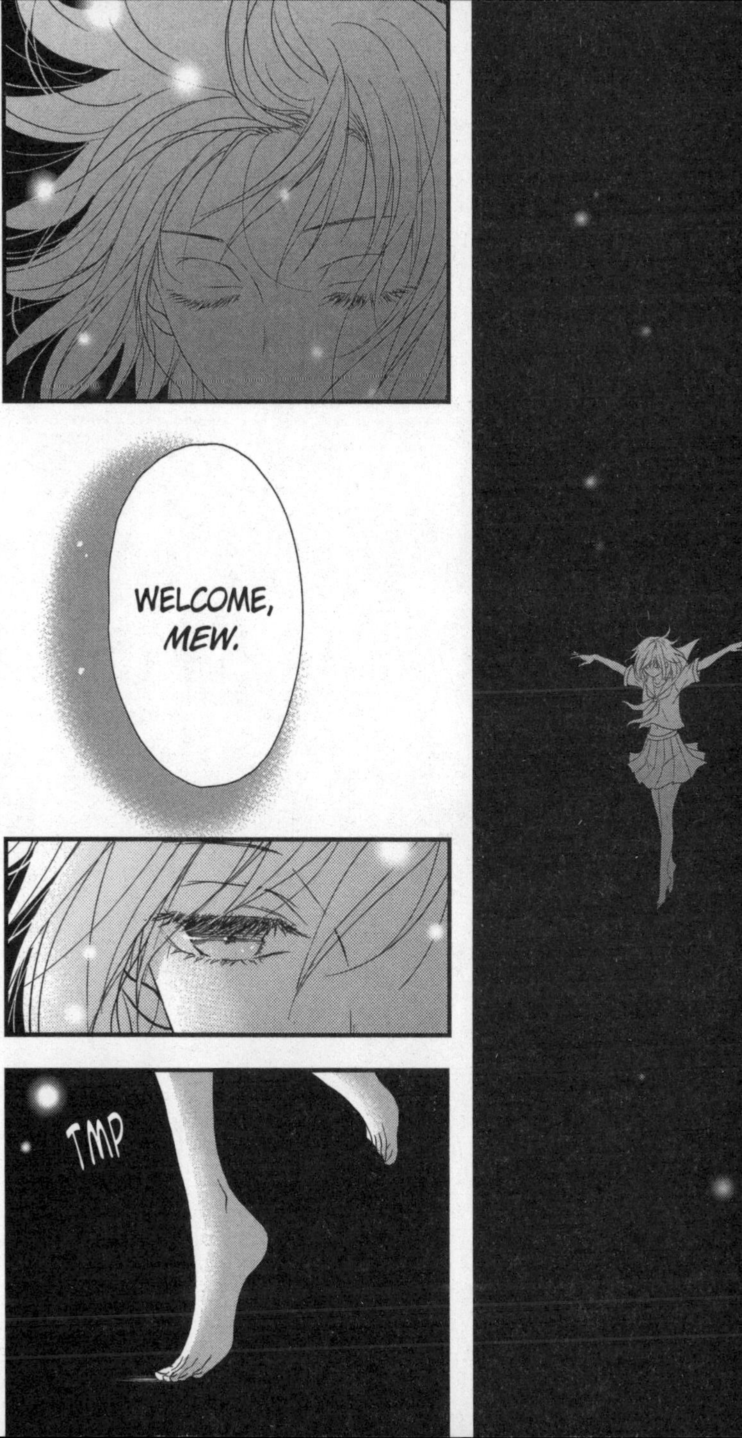
WELCOME, MEW.
TMP

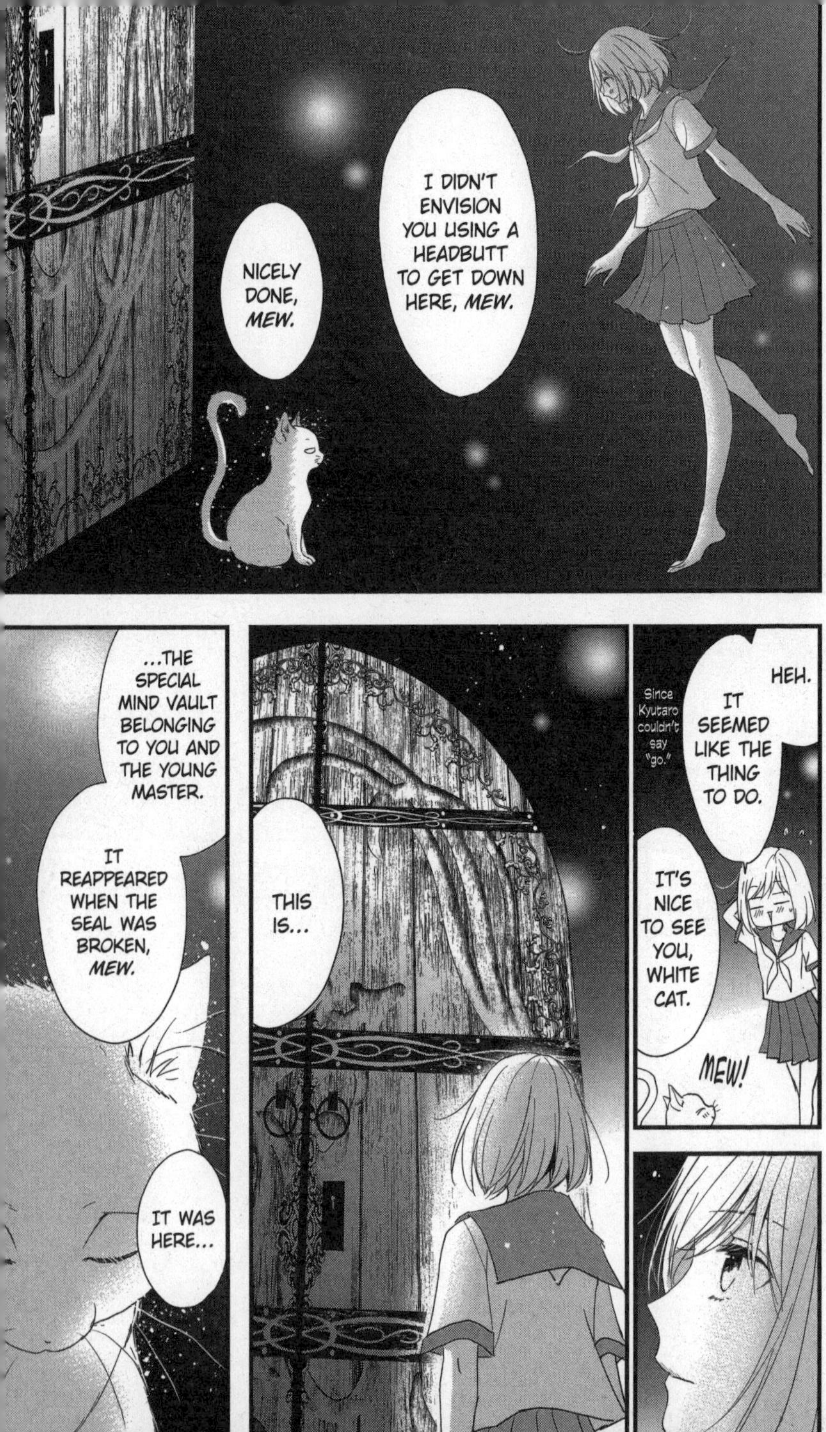
I DIDN'T ENVISION YOU USING A HEADBUTT TO GET DOWN HERE, *MEW.*
NICELY DONE, *MEW.*
HEH.
IT SEEMED LIKE THE THING TO DO.
Since Kyutaro couldn't say "go."
IT'S NICE TO SEE YOU, WHITE CAT.
MEW!
THIS IS...
...THE SPECIAL MIND VAULT BELONGING TO YOU AND THE YOUNG MASTER.
IT REAPPEARED WHEN THE SEAL WAS BROKEN, *MEW.*
IT WAS HERE...

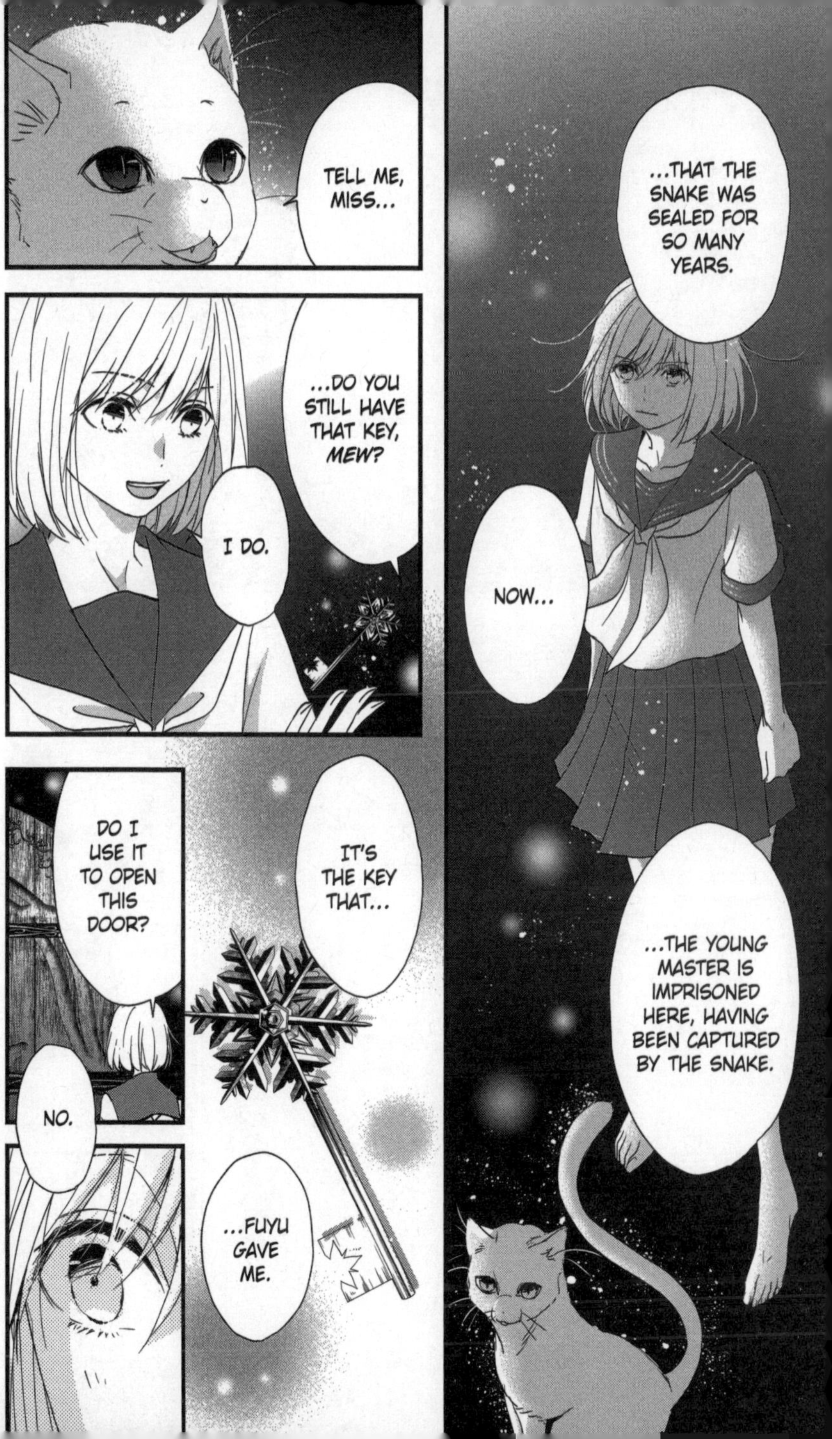
...THAT THE SNAKE WAS SEALED FOR SO MANY YEARS.
NOW...
...THE YOUNG MASTER IS IMPRISONED HERE, HAVING BEEN CAPTURED BY THE SNAKE.
TELL ME, MISS...
...DO YOU STILL HAVE THAT KEY, *MEW?*
I DO.
IT'S THE KEY THAT...
DO I USE IT TO OPEN THIS DOOR?
NO.
...FUYU GAVE ME.

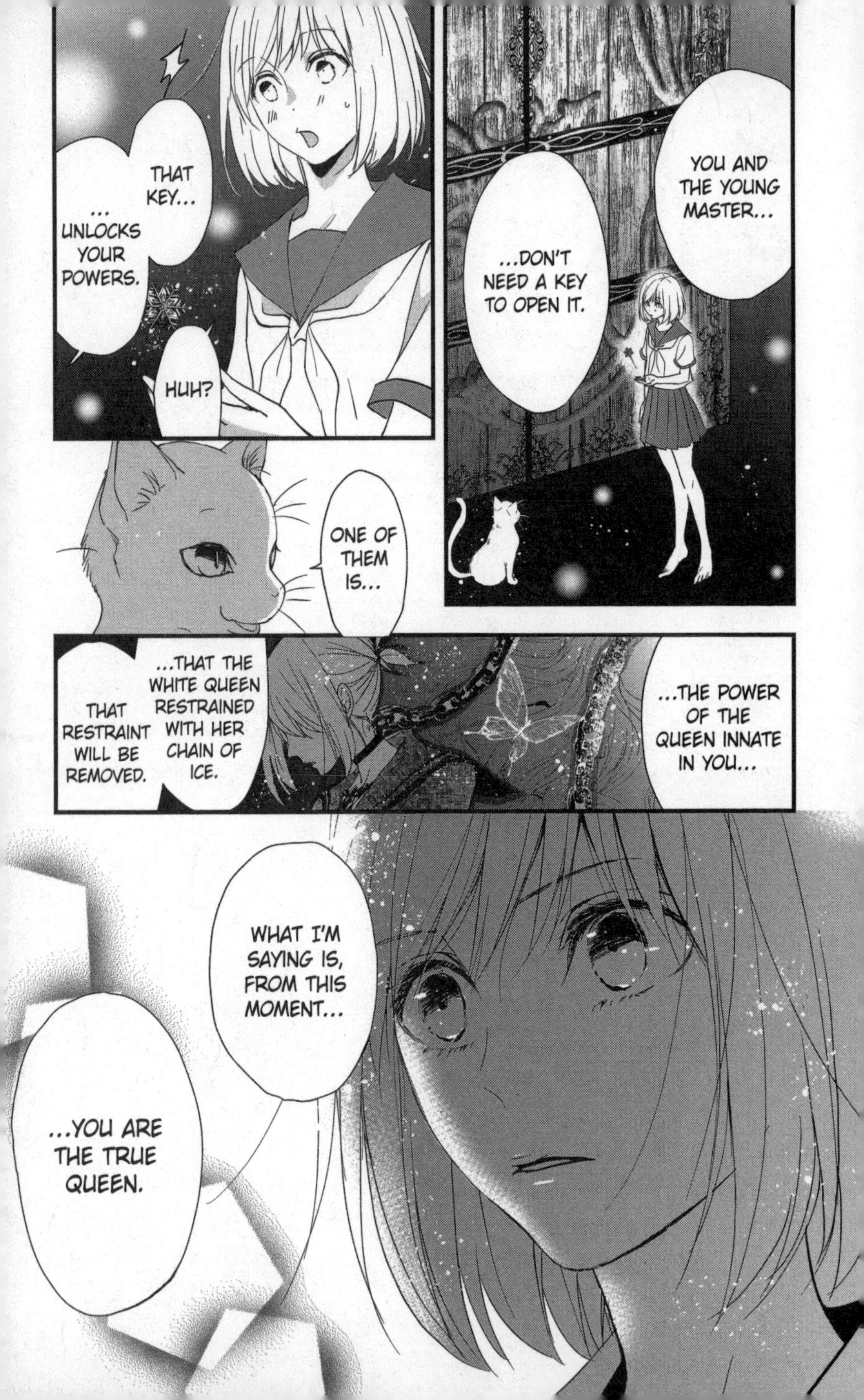
YOU AND THE YOUNG MASTER...
...DON'T NEED A KEY TO OPEN IT.
THAT KEY... ...UNLOCKS YOUR POWERS.
HUH?
ONE OF THEM IS...
...THE POWER OF THE QUEEN INNATE IN YOU...
...THAT THE WHITE QUEEN RESTRAINED WITH HER CHAIN OF ICE.
THAT RESTRAINT WILL BE REMOVED.
WHAT I'M SAYING IS, FROM THIS MOMENT...
...YOU ARE THE TRUE QUEEN.

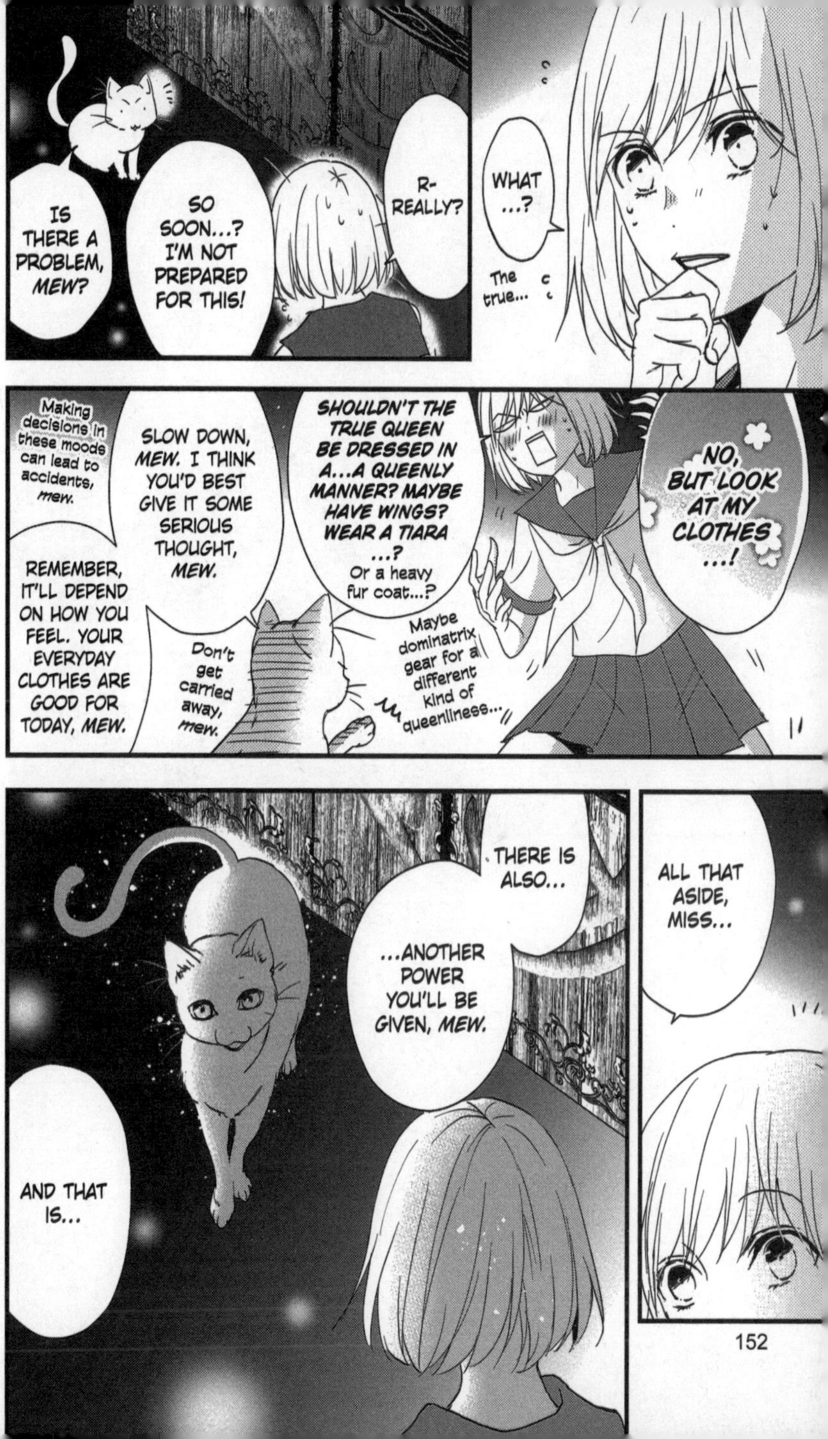
WHAT ...?
The true...
R-REALLY?
SO SOON...? I'M NOT PREPARED FOR THIS!
IS THERE A PROBLEM, MEW?
NO, BUT LOOK AT MY CLOTHES ...!
SHOULDN'T THE TRUE QUEEN BE DRESSED IN A...A QUEENLY MANNER? MAYBE HAVE WINGS? WEAR A TIARA ...?
Or a heavy fur coat...?
Maybe dominatrix gear for a different kind of queenliness...
SLOW DOWN, MEW. I THINK YOU'D BEST GIVE IT SOME SERIOUS THOUGHT, MEW.
Don't get carried away, mew.
Making decisions in these moods can lead to accidents, mew.
REMEMBER, IT'LL DEPEND ON HOW YOU FEEL. YOUR EVERYDAY CLOTHES ARE GOOD FOR TODAY, MEW.
ALL THAT ASIDE, MISS...
THERE IS ALSO...
...ANOTHER POWER YOU'LL BE GIVEN, MEW.
AND THAT IS...

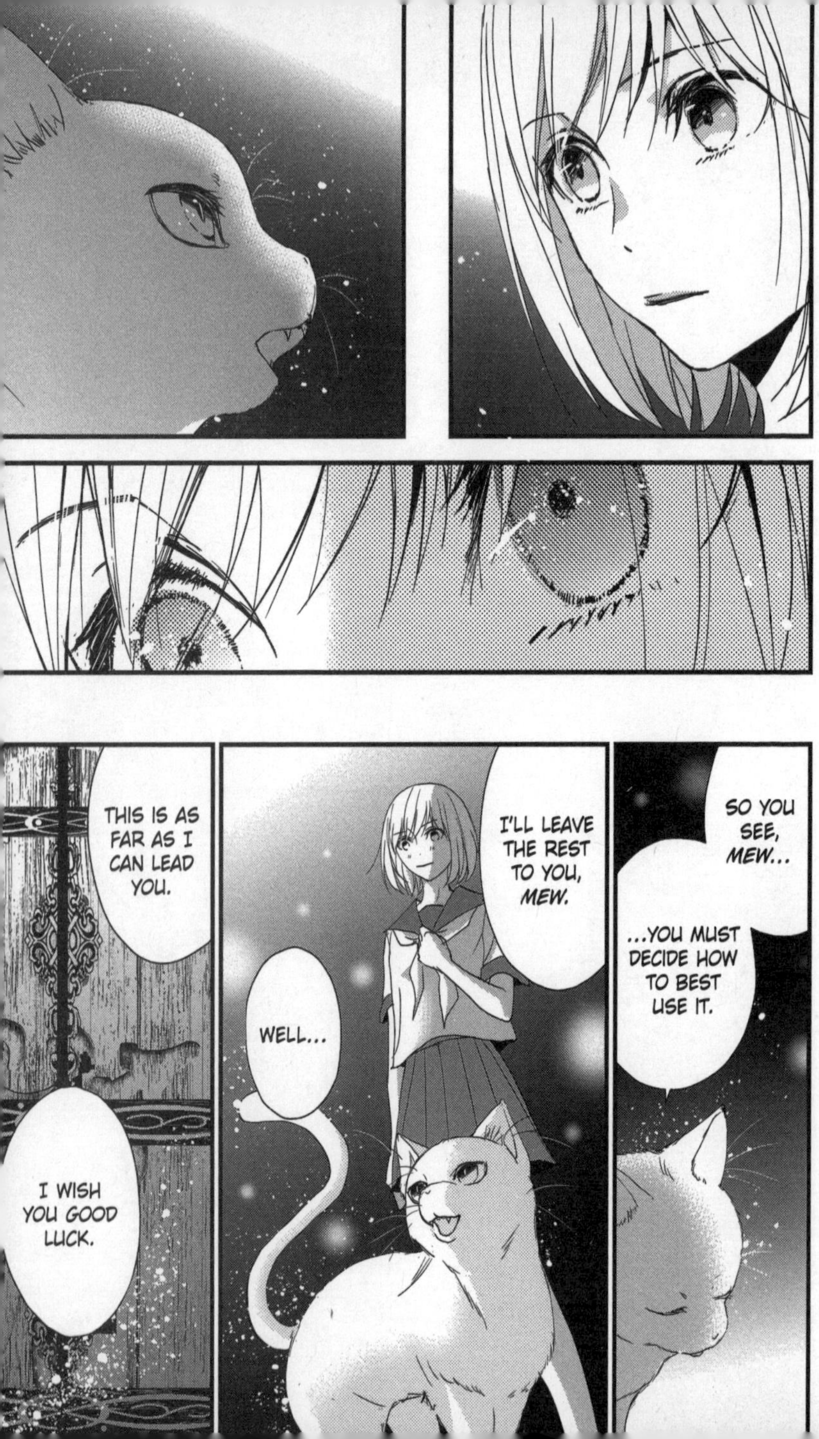
SO YOU SEE, MEW...
...YOU MUST DECIDE HOW TO BEST USE IT.
I'LL LEAVE THE REST TO YOU, MEW.
WELL...
THIS IS AS FAR AS I CAN LEAD YOU.
I WISH YOU GOOD LUCK.

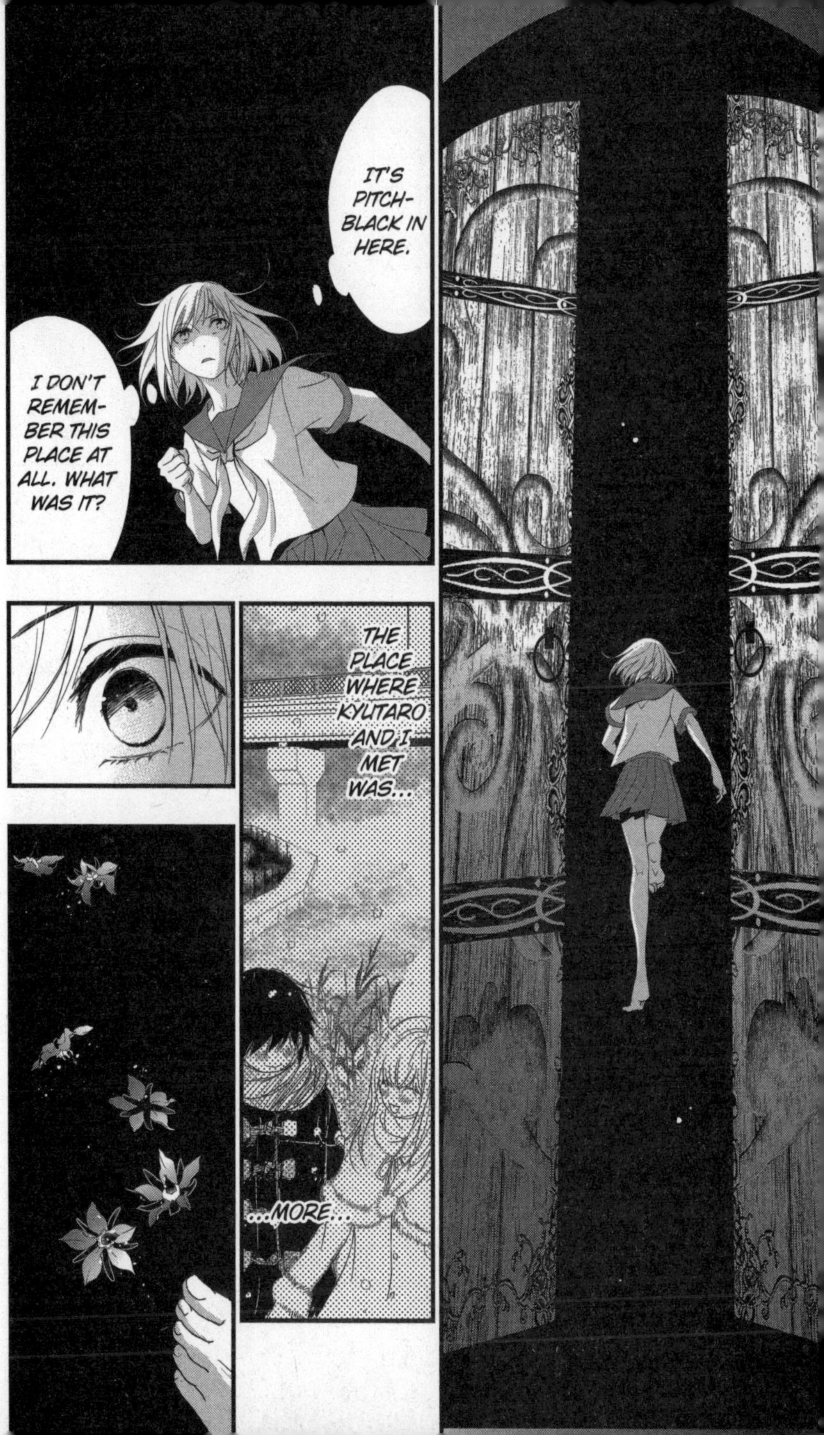
IT'S PITCH-BLACK IN HERE.
I DON'T REMEMBER THIS PLACE AT ALL. WHAT WAS IT?
THE PLACE WHERE KYUTARO AND I MET WAS...
...MORE...

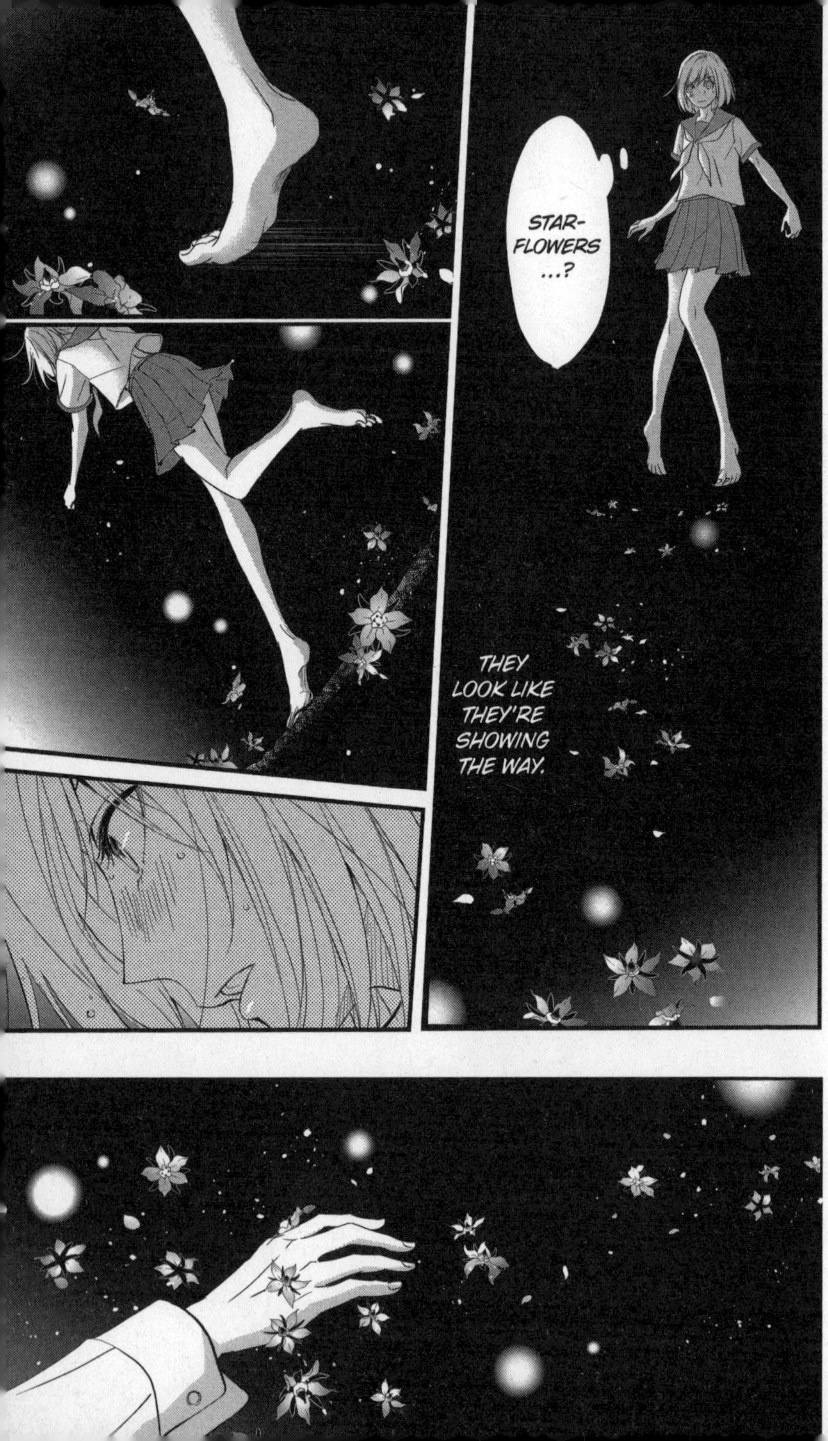
STAR-FLOWERS ...?
THEY LOOK LIKE THEY'RE SHOWING THE WAY.

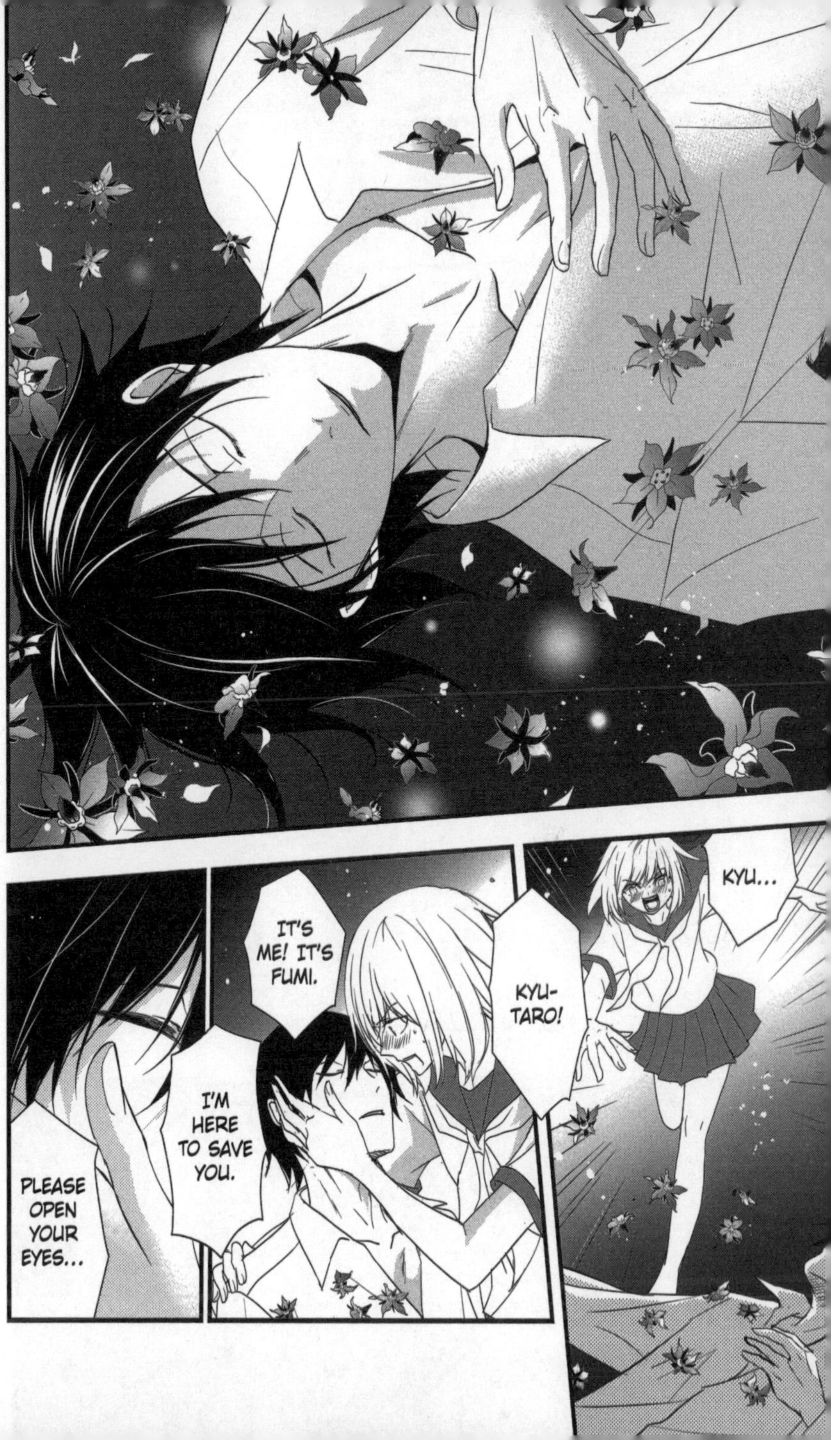
KYU...
KYU-TARO!
IT'S ME! IT'S FUMI.
I'M HERE TO SAVE YOU.
PLEASE OPEN YOUR EYES...

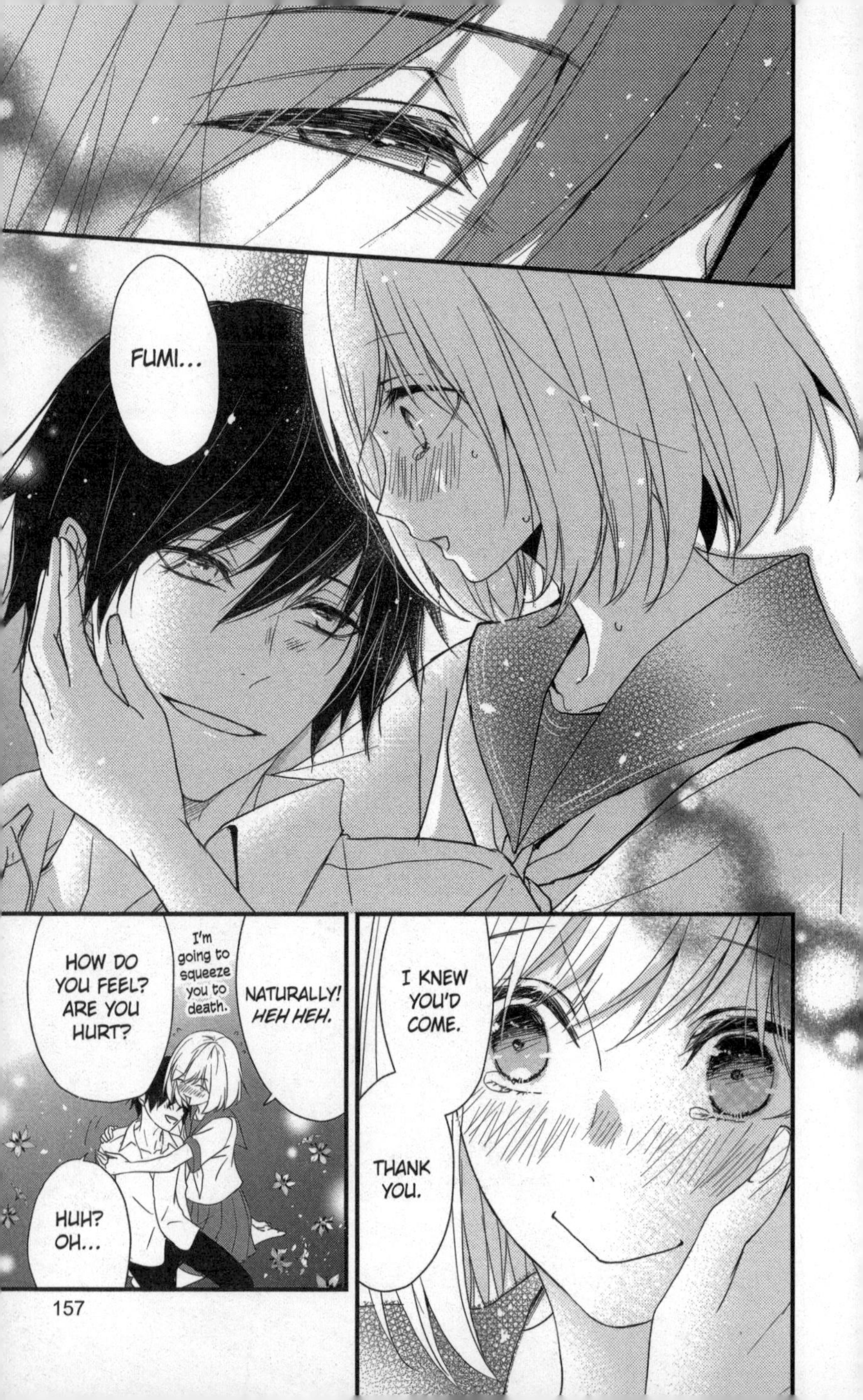
FUMI...
I KNEW YOU'D COME.
THANK YOU.
NATURALLY! HEH HEH.
I'm going to squeeze you to death.
HOW DO YOU FEEL? ARE YOU HURT?
HUH? OH...

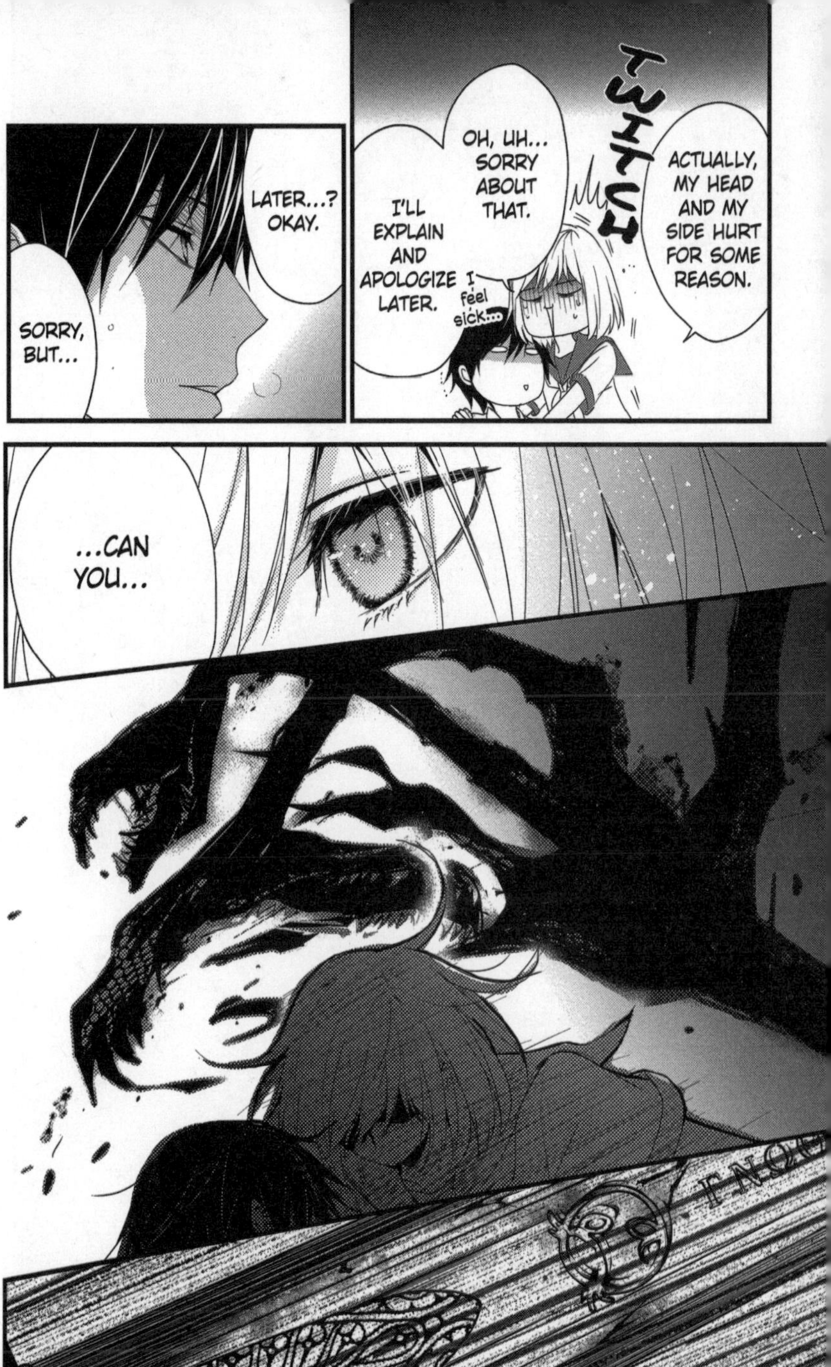
ACTUALLY, MY HEAD AND MY SIDE HURT FOR SOME REASON.
TWITCH
OH, UH... SORRY ABOUT THAT.
I'LL EXPLAIN AND APOLOGIZE LATER.
I feel sick...
LATER...? OKAY.
SORRY, BUT...
...CAN YOU...

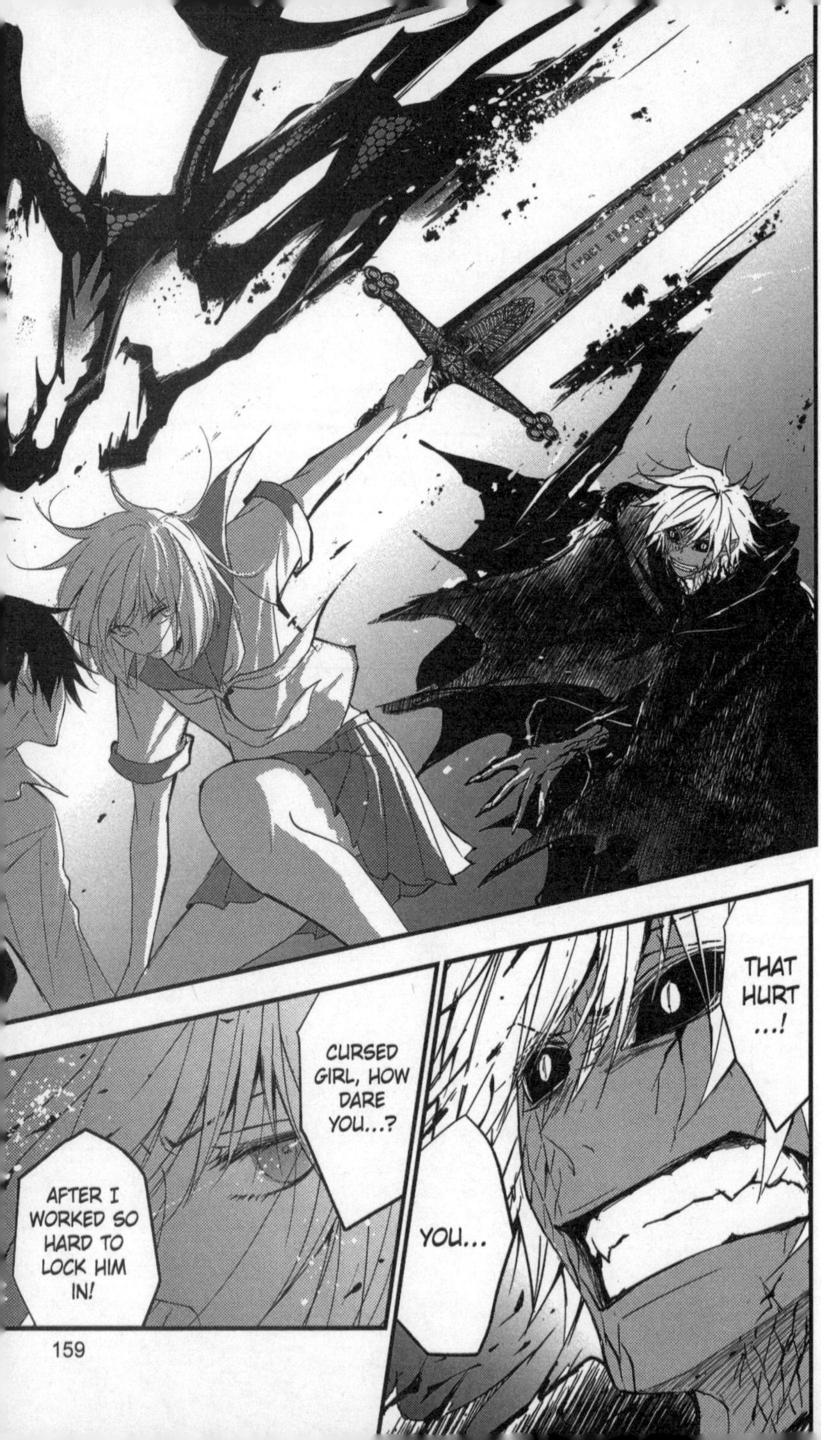
THAT HURT ...!
CURSED GIRL, HOW DARE YOU...?
YOU...
AFTER I WORKED SO HARD TO LOCK HIM IN!

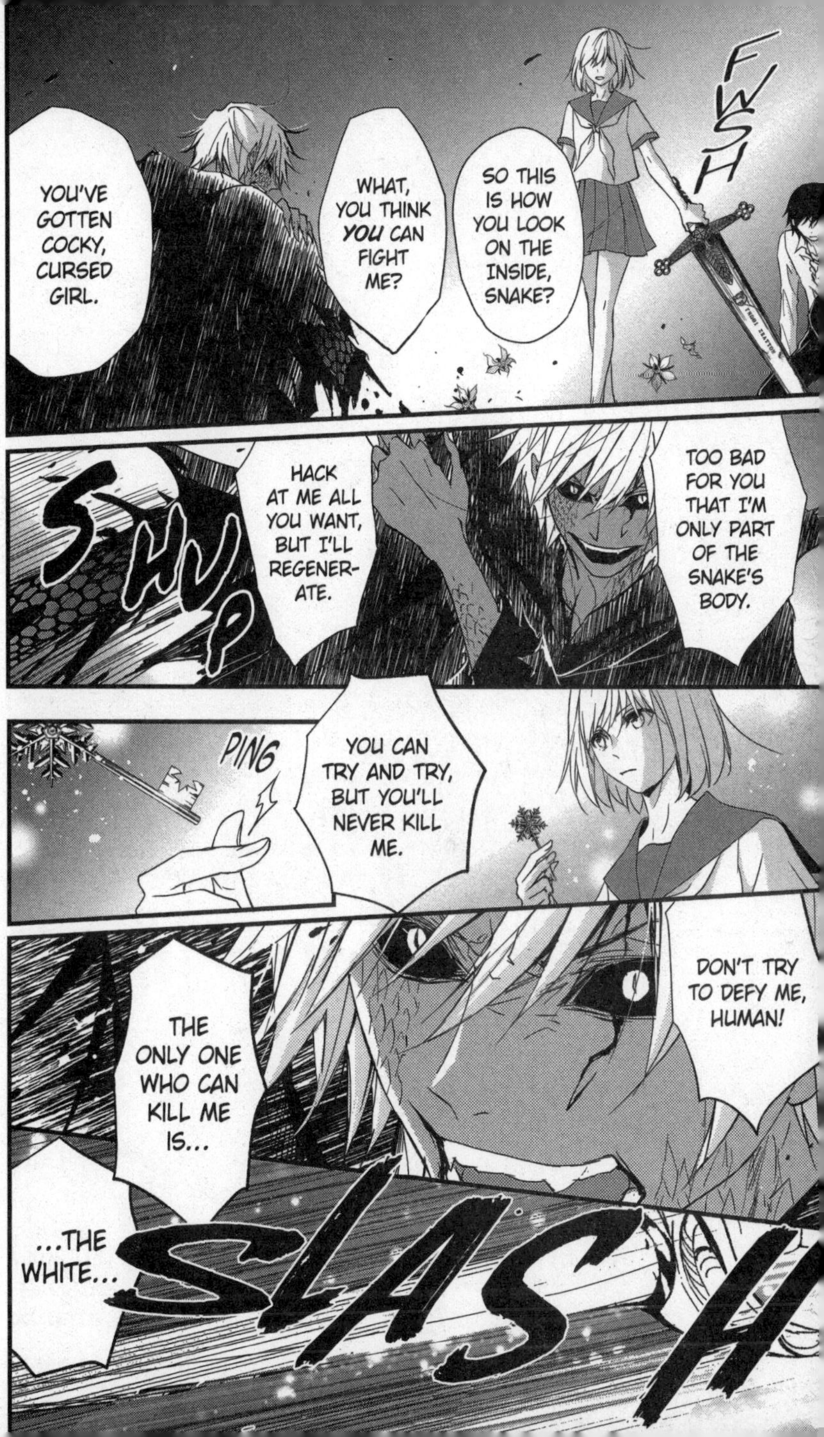
FWSH
SO THIS IS HOW YOU LOOK ON THE INSIDE, SNAKE?
WHAT, YOU THINK *YOU* CAN FIGHT ME?
YOU'VE GOTTEN COCKY, CURSED GIRL.
TOO BAD FOR YOU THAT I'M ONLY PART OF THE SNAKE'S BODY.
HACK AT ME ALL YOU WANT, BUT I'LL REGENER-ATE.
SHUP
YOU CAN TRY AND TRY, BUT YOU'LL NEVER KILL ME.
PING
DON'T TRY TO DEFY ME, HUMAN!
THE ONLY ONE WHO CAN KILL ME IS...
...THE WHITE...
SLASH

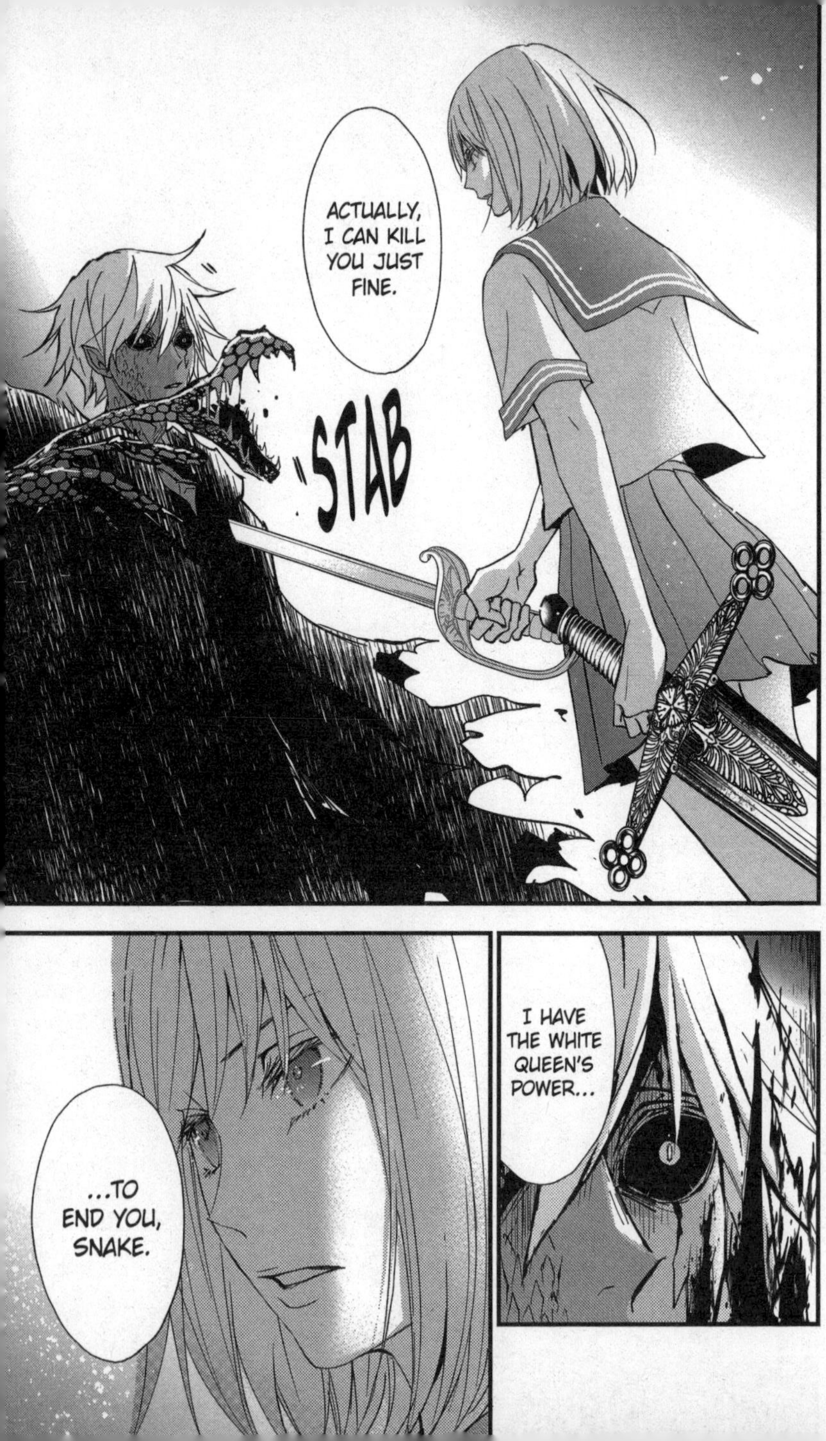
ACTUALLY, I CAN KILL YOU JUST FINE.
STAB
I HAVE THE WHITE QUEEN'S POWER...
...TO END YOU, SNAKE.

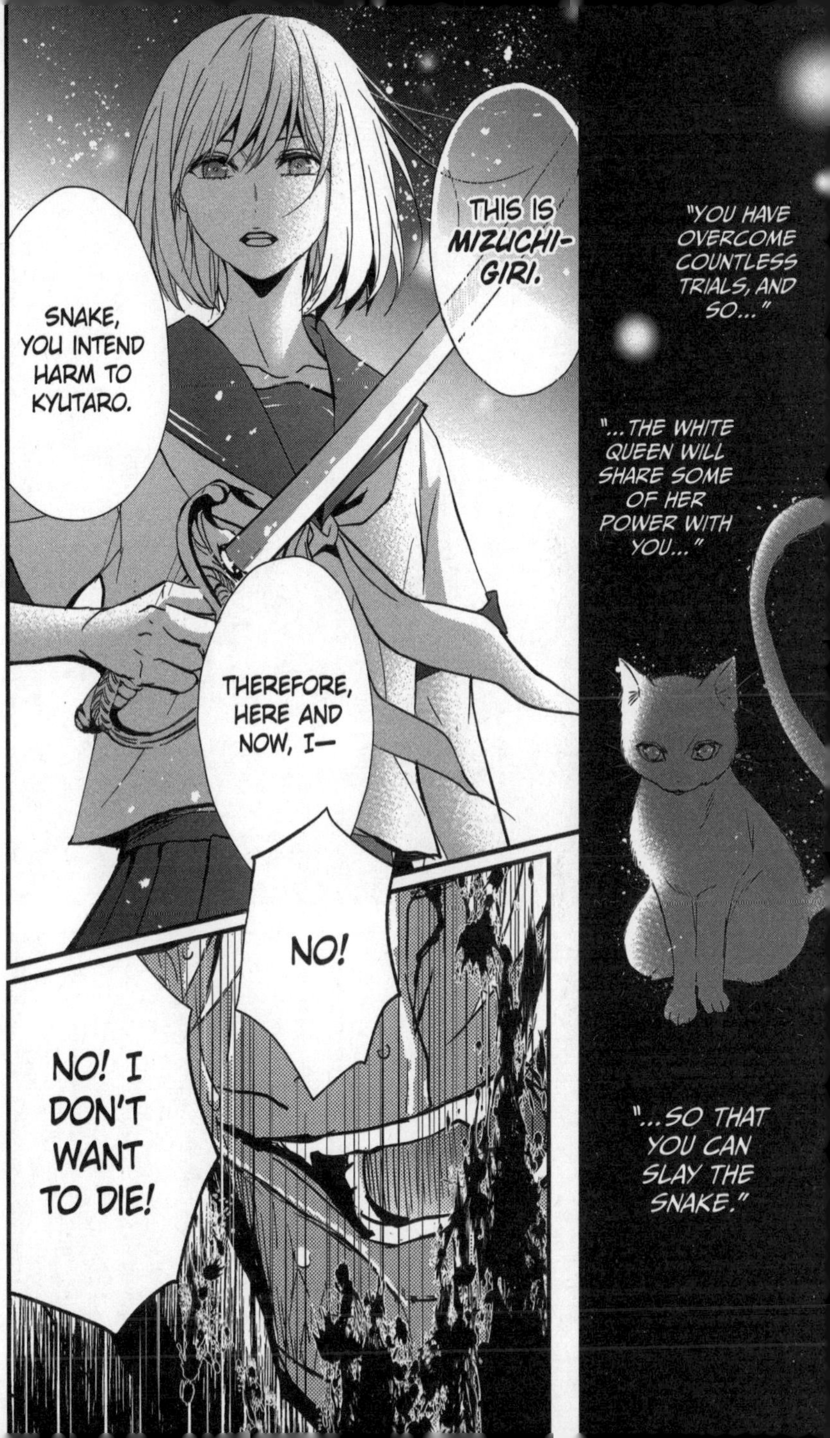
"YOU HAVE OVERCOME COUNTLESS TRIALS, AND SO..."
"...THE WHITE QUEEN WILL SHARE SOME OF HER POWER WITH YOU..."
"...SO THAT YOU CAN SLAY THE SNAKE."
THIS IS MIZUCHI-GIRI.
SNAKE, YOU INTEND HARM TO KYUTARO.
THEREFORE, HERE AND NOW, I—
NO!
NO! I DON'T WANT TO DIE!

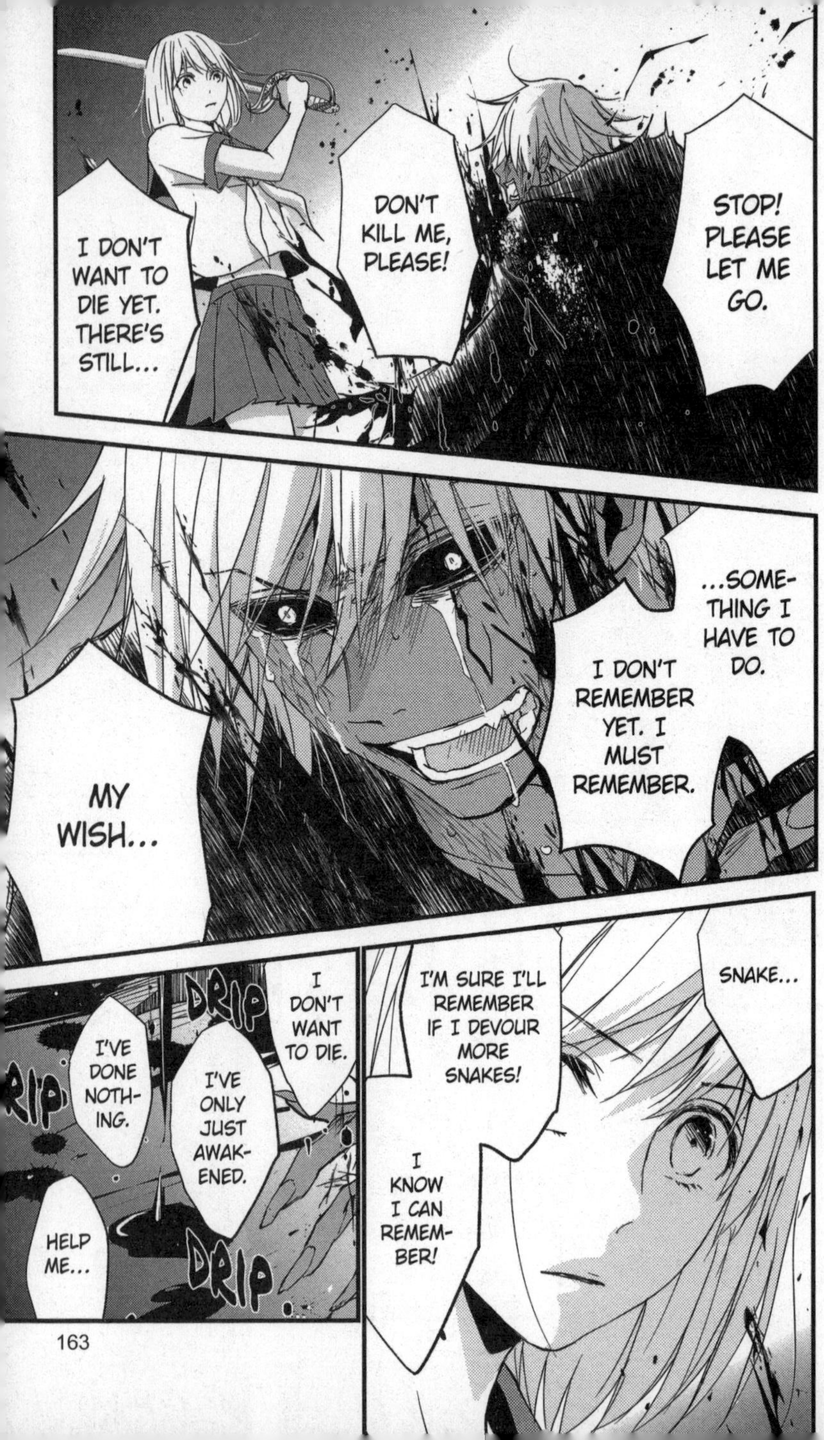
STOP! PLEASE LET ME GO.
DON'T KILL ME, PLEASE!
I DON'T WANT TO DIE YET. THERE'S STILL...
...SOME-THING I HAVE TO DO.
I DON'T REMEMBER YET. I MUST REMEMBER.
MY WISH...
SNAKE...
I'M SURE I'LL REMEMBER IF I DEVOUR MORE SNAKES!
I KNOW I CAN REMEMBER!
I DON'T WANT TO DIE.
DRIP
I'VE ONLY JUST AWAKENED.
I'VE DONE NOTH-ING.
DRIP
HELP ME...
DRIP

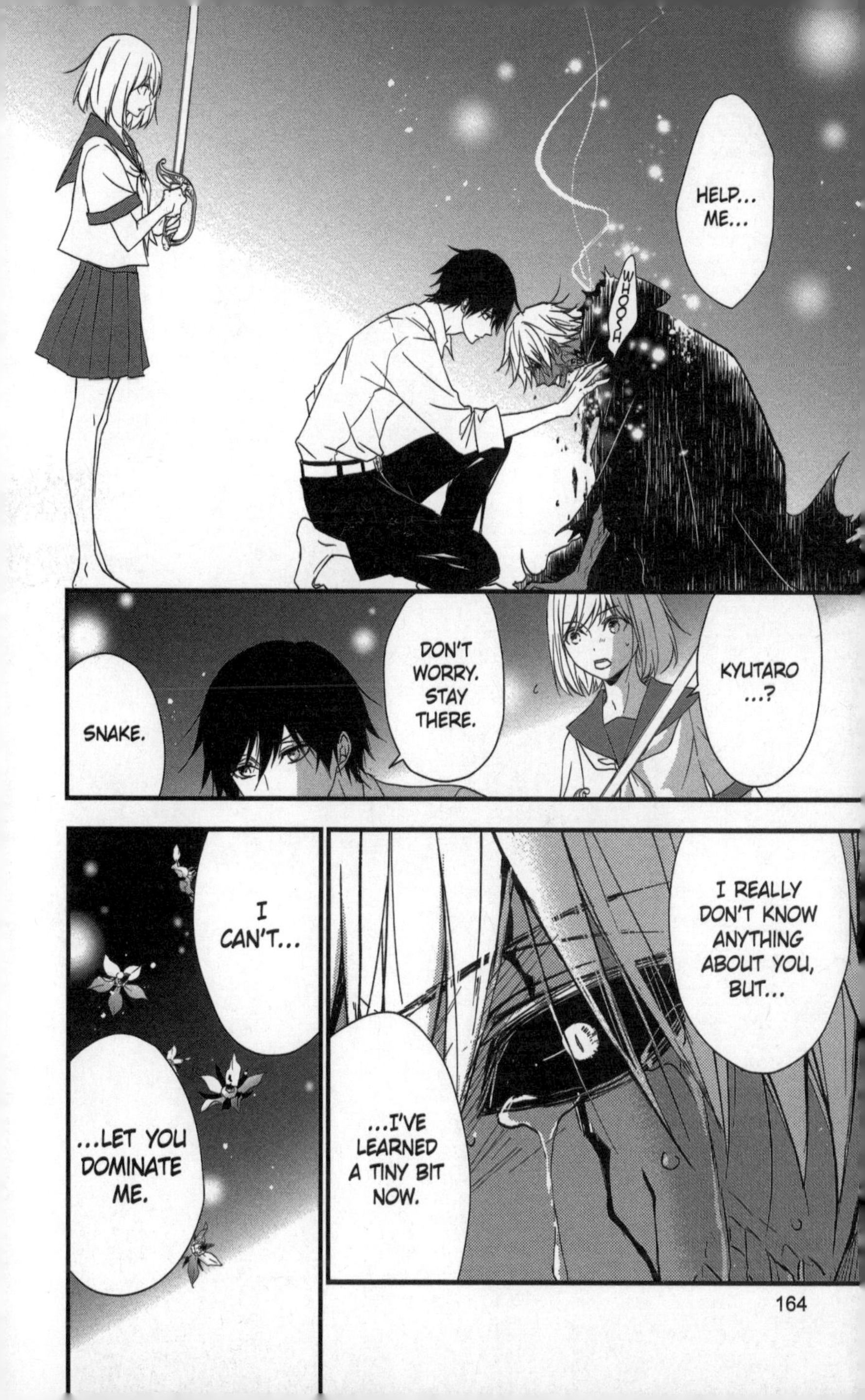
HELP... ME...
WHOOSH
KYUTARO ...?
DON'T WORRY. STAY THERE.
SNAKE.
I REALLY DON'T KNOW ANYTHING ABOUT YOU, BUT...
...I'VE LEARNED A TINY BIT NOW.
I CAN'T...
...LET YOU DOMINATE ME.

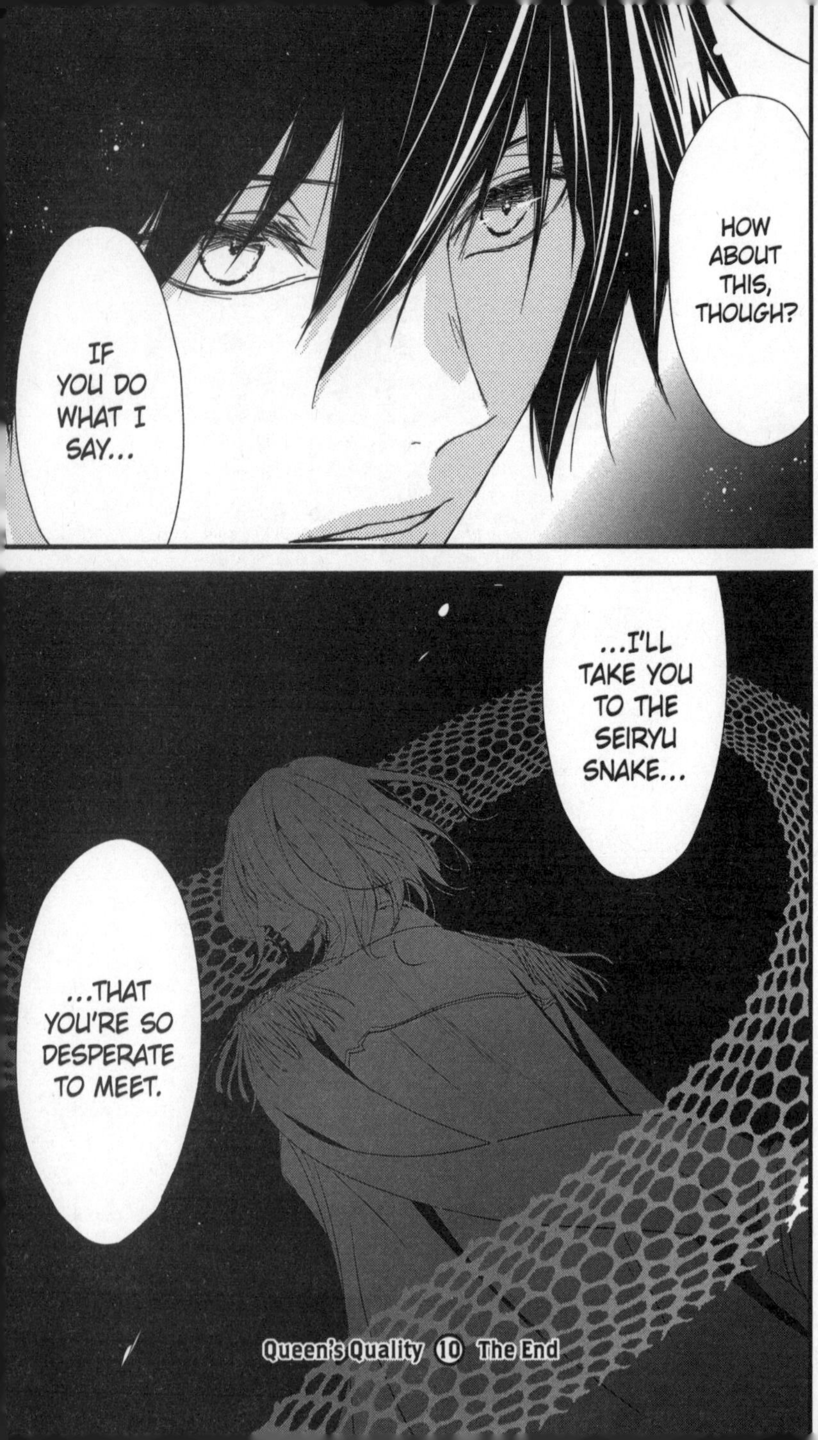
HOW ABOUT THIS, THOUGH?
IF YOU DO WHAT I SAY...
...I'LL TAKE YOU TO THE SEIRYU SNAKE...
...THAT YOU'RE SO DESPERATE TO MEET.
Queen's Quality 10 The End

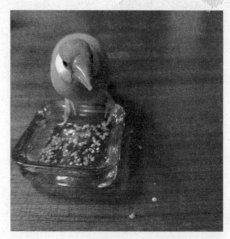

Thanks to all of you, this is volume 10!

—Kyousuke Motomi

Author Bio

Born on August 1, Kyousuke Motomi debuted in *Deluxe Betsucomi* with *Hetakuso Kyupiddo* (No Good Cupid) in 2002. She is the creator of *Dengeki Daisy*, *Beast Master* and *QQ Sweeper*, all available in North America from VIZ Media. Motomi enjoys sleeping, tea ceremonies and reading Haruki Murakami.

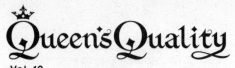

Queen's Quality

Vol. 10
Shojo Beat Edition

STORY AND ART BY
KYOUSUKE MOTOMI

QUEEN'S QUALITY Vol. 10
by Kyousuke MOTOMI
© 2016 Kyousuke MOTOMI
All rights reserved.
Original Japanese edition published by SHOGAKUKAN.
English translation rights in the United States of America, Canada, the United Kingdom, Ireland, Australia and New Zealand arranged with SHOGAKUKAN.

ORIGINAL DESIGN/Chie SATO+Bay Bridge Studio

English Adaptation/Ysabet Reinhardt MacFarlane
Translation/JN Productions
Touch-Up Art & Lettering/Rina Mapa
Design/Julian [JR] Robinson
Editor/Amy Yu

Printed in the U.S.A.

Published by VIZ Media, LLC
P.O. Box 77010
San Francisco, CA 94107

10 9 8 7 6 5 4 3 2 1
First printing, December 2020

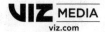

viz.com

shojobeat.com

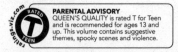

This is the Last Page!

It's true: In keeping with the original Japanese comic format, this book reads from right to left—so action, sound effects and word balloons are completely reversed. This preserves the orientation of the original artwork—plus, it's fun! Check out the diagram shown here to get the hang of things, and then turn to the other side of the book to get started!

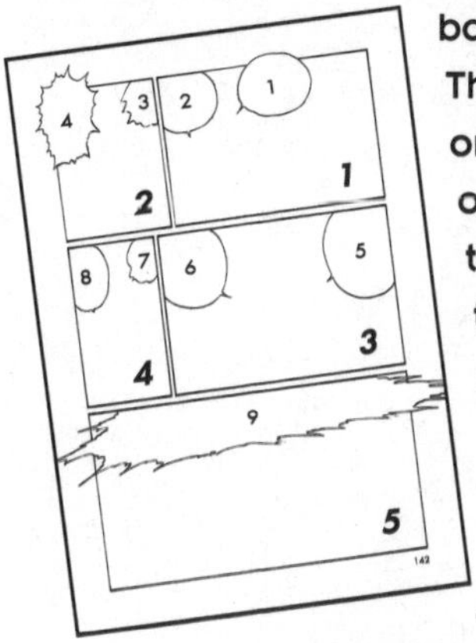
1
2
1
3
4
2
5
6
3
7
8
4
9
5
142

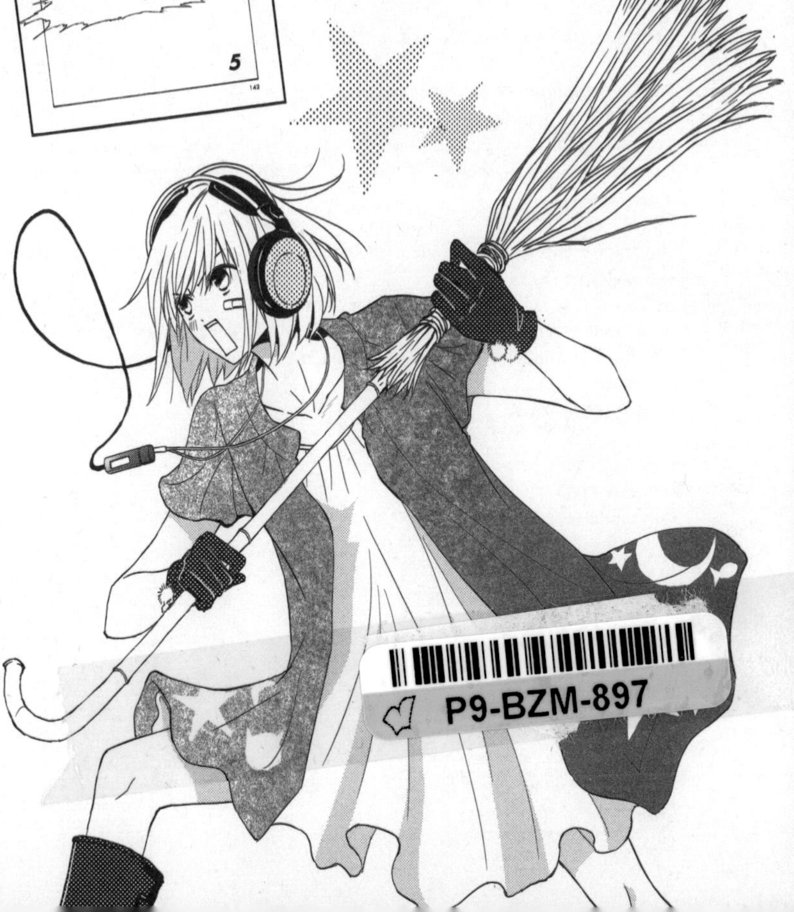

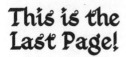